Contents

0148407

IFK3Q
16.56
(Cor)

This book is due for return on or before the last date shown below.

0521551102

Theories of theories of mind

Theories of theories of mind

edited by

Peter Carruthers

Professor of Philosophy and Director, Hang Seng Centre for Cognitive Studies, University of Sheffield

and

Peter K. Smith

Professor of Psychology, University of Sheffield

Published in association with the Hang Seng Centre for Cognitive Studies, University of Sheffield

CAMBRIDGE
UNIVERSITY PRESS

Published by the Press Syndicate of the University of Cambridge
The Pitt Building, Trumpington Street, Cambridge CB2 1RP
40 West 20th Street, New York, NY 10011-4211, USA
10 Stamford Road, Oakleigh, Melbourne 3166, Australia

First published 1996

Printed in Great Britain at the University Press, Cambridge

A catalogue record for this book is available from the British Library

Library of Congress cataloguing in publication data

Theories of theories of mind / edited by Peter Carruthers
and Peter K. Smith
    p.   cm.
Chiefly papers presented at a series of workshops, held in 1992 to
July 1994.
Includes bibliographical references and index.
ISBN 0 521 55110 2 (hardback) – ISBN 0 521 55916 2 (paperback)
1. Philosophy of mind–Congresses.   2. Philosophy of mind in
children–Congresses.   3. Cognition in children–Congresses.
I. Carruthers, Peter, 1952– . II. Smith, Peter K.
BD418.3T44   1996
128′.2–dc20   95-14610 CIP

ISBN 0 521 55110 2 hardback
ISBN 0 521 55916 2 paperback

for

SIR Q. W. LEE

Chairman, Hang Seng Bank of Hong Kong

*– whose vision and generosity made possible this
and a projected nine further volumes*

List of contributors

JANET ASTINGTON   Institute of Child Study, University of Toronto.

SIMON BARON-COHEN   Departments of Psychology and Psychiatry, University of Cambridge.

GEORGE BOTTERILL   Department of Philosophy, University of Sheffield.

JILL BOUCHER   Speech Science Department, University of Sheffield.

PETER CARRUTHERS   Department of Philosophy, University of Sheffield.

GREGORY CURRIE   Department of Philosophy, Flinders University of South Australia.

MARTIN DAVIES   Experimental Psychology, University of Oxford.

JUAN-CARLOS GÓMEZ   Departamento de Psichologia Basica, Universidad Autonoma de Madrid.

ALISON GOPNIK   Department of Psychology, University of California at Berkeley.

ROBERT GORDON   Department of Philosophy, University of Missouri-St Louis.

PAUL HARRIS   Experimental Psychology, University of Oxford.

JANE HEAL   St John's College, Cambridge.

DAVID KLEIN   Wall Street, New York.

ALAN LESLIE   Department of Psychology, Rutgers University.

SHAUN NICHOLS   Department of Philosophy, College of Charleston.

JOSEF PERNER   Institute fuer Psychologie, Universitaet Salzburg.

DANIEL POVINELLI   Laboratory of Comparative Behavioural Biology, New Iberia Research Center.

GABRIEL SEGAL   Department of Philosophy, King's College London.

PETER K. SMITH   Department of Psychology, University of Sheffield.

STEPHEN STICH   Department of Philosophy, Rutgers University.

TONY STONE   King Alfred's College of HE.

JOHN SWETTENHAM   Departments of Psychology and Psychiatry, University of Cambridge.

ANDREW WHITEN   Department of Psychology, University of St Andrews.

Preface

In 1992 the *Hang Seng Centre for Cognitive Studies* was founded at the University of Sheffield, with generous funding from the Hang Seng Bank of Hong Kong. We decided that the best use that could be made of those funds would be to run a series of workshops on inter-disciplinary topics, building up to an international conference every two years, which would then form the basis for a publication. We chose *theory of mind* as our first topic – this being an obvious area in which there might be fruitful interaction between psychologists and philosophers – and sent out a number of invitations. Three weekend workshops were held in the academic year 1992/3, and two in 1993/4. The concluding conference was held at Earnshaw Hall, University of Sheffield, in July 1994.

This volume is much more than a set of conference papers, however. Almost all of the contributors attended one or more (often all) of the workshops, commenting on the work of others and/or contributing a paper themselves. Moreover, all of the conference contributors were asked to submit their papers two months in advance. These were then copied around the other contributors, and the editors gave detailed feedback and comments, both pre- and post-conference. Finally, a selection was made from these papers for inclusion in the volume, and the authors then had the opportunity to rewrite in the light of conference discussions, and in the knowledge of what others had done. The result, we believe, is a highly integrated and original, and genuinely inter-disciplinary volume of essays.

The workshop series played a crucial role, not only in allowing the contributors to develop and hone their ideas under criticism over a period of time, but also in breaking down disciplinary barriers. Individual philosophers and psychologists have collaborated in the past, of course; but each discipline still has its own language, assumptions, and ways of thinking and arguing. These differences were very evident in early meetings, where it was generally obvious whether the speaker was a philosopher or a psychologist, and in which there was a good deal of mutual incomprehension. But this really did change with time, and by the final conference the distinctions were much less obvious, with participants capable of moving freely across disciplinary boundaries. As a result, we believe that all the papers in this volume will be both accessible and interesting to people from a range of different academic disciplines.

We would very much like to thank all those who participated in the workshop series and concluding conference, whose comments and contributions to discussions did so much to help shape the final volume. Special thanks should go to all those who contributed a talk at one or other venue, but who, for one reason or another, do not have a paper included in the present volume. They are: Tony Charman, Norman Freeman, Charlie Lewis, Adam Morton, Jim Russell, Clive Witcomb, and Andrew Woodfield. Thanks also go to Clive Witcomb for his help with the editing, and for the preparation of the index. Finally, in addition to our obvious and heart-felt debt to the Hang Seng Bank, we should like to thank the British Academy for a grant to assist in the funding of the conference.

1   Introduction

Peter Carruthers and Peter K. Smith

Since Premack and Woodruff's classic (1978) paper, the term 'theory of mind' has come to designate a particular research-domain, whose goal is to provide an explanation of the ability – which may or may not be unique to human beings – to explain and predict the actions, both of oneself, and of other intelligent agents. It is also the term used to designate one controversial characterisation of the basis of this ability. So-called 'theory-theorists' maintain that the ability to explain and predict behaviour is underpinned by a folk-psychological *theory* of the structure and functioning of the mind – where the theory in question may be innate and modularised, learned individually, or acquired through a process of enculturation. There are, then, many different theories of theory of mind in its research-domain sense; and the theory-theory account of our theory of mind abilities, too, admits of a number of different variants. Moreover, both sets of questions are now of common concern to a number of different disciplines, including philosophy, primatology, cognitive science, and developmental psychology. These multiplicities are reflected in the title of this volume, and in its contents. In this brief introductory chapter we shall provide the reader with a map of the area, laying out the issues and options, and linking these to the chapters that follow.

1   A recent history

Curiously, the modern phase of work on theory of mind by developmental psychologists began with a paper in primatology – Premack and Woodruff, 1978 – which raised the question whether chimpanzees have a theory of mind. This question proved immensely difficult to answer, although it has spawned a good deal of very interesting research since (continued in Part IV of this volume). But what it certainly did do, was to force all psychologists to think very hard about what it *is* to possess a conception of the mind of another creature, and also about the behaviour which might show whether or not such a conception is possessed. This thinking bore fruit a few years later (seeded, it should be said, by suggestions from the philosophers Daniel Dennett and Gilbert Harman in their commentaries on Premack and Woodruff's paper) with the publication of Wimmer and Perner's 1983 article, containing the now-famous *false-belief task* for use with children – about which more will be said shortly.

In fact the developmental study of theory-of-mind skills in children had had, in a sense, a history going back at least to the seminal work of Piaget on children's thinking and egocentrism in the 1930s to 50s, and the following work on empathy and role-taking skills in the 60s and 70s. But while this research was of value, the topic did not 'take off' then in the way that it has in the 80s and 90s. There may be several reasons for this. First, until the late 1970s developmental psychologists in this tradition were perhaps too narrowly focused within the framework of Piagetian theory – whether aiming to confirm, or disprove, its tenets. Second, and relatedly, there was not then the influx of ideas from philosophy, primatology, and cognitive science which has proved so fruitful more recently. And third, the research lacked the focus of a clear experimental paradigm, which only appeared with the invention of the false-belief task in the early 80s.

The original false-belief task involved a character, Maxi, who places some chocolate in a particular location and then leaves the room; in his absence the chocolate is then moved to another location. The child is then asked where Maxi will look for the chocolate on his return. In order to succeed in this task, the child must understand that Maxi still *thinks* that the chocolate is where he left it – the child must understand that Maxi has a false belief, in fact. The task works, because in order to succeed in it the child must be able to *contrast* its own perception of the real situation with the belief of the target agent – in order to get the right prediction, the child must be capable (in one way or another), not just of representing the state of the world, but of representing Maxi's representation of the world.

The surprising initial finding was that children became able to succeed in this task between the ages of 4 and 5, some two or three years earlier than Piaget would have predicted. A small industry then developed, replicating and refining the task, and attempting (with some success) to push the critical age of acquisition still lower. Other sources of evidence also began to be looked at – for example, relating to children's early verbalisations concerning mental states, their understanding of emotions, and their ability to deceive others. And researchers began to investigate the developmental stages through which theory-of-mind abilities are acquired. (For extensive discussion, bold theorising, and reviews of the literature, see Wellman, 1990 and Perner, 1991a.) Others continued to investigate the possibility of theory-of-mind abilities in non-human primates. And yet others again began to look at the possible *absence* of theory of mind in some humans, particularly in connection with autism (see Baron-Cohen *et al.*, 1985).

Most psychologists through this period have remained neutral on the nature of the *end-state* of theory of mind acquisition. Many, for example, have been careful to speak of theory of mind (or mind-reading) *abilities*, without commitment as to whether these abilities are underpinned by anything resembling a theory. But increasingly there has been a realisation that questions concerning the process of theory of mind acquisition cannot be kept wholly separate from questions concerning the nature of what is acquired, and a number of developmental psychologists have taken stands on the latter issue. For example, Wellman (1990) and Gopnik (1993) have declared themselves for a theory-theory account of our mature mind-reading abilities, and Harris (1989) has defended the simulationist alternative. (More will be said about the contrast between theory-theory and simulationism shortly.)

Philosophers, of course, have had a long-standing interest in the basis of our (adult) knowledge of the minds of ourselves and others, going back to Descartes and beyond. With the demise of Cartesianism in the 1940s and 50s, and the collapse of behaviourism in the 60s, some or other form of theory-theory has come to be dominant, at least since David Lewis' classic (1966) paper. According to this view, our access to the minds of other people (and also our access to our own mental states) is mediated by an implicitly held *theory* of the structure and functioning of the human mind; and the different types of mental state are individuated by their functional role as described within this theoretical system. Until the mid-1980s philosophers were not overly interested in the process of acquisition, as such, assuming it to involve some or other form of enculturation. But that has now changed dramatically, for two distinct reasons.

The first is that philosophical interest in theory of mind has recently come to intersect with another perennial debate, between Rationalists and Empiricists, concerning innate versus learned knowledge; and this debate is, of course, at least partly a developmental one. In particular, Fodor (1981, 1987, 1992) has proposed that our knowledge of folk-psychological theory is innate, developing in the child through a process of maturation rather than of learning.

The second reason arises out of the challenge mounted to the theory-theory orthodoxy by Robert Gordon (1986) and, independently, by Jane Heal (1986), who each proposed a simulationist alternative. According to this view, what lies at the root of our mature mind-reading abilities is not any sort of theory, but rather an ability to project ourselves imaginatively into another person's perspective, *simulating* their mental activity with our own. This view has been developed further by Gordon (1992a) and cultivated rather differently by Goldman (1989, 1992b, 1993a). And it rapidly began to dawn on people that simulationism and theory-theory might have different implications for (and be tested against) the process of normal theory of mind development; and also that they might provide competing explanations of some of the experiences and difficulties of people with autism.

By 1992 the time was then ripe for philosophers and psychologists to begin to interact with one another much more directly and fruitfully on these issues; and the stage was thus set for the project leading up to the present volume. But before introducing the reader to its contents, it may be helpful to lay out the issues and options in a little more detail.

2   A map of the area

We focus first upon the end-state of theory of mind acquisition, namely how a mature adult explains and predicts the actions of self and others. The basic theoretical choice is between theory-theory and simulationism, with also the possibility of some form of simulation/theory mix. Each of these options then admits of further sub-divisions. If mature theory of mind abilities are underpinned by a theory, then this theory may be more or less implicit (more or less accessible to consciousness and oral report); and it may be more or less deeply *theoretical* (for example, consisting of a more or less tightly structured and inter-related set of principles). If those abilities are underpinned by simulation, on the other hand, then one can either maintain that simulation presupposes first-person awareness of one's own mental states, with the inference from self to other being a kind of argument from analogy (as Goldman has claimed); or one can maintain that simulation involves a kind of imaginative identification which can operate without introspective self-awareness (as Gordon has claimed). And then of course there are a whole range of possible simulation/theory mixes, maintaining that some specified components of our theory of mind abilities are underpinned by simulation and others by theory.

A separate issue is how these theory of mind abilities develop; although the theoretical choices above have implications for the process of development. It is hard to see, for example, how anyone could consistently maintain that the end-state is one of simulation, while claiming that theory of mind *acquisition* is a process of theorising. For how could theorising lead to something which is *not* a theory, namely an ability to simulate? It is almost as hard to see how an ability to simulate could be acquired entirely through enculturation, or social learning. In fact, simulationists maintain that the ability to simulate is grounded in an innate genetic endowment. This is variously characterised as the ability to imagine; the ability to think counter-factually; the ability to entertain suppositions; or the ability to take one's practical reasoning system 'off-line'. But simulationists would also allow that there is an *element* of learning involved in development, since children have to learn *which* of their mental states to vary when they simulate another person, in order to constitute their then-altered perspective.

It is almost equally hard to see how anyone could maintain that the end-state is one of theory while the process of acquisition is one of simulation. For why should simulation drop out once we have attained mature theory of mind abilities (by hypothesis, a mature theory), if it was nevertheless the crucial engine of acquisition? And, indeed, there is no one who attempts to defend this option. Those who are theory-theorists about the end-state mostly face a three-way choice concerning the mechanism of acquisition: it can either be a matter of growth in an innate module; it can be learning by theorising; or it can be learning through teaching and enculturation (or any pair-wise combination, or indeed any combination of all three processes).

Some theory-theorists maintain that the process of acquisition is one of biological growth. They believe that folk-psychology (or at least some of the core components thereof) is embodied in an innate, genetically endowed, theory of mind module which grows in the normally developing child (perhaps passing through a number of intermediate theory-like stages). Normal development may require triggering experiences from the environment, of course; and these may include the experience of enculturated talk about the mind. And there may also be an element of learning around the periphery. But on this view, the core process is *not* one of learning or theorising.

Other theory-theorists maintain that theory of mind is *learned* on the basis of experience. In one version, the child is pictured as a little scientist, constructing and revising theories in the light of incoming data. In the other version, the child is seen more as a little science *student*, picking up the folk-psychology of its culture through interacting with – and listening to the talk of – its carers and older siblings. Almost everyone now holding one or other of these positions maintains that there is *some* innate initial basis – some innate starting point of attention-biases or similarity-spaces which gives a kick-start to the process of theory of mind acquisition. But that process itself is conceived to be one of learning.

Finally, those who maintain some or other form of simulation/theory mix for the end-state of development are free to adopt almost any combination of the above possible processes of acquisition. No wonder that the theory of mind literature has grown increasingly complex, and that the issues are so difficult to resolve!

A widely accepted hypothesis is that autism involves at least some sort of theory of mind deficit. People with autism have notorious problems in communication and social interaction, and in reading the minds of other people – well-documented in their difficulties with false-belief tasks, for example. And the various proposals canvassed above, concerning the process of normal theory of mind acquisition, carry different implications for the understanding of these phenomena. For simulationists, autism must result (at least in part) from a damaged capacity to imagine, or to engage in counter-factual reasoning. For modularist theory-theorists, autism will result (again, perhaps only in part) from a damaged or destroyed theory of mind module. And for either sort of learning theory-theorist, it must either be the capacity to learn from experience which is damaged, or autism may result from the lack of (or damage to) the innate initial basis of normal development. This is then fertile testing-ground for a whole range of specific hypotheses concerning normal theory of mind development.

The question whether or not non-human primates possess theory of mind abilities connects with a number of the above issues in a variety of complex ways. For example, if chimpanzees (or other great apes) were to turn out to possess some simpler version of our human folk-psychology, then this might contain valuable clues to the underlying basis for, and also the evolution of, our own capacities. But part of the interest of the primate research is also methodological. For any tests of theory of mind competence in non-human primates must, perforce, be non-language-involving; and the construction of such tests may then cast important new light on the course of theory of mind development in young children.

3   A guide to the volume

Parts I and II of the volume divide, very roughly, into chapters on the end-state of theory of mind development, and chapters focusing on the process of development itself; though often with very considerable overlap. Many of the chapters in Part I are distinctive in proposing some form of simulation/theory mix (see Carruthers, ch. 3; Heal, ch. 5; Perner, ch. 6; Botterill, ch. 7).

Gordon (ch. 2) presents and argues for a radical form of simulationism, according to which our very concepts of the mental are acquired through a process of simulation, without subjects needing to have introspective access to their own mental states as such – though he is now prepared to allow a limited place for introspection of what are in fact mental states, but not initially categorised *as* mental, but rather as states of the body. Carruthers (ch. 3) then criticises both the Gordon and Goldman versions of simulationism, on the grounds that neither can account adequately for our introspective knowledge of our own occurrent thought-processes, in particular. (Gordon, he alleges, is a quasi-behaviourist, whereas Goldman is claimed to be a sort of Cartesian.)

Nichols *et al.* (ch. 4) explore the explanatory potential of off-line simulation accounts of a variety of cognitive capacities, to compete with the sort of information-based explanations more usual in cognitive science. They consider how off-line simulation might be appealed to in explanation of counter-factual reasoning, of empathy, and of mental imagery, as well as considering its more usual role in purported explanations of our theory of mind abilities. In the latter connection, they present new evidence that behaviour prediction is *not* done by simulation; but they argue that the other three possibilities are well worth further exploration. Besides an explicit criticism of the simulationist account of our theory of mind abilities, this chapter also contains an implicit criticism. For many simulationists have argued for their position on grounds of simplicity, claiming that off-line simulation will need to be appealed to in any case, to explain counter-factual reasoning and empathy, for example. Nichols *et al.* attempt to undercut this argument, since they clearly think that it will be a *different* system which is taken off-line in each case.

Heal (ch. 5) and Perner (ch. 6) both argue for a simulation/theory mix. Heal argues that while simulation must be employed to enable us to predict what people will come to believe on the basis of their other beliefs, we must also possess a body of theoretical knowledge concerning the causal roles of various types of propositional attitude. Perner makes a new proposal to distinguish simulation from tacit theory, and presents a range of experimental data to suggest that simulation cannot be by any means the whole story.

Botterill (ch. 7) makes a useful distinction between different versions of theory-theory, depending upon how deeply *theoretical* the body of information is supposed to be, and argues tentatively in favour of strong theoriticity. Stone and Davies (ch. 8) then lay out their view of the State of the Art, meanwhile commenting on the other chapters in Part I.

Segal (ch. 9), and Baron-Cohen and Swettenham (ch. 10), open Part II of the volume by defending and developing modularist forms of theory-theory. Segal begins his chapter by distinguishing a number of different notions of 'modularity'; he then contrasts one sort of modularist account of development with the child-as-scientist alternative, and argues on a variety of grounds that the former is preferable. Baron-Cohen and Swettenham assume the correctness of a modularist framework, and explore the relationship between the theory of mind module (ToMM) and a postulated precursor module, the shared attention mechanism (SAM), using the results of a recent large screening study in which young children were tested for autism.

Gopnik (ch. 11) and Astington (ch. 12) are both learning-theorists; but of different sorts. Gopnik takes issue with modularity accounts, and defends her version of the child-as-scientist account of theory of mind acquisition. Astington argues that renewed consideration should be given to enculturation accounts – placing greater emphasis on learning from adults and on the role of language in theory of mind acquisition – and presents a range of empirical data in their support.

Harris (ch. 13) raises a little-noticed problem, which is a difficulty for simulationists and theory-theorists alike, namely: why is it that beliefs are so much more difficult for children to understand than desires? His novel proposal is that the notion of desire has its essential place in the understanding of agency, which comes more easily to children because they are acquainted with their own agency from the start; whereas the notion of belief has its locus in the understanding of communication, requiring some linguistic competence as a prerequisite.

The three chapters in Part III focus on autism. Boucher (ch. 14) presents and defends the criteria for an adequate explanation of autism, arguing that theory-theory explanations fall short of a number of them. Her view is that autism probably has multiple bases. Currie (ch. 15) compares and contrasts theory-theory with simulationist explanations of autistic phenomena, arguing tentatively for the superiority of the latter. And finally Carruthers (ch. 16) tries to show how a theory-theorist can explain features of the autistic syndrome (specifically, absence of pretend play and executive function deficits) which might otherwise appear problematic for the 'mind-blindness' theory of autism.

The four chapters in Part IV round out the volume by considering a variety of issues arising from the domain of primatology. Whiten (ch. 17) considers a number of proposals for marking the distinction between clever behaviourism and genuine mentalism. Povinelli (ch. 18) explores at length the prospects and potential significance of discovering theory of mind abilities in non-human primates, and presents dramatic new evidence suggesting that chimpanzees do not even have an understanding of visual attention. Gómez (ch. 19) discusses some of the difficulties inherent in testing for theory of mind abilities in non-human primates, and presents the results of experiments conducted with a captive orang-utan. Finally, Smith (ch. 20) concludes the volume with a comment on the previous chapters in Part IV, and with the suggestion (similar to the one made by Harris in ch. 13) that theory of mind abilities may be dependent upon language.

This volume may not have definitively resolved any of the outstanding issues concerning the nature of theory of mind abilities and their attainment. But it has at least clarified those issues, and put up a number of new possibilities worthy of further investigation. It also provides an exemplar, we believe, of the sort of inter-disciplinary collaboration necessary for future progress in this area.

uired – theory-theory versus
heory

2   'Radical' simulationism

Robert M. Gordon

The theory outlined in this chapter is what has sometimes been called the 'radical' form of the simulation theory. It conceives simulation as more than just a heuristic for finding out the mental states of others and predicting their behaviour quickly and economically, using a minimum of specially dedicated brain power. Beyond this, the theory holds that even our ability to grasp the concepts of mind and the various mental states depends on our having the capacity to simulate others.

Before discussing the radical position, I present a broad characterisation of the simulation theory in general and a new argument that clearly favours it over competitors.

1   Hot and cold methodologies contrasted

Concerning the 'theory of mind', or more broadly the methodology, by which people anticipate and predict one another's actions, there are basically two kinds of theory. One kind holds that we use what I call a *cold* methodology: a methodology that chiefly engages our intellectual processes, moving by inference from one set of beliefs to another, and makes no essential use of our own capacities for emotion, motivation, and practical reasoning. So-called 'theory' theories are of this kind, both those that hold we develop or somehow acquire something comparable to a scientific theory and those that say the work is done by a 'theory' in an extended sense, a set of rules of symbol manipulation embodied, like a Chomskian universal grammar, in an innate module. The other kind imputes to us a *hot* methodology, which exploits one's own motivational and emotional resources and one's own capacity for practical reasoning. The simulation theory in its various formulations (e.g., Gordon, 1986, 1992a; Goldman, 1989, 1992b; Harris, 1989, 1992; Heal, 1986) is of this kind.[1]

To contrast the two methodologies, I will use an example given by Jerry Fodor, the originator of the innate module theory. In Shakespeare's *A Midsummer Night's Dream*, Lysander, cast under a magic spell, abandons

11

Hermia while she's asleep in the forest. When Hermia wakes up and doesn't find her lover beside her, she concludes that his rival Demetrius murdered Lysander. Fodor (1987) explains how Hermia might have arrived at this conclusion. He suggests that it is a product of 'implicit, non-demonstrative, theoretical inference' that leads her to think that Demetrius had certain desires and emotions, that he made certain practical inferences, and that he performed an act of a certain type. The reasoning goes something like this. Demetrius is a rival of Lysander, and rivals want each other to get out of the way. And Demetrius has the following belief: Lysander will not be out of the way unless he is dead, and I Demetrius can bring about Lysander's death. Hermia plugs these ascriptions into the law, 'If one wants that P, believes that not-P unless Q, and also believes one can bring it about that Q, then (ceteris paribus) one tries to bring it about that Q.' Hence Hermia says to Demetrius, 'It cannot be but thou hast murder'd him.'

This imputes to Hermia, without a doubt, a *cold* methodology: Hermia has certain initial beliefs, and these together with certain rules lead to other beliefs, including, ultimately, the belief that Demetrius murdered Lysander. It makes no essential difference that Hermia's beliefs and inferences are about Demetrius' emotions, desires, and practical reasoning: her own emotional and motivational resources and capacity for practical reasoning do not come into play, except in those ways in which theoretical reasoning in general may be influenced, for better or worse, by emotions and attitudes. Although there are important differences between the Fodorian cold methodology and other cold methodologies, they need not concern us here.

The simulation theory would suppose that Hermia arrived at her 'conclusion' concerning the decisions and actions of Demetrius by moving, not just from belief to belief, but through a variety of mental states culminating in a decision – not a decision she herself was prepared to act on, but one made with the express purpose of anticipating or predicting Demetrius' decisions and actions. Before making these decisions, she would transport herself in imagination into his situation to the extent to which it seemed, to a first approximation, relevantly different from her own; but not strictly transport *herself*, Hermia, but rather a self *transformed*, insofar as seemed necessary, into someone who would behave as she had known *Demetrius* to behave. For example, she might imagine loving someone and having a rival for that person's love: possibly, even, loving *Hermia* and having *Lysander* as a rival. And she would try to motivate past deeds and emotions of Demetrius that would not have come naturally to her in similar circumstances. Thus transported and transformed, and with whatever changes in emotion, desire, belief, and so forth, these changes induced in her, she would make decisions 'in the role of' Demetrius. In other words, she would simulate Demetrius, using her own motivational and emotional resources and her own capacity for practical reasoning, adjusted or calibrated as necessary. This would be a hot methodology.

One important advantage of the methodology just sketched is that it can readily exploit other kinds of 'hot cognition'. To illustrate this advantage, I will invent an additional scene for Shakespeare's play. In the imagined scene, Hermia relates that on the previous evening she had been speaking intimately with Lysander when Demetrius walked past. She noticed Demetrius giving a brief glance in their direction, and then looking a strange way – part smile, part grimace, perhaps – that she found very difficult to categorise or describe in terms of emotions expressed. Despite her inability to describe it, she explains, that look helped persuade her that Demetrius was apt to do harm to Lysander – that look, taken together with other evidence.

Ineffable factors do not sit well with Fodor's theoretical inference account. It is hard to see how a facial expression one is unable to categorise might translate into a predicate that can be plugged into a Fodorian law.[2] Alternative cold methodology theories, such as those that invoke connectionist prototypes, might do a better job of explaining how an ineffable look could have helped persuade Hermia that Demetrius was apt to act a certain way. But a hot methodology would be more promising. For the sight of Demetrius' facial expression would probably have produced a similar expression on Hermia's face – even if not a visually detectable expression, at least the corresponding pattern of muscular innervation.[3] And these copy-cat innervation patterns, at least when they replicate another's expression of emotion, tend to produce an emotion in us, typically (where there are no relevant cultural differences), an emotion similar to the one that caused the other's original expression. Even the *voluntary* movement of facial muscles tends to produce felt emotion and the corresponding physiological changes. Thus, by replicating the facial expressions of others, we would tend to 'catch' the emotions expressed. There are also mechanisms for catching the intentionality of another's emotion – for example, the gaze-tracking response that transfers one's attention from the other's facial expression to the 'cause' or 'object' of the emotion.

It is plausible that our capacity to *recognise* and *name* the emotion expressed on another's face owes much to subliminal contagion of the sort described. And there is no reason why a cold methodology couldn't exploit such hot cognitions. A named or at least recognised emotion could, for example, be plugged into a Fodorian law. But if Hermia were predicting Demetrius' decisions and actions by *making* decisions, then the emotion she picked up from Demetrius' expression could have influenced her 'conclusion' that Demetrius murdered Lysander, whether or not she was able to recognise, name, or describe the emotion. For emotions can influence our decisions, can move us to *decide* and to *act* in ways we would not have decided and acted in their absence, with or without recognition. That is the key. Decisions made in the role of another agent can be influenced by unrecognised emotions, *including* any emotions picked up from the person whose actions are being predicted. (Presumably Hermia's copy-cat emotions would have been segregated, at least to a degree, from those that arose in the normal way from her own perceptions and memories. Thus they could be prevented from influencing either *her own* decisions or decisions made in the role of someone other than Demetrius. In other words, the emotion picked up from Demetrius would be confined to her first-person representation of Demetrius.)[4] In short, if Hermia were predicting Demetrius' actions by simulating Demetrius, then she wouldn't have to *categorise* her second-hand emotion at all – she would have only to *use* it, that is, to allow it to do its usual work of influencing behaviour.

The broader significance of this point is that, given a hot methodology, our competence in predicting the actions of others may not depend as much as has traditionally been thought on a capacity to recognise and categorise their mental states. At least this is so in the case of emotions conveyed through facial expression (and probably also emotions conveyed through vocalisation or bodily posture and motion). But suppose, as is plausible, that it is also true that a person's *desires* and *beliefs* are apt to be contagious in some degree (though probably by a mechanism far more sophisticated than facial mimicry). Then second-hand desires and beliefs, too, need only be 'used' and allowed to have their influence on behaviour, rather than recognised and categorised. Even possession of the concepts of desire and belief would be less important to our competence in predicting actions than philosophers and psychologists have supposed.

2   Two simulation theories, and a move toward reconciliation

There are basically two kinds of hot methodology theory that go under the name, 'the simulation theory'. According to one of these, one first recognises one's own mental states under actual or imagined conditions and then infers, on the basis of an assumed similarity or analogy, that the person simulated is in similar states. The recognition of one's own mental states is thought to be grounded in introspective access to these states, or at least in comparison of their qualitative features with a standard held in memory; and this is thought to require possession of the relevant mental state concepts. Harris and especially Goldman have promoted such a view in several of their writings. (The view is sometimes characterised as 'Cartesian', even though its proponents are not committed to some of the more objectionable tenets of Descartes' theory of mind.) If simulation thus conceived is the methodology by which people attribute mental states to others, one consequence would seem to be that children could not ascribe a given type of mental state to others unless they could ascribe it to themselves, and the capacity for self-ascription would presumably *precede* the capacity for other-ascription.

In other papers (Gordon, 1992a; Gordon, 1995a), I argue against this version of the simulation theory. Against the thesis that we make inferences from what we ourselves would do in the imagined circumstances to what the other will do, I emphasise imaginative transformation into the other (as briefly set out in the first section). In reply to the thesis that simulation requires a capacity to ascribe mental states to oneself, particularly by recognition of their distinctive qualitative 'feel'[5] (Goldman, 1993a), and the corollary that it requires possession of the relevant mental state concepts, I argue that such self-ascription relies instead on what I call *ascent routines*. For example, the way in which adults ordinarily determine whether or not they believe that p is simply to ask themselves the question whether or not p. Thus, if someone were to ask me, (Q1) 'Do you believe Mickey Mouse has a tail?' I would ask myself, (Q2) 'Does Mickey Mouse have a tail?' (with certain constraints on how I obtain the answer to Q2). If the answer to Q2 is Yes, then the presumptive answer to Q1 (the best I can do without taking into consideration possible conflict between verbal and non-verbal behaviour) is Yes (or, 'Yes, I do believe Mickey has a tail'). The answer to Q1 is No if either the answer to Q2 is No or no answer is available within the constraints.

I call this procedure an *ascent routine* because it answers a question by answering another question pitched at a lower semantic level – the former being a question about a mental state that is about x, the latter a question directly about x. What is of particular interest is that it allows one to get the answer to a question about oneself, and specifically about one's mental states, *by answering a question that is not about oneself, nor about mental states at all*. The latter is what I will call an 'object-level' question.[6] Moreover, the answer thus obtained will usually be the *right* answer, or at least the one borne out in the long run by situational and behavioural evidence available to others. Thus children would have the wherewithal for *securing the right answer* to questions they lack the sophistication to understand. They need only grasp the 'object-level' question, such as, 'Does Mickey Mouse have a tail?' to generate the right answer to a question they don't understand, namely, 'Do you believe [or: Is it your belief] that Mickey Mouse has a tail?'

It should be emphasised that, even if it enables children to generate the right answers to questions about their beliefs, the ascent routine does not equip them to make *genuine, comprehending* ascriptions of belief. Just instructing children to use the ascent routine whenever they hear a question of the form, 'Do you believe (or: think) that p?' would not equip them to understand in what way the question is a question *about themselves* rather than simply a question *about* (for example) *Mickey Mouse.* The point is not that they would fail to understand that, 'Mickey has a tail', and 'I believe Mickey has a tail', are not logically equivalent: that an individual may (logically) believe something that is false and may fail to believe something that is true. The point is rather that they would have no means of understanding how, 'I believe Mickey Mouse has a tail', could be about an individual (other than Mickey Mouse) at all. They fail to grasp several components of the concept of belief, but the one that is paramount, because it is presupposed by all the others, is the general idea that a fact (about Mickey Mouse, for example) can have a *mental location*: can be, in other words, a fact *to* some individual.

Unless the Mickey Mouse example is atypical, even we who do possess the concept of belief rely on an ascent routine for answering questions about what we believe.[7] And our answer to the object-level question, such as the question about Mickey Mouse, does not generally require recognising something by qualitative feel. There are, however, mental states other than belief for which a stronger case can be made for recognition by qualitative feel. Pain is the state most often mentioned in this connection. Indeed, even where belief is concerned, it might be said that at least *strength or degree of belief* can sometimes be recognised by qualitative feel. Not long ago, it seemed to me that consistency in my opposition to the 'Cartesian' view of simulation demanded a position squarely opposed to any recognition by qualitative feel. I was mistaken. For what I oppose is the claim that simulation requires recognition of our own mental states *as such*, along with the corollary that it requires *possession of the concepts* of the various mental states simulated in others. There is, however, no reason to rule out *a priori* the possibility that some of the object-level questions can be answered on the basis of qualitative feel, and no reason to rule out *a priori* the mechanism Goldman proposes, comparison of qualitative features with a standard held in memory. The ascent routine story simply does not stipulate *how* the object-level question is to be answered.[8]

Is there an ascent routine for pain? What we should look for is a type of question that even people who do not possess the concept of pain can answer, such that their answers would generate the right answers to questions about their pains. Consider children who have learned, not only to *express* pain ('Ouch!' 'That hurts!'), but also to *describe* their pains, in part by localising them ('My foot hurts') and in part by characterising their qualities ('It's a sharp pain'). Let's grant for the sake of argument that the child who can inform others *where* it hurts, who can say, 'My x hurts', where 'x' refers to a part of the body, must understand the use of the pronoun 'my' *in regard to body parts*. That is, the child understands that the foot that hurts is 'part of me'. Nonetheless, this does not ensure that the child understands that the *hurting* or *pain* is also 'part of me': that it too is 'in *me*', that it is '*my*' hurt', '*my*' pain'. Consider the alternative: the child understands the *hurting* to be a property of the foot in just the way that its size, shape, and colour are properties of the foot. Or, for a closer analogy, the hurting is a temporary condition of the foot, like the property of being swollen. There may be warrant for calling the hurting a *qualitative* property of the foot, and it is at least conceivable that the mechanism underlying our attributions of that property to parts of the body is qualitative comparison with a standard held in memory. (It is especially plausible that *qualitative descriptions* of pain are produced in this way.) It may be that the child has a basis for saying that his foot hurts, or that there is a pain in his foot: the basis is, *the way the foot feels*. Yet there is nothing *mental* about what the child is attributing to his foot when he says it hurts.

The point is not simply that the child fails to understand that when his foot hurts, no one but he feels it hurt: that the hurting or pain is only in the individual whose body part hurts (empathy aside). The point is rather that he fails to grasp any sense in which the hurting or pain is *in* x, or is the pain *of* x, is x's pain, except the non-mental sense, in which being in or belonging to x is just being in or being a property of a part of x's body. He isn't yet at a point at which it even makes sense to him to *assert or deny* that the hurting or pain is only *in*, is only the pain *of*, the individual whose body part hurts. The child may speak of 'pain', but he does not conceive of this 'pain' as a kind of mental state. Hence he doesn't have the concept of *pain*. The object-level question about his foot is all he can understand; yet it is all the information he needs for answering (though not for understanding) the corresponding question about himself, namely whether he feels pain in his foot.[9]

3   Simulation places facts and pains at a mental location

If, as I claim, simulators need not be able to recognise their own mental states *as such*, for example, as '*my*' pain (and not just a pain that is 'in my foot'), and they need not even have the relevant mental state *concepts*, then it is appropriate to ask: how can simulation be used to attribute mental states *as such* to others? If simulation does not require that one already possess the relevant concepts, and thus the capacity to make *genuine, comprehending* ascriptions of mental states, then it must provide a bootstrap by which one can acquire these concepts and capacities. Greater conceptual understanding must come out of the simulation process than goes in. Is this possible?

I believe it is, but I offer here only a brief sketch of an explanation *how* it is possible. Recall the kind of understanding that was lacking in the children described in the previous section. Chief among the components of the concepts of belief, or of pain, that they failed to grasp, and presupposed by the rest, was the idea of something's being *at a mental location*. They didn't understand that a pain can be (much less that it must be) *mentally* at a location, that it can be *someone's* pain, and not just a pain in a part of someone's body. So they could not have understood the question, 'Does your foot hurt?' as a question about how their foot feels *to them*. Likewise, they didn't understand the idea of a fact being a fact *to* someone.

The very process of embedding ascent routines in simulations remedies this deficiency. It gives sense to the idea of a mental location. When an ascent routine is used within the context of a simulation, a new logical space is opened. One can understand the object-level question (Q2), 'Does Mickey Mouse have a tail?' to have answers *at* various locations in this space. For example, one child, Jane, might simulate another, Mary, and then ask herself, in the role of Mary, the object-level question, 'Does Mickey have a tail?' Simulation links the answer to the particular individual whose situation and behaviour constitute the evidence on which the simulation is based – the individual whom one is *identifying with* within the simulation. This, it seems to me, gives sense to the notion of something's being a fact *to* a particular individual. Thus when Jane, in the role of Mary, generates the response, 'Yes, I (Mary) believe Mickey Mouse has a tail', she will understand the 'I' to refer to that particular individual, Mary; and when, simulating another individual, Joe, she generates the response, 'Yes, I (Joe) believe Mickey Mouse has a tail', she will understand the 'I' to refer to Joe.[10]

I am not saying that simulation will give these children the concept of belief or the concept of pain. For there are components of these concepts that simulation alone would not enable the children to grasp. Indeed, the further lessons needed for understanding belief are quite different from those needed for pain. For example, unlike a *pain*, a fact need not have a mental location: something may be a *fact* even if it is not a fact *to* anyone. Thus it may be the case that p even if no one ever knows or is aware that p, or indeed even just happens to believe that p. More formally,

(B1) The following is possible: it is a fact that p, and it is true of no individual x that, to x, it is a fact that p.

And further:

(B2) The following is possible: it is not a fact that p, and, to some individual x, it is a fact that p.

(B3) The following is possible: to some individual x it is a fact that p, and to some individual y (not identical with x) it is not a fact that p.

In the case of pain, however, matters are quite different. Pains always have a mental location. There are no pains that are not the pains *of* someone (or, more broadly, something). More specifically, if a part of x's body hurts, then it hurts x, the pain is in x (it is not just 'out there' in x's foot, in the way the swelling of the foot may be). More formally,

(P1) The following is *necessary*: If ø hurts, and ø is a part of x's body, then ø's hurting is a state of x.

And further:

(P2) The following is *necessary*: If ø hurts, and ø is not a part of x's body, then ø's hurting is not a state of x's.

I am not suggesting, of course, that to understand belief and pain children must somehow learn, or their brains must come to represent, these generalisations *as such*, in discursive form. Rather, I would suppose that children, once they can by simulation assign mental locations to facts and pains, will learn *how* to do so. They will learn, for example, never to carry *pains* along with them into a simulation: for example, Jane will learn not to take along with her, when simulating any other individual, either 'the pain in my foot' or 'the pain in Jane's foot'. For otherwise, if Jane has a pain in her foot, then she would be representing the other individual either as feeling a pain in *her own* foot or as feeling the pain in *Jane's* foot. Facts, however, would be treated differently, for in simulating others we don't modify the facts without reason: if Mickey Mouse has a tail, then Mickey Mouse has a tail *to Mary*, unless there is a special reason, such as an epistemologically relevant difference between Mary and me, or some behaviour of hers best explained by a contrary hypothesis. In short, the procedure we learn is: leave all pains at the gate, and carry all facts through, unless specifically notified by Customs.

I hope that upon reaching the end of this essay the reader does not find 'radical' simulationism all that radical. For one thing, the hypothesis that we ascribe mental states to ourselves by ascent routines proves compatible with the hypothesis that the pain in the foot, for example, is recognised by its qualitative features, by the way it feels. For recognition of a pain 'out there' in the foot – or, for that matter, 'out there' in the tooth, or in the head – requires only object-level thinking, and no understanding of mental states as such. And what is needed to elevate such object-level thinking to an understanding of mental states *as such* is the ability to *reconceptualise* such 'objects' as the pain in the foot – or the facts about Mickey Mouse – as having a mental location. When the relevant ascent routine is used within a simulation, I suggested, a logical space is opened that enables us to think of pains and facts as located in (or at) individual minds. Thus simulation and ascent routines fit hand-in-glove. And if it *isn't* simulation that makes such reconceptualisation possible, then it must be something else; and competing theories will have to explain how this something else enables us to conceive the pain in the foot as *someone's* pain, and Mickey's having a tail as, possibly, a fact *to* someone.

NOTES

1 For a collection of essays pro and con the simulation theory, see Davies and Stone, 1995 and Stone and Davies, 1995.

2 One might want to reply that, even if Hermia is unable to categorise the expression and the inner state it expresses, her innate ToM module might be able to. After all, our powers of parsing natural language sentences far outstrip the meagre set of grammatical distinctions to which most native speakers have conscious access: why not the same for folk psychological distinctions? The answer, in brief, is that Fodor and others who posit a *ToM* module suppose that what explains our competence in predicting behaviour is *folk psychology*, the principles that underlie our common-sense concepts of mental states, whereas those who posit a *grammar* module would deny the corresponding claim, that what explains our grammatical competence is *folk grammar*, the principles that underlie common-sense notions of grammar (see Gordon, 1992b).

3 According to Meltzoff and Gopnik (1993), from which I borrow much of this account of the 'pick-up' of facial expressions, facial mimicry appears to originate in a prewired mapping: visually perceived faces translate directly into motor output. That is why infants can mimic in the absence of visual (e.g., mirror) feedback, which would enable them to compare their own motor output with the pattern they observe on the other's face.

4 For further discussion of the pickup of emotional expression in connection with Humean 'sympathy' and Adam Smith's 'impartial spectator', see Gordon (1995b).

5 I am using this term to stand in for any mode of appearance, including visual appearance, or look.

6 I am leaving aside the special case in which the belief question concerns a belief about a mental state. Generally, such a question would call for *iterated* ascent routines.

7 I am inclined to say we do so exclusively, except when we base self-ascriptions on situational and behavioural evidence; but I believe nothing I say in this essay commits me to so strong a claim.

8 Several people helped me see that I had been drawing the line at the wrong place: especially Peter Carruthers, Martin Davies, Jane Heal, and Josef Perner.

9 A similar thesis seems to me to be suggested, although within a very different philosophical framework, by Hume's famous observation about self-perception: 'For my part, when I enter most intimately into what I call myself, I always stumble on some particular perception or other, of heat or cold, light or shade, love or hatred, pain or pleasure. I never can catch myself at any time without a perception, and never can observe any thing but the perception' (Hume, 1739/1978).

10 Thus each 'I' uttered (or thought) within a simulation becomes for the simulator a genuine indexical term. This appears to contradict Ruth Millikan's claim

that so-called 'essential indexicals' are not really indexical: 'The universal self name [the mental 'I'] would not be an indexical for the selves who named themselves with it, and when read by someone else, it could function only as a natural sign, not as a sign in the language of thought' (Millikan, 1993).

3 Simulation and self-knowledge: a defence of theory-theory

Peter Carruthers

In this chapter I shall be attempting to curb the pretensions of simulationism. I shall argue that it is, at best, an epistemological doctrine of limited scope. It may explain how we go about attributing beliefs and desires to others, and perhaps to ourselves, in some cases. But simulation cannot provide the fundamental basis of our conception of, or of our knowledge of, minded agency.

1   Theory-theory

Let me begin by pinning my colours to the mast: I am a theory-theorist. I believe that our understanding of mentalistic notions – of belief, desire, perception, intention, and the rest – is largely given by the positions those notions occupy within a folk-psychological theory of the structure and functioning of the mind. To understand one of these notions is to know – at least implicitly – sufficiently much of the corpus of folk-psychology, and to know the role within that theory of the notion in question. I also maintain that children's developing competence with these mentalistic notions involves them in moving through a series of progressively more sophisticated theories – for example, moving from desire-perception theory, through a copy-theory of belief, to full-blown, intentionalistic, belief-desire theory (see Wellman, 1990).

This theory-theory approach is definitely to be preferred, in my view, either to various forms of Cartesianism and neo-Cartesianism on the one hand, or to behaviourist and quasi-behaviourist accounts of our conception of the mental on the other – preserving for us the realism of the former without the first-person primacy, and something of the essential potential publicity of the latter without its associated anti-realism. As we shall see later, any radical form of simulationism is in danger of slipping into Cartesianism in the one direction, or into some form of quasi-behaviourism in the other.

I also believe – to pin my colours to another mast – that at least the core of this folk-psychological theory is given innately, rather than acquired through a process of theorising, or learning of any sort. It makes its appearance in the individual through a process of ontogenetic development (though perhaps also requiring triggering experiences of particular sorts). And the different mentalistic theories that young children entertain should be thought of as different stages in the maturation of their theory-of-mind faculty, perhaps corresponding to, and replicating, the different stages in the history of its evolution in the human species (see Segal, this volume).

I favour such a nativistic theory-theory because if, firstly, young children are pictured as little scientists, constructing a mentalistic theory as the best explanation of the data (which data? – even action-descriptions presuppose folk-psychology!), then it beggars belief that they should all hit upon the *same* theory, and at the same tender age too (at about the age of four, in fact). But if, secondly, the theory is supposed to be learned by the child from adult practitioners, then it is puzzling how this can take place without any explicit teaching or training; and also how the theory itself, as a cultural construct, could remain invariant across cultures and historical eras. In contrast, the suggestion that folk-psychology might be innate is not at all implausible, given the crucial role that it plays in facilitating communication and social co-operation in highly social creatures such as ourselves. The nativist hypothesis also coheres well with what we know about the development of social competence in our nearest cousins, the apes (see Byrne and Whiten, 1988); and with what we know about the absence of mentalistic abilities in the case of people with autism (see Baron-Cohen, 1989c; Leslie, 1991; Carruthers, ch.16 this volume).

This nativistic version of theory-theory is not one that I need to depend upon here, however, except insofar as it may be necessary to remove one support for simulationism. For the picture of two- and three-year-old children as little scientists constructing their theories through a process of data collection, hypothesis formation, and testing, is otherwise apt to seem extravagant, even if they are partly guided in this process by the implicit theory-deployments of the adults around them. (See Goldman, 1989, pp. 167-8, and Gordon, 1986, p. 170, where these arguments are made much of in support of simulation-theory; see also Gopnik and Wellman, 1992, pp. 167-8, for a non-nativist reply.) There is some reason to think, indeed, that the hypothesis of child-as-scientist is not only extravagant, but close to incoherent. For recall that it is agreed on all hands by developmental psychologists that children do not acquire the concept of false belief until sometime in their fourth year. Then how could the child-scientist possibly realise that their previous mentalistic theory was false or inadequate, and hence replace or modify it, prior to acquiring such a concept? It is difficult to understand how anyone – whether child or adult – could operate as a scientist, who did not yet possess the concept of false belief.

2   Simulation within a theory

Now how, on the theory-theoretic account, does one set about attributing beliefs, desires, and intentions to others? Partly, and most fundamentally, through deploying one's theoretical knowledge. It is in virtue of knowing such things as: the relationship between line of vision, attention, and perception; between perception, background knowledge, and belief; between belief, desire, and intention; and between perception, intention, and action; that one is able to predict and explain the actions of others, on this account. One may also deploy theoretical knowledge of the distinctive manner in which propositional attitudes will interact with one another in processes of reasoning in virtue of their form, deploying such principles as: that someone who wants it to be the case that Q, and believes that if P then Q, and believes that P is within their power, will, other things being equal, form an intention to cause it to be the case that P; that someone who has formed an intention to bring it about that P when R, and who believes that R, will then act so as to bring it about that P; that someone who believes that all Fs are Gs, and who comes to believe that F-of-a, will also believe that G-of-a; and so on. But it is also very plausible that this theoretical knowledge may be supplemented, on occasion, by a process of simulation.

General theoretical knowledge – that is, the sort of non-content-specific knowledge that might very plausibly be held to be innately given – is all very well as a framework, but plainly needs to be supplemented in some way if one is to be able to provide fine-grained intentionalistic predictions and explanations. There appear to be only two options here: either to supplement one's initial folk-psychological theory with a whole lot of further more specific theoretical knowledge, concerning what people with *particular* beliefs and desires may be inclined to do or think; or to simulate, *using* the inferential connections amongst one's own contentful states to derive a prediction for, or explanation of, the other. It may be that both of these options are realised in us, to some degree. But there are arguments to suggest that we do – perhaps must – use simulation sometimes, at least.

One's grasp of the immediate inferential connections entered into by someone's beliefs and desires will sometimes be crucial in the attempt to provide predictions and explanations of either their mental states or their behaviour. Thus, for example, if I attribute to someone the belief that a particular brick is cubic, then I should predict that they will be surprised if it should turn out to look oblong when viewed from another angle. Now, suppose that something along the lines of the theory of concepts proposed by Peacocke (1986, 1991) is correct in this regard – that is, suppose that the conditions for possessing any given concept may include a set of canonical grounds for, and/or a set of canonical commitments of, thoughts containing it. So a condition for possessing the concept *cubic* will be, for example, that if one is prepared to judge, of a particular perceptually presented object, 'That is cubic', then one will be primitively disposed to accept that the object will continue to appear as such when viewed from any other angle in normal conditions. (See Peacocke, 1986, pp. 15ff.) It will be, then, precisely this feature of the possession-conditions of *cubic* that underlies the prediction made earlier, concerning the conditions under which the subject will show surprise. And so on for many other concepts.

The upshot is that in order to predict what someone who entertains a thought containing a concept such as *cubic* will do or think, I shall have to predict the inferential role of that concept. I *could* do this by deploying a portion of what would be an extensive theory of concepts, whose clauses would severally specify the possession-conditions for the full range of concepts available. But it is immensely implausible that I should ever have had the opportunity to learn such a theory, and even more implausible that it should be innate (remember, many of *these* concepts, about whose possession-conditions I would be supposed to have a theory, would definitely *not* be innate, including such concepts as *cow, horse,* and *car*). There is, moreover, an easy alternative – I can *simulate* the role of the concept in the mental life of the other by relying on my grasp of that same concept, inserting thoughts containing it into my reasoning systems, in order to see what I should then be disposed to do or think as a result.

The sort of limited role for simulation sketched above is something that a theory-theorist should have no principled objection to, in my view. (As I understand it, Heal defends a limited form of simulationism of this sort – see her 1986, 1995, and this volume; as does Wellman, 1990.) Such a proposal leaves in place the fundamental, and defining, framework of theory beloved of theory-theorists, while allowing simulation a role in generating fine-grained predictions and explanations of the thoughts, feelings, and actions of other people. On such a view it will be, at least partly, an empirical matter just which sorts of mental-state attributions employ simulation, and which operate purely theoretically – indeed, a good many of the empirical debates in the literature can be seen as directed at this question. My quarrel with simulationism only begins when the latter attempts to usurp the role accorded to theory in the account sketched above. My particular focus will be on the treatments that the various accounts can give of *self-knowledge* – of the knowledge that one has of one's own mental states. I shall begin by outlining what I take to be a plausible theory-theoretic account of the matter, before criticising the two main simulationist alternatives.

3   Self-knowledge as theory-laden recognition

What account is the theory-theorist to provide of our knowledge of our own mental states? In particular, must such a theorist be committed to the implausible view that we know of our own mental states just as we know of the mental states of other people – by means of an inference to the best explanation of the (behavioural) data, operated within the framework of a folk-psychological theory? Most theory-theorists have not thought it necessary to travel this route, maintaining, rather, that self-knowledge should be thought of as analogous to the theory-laden perception of theoretical entities in science. Just as a physicist can (in context, and given a background of theoretical knowledge) sometimes *see* that electrons are being emitted by the substance under study; and just as a diagnostician can *see* a particular sort of tumour in the blur of an X-ray photograph; so, too, can we each of us sometimes see (that is, know intuitively and non-inferentially) that we are in a state accorded such-and-such a role by folk-psychological theory.

In saying that our beliefs about our own mental states are arrived at non-inferentially, of course I only mean to exclude the intervention of conscious, person-level, inferences. For it is highly plausible to claim that *all* perception is inferential, at some level. Indeed, it may be that the above analogy proves to be somewhat less than perfect when one considers the kinds of sub-personal inferences that might be involved. In particular, in the scientific case the perception of an electron, or of a tumour, will presumably be mediated by sub-personal inferences that somehow access and deploy the conscious theoretical knowledge of the person in question. But this may not always be so in the case of knowledge of our own mental states, since much of folk-psychology may be only implicitly, not consciously, known.

Thus, it may be part of the normal functioning of the mind that a mental state, M, if conscious, will automatically give rise to the belief that I have M, without all the principles of folk-psychology that play a part in generating that belief being accessible to me. But still, what I will recognise when I recognise that I have M is a state having a particular folk-psychological characterisation. Although the process of acquiring self-knowledge may involve theories, or aspects of theories, that are only implicitly known by the subject, still the upshot of that process – the knowledge that I am in M – will nevertheless be theory-involving. On the theory-theory account, what I recognise my own mental states *as*, are states having a particular folk-psychological role, even if I am unable to provide, consciously, a complete characterisation of that role.

I have explained how a theory-theorist can claim that we have knowledge of our own mental states 'immediately', without conscious inference (and in the normal case, surely, without *any* sort of inference from observations of our own behaviour). But my view is that such an account should only be endorsed for self-knowledge of *occurrent* mental states, such as pains, perceptions, acts of wondering whether, forming an intention to, and judging that. In particular, it does *not* apply to standing states such as beliefs, desires, and long-term intentions. Rather, our knowledge of such standing states is normally achieved by activating them into corresponding occurrent events, to which one does then have immediate access. So what enables me to have knowledge that I believe that P is not, in the first instance, that my state is reliably disposed to give rise to the belief that I believe that P. Rather, it is that my belief is apt to emerge in an occurrent *judgement* that P, where such a judgement is an event of which I will have immediate non-inferential knowledge.

The suggestion above is supported by the intuitive epistemology of self-attributions of belief, desire, and intention, noted by a number of writers (see, for example, Evans, 1982, p. 225; Gordon, 1995 and this volume). Thus, what I do when I attempt to determine whether or not I believe that world deforestation will be disastrous is ask myself, first, the first-order question, 'Is it the case that world deforestation will be disastrous?'; if I find myself inclined to answer, 'Yes', then I make a semantic ascent, and am prepared on that basis to issue the second-order statement, 'I believe that world deforestation will be disastrous.' Thus the primary way in which I have knowledge of my own standing-state beliefs is through the manner in which those beliefs are apt to emerge in occurrent judgements with the same content, and it is only the latter of which I should be said to have quasi-perceptual knowledge.

The above point is important for a number of reasons, not least the way in which it enables us to handle self-*mis*-attributions of belief, desire, or intention. It is well known that in a variety of situations subjects will confabulate false explanations of their own behaviour (see Nisbett and Ross, 1980). For example, if asked to choose from what is, in fact, an identical array of objects, subjects will consistently choose from the right-hand side; but if asked to explain their choice they will claim that the object in question was more attractive, or a brighter colour, or something of the sort. I hypothesise that in all such cases the reasoning that leads to action is not conscious – that is, in the present context, it consists in occurrent events that are *not* apt to emerge in self-knowledge of their own existence. So what one does in such cases, knowing that there must be *some* explanation for one's action, is to construct an explanation *post hoc*, either by deploying relevant theoretical knowledge, or by using a simulation strategy. This enables the explanation to be wildly at variance with the facts, just as it can be in our attempted explanations of the behaviour of others. It will only be in those cases where the reasoning that leads to action consists in occurrent conscious thoughts, that one would expect a much higher degree of reliability in self-attribution, according to the account sketched here.

There is one important problem with the account still remaining, however. For I have conceded that one may have to use simulation to discover the causal roles of some particular beliefs and desires (and also, by implication, the occurrent counterparts thereof). So when I have self-knowledge of the occurrence of these events, what am I aware of them *as?* Since, by hypothesis, the background folk-psychological theory is not sufficient to individuate the particular events in question (at least as objects of knowledge), quite what, then, *does* individuate them? Here I suggest that it is the linguistic *form* of those events. Our conscious occurrent judgements may mostly consist in deployments of imaged sentences, generally the very same sentences that one would use to express those judgements aloud. So self-knowledge of the judgement is mediated by self-knowledge of the occurrence of the vehicle of the judgement, namely an imaged sentence. (For more detailed development and defence of this view, see my 1996.) Then when the thought occurs to me that world deforestation will be disastrous, I shall immediately know what I have just thought because I can recall – and hence reliably report and reproduce – the very form of words that my thought employed; namely, 'World deforestation will be disastrous.'

I have sketched my preferred theory-theoretic account of self-knowledge of mental states, which models the latter on the case of theory-dependent perceptual knowledge. This account is, I think, an attractive one, having both intrinsic plausibility and substantial explanatory power. I shall now contrast that account with two different forms of simulation-theory – each of which is more ambitious than the kind of limited simulationism discussed above – due to Goldman and Harris on the one hand, and Gordon on the other. Each of these runs into insuperable trouble, I shall argue, in its treatment of self-knowledge in particular.

4   Simulationism and the priority of introspection – Goldman and Harris

The versions of simulationism developed by Goldman (1989, 1992b, 1993a) and Harris (1989, 1992) are ambitious – and distinctively anti-theoretical – in the sense that they purport to provide the very basis for the child's ability to ascribe mental states to other people; but they take self-knowledge of mental states for granted. On this view, when I explain or predict the behaviour of another person, I pretend to adopt some beliefs or desires which issue, as a result of the normal operating of my practical reasoning processes, in a pretend intention to perform the action to be explained or predicted. But for this to work I have to be able to recognise, in my own case, the beliefs, desires, and intentions in question (or at least the pretend versions of them). Having access to my own mental states, I use simulation to ascribe mental states to others.

What kind of access am I supposed to have to my own mental states, on this account? In particular, when I recognise in myself a given mental state, M, what do I recognise it *as*? Not, presumably, as a state normally occupying a particular causal role, or satisfying a certain theoretical description, since this would then be just another version of theory-theory. As what, then? It is hard to see how there can be any alternative but to say: as a particular distinctive *feeling*, or *quale*. On such a view, the basic mentalistic concepts, instances of which serve as inputs to the process of simulation, are *purely recognitional* ones. I begin by distinguishing between one type of mental state and another purely on the basis of their intrinsic, subjectively accessible, qualities. I may then later, through observing regularities in my subjective life, and through success in simulating the mental lives of others, come to have a body of theoretical knowledge about these states. But such knowledge is derivative, not fundamental.

The above statement of this form of simulation-theory fits Goldman's (1993a) characterisation of his position very well, and is at least consistent with Harris's somewhat less explicit presentation of the nature of self-knowledge (see his 1989, pp.54–7). However, Goldman once attempted to avoid the conclusion that mentalistic concepts must be grounded in capacities to recognise subjective qualities. He wrote as follows:

If the simulation-theory is right, however, it looks as if the main elements of the grasp of mental concepts must be located in the first-person sphere. Is this objectionable? We should recall, first, how problematic purely third-person accounts of the mental have turned out to be. Second, we should note that the simulation approach does not confine its attention to purely 'private', 'internal' events. It also invokes relations between mental states, on the one hand, and both perceptual situations and overt actions. Thus, there may well be enough ingredients of the right sort to make sense of a first-person-based grasp of mental concepts. (1989, p.183)

This was wholly unconvincing. First, that purely third-person accounts of mental concepts are problematic provides no support whatever for accounts that are purely first-personal. For there remains the intermediate theory-theoretic account sketched in section 3 above, which allows for the existence of first-person recognition of mental states, but maintains that this is recognition of them *as* states with particular theoretical characterisations. Second, if knowledge of the relations between mental states, and with perceptual situations and overt actions, is supposed to be constitutive of grasp of mental concepts, then what we have here is just another version of theory-theory. If, on the other hand, Goldman meant that these relations are to be learned subsequent to our grasp of mentalistic concepts, then it really is the case, after all, that such concepts must consist, at bottom, in pure recognitional abilities for distinctive feel.

What would be wrong with that? For most contemporary philosophers it is sufficient to refute the Goldman-Harris suggestion, to point out that it commits them to a form of neo-Cartesianism. But lest we reject the position too hastily, let us consider whether or not it is really vulnerable to the standard objections to Cartesian accounts of the mental. Firstly, it need not be committed to the ontological aspects of Cartesianism, of course, since the thesis only concerns the nature of our most basic mentalistic *concepts*, not the nature of mental *phenomena*. So the position is fully consistent with the sort of physicalism which is obligatory, now-a-days, for all right-thinking men and women.

Now secondly, what of the objection that Cartesian conceptions of the mental must inevitably render our knowledge of the mental states of other people problematic? This was a popular line of objection to Cartesianism in the 50s and 60s, when it was often claimed that by starting from acquaintance with my own mental states, and then having to argue by analogy to the mental states of others, I should be making what is, in effect, a weak induction from just one instance (see, for example, Malcolm, 1958). This objection, too, is easily answered, as Goldman himself points out (1989, pp.181–2), provided that we are prepared to accept a reliabilist conception of knowledge – provided, that is, we accept that knowledge is *reliably acquired* true belief rather than being, as tradition would have it, *justified* true belief. For, given reliabilism, my beliefs about the mental states of others will count as known provided that the process by which I arrive at them is in fact a reliable one. And it may be that simulation is just such a process.

Finally, what of the point that not every different type of mental state really does have a distinctive feel to it? While recognition of feel may be plausible for experiential states such as pains, tickles, and sensations of red, it is, surely, hugely *im*plausible for beliefs, desires, and intentions. So my concepts of the latter cannot consist in any bare recognitional capacity. Here Goldman and Harris can reply that it is only *occurrent* mental events that have qualia – our concept of belief then being the concept of a standing-state that is *apt to emerge in* an event (an occurrent judgement) with a particular distinctive feel.

Thus if Goldman and Harris can make out the case that every occurrent mental state – in particular, every act of judging, wondering whether, wishing, and hoping – has a distinctive feel to it, appropriate to be an object of bare recognition, then it appears that they may be home and dry. But this now looks like a more promising avenue of criticism. For there are a potential infinity of such states, in virtue of the unlimited creativity of thought. Are we to suppose that each of us possesses, miraculously, an unlimited set of corresponding recognitional capacities? And anyway, what *does* it feel like to judge that today is Tuesday, as opposed to judging that today is Wednesday? Are there really any distinctive subjective feelings here to be had?

The only way forward for this form of simulationism that I can see, is to borrow the claim defended briefly above, that conscious propositional episodes of judging, wondering whether, and so on, consist in deployments of imaged sentences; and to couple this with the claim that we can immediately recognise such images in virtue of the way they feel to us. This enables the account to harness the creative powers of language to explain our capacity to recognise in ourselves an unlimited number of propositional episodes, and makes it seem plausible that there will, indeed, be a feeling distinctive of judging that today is Tuesday – namely the distinctive feel of imaging the *sentence*, 'Today is Tuesday.' Thus, I can, on this account, recognise in myself the new act of wondering whether there is a dragon on the roof (never before encountered), because this action consists in the formation of an image of the sentence, 'Is there a dragon on the roof?' (which is a state a *bit like hearing* that sentence), and because I can recognise this image in myself in virtue of being capable of recognising the distinctive feels of its component parts.

While such a view can avoid the standard objections to Cartesianism, there remain a great many difficulties with it. Notice, to begin with, that I should have to do a good deal of inductive learning from my own case before I could be capable of simulation, on this account. I should have to learn, in particular, that whenever I am aware of the distinctive feel of an intention, where the feel is similar to that of hearing an utterance of the form of words 'P', that I thereafter generally find myself performing actions describable as 'P'. For only so will I have any way of generating a predicted action for another person from the pretend-intention with which my simulation of them concludes. And since these feelings do not wear their causal efficacy on their sleeves, I should also have to reason to the best explanation, having discovered reliable correlations between feelings of various types, to arrive at a theory of the causal sequences involved.

(Notice that simulationism now inherits all the difficulties of the child-as-scientist theory-theory account. For the child has to be pictured as building up a body of theoretical knowledge of the causal relations amongst states which it can introspectively recognise immediately on the basis of their feels. It remains remarkable that all normal children should end up with the same body of knowledge at about the same time. And it remains mysterious how anyone is to engage in a practice of inferring to the best explanation who does not yet possess the concept of false belief.)

Notice, too, just how *opaque* an explanation of action would seem at this early stage. It would have the normal form: '*This* feel and *that* feel caused *that* feel. [This belief and that desire caused that intention.] And that latter feel caused me to do P. [That intention caused my action.]' The suggestion that one could get from here to anything recognisable as belief-desire psychology is about as plausible (that is, immensely *im*plausible) as the claim that we can get from descriptions of sequences of sense-data to full-blown descriptions of physical reality.

Philosophers and psychologists alike have long since given up believing that children learn to construct the world of three-dimensional physical objects, and then arrive at something resembling common-sense physics, by establishing inductive correlations amongst sense-data and reasoning to the best explanation thereof. The idea that children have to construct folk-psychology from their first-person acquaintance with their own feelings, supplemented by simulation of the feelings of others, should seem equally indefensible. For in both domains, note, the classifications made by the folk have to reflect, and respect, a rich causal structure. Even if we agree that all mental states have introspectively accessible feels, fit to be subjects of immediate recognition, it still remains the case that such feelings are useless for purposes of explanation until supplemented by much additional causal knowledge. And the question of how we acquire such knowledge is no more plausibly answered by simulationism than by child-as-scientist versions of theory-theory.

I have argued that the version of simulationism due to Goldman and Harris must face severe difficulties. Let me now conclude this section with two rather more precise sources of worry for their account. The first is that there are cases where we can have, and know that we have, distinct propositional episodes, where it is nevertheless implausible that there would be any difference between them in terms of introspectible feel. For example, consider the difference between *intending* and *predicting* that if the party should turn out to be a bore then I shall fall asleep. Each state will consist, on the above account, in an image of the very same sentence – the sentence, namely, 'If the party is a bore I shall go to sleep.' So the claim must be that imaging this sentence in the mode of intention is subjectively, introspectively, different from imaging it in the mode of prediction. This certainly does not fit with *my* phenomenology. Granted, I will immediately know that I have formed an intention, if I have; but not on the basis of the distinctive way the event *felt*.

The second difficulty is the converse one – that there are cases where propositional episodes would be distinct, on the above account, which are, in reality, the same. Thus two token actions of judging that the dog bit the postman might consist, in the one case, of an image of the sentence, 'The dog bit the postman', and in the other case of an image of the distinct sentence, 'The postman was bitten by the dog.' Since the sentences are different, so are the images, and so too, on the account above, must be the mental states in question. But they are not. These are tokens of the very same type of thought.

Note that these examples present no difficulty for the sort of theory-theoretic account of introspective knowledge considered earlier. For our cognitive systems might very well be able to tell the difference between intending that P and predicting that P (which will, for the theory-theorist, be a difference in distinctive causal role) on the basis of differences that are not available to consciousness, or at any rate differences that are not phenomenological. Similarly, the imaged sentences about the postman will both be counted as constitutive of the very same thought, in virtue of my background theoretical knowledge that active-passive transformations have no significant effect upon causal role.

5   Simulationism without introspection – Gordon

Gordon has an even more ambitious story to tell about how it is possible to represent the beliefs and desires of another person. He claims, in particular, that this can occur without introspective access to one's own mental states, without yet having any mentalistic concepts, and without engaging in any sort of analogical inference from oneself to the other. (See his 1986, 1992a, 1995, and this volume.) The story is, first, that I put my own practical reasoning system into suppositional mode by pretending to *be* the other person, A. Then within the scope of such a pretence, my uses of the first-person pronoun refer to A, and my expressions of pretended belief in the form 'P' or 'I believe that P' therefore represent the beliefs of A. To this is added the claim that basic competence in the use of utterances of the form, 'I believe that P', 'I want that P', or 'I intend that P' require, not introspective access to the states of belief, desire, or intention in question, but only an ascent routine whereby one *expresses* one's beliefs, desires, and intentions in this new linguistic form. Here we have the materials for an account of how simulation can enable a child to boot-strap its way into acquiring mentalistic concepts without introspective access, and of how it can attribute the corresponding states to others without relying on an analogical inference.

There is one respect in which Gordon's account is in need of supplementation, I believe. For *representing* A as believing that P is not the same thing as *ascribing* to A the belief that P, or as *asserting*, or *judging*, that A believes that P. (Similar remarks apply, *mutatis mutandis*, to representing versus ascribing a desire or an intention.) Pretend-asserting 'P' or 'I believe that P' while simulating A is surely one thing, making, assertorically, the attribution, 'A believes that P' is quite another. For the first assertion occurs *within the scope of a pretence*, and is therefore not properly an assertion at all. How, then, is a simulator to get from the former to the latter? Will this re-introduce, after all, an inference from me to you? I think not, or not necessarily. Gordon should claim that what is distinctive of simulation, as opposed to other forms of imaginative identification, is that I am primitively disposed to complete the process by transforming pronouns, or by substituting a name for the first-person pronoun. So when I conclude my simulation of A with the pretend-assertion, 'I believe that P', I am then disposed to assert, outside of the scope of a simulation, 'He believes that P' or, 'A believes that P.'

Is this reply really sufficient to save Gordon from trouble? For does it not look like there must be at least a *tacit* inference from me to you? For the transforming of pronouns is only going to be valid on the (tacit) assumption that you are relevantly similar to myself. I think Gordon should concede this point, since it does not damage his main case. The only sort of inference from me to you that Gordon is committed to rejecting is one which would require us to have introspective access to our own mental states, and/or one which would require us to possess the concepts of belief and desire in advance. The tacit inference from me to you which is involved in the transformation of pronouns at the end of a process of simulation seems to require neither.

Now, I applaud Gordon's rejection of the introspectionist account of knowledge of our own beliefs and desires. Beliefs and desires are standing states; they are not experiences, nor even occurrent events. We therefore cannot have knowledge of them by virtue of introspecting their distinctive qualities. I also applaud what Gordon calls the *answer-check* procedure as an account of the way in which we give reports of our own beliefs and desires. But this is not because I agree that we only begin to acquire the concept of belief by being trained to preface our assertions with 'I believe that'. Rather, it is because I think that the primary way in which beliefs and desires, as standing states, become occurrent, and contribute to the causation of behaviour, is by emerging in acts of thinking *with the same content.* What is distinctive of my conscious standing-state belief that February contains twenty-eight days except in a leap year, is that I am, in appropriate circumstances, disposed to judge (think to myself), 'February has twenty-eight days, except in a leap year.' And what is distinctive of my conscious standing-state desire to have a holiday in France, is that I am disposed, in suitable circumstances, to think to myself, 'If only I were on holiday in France!', or, 'I want to have a holiday in France.' Whether or not I express these thoughts is irrelevant, in my view.

However, I *do* think that our *occurrent* thinkings *are* introspectible. By this I mean at least that we are each of us aware, immediately and non-inferentially, of what we have just judged, wondered whether, or made up our minds to do. (Remember, by a non-inferential process I mean only one that involves no conscious inferences.) We are also aware of the sequences of our thoughts, and will know, at least shortly afterwards, what led us to think one thing after another, and what sequence of reasoning led up to our decisions. (If saying this puts me in the opposite camp from Wittgenstein, Ryle, and Malcolm – see Gordon, 1995, note 2 – well then, so be it. My counter-charge is that Gordon is committed to something resembling the unacceptable behaviourism of these writers.) Acknowledging these facts does not have to make one into a Cartesian. They can equally well be accommodated by a functionalist theory of the mental, supplemented by a theory-theory account of our understanding of mentalistic concepts, as we saw in section 3 above. As a functionalist I can claim that it is distinctive of conscious thinkings that they are apt to give rise to the knowledge that those thinkings have just taken place, where the concepts deployed in such items of second-order knowledge are embedded in a common-sense theory of the workings of the mind.

Can Gordon find a place for the introspective phenomena mentioned above? I can't see how. For how could he possibly make an account of introspective knowledge ride on the back of this sort of radical – introspection-less – story about simulation? Indeed, I can't see how, from the process of simulation as Gordon describes it, I could even so much as *get the idea that* processes of reasoning often lead up to decisions, let alone get to know of the details of those processes in my own case. Let me elaborate.

According to Gordon, the child begins by being disposed to make assertions about the world, and by being disposed to express (not describe) its own desires and intentions. On this basis some new locutions can easily be introduced – the child can be trained to preface its assertions with, 'I believe that', its expressions of desire with, 'I want', and its expressions of intention with, 'I intend'. Having got so far, it can then begin to use increasingly sophisticated forms of simulation to attribute beliefs, desires, and intentions to other people, and can come to realise that an assertion of the form, 'A believes that P', can be appropriate when an outright assertion of the form, 'P', is not, and vice versa. (People can have false beliefs, and can be ignorant.) The child can also, on this basis, form a descriptive conception of the belief that P as: that state which is apt to issue in (cause) the utterances 'P' and/or 'I believe that P'. It can also form a descriptive conception of the difference between standing-state and occurrent beliefs, characterising the latter as a belief-state which is currently engaged in the causation of behaviour. But none of this would begin to give the child introspective access to its own occurrent beliefs (judgements), except by inference (presumably employing simulation) from its own recent behaviour; nor would it yet have any idea that it often engages in trains of thinking.

Can one imagine the process of self-simulation becoming so smooth and swift as to give us almost instantaneous knowledge of our own occurrent thoughts, independently of any disposition that we might have to verbalise those thoughts aloud? If so, then simulation might be able to boot-strap us into something at least resembling introspection. But the answer to the question is clearly negative. For simulation requires data to operate upon. In the case of attributions of occurrent thought, there must, in particular, be some overt behaviour to explain. Any process of simulation which concludes with a thought-attribution of the form, 'A has just judged that P', must *begin* with a representation of an action-to-be-explained, the process of simulation then consisting in trying out various pretend-judgements until hitting upon one that issues in a pretend-intention to perform the action in question.

Thus one can, by using simulation, only come to know of an occurrent thought *after* the behaviour which it causes. But since many thoughts occur some time prior to the actions that they rationalise, simulation will never be able to issue in thought-attributions to oneself that are, in general, anything like simultaneous with the thoughts ascribed. Moreover, since many occurrent thoughts never issue in action at all, they must forever lie beyond the reach of a simulationist strategy, no matter how swift and smooth it may become.

6   Three sets of empirical commitments

I have argued, on the basis of a variety of armchair (or rather typing-stool) considerations, that theory-theory is preferable to either form of simulation-theory in terms, at least, of its treatment of first-person knowledge. It is worth noting that some of the empirical data, too, pull in the same direction, specifically relating to the developmental sequence of self- and other-attributions of propositional attitudes. This is a good testing-ground for me, since each of the three theories I have considered makes distinct predictions about the normal order of development.

The theory-theory predicts that there should be no difference in the development of self- and other-attributions. As more sophisticated mentalistic theories and concepts become available, either through learning or maturation, so they can feed into more sophisticated attributions either to oneself or to other people. So we should expect a pattern of development in which children make essentially the same sorts of characteristic errors in self- and other-attributions at the same developmental stages.

The Goldman-Harris theory, on the other hand, predicts that competence in self-attribution should be achieved *before* competence in other-attribution. For simulation, in this version of the story, consists in projections of mentalistic attributions from oneself to a simulated other. So the predicted pattern of development will be a movement from common errors in both self- and other-attribution, through a stage at which there are characteristic errors still occurring in other-attribution which have disappeared in the case of self-attribution, to a stage of overall competence.

Finally, Gordon's form of simulationism predicts (counter-intuitively) that competence in self-attribution should only be achieved *after* competence in other-attribution. For on such an account (as Gordon himself notes, 1995), attributing mental states to oneself with full understanding (not just using the *answer-check* procedure followed by semantic ascent) requires a dual (and hence more difficult) simulation – in fact I must simulate another person (or myself at a later time) simulating myself.

Pleasingly, the available empirical data count in favour of theory-theory on this matter. At the stage at which children are still making errors in allowing for the possibility of false belief, or in distinguishing between different sources of belief, or in describing the appearance of an illusory object (such as the 'rock-sponge'), they are just as likely to make these errors in relation to their own states as to the states of other people, and vice versa. (See Gopnik and Wellman, 1992, pp.160–6, and Gopnik, 1993, pp. 3–8 and 90–3.) And when these errors disappear, they disappear across both self- and other-attributions together.

Conclusion

Granted, simulationism may have some valuable things to tell us about the way in which we go about predicting and explaining the mental states and actions of other people, and of our own past selves, in some circumstances. But it has, I claim, nothing of value to tell us about the manner in which those states are conceptualised or introspectively known. If I am right, then the only defensible form of the doctrine will be: *simulationism circumscribed by theory*.

To oversimplify the history just a little: first there was Cartesianism, then there was behaviourism, and then there was theory-theory. This sequence was generally perceived to be progressive. Now we have simulationism, which is claimed to advance our understanding still further. But it is, in reality, a step back – either to Cartesianism, in the Goldman-Harris version of it, or to quasi-behaviourism, in the Gordon version. So theory-theory still rules OK!

ACKNOWLEDGEMENTS

I am grateful to the following for their comments on an earlier draft: George Botterill, Jack Copeland, Paul Harris, and Peter J. Smith.

4   Varieties of off-line simulation

Shaun Nichols, Stephen Stich, Alan Leslie, and David Klein

1   Simulation and information

In the last few years, off-line simulation has become an increasingly important alternative to standard explanations in cognitive science. The contemporary debate began with Gordon (1986) and Goldman's (1989) off-line simulation account of our capacity to predict behaviour. On their view, in predicting people's behaviour we take our own decision-making system 'off line' and supply it with the 'pretend' beliefs and desires of the person whose behaviour we are trying to predict; we then let the decision maker reach a decision on the basis of these pretend inputs. Figure 4.1 offers a 'boxological' version of the off-line simulation theory of behaviour prediction.[1]

The off-line simulation theory of behaviour prediction is a radical departure from the typical explanations of cognitive capacities. In explaining a capacity in some domain (e.g., our ability to solve mathematical problems), the usual strategy in cognitive science is to suppose that the subject has a body of information about that domain (see, e.g., Fodor, 1968a). For example, our ability to predict the motion of projectiles is thought to depend on a body of information about mechanics – a folk physics. Of course, much if not all of these information bases or theories may be tacit or 'sub-doxastic' (Stich, 1978). Further, different theorists have different ideas about how the information is encoded. Some think that the information is encoded in sentence-like structures (Fodor, 1975); others think the information is represented by non-sentential mental models (Johnson-Laird, 1983); still others think that the information is represented by the connection strengths between the nodes of a neural network (Churchland, 1989). Despite the serious and sometimes harsh disagreement between these theorists, they all explain cognitive capacities by appealing to *some* kind of information regarding the domain. In contrast, an off-line simulation account of a capacity claims that the capacity *doesn't* depend on information about the domain. According to such accounts, whether or not a subject has information about the domain is irrelevant to the capacity. Instead of appealing to information about the domain, such theories

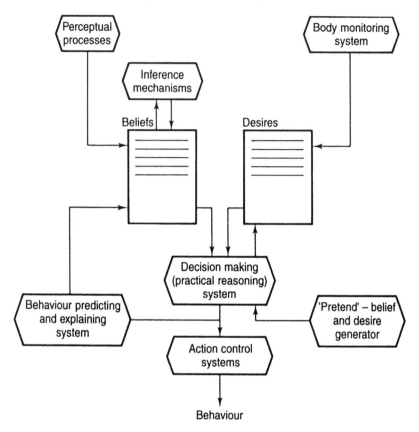

Figure 4.1 Simulation-based account of behaviour prediction

appeal to a mechanism that is already present, but claim that the mechanism is used to support another function. As a result, off-line simulation accounts present a strikingly different picture of cognitive capacities. Indeed, it seems that if off-line simulation can provide plausible accounts of a number of important capacities, it may well constitute a new paradigm in cognitive science.

Given the radical departure off-line simulation takes from information-based theories, simulation may be viewed either as a promising alternative or as an insidious threat to traditional theories in cognitive science. Either way, off-line simulation deserves our careful attention. In this paper, we want to show just how extensive the simulation alternative is. In this first section, we will try to put the notion of off-line simulation into a broader perspective than has been considered in the literature. We will also discuss how cognitive penetrability provides a wedge for empirically determining whether a capacity requires an information-based account or an off-line simulation account. In the second section, we'll present some empirical results on the cognitive penetrability of our capacity to predict behaviour. In the final section, we'll consider some recent extensions of off-line simulation theory. We'll look at simulation-based accounts of counterfactual reasoning, empathy and mental imagery.

1.1   Off-line simulation

Although the off-line simulation theory of behaviour prediction has received the most attention (see, for example, the essays in Davies and Stone, 1995), the basic idea of off-line simulation can be cast in a much broader framework. To explain this framework, it will be helpful to recount a familiar presupposition in cognitive science. One guiding assumption in cognitive science for the past quarter century is that the mind is composed of different cognitive components that are individuated by their functions (Fodor, 1968a, Dennett, 1978). For instance, beliefs are distinguished from desires by the fact that beliefs serve a different function from desires. Hence, cognitive scientists tend to posit distinct belief and desire components. Similarly, we distinguish the capacity to draw theoretical or logical inferences from the capacity to draw practical or desire-based inferences. These capacities too are distinguished by their functions. Distinguishing cognitive components by their functions results in a 'functional architecture' of the mind. A prevalent and colourful way of presenting models of such functional components is by supposing that the mind is made up of various boxes, each of which has a different function.[2] Figure 4.1 is one example of such a 'boxology'.

The basic idea of the off-line simulation theory of behaviour prediction is that the practical reasoning component is taken off line and used for predicting behaviour. However, there's no reason to suppose that the idea of off-line simulation can't be extended to components other than the practical reasoning system. In fact, given a boxology (a functional architecture), *each* component can be viewed as a possible engine of simulation. In principle, *any* component can be taken off line (detached from its usual function) and be used to perform some other function. That is, each component could conceivably be disengaged from its normal purpose and used to support or produce another capacity.

There are a few points worth emphasising about the breadth of this idea. First, it's possible that the same component or mechanism can support several different types of simulation-based capacities. For instance, it's conceivable that the practical reasoning mechanism is taken off line to support our capacity for behaviour prediction as well as our capacity for conditional planning. Indeed, it seems that this is exactly what Goldman has proposed (1993b).

Second, off-line simulation isn't restricted to processing components. The possibility of disengaging a component from its normal functions is clearest for processing or computational mechanisms, like the practical reasoner or the inference device. But it is also true for storage components like the belief box and the desire box.

Previous discussions of off-line simulation accounts have typically characterised the off-line input as 'pretend' input. For example, both Gordon (1986) and Goldman (1989) appeal to pretence in sketching the off-line simulation account of behaviour prediction. Now, it's not entirely clear what 'pretend' is supposed to mean in this context; but perhaps some notion of pretence is essential to characterising an off-line simulation account of behaviour prediction. However, there's no in-principle reason to suppose that *all* off-line simulation theories must be tied to the capacity for pretence. What *is* required is that the component is detached from its normal function. So, the inputs must have a different source than the usual source, but that source needn't be linked to pretence. Indeed, as we've presented it, off-line simulation doesn't necessarily invoke 'inputs' at all. If the mental box that we are taking off line is a processor of some sort (e.g., the practical reasoning device), then inputs are, of course, required. But if the box we are taking off line is a storage system (e.g. the belief box), then it is less than clear that anything appropriately called an 'input' is needed. Consider, for example, using the belief box in the kind of simulation suggested by Paul Harris (1992). Asked to predict what Bill Clinton will think when asked, 'What is the capital of California?', we check to see what we think the answer to the question is. Since we suppose that Clinton is at least as much an expert on United States state capitals as we are, we predict that Clinton will think what we do. There's *some* sort of probe to the belief box here, of course, but it plays a very different role from the pretend inputs posited for practical reasoning or inference simulation.

We've been stressing the potential fertility of off-line simulation. Since virtually any cognitive component is a potential engine of simulation, it seems that off-line simulation accounts might be offered for many different capacities. Indeed, in the last few years, simulation-based accounts *have* been offered for a wide range of cognitive capacities. We have already seen the off-line simulation account of behaviour prediction. On that account, the practical reasoning mechanism is taken off line and used to generate predictions rather than behaviour. We'd now like to sketch two off-line simulation accounts that exploit cognitive mechanisms other than the practical reasoner.

Paul Harris (1992) argues that simulation can provide an excellent account of our capacity to predict the grammaticality judgements of those from the same linguistic community. Suppose you were given a list of grammatical and ungrammatical sentences and asked to predict the judgements other English speakers would make about the grammaticality of the sentences. How do you make such predictions? An information-based account of this capacity would say that you have a body of information about the grammaticality judgements of others in your linguistic community. Harris presents a rather different account of how you would go about predicting such judgements. He writes, 'The most plausible answer is that you read each sentence, asked yourself whether it sounded grammatical or not, and assumed that other English speakers would make the same judgements for the same reasons' (Harris, 1992, p. 124). According to Harris, then, our capacity to predict grammaticality judgements doesn't depend on our having a body of information about the grammaticality judgements of others. Rather, we use part of our *own* grammaticality system, taken 'off line', to determine the grammaticality judgements of others.

Harris' account of grammaticality judgement predictions suggests an off-line simulation account of a quite different capacity. The prediction of behaviour is the most heralded of our folk psychological capacities, but we also have a capacity to predict what *inferences* others will draw. This capacity would be exploited in the following thought experiment from Stich and Nichols (1995). Suppose you are told the following: 'Sven believes that all Italians like pasta. Sven is introduced to Maria, and he is told that she is Italian.' Now, you are asked to predict what Sven will say if asked whether Maria likes pasta. How do you arrive at your prediction? Well, an information-based account of the capacity would claim that you have a body of information about how people draw inferences. This might be thought of as a tacit theory of reasoning. On the basis of this theory and the information about Sven, you arrive at the conclusion that if asked, 'Does Maria like pasta?', Sven will assent. A quite different account of the capacity is suggested by off-line simulation. On this account, inference prediction proceeds as follows. Hypothetical inputs are fed into your own inference mechanism; the inference mechanism produces the appropriate inference given the pretend inputs; this output is then embedded in the appropriate belief sentence. So, on the above example, you feed your inference mechanism with the pretend beliefs that all Italians like pasta and that Maria is an Italian. Your inference mechanism then produces the conclusion that Maria likes pasta. But this conclusion isn't directly fed into your belief box. Otherwise *you* would come to believe that Maria likes pasta. Rather, this conclusion is embedded in a belief sentence with Sven as the subject. Through this process, you come

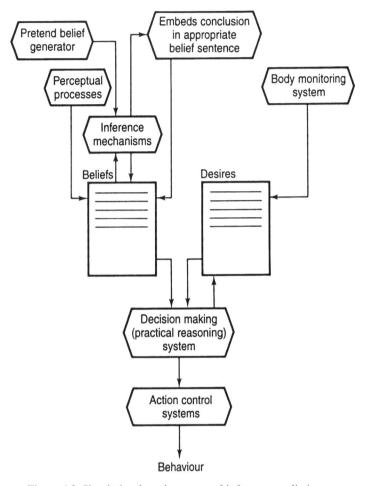

Figure 4.2 Simulation-based account of inference prediction

to believe that Sven will infer that Maria likes pasta. Figure 4.2 is a box-ological rendition of this account.

In addition to the foregoing accounts, off-line simulation accounts have been suggested for conditional planning (Goldman, 1992a; Harris, 1992), counterfactual reasoning (Goldman, 1993b), empathy (Goldman, 1993b), and mental imagery (Currie, forthcoming). There is even an account of phoneme recognition from the earliest days of cognitive science that has the relevant features of off-line simulation. Halle and Stevens' analysis by syn-thesis account of phoneme recognition is perhaps the earliest detailed 'off-line simulation' account in cognitive science (Halle and Stevens, 1962). On their account, our capacity for phoneme recognition exploits our phoneme *production* system. Crudely put, the idea is that when given phonemic input (i.e., when spoken to), the phoneme production system is taken off line (detached from its normal function) to generate hypotheses for matching the phonemic input. Recognition occurs when a match is found between the phonemic input and one of the hypothetical outputs of the phoneme production system.[3]

So, simulation-based theories can be offered for a wide range of cognitive capacities, and such accounts can provide enticing alternatives to standard information-based accounts. Off-line simulation even makes a sort of evolutionary sense. The literature in evolutionary biology is rife with examples in which a mechanism that was selected for one function, ends up being used for another. For instance, Gould and Vrba report that the wings of the Black Heron serve two important functions. The Heron uses its wings in flight, but it also uses them as a fishing aid. It fishes in shallow water, and it uses its wings to shade the water; this facilitates the bird's ability to see the fish (Gould and Vrba, 1982, pp. 8–9). Clearly, since this can enhance the bird's feeding, it might now be an important selective feature. Gould and Vrba introduce the notion of exaptation, which captures such cases. Exaptations are characters that are 'evolved for other usages . . . and later "coopted" for their current role' (Gould and Vrba, 1982, p. 6). Or, as Vrba puts it, 'An exaptation is a character that is currently useful (and subject to selection) in a particular role, but that was not shaped by step-by-step selection for that role' (Vrba, 1989, p. 130). Gould and Vrba argue that exaptations form an extremely important category in evolutionary biology. If we import the notion of exaptation into evolutionary psychology, then capacities produced by off-line simulation look to be excellent candidates for exaptations. For instance, in the off-line account of behaviour prediction, a psychological mechanism that was built (selected) for one purpose is coopted for another.

Off-line simulation can offer accounts for a wide array of cognitive capacities. And it's quite possible that in some cases the simulation story is appropriate while in other cases it's misguided. Indeed, we suspect that some cognitive capacities probably *are* subserved by off-line simulation. For instance, Harris' simulation account of the capacity to predict grammaticality judgements is quite plausible. However, we are still extremely sceptical of the off-line simulation theory of behaviour prediction, and in section 2 we will present some empirical results against the theory. But before we present our data, we need to get clear about how to empirically distinguish off-line simulation accounts from more traditional information-based accounts.

1.2   Information, simulation, and cognitive penetrability

Stich and Nichols (1992) argued that demonstrating that behaviour prediction is 'cognitively penetrable' would be strong evidence that behaviour prediction derives from a theory or information base rather than off-line simulation. A capacity is cognitively penetrable in this sense if that capacity is affected by the subject's knowledge or ignorance of the domain. The point was that if behaviour prediction derives from off-line simulation, then the subject's knowledge or ignorance of generalisations about human behaviour should be irrelevant to the subject's performance on behaviour prediction tasks. However, the relevance of cognitive penetrability for the simulation debate extends far beyond the issue over behaviour prediction. We would maintain that, for any cognitive capacity, demonstrating that that capacity is cognitively penetrable indicates that the capacity derives from an information base rather than from off-line simulation.

For present purposes, the crucial difference between information-based accounts and simulation-based accounts is that an information-based account claims that the capacity depends on information about the domain but a simulation-based account claims that information about the domain is irrelevant to the capacity. This difference is exactly what matters for cognitive penetrability. Insofar as a capacity is affected by the subject's knowledge or ignorance of the domain, that capacity is 'cognitively penetrable'. As a result, any capacity that depends on information about the domain will be cognitively penetrable. By contrast, a simulation-based account of a capacity claims that the subject's information about the domain is irrelevant. Accordingly, if a capacity derives from off-line simulation, that capacity should not be cognitively penetrable. In other words, the subject's knowledge or ignorance of the domain should be irrelevant to their performance on tasks exploiting the capacity.

To avoid confusion over the matter, we want to clarify a difference between our notion of cognitive penetrability and Pylyshyn's notion (1980). On Pylyshyn's notion, a capacity is cognitively impenetrable insofar as it is unaffected by the subject's beliefs and desires outside of the information base devoted to the domain. The notion of cognitive penetrability important to the simulation debate is rather that a capacity is cognitively impenetrable only if the subject's cumulative knowledge or ignorance of the domain is irrelevant to the subject's performance on tasks exploiting the capacity. It's perfectly conceivable, then, that a capacity might be cognitively impenetrable in Pylyshyn's sense without being cognitively impenetrable in the sense relevant to simulation. For example, it's possible that our capacity to predict behaviour depends on a folk psychology module in Fodor's sense (1983). If, so then folk psychology would be both a theory (and thus cognitively penetrable in our sense) and cognitively impenetrable in Pylyshyn's sense.

Perhaps the easiest way to test whether a capacity is cognitively penetrable in our sense is to test subjects on a task for which they plausibly lack the relevant information about the domain. According to an information-based account, where subjects lack important information about the domain, they will perform poorly. On the other hand, according to simulation-based accounts, since subjects don't depend on information about the domain to perform the tasks, the subject's ignorance about the domain should make no difference to the subject's performance.

We've been urging that off-line simulation offers an alternative to standard information-based explanations. Furthermore, for a wide range of capacities including behaviour prediction and inference prediction, these two possibilities exhaust the current playing field. As a result, in many cases, cognitive penetrability seems to be a decisive test. Showing that a capacity is cognitively penetrable suffices to show that that capacity requires an information-based account. For to show that a capacity is cognitively penetrable is just to show that the capacity depends on information about the domain. However, if a capacity is not cognitively penetrable, then an information-based account is inappropriate, and typically the only other option is a simulation-based theory.

Off-line simulation is not, of course, the only kind of simulation. Another familiar notion of simulation comes from computer science. On this notion of simulation, one tries to predict the behaviour of a system by exploiting a computer model of the system (e.g., Widman and Loparo, 1989, p. 15). Such models may be characterised by mathematical equations or rules. For example, suppose we wanted to be able to determine how long it would take a forest fire in Yellowstone to reach surrounding towns under prevailing conditions. The speed at which the fire will burn depends partly on the moisture conditions, the wind conditions, and the density of the forest. As a result, a good computer model would include equations that capture the impact of these variable conditions as well as information about the size of the forest and the location of the towns. This notion of simulation relies on a model that is constituted by an internally represented body of information; as a result, we'll call it information-based simulation.

Information-based simulation differs from off-line simulation in important ways. As we have taken pains to point out, one way to demonstrate that a capacity derives from off-line simulation is to show that the capacity does not depend on a body of information about the domain. However, to show that a capacity depends on information-based simulation, one would have to show that the subject *is* exploiting a body of information about the domain. Simulation theorists sometimes seem to conflate the distinction. For example, as Stich and Nichols (1992) note, Goldman enlists research on information-based simulation as support for off–line simulation. Goldman writes:

> several cognitive scientists have recently endorsed the idea of mental simulation as one cognitive heuristic, although these researchers stress its use for knowledge in general, not specifically knowledge of others' mental states. Kahneman and Tversky, 1982, propose that people often try to answer questions about the world by an operation that resembles the running of a simulation model. The starting conditions for a 'run', they say, can either be left at realistic default values or modified to assume some special contingency (Goldman, 1989, p. 174).

Gregory Currie also invokes information-based simulation in the debate over off-line simulation. He writes: 'What goes on in the simulator is a substitute for real action; it gives us, under optimal conditions, the information that action would give us about the success or failure of a strategy, without the costs of failure' (Currie, 1995, p. 10). Currie defends his appeal to information-based simulation as follows: 'Simulation theorists have stressed that simulation may employ theory without ceasing to be simulation (see e.g. Goldman's distinction between 'process' and 'theory' driven simulation in his 1992). But this point continues to be overlooked by opponents of simulation theory' (Currie, 1995, p. 13, n. 16).

We would scarcely deny that there are important similarities between the two kinds of simulation. However, in the present context, it's extremely important to keep the distinction clear and prominent. In the first place, as we've noted, information-based simulation theories have radically different empirical commitments than off-line simulation theories. Information-based theories *must* exploit information about the domain. Off-line theories on the other hand, expressly do not exploit information about the domain. So, in order to evaluate a simulation theory, it's vital that we know whether the proposal is information-based or off-line.

Further, it's relatively uncontroversial that we have the capacity for information-based mental simulation. There are, of course, a number of unresolved questions about this kind of mental simulation. There are debates about how the models are encoded and what mechanisms underlie the capacity. However, virtually no one denies that we *have* such a capacity. By contrast, the claim that we have a capacity to take our decision making mechanism off line is enormously controversial.

In this section, we've been concerned to clarify the theoretical groundwork for off-line simulation. In the next section, we take an empirical turn. We will present results on the cognitive penetrability of behaviour prediction.

2   The cognitive penetrability of behaviour prediction: some experimental results

When subjects do a good job at predicting the behaviour of other people, it is often difficult to determine whether they are relying on simulation or internalised information. For if they are relying on internalised information, it may well be the case that this information is not readily available to conscious access. Thus the mere fact that subjects can't report the relevant information, or recognise various characterisations of the information they are using, provides no reason to conclude that they are not invoking a tacit theory. When subjects do a poor job of predicting the behaviour of other people, however, the situation is quite different. For in these cases, the explanatory resources of the theory-theory are considerably greater than those of the simulation theory. On a simulation account like the one portrayed in Figure 1, mistaken predictions can arise in one of two ways.

 (i) The predictor's Decision Making (or Practical Reasoning) mechanism is different from the target's.
(ii) The Pretend Belief and Desire Generator has not provided the Decision Making System with the right pretend beliefs and desires – i.e. with the ones that actually motivate the target person whose behaviour is to be predicted.

If an experimental situation can be designed in which subjects systematically mispredict the behaviour of targets, and in which it is unlikely that either (i) or (ii) is the source of the problem, then the simulation account will be seriously challenged. Often, however, these cases will be easily accommodated by the theory-theory, which can attribute the error to the fact that the internalised information on which the subject relies is mistaken or incomplete. If there is some psychological process that is unknown to folk psychology, and if this process affects people's behaviour in a given sort of situation, then it is not surprising that subjects who rely on folk psychology to predict how others will behave in that situation will be mistaken in their predictions.

Stich and Nichols (1992) reported an informal experiment that turned on just such an unsuspected psychological phenomenon. The phenomenon in question was first reported by Ellen Langer (1975). She called it 'the illusion of control', but we prefer a less theory-laden label; we'll call it 'the Langer Effect'. In one of her experiments, Langer organised a football pool in the office of an insurance agency a few days prior to the Superbowl, selling tickets at $1.00 each. Some subjects were offered a choice of tickets; others were offered only one. The day before the big game, Langer said she would be willing to buy the tickets back from the subjects, and asked how much they wanted for them. The surprising result was that subjects who had no choice of tickets sold them back for an average price of $1.96, while subjects who had a choice sold theirs back for an average price of $8.67.

In their informal experiment, Stich and Nichols (1992) read a description of Langer's experiment to a group of undergraduates and asked them to predict what Langer's subjects would do. Not surprisingly, the students got it wrong. They predicted no significant difference between the price asked by the no-choice subjects and the price asked by the subjects who were given a choice. Stich and Nichols tried to use this result as an argument against simulation accounts of behaviour prediction. But the Simulation Theorists were not convinced. Both Harris (1992) and Goldman (1992b) complained that the way in which the facts were presented to the students made it very unlikely that they would use the right pretend beliefs and desires in generating their predictions. Each participant in Langer's experiment was exposed to only one condition – either choice or no-choice. And there was a delay of several days between buying the ticket and being asked to sell it back. In contrast, the students who were asked to predict how Langer's subjects would behave were told about both conditions, and the time delay between being told about the purchase and being asked to predict the sell-back price was only a minute or two. Given these differences, Harris and Goldman protested, it would hardly be surprising if the students used the wrong pretend-inputs in making their prediction. In a later paper Stich and Nichols (1995) concede that the criticism is a fair one. The experiments we are about to report were designed to side-step the shortcomings in Stich and Nichols' informal experiment.

The first issue that needs to be addressed is the importance of the time lag in Langer's original experiment. Was this an essential factor in producing Langer's effect? To answer this question, we conducted an experiment similar to Langer's, but with no significant time lag. Subjects, who met one-on-one with the experimenter, were told that they would be asked to judge the grammaticality or ungrammaticality of fifteen sentences to be read by the experimenter. Before reading them the sentences, it was explained that to reward them for their participation, a lottery had been arranged. The prize was $30.00. At this point, some of the subjects were given a numbered lottery ticket by the experimenter. Other subjects were invited to select one of three lottery tickets that were offered. The experimenter then read the fifteen sentences, and had subjects record their judgements on an answer sheet. The grammar-judgement task lasted about five minutes. When it was complete, the subjects were told that it might be necessary to run more subjects than planned. And since the experimenter wanted to give all subjects a reasonable chance at winning the lottery, he might want to buy back some of the lottery tickets. Subjects were asked to set a price at which they would be prepared to sell the lottery ticket back to the experimenter, and to record that price on their answer sheet. There were a total of thirty subjects, fifteen in each condition. The mean price set by subjects in the no-choice condition was $1.60; the mean price set by subjects in the choice condition was $6.29. (p < .05). These results clearly indicate that the Langer Effect can be obtained without any significant delay between the time the subjects receive the lottery tickets and the time they are asked for a price at which they will sell them back.

The next question to be addressed is whether observers can accurately simulate the decision making process that leads subjects in Langer-style experiments to set the prices they do. In order to assist observer-subjects in generating the best possible pretend inputs (if that is indeed what they do) we produced a pair of video tape recordings of a subject (actually a confederate) participating in the experimental procedures just described. The two tapes were identical except for the first two minutes in which the grammatical judgement task was explained and the lottery ticket was given (on one tape) or chosen (on the other tape). Each tape was shown to a separate group of observer-subjects. The observer-subjects were provided with answer sheets identical to the one provided to the subjects in the Langer-style experiment. Observer-subjects were asked to predict what the experimental subject on the tape would say about the grammaticality or ungrammaticality of each of the fifteen sentences. They were also asked to predict the price the subject on the tape would set for selling back his lottery ticket. There were 38 observer-subjects in the choice condition and 39 in the no-choice condition. The mean predicted buy back price was $7.82 in the choice condition and $9.37 in the no-choice condition. (The difference is not statistically significant.) These numbers are quite high, since several less than co-operative observer-subjects in each group gave absurdly high numbers. To correct for this, we reanalysed the data after discarding all predictions higher than $15.00. On this analysis, the mean in the choice condition was $4.62; the mean in the no-choice was $3.47. (Once again, the difference is not statistically significant.) These results are summarised in Table 4.1. For completeness we also calculated the success rate of observer-subjects on the grammatical judgement prediction task. All of the authors judged all of the sentences used to be clearly grammatical or clearly ungrammatical. Using our judgements as a criterion of correctness, the observers predicted correctly 84% of the time, with no significant variation between the two conditions.

It is our contention that these experimental results pose a serious problem for those who think that behaviour prediction relies on the sort of simulation sketched in figure 1. For, as we noted earlier, this sort of simulation has only two straightforward ways of accounting for systematically mistaken predictions. Either the predictors' decision-making system differs from the targets', or the predictors are providing their decision-making

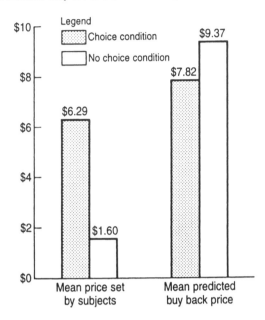

Table 4.1

system with the wrong pretend inputs. In the present experiment, the first option is very implausible, since the predictors and the subjects in the Langer-style experiment were drawn from the same population. There is every reason to believe that if the predictors had been subjects in the Langer-style experiment they would have behaved in much the same way that the actual subjects did. Moreover, the conditions for producing pretend inputs were about as good as they could possibly be, since predictors observed the target on video tape as he was making his decision. Moreover, post-experiment interviews with a number of subjects indicated that all of them correctly remembered whether or not the target they observed had been given a choice of lottery tickets. On the theory-theory account of how behavioural predictions work, these results are easy enough to explain. Folk psychology includes no information about the Langer Effect, so predictors get it wrong. Perhaps Simulation Theorists can produce a plausible alternative explanation of these results. But we haven't a clue what it might be.

3   Off-line simulation: new directions

The results reported in the last section make us sceptical of the off-line simulation account of behaviour prediction. However, off-line simulation might provide a plausible account of other important capacities. In the first section we stressed the fertility of the idea of off-line simulation. And in the last few years, off-line simulation accounts have been offered for three crucial but strikingly different capacities: counterfactual reasoning, empathy, and mental imagery. In this section, we want to discuss each of these capacities in relation to the simulation debate. We don't, however, propose to decide whether off-line simulation is the correct account for any of these capacities. We only hope to chart the philosophical and psychological space.

3.1   *Counterfactual reasoning*

Counterfactuals play an enormous and vital role in our inferential lives. Counterfactual thoughts range from the pedestrian – if I'd brought my umbrella I wouldn't be wet – to the profound – if I travelled at the speed of light, I'd turn into energy. The importance of counterfactuals is reflected in the amount of attention they've received in both philosophy and psychology. In the philosophy of language, there is an extensive literature on counterfactuals (e.g., Goodman, 1947; Stalnaker, 1968; Lewis, 1973). There is also a sizeable literature in cognitive social psychology on the generation of counterfactuals (e.g., Kahneman and Tversky, 1982; Markman *et al.*, 1993; Roese and Olson, 1993). In the philosophy of language, there are two closely related projects concerning counterfactuals. One project is to provide an account of the truth conditions for counterfactual conditionals. The goal is to determine what makes such sentences true or false. This project parallels the attempt to provide a semantics for belief sentences. In addition to outlining the semantics of counterfactual conditionals, philosophers of language have tried to produce a logic for counterfactuals. That is, philosophers have tried to determine which inferences are valid given counterfactual premises. This project parallels the attempt to provide a logic for material conditionals, modal operators, temporal terms, etc. For each of these traditional philosophical endeavours, there is a complementary psychological project. Whereas philosophers of language have discussed how counterfactual conditionals *should* be evaluated, the psychological issue is how people *actually* go about evaluating counterfactuals. Similarly, while logicians try to determine what inferences are valid given counterfactual premises, the psychological question is what kinds of inferences people are willing and unwilling to make given counterfactual premises.[4]

Simulation theory offers an extremely interesting perspective on the psychological projects. The question posed by the simulation debate concerns the psychological mechanisms responsible for counterfactual reasoning.

When people actually evaluate counterfactuals or make inferences over counterfactuals, are they using some kind of off-line simulation, or are they guided by a body of counterfactual-specific rules or information?

Goldman (1992a) assumes that counterfactual reasoning requires an off-line simulation account. By 'counterfactual reasoning', he seems to mean the evaluation of counterfactual conditionals. He writes, 'When considering the truth value of "If X were the case, then Y would obtain", a reasoner feigns a belief in X and reasons about Y under that pretence' (1992a, p. 24). Goldman likens this kind of counterfactual reasoning to off-line simulation of behaviour prediction. He takes counterfactual reasoning to be an example of a process that exploits the same mechanisms as the off-line account of behaviour prediction (1992a, pp. 22–4).

We are sceptical of Goldman's view that the evaluation of counterfactual conditionals can be assimilated to the off-line simulation of behaviour prediction. As mentioned in section 1, it's common to distinguish the mechanisms devoted to theoretical reasoning from those devoted to decision making. In figure 4.1, this distinction is depicted by separate boxes for the decision making system and the inference mechanisms. The off-line simulation account of behaviour prediction depends on the decision making system, not the inference mechanisms. However, evaluating counterfactuals seems to be a process by which we come to beliefs, not a process by which we come to decisions. That is, the evaluation of counterfactuals, unlike off-line simulation of behaviour prediction, concerns theoretical inference mechanisms, not the decision-making system.

Although off-line simulation of behaviour prediction provides a poor model for the evaluation of counterfactuals, off-line simulation of *inference* prediction does provide a credible model for how we evaluate counterfactuals. If we suppose that the reasoning processes that are taken off line are the theoretical reasoning processes, then Goldman's account becomes much more plausible. On such an account, we evaluate sentences of the form 'If X were the case, then Y would obtain' as follows: Our inferential mechanisms are taken off line and fed the pretend belief that X. Given that pretend belief, we let our inferential mechanisms work off line to see what can be concluded about Y. In keeping with the off-line simulation theory, we suppose that the inferential mechanisms operate over that feigned belief as if it were a genuine belief.

We think that off-line simulation provides a plausible and interesting account of how we evaluate counterfactual conditionals. But it doesn't have a corner on the market – there are other plausible models of this capacity that don't derive from off-line simulation. One possibility is that the evaluation of counterfactuals depends on a body of meta-linguistic principles concerning entailment relations among sentences. Such principles would be stored in the belief box; however, like the principles of folk physics and folk psychology, they may not be readily accessible to consciousness. According to this meta-linguistic theory, we know, perhaps tacitly, that certain sentences follow from other sentences. And we can see, as a result, that if some sentences were true, other sentences would also be true. To clarify the nature of this account, let's consider an example. Most would take the following counterfactual to be true:

If Bill Clinton had lost the election, Hillary Clinton would not be the First Lady.

On the current proposal, we evaluate this sentence in the following way. We know that the following sentences are true: 'The First Lady is the wife of the President'; 'Hillary Clinton is Bill Clinton's wife'; 'The loser of the election doesn't become President.' In addition, we know various entailment relations among sentences. Given our knowledge of the entailment relations, plus our knowledge of the true sentences, we reason that if 'Bill Clinton lost the election' were true, 'Hillary Clinton is not the First Lady' would also be true. This account involves neither pretence nor taking the inference mechanisms off line. Rather, it relies on a body of information about relations between sentences.

Another possible alternative to the simulation account is that the evaluation of counterfactual conditionals depends on a body of counterfactual-specific rules in the inference mechanism. Just as we have a set of rules that guides our evaluation of the material conditional, so too, according to this view, we have a set of inference rules devoted to evaluating counterfactual conditionals. Again, such an account needn't appeal to pretence nor to taking the inference mechanisms off line.

It is, of course, an interesting question which, if any, of these accounts is right. But it's not our purpose here to decide that. Indeed, we suspect that given the current state of the evidence, it's difficult to determine with any confidence whether off-line simulation provides an adequate account of how we evaluate counterfactuals. One way to test the off-line simulation account under consideration might be by exploring how well autistic people are able to evaluate counterfactuals. We have followed Goldman in supposing that the off-line input would be 'pretend' input. One of the central features of autism is the lack of pretend play, and both Goldman (1989) and Gordon (1986) argue that the fact that autistic people fail theory of mind tasks indicates that pretence is involved in those tasks. We're sceptical that the performance of autistic people on theory of mind tasks can be fully explained by their problems with pretence. However, we do think that studying autistics' reasoning about counterfactuals might provide some evidence to help assess Goldman's off-line account of how we evaluate counterfactual conditionals. If the capacity to evaluate counterfactuals depends on the capacity for pretence as Goldman suggests, then autistic people should perform poorly on tasks that require them to evaluate counterfactuals. One way to run such an experiment would be to assemble a list of counterfactual conditionals and see whether autistic people do as well as their mental peers at determining whether the sentences are true or false. According to the off-line account under consideration, autistic people should perform poorly on this task.

Leslie (1987b, 1988a, 1994a) has detailed a quite different set of connections between pretence, autism, and theory of mind. Leslie shows that the capacity for pretence emerges very early in development between 18 and 24 months of age. He points to a critical feature of this capacity, namely, the 'yoking' in development between the capacity for pretending by oneself and understanding pretence-in-others. As soon as the child is able deliberately to entertain counterfactual suppositions as evidenced by solitary pretence, she is also able to understand when other people deliberately entertain counterfactual suppositions, that is, pretend. By two years of age, an infant can share pretend scenarios with others and demonstrate that she understands the specific content of the other person's pretence. In this regard, pretending is strikingly different from believing. Infants only a few months old have beliefs (about the mechanical properties of hidden objects, for example) but, as far as anyone can tell, they are not able to understand beliefs-in-others until a considerable time later – about two years later on the most optimistic estimate.

Leslie's model accounts for the above facts in the following way. In terms of 'boxology', having a belief can be thought of as placing a representation in the 'belief box' – that is, as a particular kind of functional relation between the organism and one of its representations; while having a desire is placing a representation in the 'desire box' – that is, as another kind of functional relation between the organism and its representations. Since young infants, by assumption, can both have beliefs and have desires, we assume that early on infants possess a belief box, a desire box and some representations. But, according to Leslie, in terms of boxology, there is no such thing as the 'pretend box', and thus no such thing as simply 'having a pretend'. Instead, pretending is a special case of placing a representation in the 'belief box', where the representation says in effect, 'someone is pretending such and such'. In a system of this type, solitary pretence and understanding pretence-in-others are inevitably yoked, whereas having beliefs and understanding beliefs-in-others are not. Like pretence, understanding beliefs-in-others depends upon the development of representations of propositional attitudes (what Leslie calls the 'metarepresentation').

Leslie's metarepresentational model has had an important application to understanding abnormal development. Autistic children show a set of behavioural abnormalities that can occur even if the child has a borderline to normal IQ level. These behavioural signs (Wing and Gould's (1979) 'triad') comprise social incompetence, communicative impairment and a lack of normal pretend play. Putting these signs together with the above model led to the hypothesis that autistic children are metarepresentation-ally impaired. This in turn led to the prediction that autistic children would show a specific impairment in their understanding of belief. This impair-ment would be specific in at least two senses: first, children with autism would be impaired relative to their own general intellectual level; and second, other groups of children with comparable or lower IQ levels would not be similarly impaired. The first experimental studies of this conjecture supported the prediction (Baron-Cohen, *et al.*, 1985, 1986) showing that only 20% of a group of autistic children with a mean IQ of 82 passed a test of false-belief understanding whereas 86% of a group of Down's syndrome children with mean IQ of 64 passed. These results have subsequently been confirmed and extended by numerous studies around the world (e.g., Baron-Cohen, 1989a, 1991a; Leslie and Frith, 1988; Leslie and Thaiss, 1992; Ozonoff *et al.*, 1991a; Perner *et al.*, 1989; Reed and Peterson, 1990; Roth and Leslie, 1991; Sodian and Frith, 1992; for a short review see Leslie, 1992; and for a discussion of some current issues see Leslie and Roth, 1993). Of particular relevance to the present discussion are two recent studies which we shall describe. Leslie and Thaiss (1992) controlled for the possibility that autistic children might fail tests of false belief understanding because they are unable to meet one or some of the general problem solving or general processing demands made by such tasks. A standard task (e.g. Baron-Cohen *et al.*, 1985) has Sally place a marble in a basket and go away for a walk. While she is away, Ann removes the marble and places it in a box. The child is asked about where Sally put the marble in the beginning, where it is now, and finally where Sally will look for the marble on her return. It makes no difference to the results if children are asked where Sally thinks the marble is rather than where she will look. Such a task no doubt makes numerous general demands upon the solver. Working memory is required, language processing skills, abstract reasoning, perhaps mental imagery, 'executive functions' of various kinds and perhaps other, as yet unthought of, processes are required. How can we address so many possibilities and support the idea of an impairment specific to understanding mental states?

Fortunately there is a way. Zaitchik (1990) reported an elegant test of understanding out-of-date photographs that almost exactly mirrors the general problem solving structure of false-belief tasks. In Zaitchik's task, Sally is replaced with a Polaroid camera and Sally's belief is replaced by a Polaroid photograph. The marble is placed in the basket as before, but, instead of Sally forming a belief about the marble in the basket, the camera forms a photograph of the marble in the basket. The photograph is then placed face down on the table before the child can see it (after all the child does not get to see Sally's belief!). The marble is then removed from the basket and placed in the box. Now the child is asked where the marble was when the photograph was taken, where the marble is now really, and finally, where, in the photograph, is the marble? For normal children, these two tasks, out-of-date photographs and out-of-date beliefs are nearly equivalently hard. Most normal three-year-olds fail both tasks, while most normal four-year-olds pass both tasks. However, experimental analysis shows that for normal children there is a small but reliable effect that if they pass only one of these tasks, it is false belief rather than photographs. Autistic children, by contrast, while failing false belief, perform at or near ceiling on photographs tasks. Similar results are obtained if simple maps or drawings are used instead of a camera and photographs (Charman and Baron-Cohen, 1992; Leslie and Thaiss, 1992). If false-belief tasks require 'imagery' for their solution, then presumably so do the photographs, maps, and drawings tasks. Of course, 'simulation', specifically of mental states, might be the problem. But, as Leslie and German (1994) show, the best explanation for that remains impaired metarepresentational processing.

Although the Leslie and Thaiss (1992) results above undermine the idea that autistic children fail false-belief tasks because they cannot process counterfactual information, a recent study has looked at this directly. Scott et al. (1994) tested normal four-year-olds, Down's syndrome children and children with autism on a task that required them to solve simple counterfactual syllogisms. For example, the children were told 'All pigs can fly. Porky is a pig' and then asked 'Can Porky fly?' The normal four-year-olds and Down's syndrome children performed rather poorly on such syllogisms showing a lot of 'reality intrusion' errors. The autistic children, on the other hand, performed very well, clearly demonstrating their mental age advantage. In an attempt to help the normal and Down's children, the children were asked to form a picture of a pig in their heads and then to make this 'pig in the head' fly. To determine what the children had understood about this talk of 'pictures in the head', they were asked whether the pig was real or 'just in their head' and whether the experimenter could see the pig in their head. Most of the normal and Down's children correctly answered that the pig was 'just in their head', and, no, the experimenter could not see it. However, less than half the autistic children got these questions right. They seemed to be confused by this discourse concerning a mental entity. The children were then presented with another set of counterfactual syllogisms, but this time they were asked to form a picture in the head of the situation described. Now the normal and Down's children appeared to be released from their previous reality-bound responses, apparently appreciating that the discourse was about counterfactuals. For young normal children, thinking about mental states facilitates access to their counterfactual reasoning abilities. The autistic children, by contrast, performed drastically worse under these conditions, apparently becoming confused and showing reality intrusion errors for the first time. Counterfactual reasoning is well within the capabilities of autistic children tested; nevertheless, they had difficulty following discourse about mental states. Their difficulty with this task cannot be attributed to difficulty forming and transforming mental imagery given the results of Leslie and Thaiss (1992) and, more directly, given their normal performance on standard mental rotation tasks (Shah, 1988). As Leslie and Roth (1993) point out, metarepresentational impairment succinctly accounts for both the specific disabilities and the spared abilities in the syndrome of childhood autism. The same model also provides the only adequate account of early pretence, linking this to the capacity to acquire a theory of mind.

3.2   Empathy

As counterfactual reasoning is vital to our inferential lives, so empathy is an integral part of our emotional lives. Further, according to many writers, empathy is essential for moral reasoning and certain types of aesthetic experience. Although there is no widely accepted definition of empathy, most researchers agree that, at a minimum, empathy is a 'vicarious sharing of affect' or 'an emotional response that stems from another's emotional state or condition and that is congruent with the other's emotional state or situation' (Eisenberg and Strayer, 1987, pp. 3,5). The literature on empathy takes empathy to cover a broad range of behaviour, from reactive new-born cry and motor mimicry to deliberate role taking (Hoffman, 1984, 1987). Goldman (1993b) maintains that empathic phenomena demand a simulation account. In this subsection, we want to explore the extent to which empathy is a product of simulation. After presenting simulation-based and information-based approaches to empathy, we'll consider how well these approaches can accommodate the empathic phenomena.

3.2.1   Two models of empathy

There are, of course, many distinctions to draw among different accounts of empathy. But for present purposes, the distinction we're concerned with is between simulation-based theories and information-based theories. Before we draw this distinction, though, we should give some indication of how non-empathic emotion is supposed to work.

There is a spirited debate in psychology over the causal basis of emotions. The debate revolves around the relative contributions of physiological and cognitive factors. Still, it's fairly uncontroversial that in many instances, emotions are at least partially the product of beliefs or memories. For example, a person will likely experience fear on discovering that he is being pursued by a bear. Or, a person might feel sorrow on reminiscing about a deceased pet. In such cases, it's likely that an emotional response system takes beliefs or memories as inputs, and produces emotional states as outputs. This understanding of emotion seems to be presumed by Goldman's simulation account of empathy. In our discussion, we too will assume this conception of emotion.

Empathy as off-line simulation. Goldman places empathy in the context of simulation as follows:

> The simulation process consists first of taking the perspective of another person, i.e., imaginatively assuming one or more of the other person's mental states. Such perspective taking might be instigated by observing that person's situation and behaviour or by simply being told about them, as when one reads a history book or a novel. Psychological processes then (automatically) operate on the initial 'pretend' states to generate further states that (in favourable cases) are similar to, or homologous to, the target person's states. I conceive of empathy as a special case of the simulation process in which the output states are *affective* or *emotional* states rather than purely cognitive or conative states like believing or desiring (1993b, p. 141)

Goldman's remarks suggest the following simulation account of empathy. A pretend-belief generator feeds into our emotional response system. The emotional response system operates on that feigned belief just as it would operate on an unfeigned belief. The output from the emotional response system is then the same emotional response as it would have been if the belief weren't feigned (see fig 4.3).

This simulation account of empathy is, of course, quite different from the simulation account of behaviour prediction. In the first place, the mechanism used to support empathy is presumably the emotional response system, rather than the practical reasoning system. When empathising, we don't reason to the conclusion that we should feel a certain way. We don't *decide* how to feel. Further, unlike the off-line simulation of behaviour prediction, on the present theory, the output from the mechanism is *not* taken off line. The output from the emotional response system is a genuine emotional response. This account, then, is not 'off-line' at both ends. Rather, we might say that it's 'input deviant'. This makes the account a special case of simulation, as Goldman says. Nonetheless, it's an important application of the basic idea behind off-line simulation.

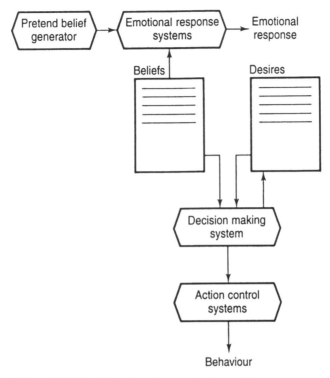

Figure 4.3 Simulation-based account of empathy

Information-based empathy. An alternative view of empathy is that in empathy, as in non-empathic emotion, the emotional response system receives input from the subject's beliefs and memories. Empathic responses might arise when the subject is reminded of events in her past similar to those of the object of empathy. So, for example, if your friend tells you that her dog has died, you might empathise with her via remembering the death of your own dog. Of course, this process of 'remembering' analogous past experiences need not be fully conscious or voluntary. Such 'information-based' accounts of empathy may come in a variety of different forms. According to one plausible version, empathic response arises as follows: a person's beliefs about the situation lead to associations with her own memories of analogous experiences; the emotional response system subsequently takes these memories as inputs and produces the appropriate emotional outputs. This account is sketched in figure 4.4. Unlike off-line simulation, such information-based accounts don't appeal to 'pretend' or deviant inputs. The inputs come from the subject's own knowledge base.

The literature on empathy often appeals to such information-based

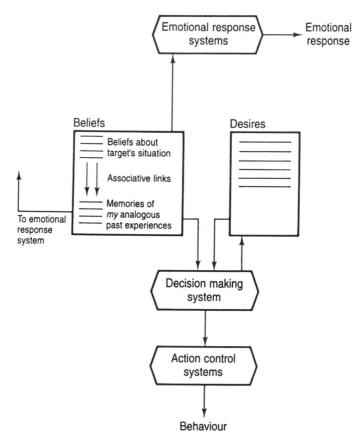

Figure 4.4 Information-based account of empathy

accounts to explain empathic phenomena. Consider, for instance, Hoffman's (1984) 'direct association' mode of empathy:

> When we observe people experiencing an emotion, their facial expression, voice, posture, or any other cue in the situation that reminds us of past situations associated with our experience of that emotion may evoke the emotion in us. The usual example cited is the boy who sees another child cut himself and cry. The sight of the blood, the sound of the cry, or any cue from the victim or the situation that reminds the boy of his own past experience of pain may evoke an empathic distress response (Hoffman, 1984, p. 105)

Eisenberg and Strayer (1987b) also suggest that an information-based account explains a good deal of empathic phenomena. They write, 'It is likely that people often empathise not because they have put themselves cognitively in another's place, but because they have retrieved relevant information from their memories' (Eisenberg and Strayer, 1987b, p. 9). In these passages, neither Hoffman nor Eisenberg and Strayer appeal to pretend input or to mechanisms being taken off line. Rather, they maintain that empathic phenomena can derive from the subject's own information base.

3.2.2   Empathy and off-line simulation

Now that we have sketched both alternatives, we can consider the degree to which off-line simulation captures empathic phenomena. Hoffman (1984) argues that there are at least six different modes of empathy. But rather than try to discuss half a dozen different types of empathy, we'll focus on the three central empathic phenomena discussed by Goldman (1993b): motor mimicry, emotional contagion, and deliberate role taking.

Motor mimicry. Everyday life as well as the laboratory provide numerous instances of people aping the motor behaviour of others. Motor mimicry is familiar from the behaviour of sports spectators. Boxing fans, for example, often bob and weave when watching boxing matches. Infants also display motor mimicry in imitating certain gestures and facial expressions. As noted earlier, a number of researchers claim that motor mimicry is a form of empathy or proto-empathy (Hoffman, 1987, Meltzoff and Gopnik, 1993, p. 358). In keeping with this, Goldman proposes a simulation-based account of mimicry: 'A natural way to explain motor mimicry is in terms of *mental* mimicry: people mentally take the role of another and fail to inhibit (to take 'off line') the behavioural upshot of this mental role taking' (1993b, p. 146).

Apparently, this account would gloss motor mimicry as follows: the subject sees the behaviour, infers the mental states that would produce the behaviour, pretends to have those mental states, and thereby produces homologous behaviour.

Simulation strikes us as quite implausible as a general model of motor mimicry. Performing this kind of simulation would require that a significant portion of folk psychology is in place. In order to perform the relevant simulation, the subject must infer the other's beliefs from her behaviour. The problem with this is that mimicry emerges *very* early. As Goldman himself notes, the capacity for motor mimicry seems to be present at birth (Meltzoff and Moore, 1983). And neither theory-theorists nor simulation theorists think that folk psychology is up and ready at birth.[5] It seems very unlikely that new-borns are capable of inferring beliefs from behaviour. As a result, it's difficult to see how simulation can explain infantile motor mimicry. Andrew Meltzoff, one of the original researchers on infant mimicry, offers a better partial explanation of the phenomenon. He suggests that 'early imitation involves a kind of cross–modal matching. Infants can, at some primitive level, recognise an equivalence between what they see and what they do' (Meltzoff, 1993, p. 222).

Of course, it's possible that the mechanisms for mimicry in infants are different from the mechanisms required for adult motor mimicry. In that case, an advocate of simulation might claim that adult mimicry, unlike mimicry in infants, sometimes does depend on simulation. However, without an argument for why adult motor mimicry is different in kind from infant motor mimicry, any such claim seems ad hoc.

Emotional contagion. Emotional contagion is, as Goldman puts it, 'familiar to all of us through the infectious effects of smiles and laughter' (1993b, p. 142). Emotional contagion is also familiar from the involuntary experience of sorrow on seeing a close friend or relative in grief. Thompson writes, 'Children as well as adults experience the direct, almost involuntary pull of another's emotional expressions in accident settings and other situations eliciting strong affect in others' (1987, p. 124).

Goldman concedes that emotional contagion may not involve role taking.[6] And there is good reason to doubt that emotional contagion derives from simulation. Like motor mimicry, emotional contagion apparently emerges very early. Simner (1971) found that new-borns cry in reaction to neonatal cries significantly more than they cry in reaction to white noise or the cries of an older infant. This has widely been taken to be a primitive form of emotional contagion (Hoffman, 1987; Goldman, 1993b, p. 142). Most infants show further emotional contagion and even more sophisticated empathic behaviour by 18 months (Thompson, 1987; Lamb, 1991).[7] The problem again for the simulation account is that it requires the subject to determine the beliefs of the object of empathy. And it seems unlikely that new-borns are even *capable* of inferring the beliefs of other new-borns. Indeed, we're not sure that *we* can infer the beliefs of crying new-borns.

Again, information-based accounts have no trouble accommodating the data. In reactive new-born cry, as in emotional contagion in general, a subject may be responding on the basis of information retrieved from the subject's own memories. As Hoffman notes, '. . . the sound of the cry, or any cue from the victim or the situation that reminds the boy of his own past experience of pain may evoke an empathic distress response' (Hoffman, 1984, p. 105). On this account, subjects don't have to infer beliefs or feed their emotional response system with pretend inputs. Hence, information-based theories, in contrast to the simulation theory, might explain how new-borns could have the capacity for emotional contagion.

There is another potential problem for the simulation account of emotional contagion. According to simulation theory, the capacity for empathy depends on the capacity for pretence. As a result, since autistic children apparently have a severely impaired capacity for pretence, the simulation theory predicts that they should have a severely impaired capacity for emotional contagion. Autistic children are typically described as being incapable of empathic responses. However, recent experimental evidence suggests that they show far more empathic response than we have been led to expect. Yirmiya *et al.* (1992) showed videotaped stories to both autistic and normal children. They describe the experiment as follows:

> Each one of the [videotaped] segments focuses on the protagonist experiencing one of the following five emotions: happiness, anger, pride, sadness, or fear (e.g., a boy is sad because he lost his dog). After watching each segment, the child is requested to report how he or she feels. . . .
>
> The performance of the autistic children was surprisingly good given the assumptions about the characteristics of autistic individuals. These children were able to give examples of feeling states from their own experience, and many of them showed considerable ability to label the emotions of others, to take the role and perspective of others, and to respond empathetically to the feelings of others (Yirmiya *et al.*, pp. 153, 156–7)

According to the simulation account of emotional contagion, we should expect autistic children to be largely unable to respond empathetically. So, the above results pose a serious challenge to the simulation account. However, autistic children did do less well than the normal children. And this is only one study. So this hardly counts as a decisive argument against the simulation account of emotional contagion. But it does mark out an area of research of considerable importance to the evaluation of simulation theories.

Deliberate role taking. The early onset of both motor mimicry and emotional contagion count as serious prima facie evidence against a simulation account of these phenomena. Hence, there seem to be significant limits to the extent to which off-line, or input-deviant, simulation can explain empathic phenomena. But at the same time, nearly everyone thinks that empathy is sometimes mediated by role taking. For instance, we sometimes *deliberately* try to take another person's perspective. Hoffman claims that the process of putting oneself in another's place, 'being deliberate, may be relatively infrequent – for example, it may be used by parents and therapists who believe they can be more effective if they experience some of their child's or patient's feelings' (Hoffman, 1987, p. 49). Perhaps then, simulation is required for these empathic phenomena. Goldman certainly seems to think that such cases of deliberate role taking establish the simulation account of empathy. He writes:

> the significance of simulation, or role taking, is . . . well established in other areas, e.g., in empathic arousal. In a study by Stotland (1969), subjects were instructed to imagine how they would feel and what sensations they would have in their hands if they were exposed to the same painful heat treatment that was being applied to another person. These subjects gave more evidence of empathic distress than (1) subjects instructed to attend closely to the other person's physical movements and (2) subjects instructed to imagine how the other person felt when he or she was undergoing the treatment (1993b, p. 95)

Goldman apparently maintains that the effects of deliberate role taking are proof that these empathic phenomena derive from simulation. Indeed, Goldman seems to identify role taking with simulation.

It does seem clear that simulation provides a possible model of deliberate role taking. If Bill wanted to empathise with John, he might deliberately try to 'put himself in John's place'. According to the simulation account, to accomplish this Bill would pretend to have some of John's beliefs. These pretend beliefs are fed into Bill's emotional response system which will operate on those feigned inputs as it would on normal inputs. The output, the emotional response, would then be similar to John's emotional response.

Although simulation thus provides a plausible account of deliberate role taking, role taking can also be accommodated by information-based accounts. For instance, an information-based account might maintain that if we want to empathise with John by deliberate role taking, we actively (though perhaps not entirely consciously) try to retrieve memories and relevant information that would lead us to feel what John is feeling. For instance, if Mark wants to empathise with John after the death of his dog, Mark can deliberately try to recall the death of his own dog. That memory might lead Mark to feel the way John does. None of this requires feeding pretend inputs into the emotional response system. Rather, on this information-based account of role taking, if you want to share in someone's grief, you should try to remember similar sad events from your own life.[8]

So, simulation isn't the only account of the processes subserving deliberate role taking. Deliberate role taking can also be explained by information-based accounts. Once we see this, data showing the empathic effects of role taking can no longer be blithely adduced as evidence for simulation. The evidence Goldman cites (Stotland 1969) does show that imagining how we would feel in a situation has a discernible effect on empathic distress. But there are different explanations of how this imaginative process transpires. One possibility is simulation: we pretend to believe that we're being exposed to painful heat. Another possibility is that we try to remember similar experiences from our past.

At present, we know of no compelling evidence to decide between these two accounts of deliberate role taking. As a result, it seems to be an open question whether simulation is *ever* implicated in empathy. One way of trying to answer this question would be by testing whether deliberate role taking is cognitively penetrable. If deliberate role taking is subserved by simulation, subjects should arrive at homologous emotional responses even if they have no memories analogous to the other person's experience. According to information-based accounts of role taking, on the other hand, if there are no analogous memories or relevant information, deliberate role taking will not produce homologous emotional responses. So, for example, on the information-based account, if a certain situation leads people to experience sorrow, but the subject has no analogous memories and no knowledge that the event makes people sad, then deliberate role taking will not lead that subject to feel sorrow. However, on the simulation account, that kind of ignorance should have no effect on empathic response.

3.3   Mental imagery

Over the last two decades, a huge literature on mental imagery has developed. This literature has largely focused on the descriptivism/pictorialism debate (Pylyshyn, 1973, 1981; Kosslyn, 1981, 1983, 1994). Descriptivists (e.g., Pylyshyn) maintain that mental images are sentence-like structures; pictorialists (e.g., Kosslyn) maintain that mental images are a kind of non-sentence based representation. In an interesting new paper, Gregory Currie (forthcoming) offers a different perspective on the mental imagery debate.[9] He argues that mental imagery derives from off-line simulation. In this section, we will try to clarify Currie's proposal somewhat. But there remains a fundamental question about Currie's proposal – we aren't sure whether Currie means to offer a novel account of imagery or whether he is arguing that existing accounts of imagery really are simulation theories. We will argue that if Currie intends to present a novel account, then his proposal requires much more elaboration, and on a couple of interpretations the account seems extremely implausible. If, however, Currie's claim is that existing accounts of imagery really are simulation accounts, then, since the notion of a simulation account is at best a vague one, we don't think the claim has any clear truth value, nor do we see why it matters one way or the other.

Currie's account of how imagery derives from simulation is largely contained in the following passage:

Vision is a process we can think of as having certain standard inputs and outputs. The standard inputs are impulses from the optic nerves which are themselves the result of light impinging on the eyes, and the standard outputs are beliefs – perceptual beliefs – about what is in our immediate environment and where it is in relation to our bodies. . . . I suggest that an episode of mental imagery runs the visual system off-line, disconnected from standard inputs and outputs. The central processing part of the visual system – that which is ultimately responsible for visual experience – is seized hold of and operated much as it would if it were taking inputs from the periphery.

Having visual images does not cause us to have beliefs about what is in our imme-diate environment in the way that vision does. But just as the simulation of belief and desire can mirror the causation of affective states by real belief and desire, so having a mental image of something – a dangerous bear, for example – can produce the affective states that seeing a dangerous bear tends to cause (Currie forthcoming, p. 4)

We find this proposal underdescribed and problematic in a number of ways. One comparatively minor problem is that it seems unlikely that affective states would be the only, or even a primary output of imagery. It's easy, for instance, to imagine a dangerous bear without feeling fear or anxiety. That is to say it's easy to imagine a dangerous bear without having the affective states that would be caused by actually seeing a dangerous bear. Although Currie's paper doesn't make it explicit, presumably the standard outputs of image generation are just mental images. Those images in turn *may* lead to affective states.

We have a more serious complaint about the inputs to the visual proces-sor. Currie tells us neither what the inputs are nor where they come from. Perhaps, in analogy with off-line simulation of behaviour prediction, Currie wants to maintain that there is a pretend input generator that feeds into the central visual processor. The resulting account would claim that in image generation, pretend input is fed into the visual processor which then operates on the pretend input as it would on actual visual input; the output of this is a mental image (which might then lead to an affective state). We've tried to make this functional architecture explicit in figure 4.5.[10]

This functional architecture still leaves many crucial questions un-answered, however. In particular, it's not clear what claim Currie is making about imagery and simulation. We're not sure whether the simu-lation account of imagery is supposed to be a novel theory of mental imagery or whether the claim is rather that certain established accounts of mental imagery *are* simulation accounts. We'll consider these possibilities in turn.

Currie's theory might be considered novel insofar as it appeals to a pretend input device for imagery. Unfortunately, Currie provides no account of the nature of the pretend input mechanism. Suppose, for instance, that I say to you: form the mental image of a polar bear in the tundra. What is the pretend input mechanism supposed to provide? If the visual processor is to work 'much as it would if it were taking inputs from the periphery', then one might expect that the inputs must be much *like* the

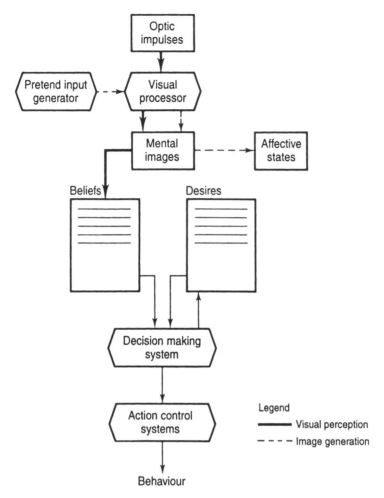

Figure 4.5 Simulation-based account of imagery

inputs from the periphery. And those, as Currie notes, are impulses from the optic nerve. Following this line of thought, the pretend input mechanism would have to take input in the form of linguistic descriptions and produce a reasonable approximation to the signals the optic nerve would produce were we actually to see such a scene. This would provide the simulationist with a novel account of imagery, but at the cost of a mechanism that stretches the bounds of credulity, to put it mildly.

Another possible interpretation of Currie's view is that mental imagery depends on the same general capacity for pretence that simulationists claim is implicated in behaviour prediction. This may be Currie's point in the following passage:

> In my view, the pretend beliefs and desires we have during simulation are no more real beliefs and desires than the simulated fighting on stage is real fighting. We might use the generic term 'imaginings' to cover these pretend states . . . That will help keep track of the commonality between simulating attitudes and simulating vision; having mental images is (a special kind of) imagining seeing (forthcoming, p. 7)

We're not at all sure we understand the supposed commonality between simulating attitudes and simulating vision.[11] In particular, we're not sure whether the pretend inputs for imagery are supposed to be pretend beliefs that might also be fed into the decision maker. It would seem to be somewhat surprising if the visual processor could take the same type of input as the decision maker. In addition, evidence from autism poses a serious *prima facie* problem for the claim that imagery and behaviour prediction depend on the same pretence mechanism. As mentioned earlier, simulationists claim that the reason autistic children fail behaviour prediction tasks is because of a gross deficiency in their ability for pretence (e.g., Currie, 1995; Gordon and Barker 1994). So, if mental imagery depended on this same capacity for pretence, simulationists would predict that autistic children should fail imagery tasks as well (Currie, forthcoming, p. 6). However, there is evidence that autistic children perform well on standard imagery tasks. For instance, they perform at normal levels on Shepard's rotation tasks (Shah, 1988). As a result, simulationists apparently can't appeal to a common pretence mechanism for behaviour prediction and mental imagery.

A final interpretation of Currie's appeal to pretence or imagination is that some 'special kind' of imagining is essential to mental imagery. The nature of this special kind of imagining is, however, left entirely unclear. We still don't know what is involved in 'imagining' to see a polar bear. As a result, it's impossible to say whether appealing to this kind of imagination represents a novel approach to imagery input. For instance, Martha Farah (1984) argues that there must be an image generation mechanism that is independent from the mechanisms of visual perception, and it's not clear how or whether Currie's special kind of imagining differs from Farah's image generation mechanism.

Perhaps, then, Currie doesn't mean to offer a novel theory of imagery. Rather, maybe the point is to argue that prevailing accounts of mental imagery really are simulation accounts. In the recent literature on imagery, there is a virtual consensus that imagery and perception share mechanisms. It's clear that Currie concurs with this. Perhaps Currie's claim is just that insofar as imagery and perception share mechanisms, imagery is a simulation-based capacity. It's difficult to see why that should be the case, though. For consider that it's quite possible that our capacity to predict and explain people's behaviour (the 'folk psychology capacity') and our capacity to predict and explain the behaviour of middle sized objects (the 'folk physics capacity') each depend on information bases (or tacit theories) which share the same inference mechanisms. But surely that's no argument that one of them must be a simulation-based capacity.

There is another established view in the literature that perhaps bears a greater resemblance to simulation theories. Kosslyn and Farah, among others, maintain that while image generation depends on an information base, there is no information base that is *devoted* to image generation. Rather, they maintain that image generation depends on a body of information that is also exploited for visual recognition.

Is Kosslyn's theory plausibly a simulation theory then? Unfortunately, there is no easy way to answer this question since the notion of a simulation theory is far from being well defined. At best it is a family resemblance notion, and one of the anchoring prototypes is the off-line account of behaviour prediction. Kosslyn's view on mental imagery has some important similarities to the off-line account of behaviour prediction. Imagery depends on mechanisms used for vision, and there is no separate information base devoted to imagery. However, there are also striking differences between Kosslyn's account of imagery and the off-line simulation account of behaviour prediction. For instance, according to Gordon and Goldman, behaviour prediction typically doesn't depend on a body of information at all. However, Kosslyn's view, as well as every other established account of imagery, does appeal to a body of information for image generation. Further, on the off-line account of behaviour prediction, the output of the practical reasoner is a proper decision, though it is not fed into the mechanism decisions are usually fed into. But in the case of imagery, the output of the imagery mechanism (whatever that mechanism is like) is considerably different from the outputs of perception. In perception, the output is either visual percepts or beliefs about the environment. But mental images are neither of these. They are not at all as rich as visual percepts. And they typically don't lead to beliefs about the environment. All they seem to do is produce beliefs about the image itself (which may, in turn, produce affective states in some cases). So, unlike the behaviour prediction case, the outputs of imagery aren't normal outputs that are taken off line.

There are, then, significant differences even between Kosslyn's account of imagery and the simulation account of behaviour prediction. Still, we have no in-principle objection to simulationists attaching their label to an established view. However, we are curious about why they should bother. One possible motivation might be to provide support for the simulation account of behaviour prediction. Currie writes, 'If the simulationist can point to other plausible cases of simulation then the claim that our access to other minds is through simulation will sound less like special pleading . . .' (forthcoming, p. 2). We find this sort of inductive argument quite puzzling. For a simulation account of image generation would presumably depend on quite different cognitive mechanisms than the simulation account of behaviour prediction. Even if the visual system is taken off line and fed deviant inputs in the process that leads to imagery, it's unclear why that would give us any reason for thinking that the *decision making system* is taken off line and fed deviant inputs in the process that leads to predictions of other people's behaviour. Further, in the previous paragraph we pointed out additional differences between accounts of mental imagery and the simulation account of behaviour prediction; these differences make it even more implausible that prevailing accounts of mental imagery can provide support for the off-line account of behaviour prediction.

The idea that simulation theory might contribute to our understanding of mental imagery is intriguing. There do seem to be some similarities between accounts of mental imagery and simulation theories. However, as far as we can tell, Currie hasn't offered a plausible simulation theory that provides a genuine alternative to prevailing accounts of imagery. And if that wasn't his intention, then we're not sure how simulation is supposed to illuminate the issue of mental imagery.

Conclusion

Throughout this paper, we've tried to emphasise the extensive explanatory potential of off-line simulation. Off-line simulation promises to offer alternatives to traditional information-based accounts of cognitive capacities. In fact, there already are off-line accounts of a number of radically different capacities, and we've tried to clarify the debate over some of these accounts. In light of the experiments reported here, the off-line simulation account of behaviour prediction still strikes us as quite unpromising. However, this need not diminish the importance of the general strategy of off-line simulation accounts. Indeed, while we are extremely sceptical of the off-line simulation account of behaviour prediction, we think that off-line simulation accounts of counterfactual reasoning, empathy, mental imagery and other phenomena clearly merit further exploration.

NOTES

1 Figure 1 is the same as figure 3 in Stich and Nichols (1992).
2 The metaphor comes from Stephen Schiffer (1981).

3   It's interesting to note that Halle and Stevens offer an argument that closely resembles a familiar argument from Gordon (1986) and Goldman (1989). Gordon and Goldman claim that the theory-theory of behaviour prediction is informationally lavish whereas the simulation alternative is informationally frugal. Similarly, in proposing their 'off-line simulation' account of phoneme recognition, Halle and Stevens argue that the most obvious information-based account of phoneme recognition would be required to posit an utterly enormous information base: 'The size of the dictionary in such an analyser increases very rapidly with the number of admissible outputs, since a given phoneme sequence can give rise to a large number of distinct acoustic outputs. In a device whose capabilities would even remotely approach those of a normal human listener, the size of the dictionary would, therefore, be so large as to rule out this approach' (1962, p. 607).

4   Given the interdisciplinary nature of this volume, perhaps it bears mentioning that counterfactual conditionals are not just conditionals with false antecedents. For material conditionals can have false antecedents; it simply makes the conditional vacuously true, as in, 'If astrology is right, then porcupines make good bed partners.' Counterfactual conditionals, on the other hand, while they typically have false antecedents, make substantive claims which may well be false. For example, the following counterfactual is presumably false: 'If astrology were right, porcupines would make good bed partners.' There is also a grammatical distinction – in English, counterfactual conditionals, unlike material conditionals, are typically expressed in the subjunctive mood.

5   Jerry Fodor (1987, 1992) and Alan Leslie (Leslie and Thais, 1992) have suggested that folk psychology is innate. But even on these views, folk psychology must be triggered. And neither Fodor nor Leslie has suggested that folk psychology is triggered before the child leaves the delivery room.

6   Goldman indicates that insofar as emotional contagion doesn't involve perspective taking, it isn't a clear case of empathy (1993, p. 143). We're not overly concerned with the terminological issues. (We're not concerned at all.) But we do think that emotional contagion is one of the most pervasive and salient cases of 'vicarious sharing of affect'. As such, it's important to determine whether it is better explained by off-line simulation or information-based accounts.

7   Thompson (1987) reports studies in which infants seem to display vicarious responses to the emotional states of others. Thompson writes, 'Among even the youngest children in the sample, the distress of others elicited orienting and, in nearly one third of the 10- to 14-month-olds, distress crying (Zahn-Waxler and Radke-Yarrow, 1982)' (Thompson 1987, p. 131). Thompson takes these and other data to indicate 'a *capacity* for empathy' develops by 18 months (p. 135).

8   Indeed actors claim that when a part calls for them to cry, they sometimes achieve this by focusing on sad memories from their own life.

9   We'd like to think Professor Currie for providing us with his unpublished paper and for allowing us to quote from it.

10 Actually, Currie's account is a bit more complicated than this as he suggests that imagery can also be generated from tacit knowledge (1994b, p. 15). We don't discuss this aspect of Currie's theory since it isn't an off-line simulation account. But we can't resist pointing out how unparsimonious his account is. He posits two radically different mechanisms (simulation and tacit knowledge) each of

which produces mental images. Perhaps imagery really *is* this fractured, but Currie provides no evidence to suggest that it is.

11 One curious feature of Currie's statement is perhaps worth mentioning. Currie writes, 'having mental images is (a special kind of) imagining seeing'. But *having* mental images is, it seems, most naturally read as: experiencing the *output* of the mental image producing process. So here he seems to be saying that the imagining, which is analogous to pretend belief, is the *output*, not the *input*. Perhaps what Currie meant to say was that having mental images *depends on* a special kind of imagining. However, this aspect of the proposal is so vague that we're really not sure what Currie means.

5   Simulation, theory, and content

Jane Heal

1   Introduction

Some, the theory-theorists, say that when we make judgements about the psychological states of others and use such judgements to predict or explain we employ some theory about the psychological. But others, the simulationists, say that we possess no such theory, or at least none complete enough to underpin all our competence with psychological notions; rather, they say, what we do in such situations is simulate others' mental states and processes in ourselves and thus get insight into what others are likely to do.

My aim in this paper is first to offer an argument in favour of simulationism but second to suggest possible limits to the simulationist strategy. I shall suggest that simulation must be central as far as dealing with the contents of others' mental states is concerned but is much less clearly of relevance in dealing with non-content. Thus philosophers and psychologists should not oppose simulation to theory, but should rather ask what is the appropriate realm of each and how they interact.[1]

The topic throughout is the nature of the fully developed adult competence with psychological notions, in the context of predicting others' future psychological states and actions on the basis of knowledge about their current psychological states. I shall not discuss the (it seems to me) importantly different question of how we arrive at judgements about other's thoughts, feelings etc. from knowledge of placement in the environment or bodily behaviour. Also I am not concerned here with the issue of what psychological concepts are and what it is to have possession of them. And finally I shall not touch at all on developmental issues or questions of how children's competence with psychological language grows and changes. I believe that there are implications for all these questions in the considerations which follow, but I shall not pursue them here.[2]

In more detail the structure of what follows is this. Section 2 offers some further clarification of three central notions, simulation, theory, and content, and some remarks on why simulation is at least an option. Section 3 reminds us of some important facts about thought. Section 4 builds on these to offer the main argument against theory-theory. Section 5 returns to the contrast between content and non-content, suggesting that even if the earlier argument persuades us to the importance of simulation, we should not overextend our claims on its behalf.

2   The central notions

By a simulation of X we shall understand something, Y, which is similar enough to X in its intrinsic nature for tendencies to diachronic development which are inherent in X to have parallels in Y. Hence, given suitably analogous stimuli or circumstances, their histories unfold in parallel and properties of the one can be read off from properties of the other according to some simple correlation scheme. The classic example is the model aircraft in the fanned draught of the wind tunnel, which is a simulation of the real aircraft in the real wind.[3]

Given this notion, the central simulationist claim is that the thinking which occurs when one person reasons, in all seriousness, to some theoretical or practical conclusion, can be simulated in a second person, who need not however be in the same way committed to the thoughts entertained. Simulationists have also claimed that this similarity can be accessed or employed so as to enable the second person to arrive at judgements about what the first will think or do.

By 'theory' we shall understand an articulated structure made up of elements, each of which either makes a claim of a kind expressible in a public language (perhaps with some extended vocabulary or notational system) or expresses a rule of inference. We are, of course, allowing that theories may be tacitly as well as explicitly known. But the kind of thing theories are is shown by the explicit specimens, for example in physics or linguistics.[4] What possession of a psychological theory would explain is our ability to make particular predictions about people, from knowledge of their psychological states. But a theory is not a mere conjunction of such individual judgements. It must embody that information not as a mere list but in some more compendious way. So the theory will contain generalisations which can be applied to individual cases.

But what form will they take and how will they be organised? Let us make a contrast here which will later be important. Consider two schematic types of medical knowledge about diseases and their likely developments. We can imagine a wise woman who is able to offer some general remarks about symptoms and their seriousness. ('High fever is often dangerous', 'Laboured breathing is generally a bad sign', 'Many skin rashes are trivial') and can also, surveying a patient, select among the visible symptoms the ones which are in fact important in the particular case. So she can say, correctly, 'This patient will recover, because the fever has broken in a sweat' or, in another case, 'This patient will not recover, because the breathing is now very laboured.' But it may well be the case that the patient who will recover is also exhibiting very laboured breathing. Our imagined wise woman, however, is unable to say why the breathing is not so sinister in that case. She knows that she is entitled to ignore it in arriving at a prognosis. But she does not know why.

Clearly however we can also imagine another practitioner, say a doctor with modern training, who possesses what the wise woman lacks, namely a framework within which the various symptoms are listed and systematically related to each other; she can talk of their interrelation and of the contexts in which each is important; she can not only predict what will happen in a particular case, but locate that case among other possible ones, by saying what would have happened in other circumstances and why. I suggest that the word 'theory' is only fully at home in describing something, whether tacit or explicit, with at least the structure of this explicit example. So I shall take it that when the theory-theorist claims that we possess a theoretically based ability to predict psychological states, he means 'theory' in this sense.

By 'content' I mean the representational aspect of a mental state, that in virtue of which it carries some specification of how the world is (or might be) and in virtue of which it can be assessed for fit with the world. We shall return in Section 5 to the distinction between content and non-content. For the moment it is enough to note two things. The first is that it is extremely implausible to suppose that full specification of content exhausts what can be said of a mental state. To say it did would be to take it that there is only one mode of occurrence of content and that every psychological state, whether a propositional attitude or perceptual state can be seen on investigation to consist of some content (perhaps immensely complex) entertained in this one mode. I do not say that I have an immediate knock down argument against this view.[5] But it has an unattractive over-intellectual flavour and it seems extremely likely that we shall need to recognise non-content to account both for the differences between propositional attitudes and also for the nature of perception and sensation. The second point to note about content is that examples of it are specified by that-clauses when we attribute beliefs, intentions, desires and emotions to people. And it is this kind of content with which we are primarily concerned in what follows.

Are we in possession of theoretical knowledge about persons and their states? And does this provide the whole of what we call on when we predict others? The answer to the first question must surely be 'yes'. We are capable of stating explicitly a fair amount about the sort of beings we take people to be, the factors which influence them and how they interrelate. For example they can perceive what is in spatial proximity to them through their various senses and can remember past events and can in these ways acquire beliefs. They have desires and, under the guidance of their beliefs, form projects on how to fulfil them. They feel emotions which are liable to influence their patterns of reasoning. And so on.[6] Being a normal adult human being with competence in using psychological notions requires grasp on all this and a lot more of the same sort, some or much of it perhaps tacitly rather than explicitly grasped.

But it does not follow from this that the answer to our second question is also 'yes', i.e. that we possess a theory, tacit or otherwise, in terms of which the whole of our ability to make predictions about individuals can be explained. What we set out in our summary of theoretical knowledge was generalities about beliefs, perceptions, emotions, projects etc. as broad classes. Such generalities say nothing directly on beliefs or projects about particular subject matters, e.g. under what circumstances a doctor will believe that a patient has measles or when a restaurant customer will order a meal. If the theory we possess, when spelled out with all its 'and so ons' is to be one which underpins such particular predictions it must grapple with content. And the claim I wish to defend is that no theory could do so fully. Of course we have bits of theory about some contents and their relations. But my suggestion will be that our primary competence with content is of the 'know how' variety and that only a small part of this can be reflected in any theoretical 'know that' about how contents relate.

The nature and possibility of simulation have been explored in the existing literature, (e.g. Gordon (1986), Heal (1986), Goldman (1989), Stich and Nichols (1992)). So I shall not rehearse the issues here. The key point is that we think and reason about situations using the same capacities, whether we take those situations to be actual or merely possible. So if I take on merely as a hypothesis what someone else actually believes then what I do in further thought simulates what he or she does, inasmuch as we both exercise the same intellectual and conceptual capacities on the same subject matter and so may move through the same sequence of related contents to the same conclusion. The ability to think about the non-actual is very remarkable. But the point that is worth stressing is that once it has been conceded we need very little more (merely grip on the general picture of the person sketched above, says the simulationist) to enable us to use our ability to think about the non-actual for the very different task of predicting others' thoughts.

3   Four important facts about thinking

I turn now from elucidating the idea of psychological simulation and defending its possibility to putting in place some of the ideas which will enable us to argue its attraction, namely by undermining its rival, the theory-theory. It will help us to get clear first what a theory adequate to deal with content would have to cope with. So I shall introduce four important facts about thinking: (1) the amount of information we possess (2) epistemic holism (3) our actual rationality and (4) our actual success in predicting others.

(1) Each normal adult human being possesses an enormous amount of information. He or she has a world view (history, physics, politics . . .) together with information about personal history (family, friends, career . . .) and perceptually given information about current physical surroundings (the location roundabout of objects, people . . .). A psychological account of a person at an instant would specify all this, and in addition would spell out the person's tastes, values, ambitions, emotions etc. To write all this out in a natural language would take volumes and volumes.[7] A person's psychological state evolves diachronically, partly under the impetus of external stimuli and partly as driven by internal factors, e.g. what problems the person is thinking about.

(2) Justification or epistemic status is a holistic notion. This is particularly important for what follows, so we should consider it further. The central claim is that the status of a thought as justified or not is determined by features of the whole set of thoughts from which it arises. An answer to a question may seem to have good support from some subset of thoughts. But if we look wider we may find further thoughts in the light of which the force of the subset is altered. For example, the information that I am in a restaurant, that I am hungry and that I have been given a menu provides good support for the decision to read the menu with a view to choosing a dish. But if I also recognise the waiter as a wanted criminal, from a distinctive scar on his hand, then I have reason to telephone the police rather than read the menu. But again, if I also have further information that my movements are being watched by the criminals who suspect that I am a police agent, then perhaps I have reason to sit tight and (at least pretend to) read the menu. And so on.[8]

Moreover no thought, whatever its subject matter, can be ruled out *a priori* as certainly irrelevant to a given question. If any one of an indefinitely large number of patterns of suitable linking elements were present then it would be relevant. And the absence of such linking patterns is a matter of what the set as a whole contains or does not contain. For example, suppose I am a doctor investigating whether a patient has measles. I have a great deal of information about symptoms and the results of physiological tests. These are obviously relevant. But it may seem equally obvious that the further information I possess that Henry VII of England was a Tudor could not be relevant. However, we need to insert only a few

further beliefs (not outrageously bizarre) into my belief set to put a connection in place. Perhaps I believe that measles has an unusual variant in
which the presence of a certain gene, common in the Tudor family, leads to
its running a non-standard course. And perhaps my patient has boasted of
his royal ancestry. (We could have used the restaurant story to make the
same point. Could the fact that the bank robber had a distinctive scar on
his hand be relevant to whether I should read this menu? It may seem
absurd, yet . . .) It is absence of any linking pattern of this kind which enti-
tles me, as the situation really is, to pay no attention to the history of
England when trying to diagnose my patient's condition. And such absence
is a matter of the structure of the belief set as a whole.

This epistemological holism is a quite different matter from semantic
holism and ought to be accepted even by semantic atomists or molecular-
ists. It does not arise from some mysterious essential interconnectedness
which thoughts of their nature have with other thoughts. Rather the central
factor underlying it is the potential complex interconnectedness of things,
both causally and evidentially. The world may present itself to us much of
the time as more or less isolated subsystems, further features of which can
be inferred on the basis of information about only the current or preceding
states of that subsystem. But each such subsystem is, we believe, embedded
in a wider spatio-temporal framework which may impinge on it or provide
clues about it. The characteristic mark of our awareness of this is our
hedging of our inferences and predictions with phrases such as 'ceteris
paribus', 'in most cases', 'in normal circumstances' and the like.[9]

(3) But what if circumstances are not normal or other things are not
equal? Factors which are *prima facie* very remote (the scar on a man's hand,
Henry VII being a Tudor) may be relevant to a question (whether to study
a menu, whether this patient has measles) because of the existence of one
of those patterns of linkage mentioned earlier. Are we then stymied?
Sometimes we are; we overlook matters, fail to follow up clues, get confused
and so forth. But not always. The remarkable fact about us is that when we
seek answers to questions, all the information in the volumes and volumes
of our world view is, to a very large extent, appropriately available to us,
not just in the sense that we can instantly provide answers to extremely
diverse questions but in the more important sense that if there are configurations of information in the total view which make something other than
a stereotypical answer proper to the question in hand then that information
tends to become prominent to us and to influence our judgement appropriately. So we are sometimes rational, not only in that we can follow
through intricate chains of deductive reasonings but also in that we can
respond flexibly to changing and unusual circumstances.

(4) Finally we must note that in predicting the thoughts of others, we take

account of the fact that they have the ability to cope sensibly when other things are not equal or circumstances are not normal. We expect of them that they will make the judgements which are justified in the holistic fashion sketched. Consider again the cases of the restaurant or the doctor, from the point of view of someone attempting to predict what the restaurant customer or doctor would do. In setting up these cases I earlier relied upon the fact that you would have no difficulty in seeing that a person with the beliefs sketched would respond in the way I outlined.

4   Simulation, relevance, and the Frame Problem

Having set in place accounts of our key terms and drawn attention to some important facts, we are now in a position to consider why the theory-theory, when it embodies a claim to be able to deal with content, is unattractive and simulationism is correspondingly strengthened. We may put the issue this way. The theory-theorist is committed to the claim that we have – tacitly at least – solved an extremely important precursor problem to the famous Frame Problem in Artificial Intelligence, namely the problem of providing a general theory of relevance. And this claim is highly implausible.

The Frame Problem is, roughly, as follows. Artificial Intelligence aims to outline how we might build machines which can perform similarly to human beings with respect to such things as sustaining a conversation or coming up with some plan of action. The object is to show how to endow a machine with knowledge and with ability to process that knowledge in such a way as to enable it to derive appropriate answers to questions it is set. But any assemblage of information has many implications, the bigger the assemblage the greater the number; and only a few of them will bear on a given question. The difficulty AI researchers have run into is that of finding a format for coding knowledge and questions, and a way in which a machine can process its knowledge in the light of its question, so as to enable it to come up with the required answer rather than coming up with some one of the vast number of other true but irrelevant claims which its knowledge base and inference rules license. Possibilities for deriving these others have to be allowed for, because they might be needed in another case, if another question had been posed. But how do we get the device to ignore them in this case?[10]

The Frame Problem is one which arises even if we do not believe in epistemological holism. Someone who thinks both that we can ignore the possibility of our being inconsistent and also that knowledge is organised in deductive systems is still faced with a version of the Frame Problem. But a system with a holistic justification structure threatens an even tougher version of the problem than a deductively based system. When deduction is central we might hope to use some combination of vocabulary and formal features in the shape of the question to narrow down the range of axioms and inference rules to be considered; and thus we might find some strategy for homing in speedily on the needed route through from information to answer. But if holism is the order of the day then relevance becomes context relative. We need not only to locate the obviously important materials but also to survey systematically the whole of the rest of the assemblage to see whether or not it contains any of the indefinitely large number of configurations of information which might, in unusual circumstances, also be important.

My claim is not that the theory-theorist must suppose that the theory he postulates itself provides a solution to the Frame Problem. That problem is about how to represent and process knowledge in an artificially created system and largely concerns the implementation level. Those studying the Frame Problem have to deal extensively with non-intentional subject matter, such as the virtues of different computer languages, the attempted syntactic specifications of various inference procedures and the like. By contrast the imagined psychological theory need deal only with items, viz. thoughts, specified intentionally.

But theory-theory and the Frame Problem are nevertheless closely connected. One thing which makes the Frame Problem so difficult is our inability to say much of a structured or systematic kind about the central notion of relevance. We want to mimic human intelligence. We can say at a high level of generality that it is characteristic of that intelligence that, given a question and a world view, a person will respond to what in that view is relevant to the question. We can also give detailed examples of relevance and so of how people actually should and do respond to this or that question. But an intermediate level competence – on which we could group the cases in a revealing way or classify kinds of relevance or point to some finite number of structural possibilities for relating information and such like – is strikingly lacking.[11] If we had it we might at least see how to think about implementing a similarly structured ability on a machine. But this intermediate level grip, a systematic way of treating relevance, is what the theory-theorist supposes we do actually, even if only tacitly, have.

To see this recall the claim of Section 2 that a theory is something which enables us to locate a given case among the range of possible cases. It specifies the possible factors bearing on outcomes, how they interrelate, and why some and not others are actually influential in a given case. Such a theory need not, of course, itself tell us what happens in unusual circumstances. To handle these we need to integrate the information provided by the theory into a wider picture. But a theory of a phenomenon ought to give us systematically based insight into the behaviour of the items theorised in normal circumstances.

When a question on a particular subject matter (medicine, restaurant behaviour . . .) presents itself to us, our remarkable cognitive system serves up to us information relevant to the question. Supposing that the subject matter is theorised, then it will serve up the theory (or the required section of it). If there are no unusual circumstances, then we apply the theory and come up with an appropriate answer. And if circumstances are not usual, the system will serve up that information also. Now matters are just the same with the supposed psychological theory. We need to have it, rather than some other irrelevant theory, come to mind when required. And its predictions are as liable as those of any other theory to be in need of correction in the light of extra information (that the person we are studying has a brain implant, is about to be hit by a meteor, etc.). Thus in operating this theory, as with any other, we shall need to rely upon the amazing powers which the Frame Problem has made us aware we have. And of course simply by being entitled to rely on those powers, the theory-theorist is not committed to supposing that he has solved any part of the Frame Problem – any more than a doctor or theorist of restaurant behaviour is so committed.

But there are two factors which make the psychological crucially different and which mean that a claim to have a psychological theory of content does involve further commitments. The first is that the subject matter of psychological theory is precisely thoughts themselves and their upshots. The second is that dealing with the unexpected or unusual is an expected and usual part of human thought. As we stressed earlier, we can cope when circumstances are not normal and we understand very well that others can do so too. So if our imagined psychological theory is to account for our competence in these cases it must give systematically organised insight into the difference between our responses in usual and unusual cases, i.e. insight into a whole range of world view/question pairs and their possible upshots. It must specify the range of psychological factors which influence thoughts and decisions in response to given questions; it must lay out how they interact; it must say why some are important to outcomes in some settings and not in others; and it must be able to tell us how and why things would have been different, given this or that variation in the starting conditions. But given epistemological holism and our actual rationality, what all this amounts to is precisely a general and systematic theory of relevance.

I do not say that it is impossible that we do possess tacitly a theory of this character. But two factors should make us very wary of postulating it. One is the oddness of supposing that we have it tacitly while at the same time possessing no inkling of how to set it out explicitly. The other, and much more important consideration, is the quite mind-boggling complexity of what is imagined. The theory has got to be able to handle world view/question pairs and come up with a predicted answer in every case where, in practice, we can predict others. Let us remember that the world views are volumes and volumes long. We may if we like, summarise much of the information very briefly with phrases like 'what most people know' or some such. But even when disguised this way and made to look less threatening, the volumes and volumes must still be handled by the theory. It must have ways of separately registering and appropriately classifying every difference in content. This is because by playing with one or another bit of that content, i.e. altering the person's world view in this or that way from the usual, we can see that we would get different predictions in the case of at least some questions. As an information storage and processing task and given the range of our actual psychological competence, dealing with this imagined theory is orders of magnitude more formidable than dealing with any other tacit theory that has been proposed, e.g. for grammar or folk physics.

The theory-theorist may try to avoid this unpleasant outcome by denying that we have this systematic theoretical grip on relevance. Instead, he says, there is a non-theoretical background machinery – our remarkable cognitive system – which delivers to us the factors relevant to any given problem. It enables us to pick out from another's world view the particular thoughts important to determining his or her behaviour in a specified case. For example, taking the customer in the restaurant recognising the criminal, it says that the other is thinking: 'Here is a menu. I am in a restaurant and want food. Therefore it is sensible to read the menu. That man is a criminal. Criminals ought to be reported to the police. Catching criminals is more important than studying menus.' The background machinery also serves up a relevant general principle, namely 'People faced with reasons for two actions, tend to do the one they judge most important.' And, applying the principle to the presented data, we get the prediction that the customer will call the police.

There are however two problems with this picture of what is going on. The first is merely verbal. It is just that the tacit theory now postulated falls considerably short of what the use of the word 'theory' suggests. The content of the supposed theory has dropped back to what was explicit in the wise woman's medical knowledge. Much work which we would expect to be done by a theory (e.g. keeping a systematic count of all potentially relevant features, specifying which are important in which circumstances) has been shuffled off onto the background ability. The second problem is more substantial, given the dialectical position. It is that in presenting this picture of matters, the theory-theorist has conceded the primary point that the simulationist is urging with respect to content. To apply the remarkable machinery to someone else's world view so as to extract from it the thoughts relevant to answering a particular question is precisely to simulate his or her thought. His or her remarkable machinery is doing exactly the same, namely sieving through varied contents to find and use the relevant ones. Each of us is relying on his or her understanding of the question and of the content of the world view to drive forward the thought process which delivers the answer.

5   Content and non-content

Let us now turn to the distinction between content and non-content and consider the question of whether use of simulation could explain our competence in handling the non-content based aspects of psychological predictions of others.

By definition non-content is an aspect of a mental state in which it differs from another mental state but where the difference does not consist in either state representing something different from the other. We should, I suggest, look for non-content in two places; first in whatever makes the difference between different propositional attitudes and second in the nature of sensation and perception. These are *prima facie* very different. The former has to do with the intuition that content plays different explanatory roles in different kinds of state and that grasping the role is different from grasping the content. The latter has to do with the plausibility of the idea that there are aspects of mental states possessing a felt 'qualitative' character, where that cannot be cashed out in terms of representational content.

Although the distinction between content and non-content is (more or less) clear in principle, it is not entirely easy to draw in practice. The difficulty is to decide when a state has representational content, i.e. when it is liable for assessment for fit with the world. With attitudes this takes us into issues about realism (e.g. on values, necessity, etc.). With felt character it takes us to the issue of qualia and of distinguishing sensational and representational elements in perception.[12] Since these are controversial there is a difficulty in finding unproblematic examples to illustrate the argument. But I hope that we can get at least some grip on the issues.

It seems clear that (if the idea of non-content is well grounded at all) each distinctive kind of non-content has a set of properties which are linked in a recurrent and stable cluster. For example, craving as a distinctive sub-variety of motivational state is, typically, marked by the following features: it arises from such things as illness or repeated ingestion of certain substances, rather than from detailed rational appraisal of the value of the craved item; it is not extinguished by knowledge of the lack of value of what is craved; it is manifested in episodes which are urgent and unpleasant; it tends to lead to actions to secure what is craved. And, to take a case of the other type, visual non-content is caused by light falling on the eyes, can be associated with spatial representational contents and has a distinctive quality space (in which it differs from those associated with hearing, taste, touch etc.).

An important assumption I shall make is that this clustering is *a posteriori*, both in the sense that possession of one feature in a cluster does not entail possession of the others and (more importantly for the argument) in the sense that it is not an *a priori* matter that a state with a particular cluster of properties exist in any creature which is a proper subject of psychological attributes. The claims that I am in effect making here are, first, that there are real psychological kinds and, second, that what these kinds are in any actual type of creature, is a matter of the contingent facts of the physiology and of the cultural formation of that type of creature. The very general conception of mind, of an active subject of experience, may fix that certain broad categories (information processing, motivation, perception . . .) must find application. But how this works out in detail, what kinds of perception, motivation etc. a given creature has, is not given *a priori* in the very notion of a psychology.

The idea we are to consider is that people can put on a kind of reproduction of non-content which will enable new information about that particular sort of non-content to be derived. We can simulate craving or visual perception and by noting the nature of what then goes on in us we can learn, for example, new things about what craving or visual perception can lead to.

The obvious, and I think only, candidate for such a reproduction is *imagining*, where we mean by this not 'falsely believing' nor yet 'merely supposing' but rather 'vividly imagining'. This is the kind of imagining which in the case of visual experience takes the form of having visual images and in the case of such things as craving takes the form of what we are inclined to describe as 'really thinking what it would be like'.

The idea that this sort of imagining is the occurrence of a (faint) copy of what is imagined is familiar and attractive. It is also notoriously controversial. But I shall suggest that simulationist claims are not significantly advanced, whichever side we take in the controversy. To test this let us consider the boldest and simplest versions of the two options.

On one view it is a naive muddle to suppose that, say, having a visual image of a rose is anything like actually seeing a rose. Rather it is a matter of supposing that one sees a rose; what makes the difference between mere conceptual supposing and what we call 'having a visual image' is that in the latter case a great amount of further detailed content (about colours, angles, etc.) is specified.

It is no surprise that this view is inhospitable to the simulationist idea, since no one takes it that what occurs in supposition, i.e. mere representation, has a significant degree of intrinsic causal resemblance to what it represents. Indeed, in general, we do not want our representations (whether these are sentences on a page or structures in the mind) to be too causally lively under their own steam, otherwise they might start dictating our empirical theories and our thoughts to us. We want them to help in calling up further representations only when (a) we have put in place through our own empirical investigations linkages, e.g. in the form of laws, between the original and the subsequent phenomena represented and (b) we ourselves direct our thoughts in such a way as to allow some of their implications to emerge. So representations of particular phenomena are, in general, causally neutral with respect to calling into existence other representations.

But what if there is, after all, something right about the naive view? I want to suggest that, contrary to what one may initially think, this does not make matters substantially better for the simulationist.

Let us allow that having a visual image is not just having representations with the content 'I am seeing . . .' but also involves the occurrence of further non-content events, significantly resembling those of actual vision. More generally, let us allow that when someone vividly imagines X and X is a mental state then something which is like X with respect to the immediate experience of the subject, occurs in the mind. The crucial point, however, is that in allowing this we have not allowed that the item need belong to the same real psychological type as X, in the sense of having the nature from which the cluster of X-distinctive properties flow. From the point of view of further properties, it may be mere delusory fool's X which occurs.

And when we consider actual cases they strongly suggest that this is so. For example, visual experience has the further property, which we did not consider earlier, of giving rise to after images. But I do not believe that someone who was unfamiliar with the phenomenon of after images could be got to be aware of it by imagining closing the eyes after seeing a bright patch. (A physiological account of this is easily forthcoming. Real seeing involves processes in the retina which give rise both to events deeper in the brain, events associated with the characteristic experiences of sight, and also to liability to after images. Having visual images may resemble seeing in that it involves visual experience-type events deep in the brain without resembling it in involving occurrences in the retina.) Considering craving, a further and hitherto unmentioned feature of it is that it sets up sensitivity to the most tenuous thought associations. One who craves X (in the dispositional sense) is liable to be reminded of X and have the active craving re-awoken by all sorts of flimsily associated items, even when the mind is focused elsewhere. But again it seems to me highly implausible that someone who was unaware of this could have it brought to his or her attention by vivid imaginings of craving.

Do the above arguments throw any doubt on the idea that simulation is possible and indeed required for the handling of content? They do not. Defence of simulation with respect to content starts from an undoubted fact, namely our ability to think – with awareness of logical implication, relevance etc. – about the non-actual. To simulate another's belief that p by engaging one's own mind on the (possibly not believed) content that p is not to have some faint experiential copy of a belief that p occur in one. Neither the belief nor the content are reproduced in this way. First, simulating belief may involve something called 'imagining'. But it is not vividly imagining believing (= faint copy of believing) which is required, but imagining (= supposing) that p. And, second, in such supposing the content that p is fully, and not merely faintly or apparently, present. Any simulationist story must of course postulate resemblance between what is done by the subject and what is done by the simulator. And there is resemblance between my hypothesising that p and your really believing that p, namely the identity of content. But this is quite different from the 'faint copy' kind of resemblance postulated between seeing and having an image.

ACKNOWLEDGEMENTS

I am indebted to Kent Bach, Peter Carruthers, David Owens, and Stephen Stich for helpful comments and discussion on an earlier draft of this paper.

NOTES

1 I am here expanding on some of the ideas in Heal (1995). A similar idea is sketched also in Perner (1994) and I am indebted to his discussion.
2 More discussion of the first and second issue may be found in Heal (1995).
3 Thus 'simulation' as I intend it is equivalent to Goldman's 'process driven simulation' rather than to his general notion of simulation, in Goldman (1989).
4 The use of 'theory' advocated here thus differs from the very generous construal offered by Stich and Nichols (1992, p.48) on which any process subserving our capacity to predict others which is *not* simulation counts as a theory, even if it contains no sentence or rule like items. For Stich and Nichols' polemical purposes at that point their wide definition is entirely appropriate. But intuitively it is a considerably stretched usage to call something a 'theory' when it lacks articulated contentful structure.
5 It may be that some have held it. Spinoza is a plausible candidate.
6 See Wellman (1990), ch.4 for a useful sketch of our folk psychological framework.
7 I ignore questions about whether there is such a thing as a complete specification or whether, at the end of the day, we have to fall back on pointing to our lives and everyday surroundings. (On this, see Dreyfus and Dreyfus

(1986)).Clearly there is such a thing as trying to make a start on the project and that is enough for this argument.

8 Even when the support given to a certain answer is deductively conclusive, holism is still in force, since my total set of thoughts is not guaranteed to be consistent. The realisation of an implication may operate to motivate discarding the premise rather than accepting the conclusion. But this ground for holism is importantly different from the one pursued in the text and I shall not be concerned further with it.

9 I do not mean to imply that all these phrases mean the same. The whole issue of 'ceteris paribus' etc. is more complex than is brought out here.

10 See Dennett (1984) and Boden (1990) for more on the Frame Problem and an introduction to the extensive literature.

11 Compare Marr's notion of a 'computational theory' for an Artificial Intelligence problem in his (1977) and (1982).

12 See Peacocke (1983).

6　Simulation as explicitation of predication-implicit knowledge about the mind: arguments for a simulation-theory mix

Josef Perner

Before discussing the relative merits of simulation and theory-theory we need to establish principled grounds for distinguishing the use of simulation from the use of a theory in order to avoid collapse between these two positions. My proposal is that simulation be characterised as the use of predication-implicit knowledge about the mind. On the basis of this characterisation I conclude that every use of a theory of mind involves an element of simulation, since our folk theory typically exploits predication-implicit knowledge about the content domain. However, I then go on to argue on empirical grounds that simulation cannot be the only ingredient in how we make mental attributions. The only viable position is a simulation-theory mix.

1　Threat of collapse: a brief review

Our folk psychology provides us with the notion of role- or perspective taking. So we thought we knew what simulation (Gordon, 1986, or 'replication', Heal, 1986) was supposed to be and how it differed from mental state attributions on the basis of a theory. The difference can be easily explained with simple examples. More concerned about urban safety than Grizzly bears my favourite example involves walking through a dark alley and noticing a seedy looking character closing in from behind. How does one feel? How will one react? Answering it by theorising one draws on knowledge that people are afraid of being mugged in dark alleys by seedy characters. The person will, therefore, feel afraid and try to run away. Doing it by simulation I imagine myself in that situation and then let myself react to this situation. I will register a slender feeling of fear and a temptation to quicken my pace. I will attribute fear and a quickening of pace to the other person.

Although the distinction seems clear at this intuitive level of analysis it has proven tricky to stipulate general characteristics of how simulation differs from theory use. As the term 'simulation' suggests, the natural idea is that one uses oneself as a model for the person whose mental states or behaviour one wants to understand or predict. However, as Goldman (1989) pointed out there are *theory driven* and *process driven* models. Only a process driven model qualifies as simulation. Its characteristic is that the driving process be isomorphic to the process that is being simulated. My reaction at this point in the discussion was that simulation is characterised by two things, the use of one's own mind as an analogue model (in the sense of having a relevantly similar causal structure) and that thereby one is using information about the functioning of one's mind without representing that one's (or any) mind functions that way (Perner, 1991b). Although this intuitive reaction needs clarification and refinement, I think, it captures intuitions about simulation in different camps (e.g., 'off-line' use, Stich and Nichols, 1992; and 'isomorphism' between processes, Goldman, 1989; but also Davies' (1994) interpretation of Gordon's (1992) position in terms of 'imaginative identification' and Gordon's (1995) notion of 'uncomprehending self reference').

The discussion in the literature continued with Davies' (1994) reaction to Goldman's suggestion that the critical feature of process-driven simulation is a structural isomorphism. Davies pointed out that this characterisation typically also holds for tacit theories: '. . . a component processing mechanism embodies tacit knowledge of a particular rule or axiom if it plays a role in mediating causally between representational states that is structurally analogous to the role that the rule or axiom itself plays in mediating derivationally between premises and conclusions' (Davies, 1994, p. 115).

2   Avoiding the threat of collapse

To prevent the ensuing threat of collapse between positions Davies distinguishes between two types of imaginative process. In one type more imagined mental states and actions are derived from the imaginatively assumed initial states. That is, it is a 'transition amongst representational states whose contents themselves concern mental states. Such contents might be of the forms: I believe that *p*; I believe that *q*' (p. 117).

Davies contrasts this with the proper simulation alternative which 'makes use of the idea of imaginative identification [where] the states of the simulator do not have contents such as these. Rather, they are 'pretend belief' and 'pretend desire' states, whose contents are simply that *p*, or that *q*.' (p. 117). To evaluate this proposal let me take my example of the quickening pace in the dark alley and make the different interpretations schematically explicit starting with simulation's close relative: reasoning by analogy (making an inference from me to you, Gordon 1995).

On a sunny day I am asked the question how someone would feel and react when followed by a seedy looking character in a dark alley way. When reasoning by analogy (RbA) I go through the following steps (the actual mental processes which are not contents of other processes are capitalised):

RbA-1. ASSUMING: I am in the dark alley situation.

RbA-2. REASONING (about myself according to what I know about myself): if I am in this situation I believe that the person is going to mug me.

REASONING: if I believe I am going to be mugged by someone I feel frightened by that person.

REASONING: if I feel frightened by someone coming from behind I tend to quicken my pace and eventually run.

RbA-3. REASONING BY ANALOGY: since my psychological make-up is similar to any typical person I conclude that anyone will feel and react as reasoned in 2.

This is *not* simulation, because I am not using myself as an analogue model (process driven) but use knowledge about myself (theory driven) as a typical specimen of the human species, and the transitions among my states (in particular in Step 2) are among states whose contents themselves concern mental states, my own mental states.

Now here is how it should be done for simulation proper in the sense of imaginative identification à la Martin Davies. I go through the following states (Step 2 of this version is marked with *D* for Davies):

SIM-1(a) IDENTIFYING with other by shifting egocentric frame, which leads to:

(b) IMAGINING being in the dark alley situation (in as life-like a fashion as possible, i.e., 'recentering my egocentric frame to other's situation').

SIMD-2. PRETEND-BELIEVING that person is going to mug me.

PRETEND-FEELING FRIGHTENED by the man.

PRETEND-WANTING to run away from the man.

PRETEND-FEELING like running (+SHOWING SIGNS OF RUNNING).

PRETEND-KNOWING that I shall be running.[1]

SIM-3(a) CLASSIFYING REACTIONS: e.g., 'wanting to run away' (directly by introspection or indirectly via ascent routines).

(b) DE-IDENTIFYING by recentering my egocentric frame to myself:

ATTRIBUTING classified reactions to other: 'Other feels like running.'

Now, this is simulation according to Davies' criterion since the states that I am going through (in Step 2) are states whose contents *do not* concern themselves with mental states. It also captures off-lineness because the 'pretend'-prefixes preserve the imaginary nature of the imagined premise in

Step 1 throughout the ensuing reactions in Step 2. Nevertheless, I feel uneasy about this move because I am not sure we are not simply conned by a linguistic trick of 'pretend-believe' being just shorthand for 'pretend to believe . . .' In that case we should conceive of simulation in the following way (only Step 2 changed):

SIM-2 PRETENDING   TO BELIEVE that the person is going to mug me,
                            TO FEEL frightened by the man,
                            TO WANT to run away from the man,
                            TO FEEL like running (+showing signs of running).
                            TO KNOW I shall run.

So, how are we to decide whether SIMD-2 or SIM-2 is the right way to look at simulation? There is one decisive argument in favour of SIM-2.

The critical condition for this procedure having any chance of success is that it exploits (wittingly or not) the fact that one's own psychological make-up is relevantly similar to the make-up of the person simulated.[2] So, it is essential that to simulate the target person's transitions from perceiving a certain situation to the ensuing beliefs, feelings, etc. we engage our own corresponding mechanism for reacting to this situation but, of course, off-line. That's what SIM-2 does. Starting from an imagined (instead of a perceived) situation it retraces the transitions among our actual beliefs, feelings, wants, etc. within the scope of off-line (pretend) execution. So it is for this reason, that our simulation recaptures the causal connections of the simulated person's mental states via the causal connections of our own corresponding mechanism that our off-line (pretend) state concerns itself with the connections between our actual beliefs, wants, etc. as in SIM-2. Whereas, in Davies' version *SIMD-2* the requirement that the sequence of pretend-states (e.g., IMAGINING a situation followed by a PRETEND-BELIEF, followed by a certain PRETEND-FEELING, etc.) bears a correspondence to the sequence of the real situation leading to a real BELIEF being followed by a real FEELING, etc. would be purely coincidental (or one would have to assume that this system of pretend-states has evolved to parallel our system of real mental states for the purpose of simulation).

So, if swayed by this argument we opt for SIM-2 then Davies' criterion is partly defeated, since my state of PRETENDING has content which concerns itself with mental states, i.e., with my BELIEVING, FEELING, WANTING, etc. and their real life connection. However, it is not completely defeated, because the way in which my PRETENDING concerns itself with my mental states in SIM-2 is different from how it concerns itself when I engage in analogical reasoning from me to other (RbA-2). And the difference between simulation vs. tacit reasoning can be pinned down on this difference.

3   Predication-implicit knowledge

The critical difference between how simulation and reasoning by analogy concern themselves with mental states is that in the latter (RbA-2) my reasoning states are concerned with mental states in full propositional form, i.e., I represent them as mental states that are predicated to me. In contrast, when simulating, my PRETENDING (in SIM-2) concerns itself with my mental states in a weak sense of 'concerning'. Minimally it concerns itself with these states by taking them off-line. One could further suspect that by taking them off-line and using them to simulate someone else these off-line states acquire representational status.[3] Fortunately for Davies' criterion, even if my PRETENDING imbues such representational status it still concerns itself with my mental states in a different way than reasoning by analogy. It just represents the states without predicating them to me or anybody else.

Dienes and Perner (in press) called such representation 'predication-implicit' knowledge, since the fact that these mental states are mine is not represented but is implicit in the fact that it is me who has them. So, my suggestion for refining Davies' criterion is to say that in simulation the transition is among mental states whose contents themselves may concern mental states, but they may do so only *predication-implicitly*.

This analysis seems to be on the right track because it fits with recent writings on the topic. In particular, my analysis of simulation is compatible with four important points:

(a) There is no inference from me to you (Gordon, 1995) required, in the classical sense of inference, although some (e.g., Helmholtz) may wonder whether the shifts in 'egocentric frame' might not be just another way of talking about unconscious, tacit inferences.

(b) The fact that the core process of simulation in SIM-2 is concerned with (represents) one's mental states in a predication-implicit way, I think, captures quite well Gordon's (this volume) notion of 'uncomprehending self-reference'.

(c) To avoid having to attribute the required success of simulation to pure coincidence, it is imperative that the sequence of predication-implicitly represented mental states are real sequences executed off-line (Stich and Nichols, 1992) and which are relevantly similar to the sequence of mental states in the simulated person. This means they function as an analogue model (Goldman, 1989).

(d) Introducing the term 'predication implicit knowledge' highlights that a central problem for simulation must be how this implicit knowledge can be made explicit. And, indeed, Davies (1994) has emphasised that without this step (SIM-3) simulation cannot meet Strawson's generality constraint, and Gordon's (1995, this volume) elaborations on 'ascent routines' are attempts to solve this problem without having to resort to introspection.

Having characterised simulation as a method for making predication-implicit knowledge about the mind explicit, I now look again at the difference between 'content simulation' and 'non-content (attitude) simulation' (Heal, 1994, this volume; Perner, 1994). I do this by distinguishing implicit knowledge about two different domains.

4   Two domains of implicit knowledge: theory implies simulation

The example of linguistic knowledge provides a good case to illustrate that our information processing mechanisms incorporate implicit knowledge about two different domains. Competent users of the language spoken in a certain language community have processing procedures that contain information (a) about the structure of their language and (b) about the structure of the processes of fellow language users. The information in (a) is typically referred to as implicit, *procedural* knowledge since the procedures are used to process language. It is predication implicit, since it reflects the distinctions and rules of the language but it does not reflect the fact that these rules are the rules of a language. In contrast, the information in (b) about the fellow language users could not be called procedural (since the procedures are not used to process fellow language users), but it is also predication-implicit since it does not reflect the fact that there are people (including oneself, i.e., uncomprehending self reference) who are characterised by having these processes. It is the making explicit of this type of implicit information that qualifies as simulation.

The classical linguist exploits the first source of information to make grammaticality judgements which in turn are used to test out hypotheses about the language's grammar to eventually build up an explicit theory of that grammar. The (folk) psycholinguist (e.g., Paul Harris, 1992, p. 124) uses the same information to predict how other speakers of the language will judge the grammaticality of sample sentences.

This folk-psycholinguistic example provides a typical case of 'content simulation' (Heal, this volume; Perner, 1994), because the primary question to answer is not what attitude the other person will take towards the sentence. It is more or less assumed that he will take an attitude of judging. The question is what the content of his judgement will be: grammatical or ungrammatical? What makes the use of simulation seemingly compulsory in this case – that's why I spoke of the 'necessity of simulation' (Perner, 1994) – is the fact that we have no theory of how people make grammaticality judgements (since we have no predication-explicit knowledge of our grammar).We simply have to use our own mind to make judgements. However, to use one's mind to make grammaticality judgements is not simulation. Hence, pure 'content simulation' is a misnomer.

Simulation, it seems, only comes into play when I use the fact that *I make a judgement* of grammaticality to attribute the same *act of judging* to the other person (a non-content/ attitude aspect). So, if simulation is involved then it is a trivial case of 'attitude simulation'. However, for that part there is no strong intuition that we have to use simulation at all, because it could conceivably be dealt with by a trivial bit of theory: 'Every competent speaker judges grammatical sentences as grammatical and ungrammatical as ungrammatical.' So it looks that, despite Heal's (1994, this volume) fears, the content aspects can be cleanly separated from the non-content (attitude) aspects and these can easily be taken care off by a simple theory. However, there we may be missing an important point.

The point easily missed here is that this simplicity of the theory is bought by the fact that I am a speaker of the language who analyses the sentence by using processes that are similar to the other language users' processes. These processes incorporate predication-implicit knowledge. And what helps keep the theory manageable is that they contain predication-implicit knowledge about the other person's mind. Thus, their use in the theory brings in an element of simulation. Consequently, even when – on the surface – I am just employing a bit of theory there is a bedrock of (content-induced) simulation on which that theory is based. This vindicates Heal's worry that content aspects cannot be cleanly separated from the non-content aspects and it helps me understand why Gordon's (1992) examples of total projection count as cases of simulation.

To summarise, my argument is that any use of a theory of mind that employs predication-implicit knowledge about the content domain necessarily involves an element of simulation. This is so because the theory tacitly plays on the fact that my content judging mechanism is relevantly similar to the person's whose mind is being considered. Heal's (1994) arguments about the inevitability of having to use our own mind to make such content judgements then implies that simulation is a virtually necessary part of any explicit understanding of the mind.

In the following I want to set a counterpoint to this conclusion, namely, that simulation is not the only ingredient in our understanding of the mind. I make this point in two ways. My point in the next section is that there can be purely implicit understanding of the mind based on empathic identification, which is only a component of simulation. In the subsequent section I argue on empirical grounds that explicit understanding of the mind cannot be purely based on simulation since we consistently observe theoretical biases in people's mental state attributions.

5   Components of simulation: empathic identification

Several component processes of simulation can be distinguished by example of the dark-alley situation:

```
SIM-1  (a)  IDENTIFY with other.        | Identific. |           |
                                        ——-         |           |
       (b)  IMAGINE being in situation. | Living     | Empathic  |
                                        | one's      | Identific-|
SIM-2       PRETEND (off-line): execution | imagin-  | ation     |
                                        | ation      |           |
            of sequence of inner states. | (Pretence) |         | Simul-
                                        ——-         ——-        | ation
SIM-3  (a)  CLASSIFY reactions.                                  |
                                                                |
       (b)  DE-IDENTIFY and                                     |
                                                                |
            ATTRIBUTE last reaction to other.                   |
                                                                ——-
```

If you just imagine being in a situation and then show some reactions we can say that you have a vivid imagination or you *live your imagination*. If that vivid imagination is triggered by observing or thinking about someone else (or yourself at another time) then I call it *empathic identification* (like with a character in a film or novel). The important point is that what distinguishes simulation from these component activities is Step SIM-3. This conforms to the view expressed by Nichols *et al.* (this volume, section 3.2) that empathy differs from simulation in that the output is not taken off-line.

Without step SIM-3 there is no genuine simulation but at best, to modify one of Gordon's phrases, 'uncomprehending empathy'. That is, one has no predicate-explicit (hence no communicable) understanding of what the significance of one's mock experiences is or who they are to be attributed to. Examples of such uncomprehending empathic identification may be the involuntary acts of body mimicry mentioned by Gordon (1992) and other empathic acts emphasised by Goldman (1992b). Although these phenomena exist, they may not be evidence for simulation, since they may exist quite independently and in addition to a different mechanism (a theory) for attributing mental states. There are some developmental data that can be taken as support for such an independence. The first example is one where empathic reactions provide an 'immature' contrast to the child's cognitively advanced understanding. Harris *et al.* (1991) report that four and six-year old children who very sharply distinguish between what is real (e.g., empty box) and what is not (e.g., imagined monsters inside) show apprehension and curiosity about the contents of the box which they know is empty but in which they imagined a creature.

The other example comes from our own research demonstrating the opposite, namely that children's empathic reactions reveal more of an understanding of false-belief (or some relevant aspect of it) than is apparent in their thought-out answers to questions. Wendy Clements tested children on the traditional, unexpected-transfer test of false belief understanding: Sam the Mouse puts his cheese in one of two boxes which are placed in front of the two mouse holes at the extreme top corners of the display. While Sam is inside in his sleeping quarters invisible to the child, the cheese is transferred to the other box. When Sam wakes up and wants his cheese, children are asked where he will look for it. Children's responses show the traditional developmental picture (e.g., Perner *et al.*, 1987). Almost all three-year olds (2 years 11 months to 3 years 2 months) answer with the second box (actual location of cheese) while most four-year olds get it right answering with the empty box (where Sam believes the cheese is). What is new is that Clements recorded where children *looked* when Sam's desire for cheese was mentioned. A surprising 80% of the three-year olds looked at the empty box. Importantly, only a few of the very young children looked there in a control condition in which the only difference was that Sam knew where the cheese was because he saw the cheese being moved before he went to bed (Clements and Perner, 1994). One should also mention that before the age of 2 years and 11 months no child either looked consistently at or answered the question with the empty location.

The behaviour by those children who look at the empty box (where Sam thinks the cheese is) but answer with the location where the cheese really is can be explained by empathic identification. There is direct anecdotal evidence that some children tend to do this. For instance, when in the story Sam goes inside to have his tea one of the children spontaneously said: 'Now *I* am going to have *my* tea, aren't *I*?' To explain our looking data we need to assume that children start identifying with story protagonists in this way by about 2 years and 11 months.[4] More specifically, in parallel with the real story events they keep track of how the world looks from Sam's perspective: the cheese is still in the old location. So when Sam's desire for cheese is mentioned their eyes wander to where, in Sam's world, the cheese is. Since this is uncomprehending identification without the benefit of Step SIM-3 of simulation children cannot use their predicate-implicit knowledge contained in their empathic reactions in order to answer the question about where Sam will go. To answer this question, it looks as if they have to rely on their immature 'theory' that Sam will go for his cheese where the cheese actually is.

Ongoing research provides a relevant variation on this theme. It separates the presumed location of the cheese (box at the bottom of a slide) from where Sam will become visible to the child again (mouse hole at top of slide). Of the twenty-two children so far tested six children answered the question about which slide Sam will use correctly. These children all looked at the mouse hole. So do most (nine) of the sixteen children who answered the question wrongly. For these children it remains undecidable whether they look at the mouse hole in expectation of Sam (our interpretation of the original finding) or because they identify with Sam and look to the top of the slide as the next significant location on Sam's way to the cheese. However, five of the children who answered the question wrongly looked at the empty box (where Sam thinks the cheese is). In these five cases the only plausible explanation is that these children *empathically identified* with Sam but *failed to simulate* (execute step SIM-3) so as to give the correct answer to the question.

This interpretation of children's looking as a result of their uncomprehending empathic identification raises a problem for introspectionist versions of simulation who all must locate difficulties in the first two steps but not in SIM-3. This step cannot pose the critical problem since it is taken for granted that even the youngest have perfect introspective access to their own mental states – which makes the final step of simulation all but trivial. This includes Harris' (1991) account which assumes that the difficulty lies in suspending default assumptions defined by the child's own perspective. Gordon (1992ac, 1995) argues vehemently against the use of introspection in simulation and suggests that the transition from empathic identification to explicit prediction or attribution of mental states is done by *recentering one's egocentric frame*.

A potentially viable explanation of our data can be obtained by combining Harris' criterion of perspective discrepancy with difficulties in recentering before the age of 4 years. Below that age (before they pass the false belief test) children can take another person's perspective (empathic identification), they also can recentre if the two perspectives are not too different (as evidenced by their correct predictions in the true belief story) but they cannot successfully recentre from the simulated world to their own world if those worlds differ in too many of the critical elements. Thus, in the case of the false belief story the attribution of action or belief fails, because the critical facts of where the object is and where I will go to get it are diametrically opposed in the two worlds.

With this recentering defect simulation becomes akin to three-year olds' 'situation theory' (Perner, 1991a). Hence, simulation theory may be able to lay its hands on the developmental data that I have explained with the development from 'situation theorists' to 'representation theorists'. However, even if simulation can explain our particular finding there are still other developmental phenomena that remain problematic.

6   Remaining problems – partial solutions

6.1   *Theoretical biases*

One type of problem is best exemplified by children's so-called 'inference neglect' (Wimmer *et al.*, 1988b), which was introduced by Stich and Nichols (1992) into the simulation debate. Sodian and Wimmer (1987) showed four- and six-year-old children and another observer that a box contained only one kind of object. Shielded from child and observer one of these objects was put inside an opaque bag. Child and observer were told that the object in the bag was from that box. When asked whether *they knew* what kind of object was inside the bag, the four-year olds answered correctly 'yes' but incorrectly that the other observer (who fully shared their perspective) didn't know. The original interpretation is that these children, even though they can make the appropriate inferences, do not understand that one can know something by inference (all objects are X, hence the one in the box must be X) without perceptual access. This finding constitutes a problem for simulation since, if children simulate the other, they should give the same response for other as for themselves.

Harris (1992, p. 137) provided the following defence of the simulation theory. Children might plausibly adopt the other person's perspective imperfectly. Their errors can be explained if they either omit the fact that the other saw the box filled with only one kind of object or if they omit the fact that the other was told that the object in the bag came from that box. Ruffman (1994) tested this possibility. To illustrate, in one of his conditions he used two dishes, a round one with red and green beads and a square dish with yellow beads. Both child and other person see this. The child, but not the other person, knows that a *green* bead has been taken from the round dish. The other person is just told that the bead came from the round dish and children are asked what colour the other person thinks the bead is. This task was administered twice. The majority (67%) of children said on both occasions that the person thinks that it is a red bead while only 11% said 'green' on both occasions and 12% oscillated between red and green. Ruffman's explanation is that children try to keep their attribution of igno- rance (other does not know which colour bead is in the bag) consistent with their belief attribution according to the rule, 'ignorance means you get it wrong'. Thus they tend to attribute a *false* belief to an *ignorant* person.

This result poses a direct problem for simulation. If children's attribu- tions were based on simulation then, because within the ignorant person's perspective there would not be any bias for red or green. Their responses should be random resulting in about 25% attributions of 'red' and 25% of 'green' on both occasions, and 50% attributions of 'red' on one and 'green' on the other occasion. In other words, children should attribute a true belief (green) as often as a false belief (red) but not favour the attribution of a false belief. Moreover, on Harris' theory children who cannot sustain the discrepancy between their own and the simulated world should fall back on the default assumptions as determined by their own world. That would mean, contrary to fact, that children should show a bias towards attributing 'true beliefs' (green).

Ruffman's results also establish, *pace* Harris' simulation explanation of the original finding, that children in these types of situation do take other's knowledge of the message (or else, some children should have answered 'yellow') and other's knowledge of the contents of the round dish into account (or else, why 'red'?). Harris' explanation of the original result by Sodian and Wimmer (1987, also replicated in one of Ruffman's other conditions) is, therefore, untenable.

6.2   *Correlations between false-belief task and nonmental problems*

In typical theory-theory tradition Perner (1991) suggested that understanding false belief relates to understanding representation. The link consists in the fact that understanding false belief requires the distinction between (a) the state of affairs the belief is *about* and (b) how that state of affairs is *believed to be* and that understanding representations requires the parallel distinction between (a) what they *represent* and (b) how they represent that *as being.* In other words, the common denominator is the ability to appreciate the possibility of 'different points of view (b) on the same thing or state of affairs (a)'.[5] On the theory view of concept acquisition (Carey, 1985; Keil, 1989) such conceptual distinctions tend not to develop in isolation but within the theoretical field of related concepts. We tested this in two ways.

Lindsay Parkin investigated children's understanding of false belief in relation to understanding misleading direction signs. Children's ability to answer the question 'Where does this sign show X is?' developed hand in hand with their ability to answer false-belief questions: 'Where does P think X is?' (PHI correlation coefficient = .66 in Experiment 1, N = 48, and .81 in Experiment 2, N = 16). Even when a common age effect was partialled out these relationships stayed highly significant (Parkin and Perner, 1994). If false beliefs are attributed by simulation then we need an explanation of why the ability to simulate belief develops in tandem with the ability to understand misleading direction signs. How could simulation theory explain this? Perhaps one possibility is that children simply simulate the sign. Since the misleading signs task shares with the false belief problem that worlds are involved that differ in the crucial facts of where X is, Harris'

(1991) theory of perspective discrepancy might explain the developmental synchrony. However, a non-trivial problem for Gordon remains in specifying adequate ascent routines for the misleading sign problem.[6]

An even tougher nut to crack might be the data by Martin Doherty. His idea was to see whether understanding false belief relates to the understanding that representations have formal properties and meaning. He investigated this with synonyms, i.e., words that differ in form but not in meaning. Three to five-year-old children were first tested for their knowledge of several synonyms (e.g., 'bunny' and 'rabbit'). On a later occasion they named one of the items again and called it, e.g., 'rabbit'. They then had to monitor that a puppet named the item correctly (use a word with the *same semantic property*, i.e., 'elephant' would not do) but differently from how the child named it (use a word with *different formal properties*, i.e., 'bunny' will do, but not 'rabbit'). In two experiments (N = 24, N = 25) the ability to monitor synonym use was strongly correlated with performance on the false-belief task (r = .76 and .84, respectively). This relationship proved to be very specific since even when verbal intelligence (BPVS) and other control variables were partialled out, the correlation stayed high (r = .70 and .74, respectively). In two further experiments (N = 38 and 31, respectively) the children themselves had to produce synonyms. Again, correlations between this task and the false-belief task was very high (r = .73 and .64, respectively) and stayed high with verbal intelligence partialled out (r = .69 and .57, respectively).

At this point in time I cannot conceive of any account of this developmental synchrony between false-belief task and synonyms task purely in terms of simulation. The only possibility I can envisage is a simulation-theory mix. For instance, the ability to simulate belief provides the basis for reflection on the fact that beliefs can (re)present states of affairs in different ways and that this reflective (predication-explicit, i.e., theoretical) insight allows the child to understand that different words can represent the same thing.

7   Summary

In this chapter I have tried to sharpen the distinction between simulation and use of a theory by characterising simulation as the explicit exploitation of *predication-implicit knowledge about the mind*. With this I tried to do justice to the points emphasised by Gordon (uncomprehending self attributions, no inference by analogy), Davies' interpretation of Gordon's view (imaginative identification) and also capture the intuitions of other's that simulation (at least any successful use of it) involves off-line functioning (Stich and Nichols) and thus implies that one functions as an analogue, isomorphic model (Goldman, 1989) for others (or oneself in a counterfactual situation).

By distinguishing two ways of exploiting implicit knowledge, i.e., information about the content domain and information about how human beings deal with that content domain, I tried to clarify the distinction between 'content' and 'non-content or attitude' simulation (Heal, this volume, Perner, 1994). My conclusion was that even when attributions seem to be made purely by theory, if that theory relies on content judgements and on the fact that these judgements are made in a similar way by the relevant group of human beings, then this reliance introduces an inevitable element of simulation into the theory use. Simulation, therefore, is a virtual necessity.

The remainder of the chapter was devoted to showing the limitations of simulation as an empirical account of our understanding of the mind. One point was that empathy phenomena should not be equated with simulation. By clearly distinguishing empathic identification from simulation a new explanation emerged for the finding that young three-year-olds look at the place where a protagonist thinks an object is but fail to give that location as an answer to a question about the protagonist's belief (Clements and Perner, 1994). The suggestion is that the looking is based on empathic identification with the protagonist. It expresses implicit knowledge about his belief which cannot be made explicit (hence not verbally communicable) and, thus, falls short of being simulation.

I also argued that simulation cannot give a complete account of our explicit knowledge about the mind since available data show various 'theoretical biases' like Sodian and Wimmer's 'inference neglect', Ruffman's 'belief-ignorance consistency' effect and the data reported by Nichols *et al.* (this volume). Moreover, simulation cannot give a satisfactory account for the findings that understanding of the mind (belief) develops in unison with insights into areas in which simulation itself does not apply (e.g., understanding synonyms).

In conclusion, since any theory use involves an element of simulation and since simulation on its own cannot account for the data, the future must lie in a mixture of simulation and theory use. However, what this mixture is and how it operates must first be specified in some detail before any testable empirical predictions can be derived.

ACKNOWLEDGEMENTS

The author would like to thank Peter Carruthers, Bob Gordon, and Shaun Nichols for their helpful online exchange of ideas over email during production of this chapter.

NOTES

1   I added this line to make it possible to attribute running without having to intro-spect one's PRETEND-WANTING or PRETEND-FEELING to run and to attribute a desire or intention to run by ascent routine from the represented (KNOWN) fact 'I shall run' (within the simulated world) to 'I intend to run' (Gordon, this volume).

2   To exploit the fact that one functions in causally relevant ways like the simulated person means that one functions as an analogue model. Gordon (1992a) took issue with this view focusing on the particular use of analogue models in engi-neering. To validate engineering models a theory is required. However, there is no need for that if one allows validation through experience in previous uses. In the case of simulation evolution made those experiences. We are just using it because we are endowed with it, without concern for a need of validation.

I can't believe he would also object to the basic fact that simulation involves use of one's own mind in a causally similar way to the simulated mind, because simulation requires this similarity for its success. Without, at least, some success it would be most unlikely that we would ever use simulation, and success would be miraculous if there were no causal basis for it.

3   In fact, Gordon (1995) seems to think that simulation serves to represent: 'When I simulate Mr Tees missing his flight, I am already *representing him* as having been in a certain state of mind' (italics mine). I should add that in this case the mental states embedded within the scope of PRETENDING in SIM-2 should not be capitalised.

4   Why this ability should start so abruptly at about this age is an interesting ques-tion for further research.

5   I have been searching for a long time for a suitable terminology for this distinc-tion. I considered 'sense-reference' (Perner, 1991) but was dissuaded from it at the Hang Seng meetings by various people (George Botterill, Peter Carruthers, Jane Heal, Gabriel Segal, Andrew Woodfield). In conversation with Bob Gordon, 'point of view' emerged as a new, seemingly more appropriate option, though it, too, may have its misleading connotations.

6   Might it go like this? The sign pointing to location A *expresses* the fact that X is in A (even though X is really in B). Identifying with the sign I imagine myself pointing to A (where X is within the world as expressed by the sign). Ascending from 'I am *pointing* to A where X is (in the simulated world)' to 'I am *showing that* X is in A' and recentering egocentric frames I conclude: 'The sign shows that X is in A.'

Folk psychology and theoretical status

George Botterill

1   Introduction

Is folk psychology a theory? Permissive use of the term 'theory' makes it too easy to say yes, and may mask differences between varieties of theory-theory just as important as the well-known disagreement with the simulationists. In this paper I want to consider to what extent the postulation of a theoretical structure can help us understand the cognitive processing involved in our understanding of minds and behaviour. I shall be arguing, largely on methodological grounds, for a particular version of theory-theory according to which common-sense psychology has a core rather like the hard core of a Lakatosian research programme (Lakatos, 1970, 1978).

My strategy will be entirely conditional: if we are going to be theory-theorists, then this is the variety of theory-theory we should go for. I will not, therefore, be directly opposing the full-blown versions of simulation theory championed by Robert Gordon and Alvin Goldman (Gordon, 1986, 1992a, 1995; Goldman, 1989, 1992b). But it is important to the variety of theory-theory I advocate that it actually needs to be complemented by the modest form of simulationism argued for by Jane Heal (Heal, 1986, 1994, this volume).

2   Why call folk psychology / theory of mind (a) theory?

We can introduce a major division within theory-theory by asking: is folk psychology a *single* theory – or at least does it have a single core theory at its centre? Talk of folk psychology need not presuppose *a* theory. After all, nobody insists that scientific psychology is *a* theory. But it's theory, for all that, since it's comprised of lots of theories, variously interrelated. Some advocates of theory-theory clearly suppose there is a theory of mind, while others think there is lots of it. Stich and Nichols' formulation of the common central idea of folk psychological theory as 'an internally represented body of information (or perhaps mis-information) about psychological processes and the ways in which they give rise to behaviour' (Stich and Nichols, 1994) is intended to be wide enough to encompass both views. But for present purposes it will be useful to distinguish the idea that there is a single core theory of mind from the view that there is a mass of theory in folk psychology. So I will label the former position *core theory-theory*.

A swift review of the main reasons why the general theory-theory position has found a seeming consensus of support among psychologists, cognitive scientists, and philosophers reveals a diverse range of attractions. There are *epistemological attractions*, associated with the special epistemic status of theories – whether one then goes on to add 'It's a theory, so it may be radically wrong' à la Churchland, or 'It's a theory that works very well, so probably it's broadly correct' à la Fodor. There are *semantic attractions*, associated with the idea that theories provide implicit definitions: on a functionalist view this promises to solve the problem of how we understand the meaning of mental state terms. There are *developmental attractions*, associated with the way in which theories are discovered and elaborated, which may be supported either by identification of specific proto-theoretical stages, or merely by the claim that a theoretical structure would facilitate an otherwise formidable learning task. Finally, there are *cognitive processing attractions*, associated with the application of theory, which hold out the hope of answering the 'How do we do it?' question by employing a frequently successful strategy – i.e., positing a body of tacit theoretical knowledge.

Without going into the question of whether these are *good* reasons for embracing theory-theory, we can readily see that they appeal to different aspects of theoreticity. Now, it may be that the analogy between folk psychology and explicit scientific theories is strong enough to sustain these divergent attractions. But, equally, it wouldn't be surprising if different conceptions of theory were in play. To tighten our grip on the idea that folk psychology constitutes theory, or a theory, we had better consider whether we can give a satisfactory account of what the distinctive characteristics of theory are.

3   What makes for a theory?

Outlining the criteria for theoretical status is an obvious place for a philosophical contribution to the debate. Given the word 'theory' is such a favourite pet of philosophers of science, one might think we could just reach for an off-the-peg account of what constitutes a theory. However, there isn't really any ready-made consensus. Certainly, there are a number of standard hallmarks proposed, in particular (1) provision of explanation and prediction, (2) counterfactual projection, (3) postulation of unobservables, and (4) implicit definition of concepts. Yet something is missing from this list. (1) and (2) are not sufficient for theoreticity, because they are exhibited by knowledge that isn't theoretical. (3) isn't a necessary condition of theoreticity because theories can have different levels of causal depth. (4) isn't a criterion that can be applied independently of identification of theoretical principles. What is missing, I think, is the requirement that theories *must contain principles that provide a systematic integration of knowledge*. I will briskly run through the main criteria for theoretical status, in the hope that the deficiencies of the others will make the importance of systematic integration more apparent.

3.1   Explanation and prediction

Perhaps the most commonly urged ground for regarding a theory as implicit in our folk psychological practices is that we use our knowledge of folk psychology to *explain* and *predict* the actions and reactions of others. Certainly explanation and prediction are two of the chief functions of theories. Yet this falls well short of providing a compelling case for theory-theory. Give or take the availability of the specific information required for predictive success, we can say: no theory without explanation and prediction. But we should hesitate to assert: no explanation or prediction without theory. Knowing a football team's star players are on the injury list may enable me to predict the team's defeat in advance, or account for it after the event. Yet such a predictive and explanatory capacity hardly supports a claim that we must therefore have access to anything like a theory of football form in particular, or theories of ball-games and team-games more generally. So we must ask more of a cognitive structure in order to deem it theory-involving than that it should yield explanations and predictions.

3.2   Counterfactual support

Counterfactual support is sometimes proposed as indicative of theoretical status, on the grounds that it distinguishes genuinely law-like (or *nomic*) principles from generalisations which are true by mere contingency. Presumably any theory worth its salt will contain principles of nomic generality. And, encouragingly, folk psychology definitely does support counterfactuals – such as *If Maxi had not believed the chocolate was there, he wouldn't have opened the wrong cupboard*. But though counterfactual projection is a necessary condition for theoretical status, it can't be regarded as sufficient. For example, it's quite plausible to maintain that: *If Mike Tyson had not been imprisoned, Lennox Lewis would never have held a world heavyweight boxing title*. As in our footballing example, there may well be a basis of knowledge of fact and causal connection that provides sufficient support for this claim. But we had better not rate the knowledge-base in question theory-involving, on pain of finding theories on any and every topic under the sun.

3.3   *Introduction of unobservables*

We are often told we can tell theories apart from mere macro-level general-isations because theories postulate unobservables. This was what the kinetic theory of gases did and why it operates at a deeper level than a macroscopic generalisation such as Boyle's law. Likewise this was what the gene theory did and why it operates at a deeper level than phenotypic generalisations about heredity. Folk psychology introduces thinking about internal and causally active representational states. Is this what makes it a theory? Fodor thinks it makes folk psychology a *deep* theory because '[i]t is a deep fact about the world that the most powerful etiological generalisations hold of unobservable causes' (Fodor, 1987, p.7), and contrasts common-sense psychology with such superficial stuff as common-sense meteorology.

Though the claim that such states as beliefs and desires are internal causes has recurrently been castigated as a para-mechanical prejudice, I think this part of Fodor's view is correct. But even if folk psychology is a deep theory, that doesn't mean it's a theory because of its depth. There are, after all, powerful theories that aren't deep in Fodor's sense. For example, the theory of evolution by natural selection is non-deep. There is some point to claiming that selectionist theories lack explanatory depth until augmented by genetic mechanisms. But they can be impressive theories in their own right, and are not much like folk weather-lore (which rather obviously fails to constitute a theory because it lacks systematic integration).

3.4   *Implicit definition of concepts*

Under this heading I do not wish to argue with the view that the best way to understand how psychological concepts like *belief, desire, hope, fear, anxiety*, etc. function is to take them as theoretical concepts, even though such views always leave us with the chicken-and-egg problem of whether we grasp the concepts through prior assimilation of theory, or *vice versa*. Here we need only note that we are hardly in a position to assess whether folk psychological concepts are implicitly defined, until we have some insight into what the principles that implicitly define them might be.

3.5   *Cognitive economy through integration*

Now, one might say that in spite of their individual inadequacy, whenever we have *all of* (1)-(4) above, for sure we have a theory. I don't know how to disprove that, but equally I don't know why it would have to be true. We might have a *de facto* sufficient set of criteria for theoreticity, and yet the string required to make up the package – the peculiar advantage conferred by possession of a theory – would fail to be apparent.

I propose that what is missing can be made good by recognising that *theories produce cognitive economy through integration of information in a small number of general principles*. I have annexed this idea from Finn Collin, who emphasises 'the power of knowledge systems high in theoreticity to reduce the number of laws and principles needed to account for the data, replacing a large class of narrow-scope principles with a smaller class of more general ones' (Collin, 1985, p. 61). It also seems to be what Gopnik and Wellman had in mind when speaking of the 'coherence and abstractness' of theories (Gopnik and Wellman, 1992, p.147).

That they link together a number of generalisations about what we would otherwise have no reason for taking to be interconnected phenomena is, surely, both an impressive and important function of theories. The most famous example of such integration is Newtonian classical mechanics. Without that theory who could ever have suspected any connection between such apparently diverse phenomena as the motions of falling bodies in the terrestrial environment, the paths of projectiles, the ebb and flow of tides, and the orbits of planets? Admittedly, this is one of the most comprehensive integrative achievements in the history of science. But it does not stand alone. The integrative synthesis of evolutionary theory in zoology and genetics is almost equally impressive.

It is worth pausing to contrast such theoretical structures with bodies of knowledge which may be practically useful, but are not theoretically integrated, such as cuisine or horticulture. Consider, for example, what an experienced and skilful gardener knows. It may be a hard task nowadays to find a canny gardener who is innocent of theory. But if we can find one, the expert knowledge of such a gardener constitutes a sort of gardening *lore*, which need not be very different from what it was in pre-Darwinian and pre-Mendelian times. Such gardening lore contains many generalisations, both about particular plant species, about cross-specific taxonomic stages or types of plants (such as *very small seeds*, *large seeds*, *seedlings*, *perennials*, *hardy annuals*), and soil conditions. The gardener's lore constitutes a body of general knowledge open to extension, but *by addition rather than projection*. Like everyone else the gardener is entitled to form expectations that are hunches based on previous experience. But he is always a student of experience, rather than a theoretical pronouncer. Can a particular type of plant be propagated vegetatively, or will one have to collect seeds? Gardening lore is not a theory that tells you the answer in advance. The only recipe is to try it and find out, or rely on the experience of someone else who has made the experiment. (Contrast this with the case of newly discovered astronomical objects. In principle, if we can discover their masses, we will be able to work out how they move. *In principle*.)

In addition to the contrast with lore, another consideration which confirms the centrality of cognitive integration to theoretical status is provided by the appropriateness of talking of theories in non-scientific areas, where the causal role of unobservables plays no part. Ethics furnishes a striking example. Common-sense morality exhibits the difficulties over projection to novel cases characteristic of lore. We think it's a virtue to be loyal and a bad thing to tell a lie. So where does this leave us when telling the truth could be very damaging to a friend? A moral theory such as utilitarianism – which is clearly theoretical because it propounds the central, unifying principle that the right action to perform is the one that maximises happiness – promises to help resolve such quandaries. Of course, the utilitarian principle on its own will not dictate the right response in a problematic case without being supplemented by reflection on possible consequences and the active exercise of situational judgement. But it does provide us with a framework that can inform as to why in general loyalty and honesty are both virtues, and provides a method for determining what morality demands when more superficial generalisations conflict. Whatever its other merits or defects, utilitarianism is a prime example of a theory both because of its systematic deployment of a central principle and *its concomitant dependence upon supplementation* – by auxiliary hypotheses (e.g., does lying in such cases constitute a precedent with debilitating general influence on character?) and case-specific information – in practical applications. This last feature is noteworthy, since it can also be discerned easily enough in the case of folk psychology.

4   Methodological advantages of core theory-theory

Suppose, then, we accept that the best account we can offer of theoretical status is this: 'Theories are information-bearing systems which yield explanations and predictions, which support counterfactual projection, which *may* postulate unobservables and *may* implicitly define concepts, and which achieve cognitive economy by integration of information under a small number of general principles.'

Such an account retains an unavoidable element of vagueness, since cognitive economy is a matter of degree. Even the humblest empirical generalisation (such as *All students in the class are taking single honours*) is more economical than a representation of the concatenation of particular facts that makes it true (*Student A is taking single honours* and *Student B is taking single honours*, etc.). Nonetheless the account does have some methodological impact on our area of concern. The more we can find in the way of systematic integration around central principles, the more the cognitive work is being done by the supposed theoreticity of theory of mind. And it is the core theory-theory view that is most strongly committed in this direction.

At the present stage of research the advantages of the core theory-theory seem to me mainly methodological. But they are not inconsiderable, and we can detail them as follows.

(i) Perhaps the most important methodological advantage of core theory-theory is that it helps sustain a distinctively theoretical account of cognitive processing by requiring differentiation of the resident core from supplementation supplied by auxiliary knowledge. A weaker version of theory-theory, according to which theory of mind may be a quite unsystematic body of general information, is not even easily distinguished from the view that folk psychology is just a remarkably pervasive kind of lore.

What's more it is a serious obstacle to progress in the simulation versus theory debate if the two sides cannot keep their respective kinds of cognitive processing apart. Of course, we can *say* that on the theory-theory view the process is theory-driven, whereas on the simulationist view it involves the off-line running of the agent's own practical reasoning system (and perhaps many other systems too). But what does this amount to, if the theory involved is no more than a mass of general beliefs? A theory of the cognitive competence that is committed to no more than the involvement of general doxastic states is liable to be pre-empted by accounts of how an inferential disposition is implemented, since one well-known view of what it is to have a general belief is that it consists in an inferential disposition. And this might be implemented by simulation. For example, suppose that the general belief is: *Anyone who believes that if p then q, and also believes p, comes to believe q* (i.e., that agents reliably make inferences according to the logical principle of *modus ponens*). Take someone who, whenever presented with another whom she takes to believe *if p then q* and to believe *p*, feeds those as pretend inputs to her own inferential system, derives *q*, and exits from this process with an attribution to the other of the belief that *q*. That's a simulationist story, but it also seems to be a perfectly adequate way of realising the general belief in question (tacitly, at least).

Imputation of a body of unstructured general knowledge, therefore, need require no more than cognitive mechanisms which appropriately control transitions between particular beliefs. The generality can be realised in the exercise of the mechanism rather than in any distinctively representational state. By contrast the structure of core theoretical knowledge requires interaction between general representations. An auxiliary hypothesis is not a mere inferential disposition. So it is only the application of a core theory that would clearly be theory-driven rather than process-driven.

(ii) A further methodological advantage of core theory-theory is that it serves the developmental attractions mentioned above far better than a weaker version of theory-theory. The role of theory in facilitating learning processes has been emphasised by several developmental psychologists (Karmiloff-Smith and Inhelder, 1974/5; Karmiloff-Smith, 1988; Wellman, 1990; Gopnik and Wellman, 1992). But if the theory were no more than a mass of loosely interconnected general information about psychological states, their likely causes, and their behavioural effects, the learning process of ontogenetic development would be fragmented.

By contrast, the idea that there is a core to folk psychology that functions in much the way that a hard core informs a Lakatosian research programme provides a direction to the learning process that may be corroborated by route-mapping normal stages of ontogenetic development. The main feature of a Lakatosian research programme is that its core theoretical principles are shielded from refutation by their empirical inadequacy, which is why they need to be supplemented by auxiliary hypotheses. The progress of a research programme consists in the introduction and revision of these auxiliaries, particularly in response to anomalous results. In a similar way anomalous behaviour – anomalous, that is, in relation to the existing stage of theory of mind development in an individual – may prompt the acquisition of auxiliary psychological information.

(iii) Core theory-theory may also assist in making a distinction that needs to be drawn between folk psychology and *folksy* psychology. There are no end of saws, adages, bits of advice, amateur psychiatry, and rule of thumb generalisations about human conduct and character. Folk psychology would be a curious rag-bag if it had to encompass all that sort of stuff. It may be a reasonable move to insist on a distinction between folk psychology proper and folksy accretions and prejudices. But how do we know we are drawing the distinction in the right place, unless we are guided by a description of the structure of the core theory? The principles I outline later can help here. For example, *He who wills the end must will the means* appears to be a corollary of those principles. Much else can be dismissed as merely folksy.

(iv) Finally, core theory-theory makes a stronger claim about how folk psychology hangs together as a common-sense theory, and the bolder claim is to be preferred as a simpler hypothesis than the postulation of a mass of general information or several distinct theories.

The last methodological point carries a programmatic commitment, placing an onus upon the core theory-theorist to unearth the fundamental principles or core structure of folk psychology. This is surely something we want to do anyway. Theory-theory that has little to say about what theory of mind actually consists in is disappointing stuff.

Besides, if we have some hypothesis as to what the core principles might be we can progress beyond methodological considerations and make the issue empirical. The way to do this would be by presenting subjects with *apparent violations of core principles*. The cognitive economy of a core theory is valuable enough to be sustained by dogmatic tenacity. So the core theory-theory would predict that in such cases subjects will resort to such theoretical expedients as *ignoring the data* or *inventing hypotheses* in order to resolve the apparent violation. But, in order to construct an apparent violation, we do at least need suggestions as to what the core principles are. Can we do better than just claiming there is a folk theory of mind?

5   Tacit theory: strongly tacit or weakly tacit?

If we had some specially dedicated, inaccessible and informationally encapsulated Fodorian module for processing information about the minds of others (cf. Segal, this volume), there would be no presumption in favour of principles consciously available to folk psychologists like us that we could go on to state. On the other hand, if the operations of folk psychology are available to consciousness, to some extent at least, then the core theory-theorist faces a more pressing challenge to come up with the principles, a challenge pointedly posed by Alvin Goldman:

Actual illustrations of such laws are sparse in number; and when examples are adduced, they commonly suffer from one of two defects: vagueness and inaccuracy . . . But why, one wonders, should it be so difficult to articulate laws if we appeal to them all the time in our interpretative practice? (Goldman, 1989, p.167)

So where should core theory-theory stand on the question of whether the putative core principles are tacitly known or available to consciousness? Now, it is true that if the principles of folk psychology were not to some degree tacit, then displaying them would not give us any trouble. Yet Goldman's challenge is difficult to meet. So the central principles are not readily available. But I think there is good reason to resist the idea that they might be tacit *in a strong sense* – in the way, for example, that the algorithms the visual module uses in processing incoming optical data (to register edges and surfaces of objects) are completely inaccessible to consciousness. By contrast, principles of folk psychology may be only *weakly tacit*. There are, after all, many areas of common-sense knowledge that rely upon unstated but recoverable (weakly tacit) principles. Even *all humans are mortal* operates in our thinking as a weakly tacit principle. And philosophical attempts to elucidate the concept of a material object are likely to come up with something like *material objects are publicly observable and three-dimensional*. That we knew all along. Common sense does not have the principle actively connected to the speech-centres. Why would it ever need to? But we were aware of it in a way we are not aware of the algorithms of the visual module. It's just that ordinarily we do not think about the underlying principle, but only its implications in a given context.

One reason for thinking the principles of folk psychology are no more than weakly tacit is the conspicuous part *explanation* plays in folk psychological practice. We – including children young enough to be quizzed by developmental psychologists – can explain why people did what they did in terms of what they hoped to achieve and what they thought they might get by so acting. But why should citing the psychological antecedents of action in this way appear to us to be explanatory, unless we have some sort of awareness of the principles involved? Contrast the case of grammatical competence in a native language, another area in which tacit knowledge is attributed. Tacit knowledge of grammatical rules can be deeply tacit because of the nature of the competence it sustains. The grammatical competence of native speakers is an ability to produce well-formed strings and to detect and reject strings that are ungrammatical. This is a remarkable enough competence in itself, but it is interestingly dissimilar from 'theory of mind competence' in that it does not involve an explanatory practice. Grammatical principles do *not* have to account for any competence on the part of native speakers in explaining why some utterances are to be accepted as grammatical and other utterances are to be rejected as ungrammatical because, in general, native speakers *do not have any such explanatory abilities*. If they did, and if they were actually quite good at giving explanations as to why certain sentences were grammatically deviant while others were not, then we would have to credit them with a degree of access to grammatical theory.

On the widely held view that explanation involves subsuming particular cases under general principles, the prominence and precociousness of explanatory practice must be a strong argument in favour of the accessibility of folk psychological principles. Unfortunately, the nature of explanation is itself too controversial a topic for any argument of this kind to be decisive. So I do not want to rest the case for core theory-theory on the weakly tacit status of the theory that informs folk psychology. Core theory-theory can still be true even if the central integrative principles are strongly tacit. That would make the articulation of the core principles a more difficult task, though we could begin to tackle it by means of a boxological specification of the functions that the principles serve. In any case, one way of trying to make progress (as I shall attempt to do in the final section) is to enunciate principles that appear indispensable to adult folk psychology, so that we can subsequently go on to see how well these relate to the empirical data supplied by developmental psychology and anthropological research into theory of mind in other cultures.

6 Part of the core: a rational agency version

If there is a core to folk psychology, then it will have to consist in rules governing transitions between the fundamental state-descriptions of folk psychology – which seem to be of the form [AGENT – ATTITUDE – CONTENT] – and linking those state-descriptions to situational input and behavioural output. The question how children come to master the contents embedded in these state-descriptions (particularly in their success on *false belief* tasks) continues to be a focus of developmental research.

I shall offer a rational agency version, in terms of belief-desire psychology, of what appear to be essential parts of the core. This sort of account of folk psychology has been criticised (e.g., by Morton, 1991, pp.111–13). But in so far as these criticisms point to the predictive weakness of principles of rational agency they seem to me ineffective, because they only serve to highlight areas in which folk psychology *is* predictively weak.

The main case for assigning a central integrating function to belief-desire psychology is that otherwise we will be unable to account either for the importance of explanation of action in terms of the agent's reasons or for our readiness to anticipate future conduct on the basis of thoughts and wants attributed. I would like to capture the content of the core principles of belief-desire psychology while remaining agnostic about their format. Expressed in natural language (or text-book style) each such principle should presumably be prefaced by a *ceteris paribus* clause, but I have omitted this to avoid tiresome reiteration.

If belief-desire psychology has a central principle, it must link belief, desire, and behaviour. It could be formulated like this:

[*Action Principle*] An agent will act in such a way as to satisfy, or at least to increase the likelihood of satisfaction, of his/her current strongest desire in the light of his/her beliefs.

The *Action Principle* is a minimal principle of behavioural rationality because it only relates behaviour to the intentional states of belief and desire, without saying anything about *their* rationality. No matter whether the attitudes themselves are rational: they can still serve *to rationalise behaviour*. If the *Action Principle* seems numbingly platitudinous, so much the better. That is exactly the way we might recognise a weakly tacit basic principle.

The core principles of a Lakatosian research programme can only be brought into contact with experience through being embedded in a network of auxiliary hypotheses and factual data. On its own the central principle is empirically vacuous: if that were all we knew of other people, we wouldn't know what to expect of them. But it is also systematically indispensable, because the need to augment it with further information in such a way as to be consistent with what we know about what people actually do guides and constrains the modification of auxiliary generalisations and specific state-descriptions. This is what Lakatos emphasised as the *heuristic* role of a theoretical core. Such a theory-driven process appears to be reflected in folk psychology in the following thought: an agent must have had *some reason* for what she did, so if prior attributions of intentional states to the agent fail to rationalise conduct, those attributions are to be corrected or supplemented.

Of course, we need to outline the functional role of belief more fully than as whatever it is that combines with desire to prompt an agent to action. We also need principles concerning the characteristic causes of beliefs, and what beliefs are liable to be induced in individuals in various situations. Something like the following would have to be counted as one of them:

[*Perception Principle*] When an agent A attends to a situation S in a given way, and p is a fact about S perceptually salient in that way, then A acquires the belief that p.

Agreed, this principle is minimally informative until supplemented by a body of knowledge about what facts are perceptually salient. Knowledge of that can only be acquired through experience, which is how the Perception Principle comes to be linked with a host of general beliefs about the perceptual capacities of human agents. That is exactly how theory of mind development should proceed according to the core theory-theorist: the child needs to learn how to flesh out the core.

Perception is one way of fixing belief. Inference is another. So we also need a principle that relates beliefs to beliefs via inference, such as the following:

[*Inference Principle*] When an agent A acquires the belief that *p* and a rational thinker ought to infer *q* from the conjunction of *p* with other beliefs that A has, A comes to believe that *q*.

This principle is in effect a normative heuristic. We could alternatively say that the default assumption is that other people are rational thinkers in their inferences – unless we have special reason to recognise that in these circumstances they are not, or that on this topic a particular person is not. Any general and fundamental principle concerning inference needs to have this special heuristic status. It cannot be a constitutive principle of what it is to hold the belief that *p* without sacrificing causal realism about inference. But equally it cannot be a non-normative generalisation about inferences without introducing the consequence that those with a theory of mind will have a general theory of inference *independent of* their own inferential dispositions. That's a very awkward consequence. What would one do if there was a mismatch, and one's own inferential dispositions gave different results from the theory of inference one applied to others?

These three principles are no more than a part of the putative core. But they do seem indispensable to the folk psychology of adult Westerners. Whether they are also part of a universal human cognitive endowment is, as Janet Astington (this volume)points out, an open question for anthropological investigation. It would certainly be surprising if there were several core theories of mind, or significantly different variants on belief-desire psychology. But I do not wish to prejudge the issue. At least we would have learned something from the rational agency version of core theory-theory, if it were to turn out that this form of folk psychology is culturally parochial.

What I will do is to conclude with a point concerning the modest form of simulationism advocated by Jane Heal. She has argued (Heal, 1994) that, given the contents of belief-attributions, deriving predictions of thinking plays a major role in folk psychology. But she thinks this is 'bad news for the theory-theory' because it is not at all plausible to suppose that in addition to our own inferential dispositions we also have a comprehensive general theory of thinking which tells us what further thoughts are to be ascribed on the basis of initial attributions. I accept that, but dispute that it constitutes anything like bad news for core theory-theory. Heal's position is eclectic (as her contribution to the present volume makes clear), since she doubts whether simulation alone has the resources to handle initial attributions of belief on the basis of information about behaviour and situation. So the claim for a simulationist role that we need to allow concerns what we may call *inference enrichment*. Yet if we consider the form that a core principle concerning inference might take (such as the *Inference Principle* suggested above), we can see that accepting Heal's point constitutes a concession to simulationism that the theory-theorist should be happy to make.

Quite generally, theoretical principles require the assistance of procedures that determine how they are to be applied to particular cases. If one wants to know what a rational thinker ought to infer from p, one needs to consider what p implies. This was already implicit in the acknowledgement that the core principle concerning inference enrichment was normative. We can call this procedure 'simulation', but calling it that does not prevent the process as a whole from being theory-driven. To apply the principles of mechanics one needs to have procedures for *measuring* masses and accelerations. Yet, clearly enough, this does not make mechanics a measuring process rather than a theory. So I see no reason why this particular form of simulationism cannot be accommodated by the core version of theory-theory. What it is incompatible with is the suggestion that an *encapsulated*

Fodorian module could process theory of mind computations. For inference enrichment through the 'simulated' use of inferential dispositions is a radically open and unencapsulated cognitive process.

ACKNOWLEDGEMENT

I would particularly like to thank Peter Carruthers for many helpful comments on an earlier draft of this chapter.

8   The mental simulation debate:
a progress report

Tony Stone and Martin Davies

1   Introduction

For philosophers, the current phase of the debate with which Part I of this volume is concerned can be taken to have begun in 1986, when Jane Heal and Robert Gordon published their seminal papers (Heal, 1986; Gordon, 1986; though see also, for example, Stich, 1981; Dennett, 1981). They raised a dissenting voice against what was becoming a philosophical orthodoxy: that our everyday, or folk, understanding of the mind should be thought of as theoretical. In opposition to this picture, Gordon and Heal argued that we are not theorists but simulators. For psychologists, the debate had begun somewhat earlier when Heider (1958) produced his work on lay psychology; and in more recent times the psychological debate had continued in developmental psychology and in work on animal cognition.

But the debate has a much longer provenance than those datings suggest; for it goes back, at least, to disputes in the eighteenth century about whether the methods that had been so successful in the natural sciences were also appropriate for the human or moral sciences. Today's friends of mental simulation stand in a tradition that includes Vico, Herder, Croce, and particularly Collingwood (1946).

1.1   Nine questions

Given the inter-disciplinary ancestry of the debate, it is no surprise that current discussion ranges over a number of distinguishable – indeed, often fairly independent – questions. We suggest that it is useful to separate out some of these questions, and here we identify nine.

(a) What is it to have mastery of the mental concepts that are deployed in our folk psychological practice? (The concept mastery question)

(b) What is the best philosophical account of the kinds of states postulated by the folk when they engage in folk psychological practice? (The metaphysical question)

(c) What are the key characteristics of our folk psychological practice –

particularly, our practices of attribution, explanation and prediction? (The descriptive question about normal adult folk psychological practice)

(d) What resources do mature adult humans draw upon as they go about the business of attributing mental states, and predicting and explaining one another's mental states and actions? (The explanatory question about normal adult folk psychological practice)

(e) What information processing mechanisms need to be postulated in order to provide a psychological explanation of the way in which humans actually attribute mental states, and predict and explain one another's actions? (The question of information-processing underpinnings of normal adult practice)

(f) What course of development do human beings follow as they develop the ability to engage in folk psychological practice? (The descriptive question about development)

(g) What explanatory account is to be given of this course of development? (The explanatory question about development)

(h) What mechanisms need to be postulated in order to explain the changes that are seen in the child's folk psychological abilities? (The question of mechanisms responsible for change)

(i) What explanatory theory can we give that explains the deficits and disorders to which the development of folk psychological practice is subject? (The question about developmental disorders)

Given the differences amongst these questions, we should not assume that a position that starts life as an answer to a philosophical question (like (a) or (b)) can be simply transposed into an answer to an empirical question (like (c)–(i)). So, there is no way to be brief over these nine questions. What we shall do, then, is to focus our comments on the explanatory question about normal adult folk psychological practice (d). Along the way, there will be some mention of the concept mastery question, and of the descriptive question about normal adult practice. The metaphysical question, and the questions about information-processing underpinnings and about development, will be left to one side.

2   The theory-theory

Here is one way in which a version of the theory-theory might be developed. It might be said that the mental concepts that comprise our everyday or folk psychology – such as *belief, desire, hope, being in pain*, and so on – are part of a linked network of mental concepts, so that understanding any one of these concepts requires understanding some or all of the others. Thus, grasping the concept of belief, for example, requires that one has mastered connections between belief and desire of the form (Churchland, 1988, p. 58–9): Persons who want that P, and believe that Q would be sufficient to bring about P, and have no conflicting wants or preferred strategies, will try to bring it about that Q; or (Botterill, this volume, p. xxx): [Action Principle] An agent will act in such a way as to satisfy, or at least to increase the likelihood of satisfaction of, his/her current strongest desire in the light of his/her beliefs. Similarly, of course, grasping the concept of desire requires mastering the same kinds of connections.

The argument in favour of this kind of view is well known. Imagine, it is said, someone who claims to have the concept of belief – indeed someone who claims to understand what it is to believe that its being the case that Q would be sufficient to bring it about that P – but who denies that someone with that belief would try, *ceteris paribus*, to bring it about that Q were she to desire that P. Then – say those who support this approach to questions about grasp of mental concepts – it is clear that, whatever concept it is that such a person is using, it is not the concept of *belief*. The same point can be made *mutatis mutandis* about grasping the concept of desire, and particularly about understanding the idea of desiring that P.

Such arguments for the view that grasp of certain concepts requires commitment to a family of inferential principles have considerable plausibility. This is especially so when grasp of a concept cannot be directly manifested by way of demonstrative identification of objects or happenings as falling under it. And indeed, many advocates of the theory-theory would stress that beliefs are unobservable, and so are not clear candidates for demonstrative identification (Fodor, 1987, p. 7).

2.1   *The analogy with science*

A theory-theorist may now take the following step. If our grasp of mental concepts depends upon our mastery of the inferential connections in a network of concepts, then there seems to be an analogy between mental concepts and those scientific concepts that get their sense from the scientific theory in which they are embedded. A concept such as *quark* can only be grasped via knowledge of a theory of sub-atomic physics. As in the case of *belief*, there is no prospect presently of being able to identify quarks demonstratively. Grasp of the concept *quark* depends upon mastery of the theory in which that concept is embedded.

In this spirit, David Lewis (1972) argues that we should see folk psychology 'as a term-introducing scientific theory, though one invented long before there was any such institution as professional science' (p. 256). The theory is formulated in the following way (ibid.): 'Collect all the platitudes you can think of regarding the causal relations of mental states, sensory stimuli and motor responses . . . Include only platitudes which are common knowledge among us – everyone knows them, everyone knows that everyone else knows them, and so on.' This analogy between mental concepts and scientific concepts is the source for one version of the theory-theory of folk psychology – a version that begins as an answer to the concept mastery question (a).

The rather limited analogy with professional science is taken a step further by those who compare the forms of explanation deployed in folk psychological practice with the deductive-nomological explanations that are usually regarded as characteristic of scientific practice. That step positions the theory-theorist to return an answer to the explanatory question about normal adult folk psychological practice (d); the answer, namely, that the resources drawn upon in folk psychological practice include knowledge of a psychological theory. But we should note that the theory-theorist's answer to the explanatory question rests upon an answer to the descriptive question (c), especially as that question relates to the key characteristics of folk psychological explanation.

Explanations in folk psychology are sometimes said to be 'rationalising' explanations. Philip Pettit (1986, p. 45), for example, describes them as 'normalising' rather than 'regularising' explanations, and John McDowell (1985, p. 389) says that 'the concepts of the propositional attitudes have their proper home in explanations of a special sort' – a sort contrasted with subsumptive or regularising explanation. But the theory-theorist's answer to question (d) about the explanation of our folk psychological practice – including our explanatory practice – begins from an answer to question (c) that says that the explanatory practice itself is not radically different in kind from giving explanations in terms of 'how things generally tend to happen' (McDowell, ibid.). Thus, Fodor states that commonsense psychological explanations (1987, p. 7): 'exhibit the "deductive structure" that is so characteristic of explanation in real science. There are two parts to this: the theory's underlying generalisations are defined over unobservables, and they lead to its predictions by iterating and interacting rather than being directly instantiated'.

According to this kind of position, then, folk psychological explanation and scientific explanation are of essentially the same kind – and draw upon the same kinds of resources. As Heal (1986, p. 135) describes the position: 'We are said to view other people as we view stars, clouds or geological formations. People are just complex objects in our environment whose behaviour we wish to anticipate but whose causal innards we cannot perceive. We therefore proceed by observing the intricacies of their external behaviour and formulating some hypotheses about how the insides are structured.' *A fortiori*, on this view, there is continuity between folk psychology and scientific psychology. Scientific psychological practice is an extension of the way that people actually do go about their everyday explanatory activities – 'but in more detail and with more statistical accuracy' (Heal, ibid.).

This is, of course, a substantive – and even controversial – claim. There is no evident incoherence in combining the idea that, when we are doing science, we can treat human beings as 'complex objects . . . whose behaviour we wish to anticipate' with the thought that ordinary folk psychological activity goes on in a fundamentally different way. Indeed, there would appear to be room for a range of views of this general type, differing over what is distinctive about folk psychological explanation. One variation on the theme would be that suggested by Pettit and McDowell. Another would stress the role of lore – rather than law – in everyday understanding and explanation (see Botterill, this volume; Heal, this volume, for examples). (See also Wolpert, 1992, for a view of science as fundamentally different in kind from commonsense thinking.) We shall return, in the concluding section of this chapter, to the idea that folk psychological explanation is fundamentally different from explanation by subsumption.

Up to this point, the weight carried by the notion of a psychological theory has depended upon an analogy with professional science. But this analogy may be somewhat problematic for the version of the theory-theory that we have been considering. After all, in many respects the practice of folk psychology looks utterly unlike that of a professional science – quantum physics, or inorganic chemistry, or molecular biology, or neurophysiology. Folk psychological practice does not bear the marks of a scientific research programme. It is not, for example, written up in learned journals or in text books; it is not subject to rigorous empirical investigation; nor does it have to be actively taught.

There are a number of strategies that could be taken by someone who seeks to articulate a version of the theory-theory, but who does not want to become entangled in these disanalogies between folk psychology and professional science. One strategy is simply to focus on the deductive-nomological form of explanation. Another strategy – not unconnected with what Fodor (1987, p. 7) says about 'generalisations [that] lead to . . . predictions by iterating and interacting rather than being directly instantiated' – is to stress the idea of a theory as providing a framework within which particular cases can be systematically related to each other (Heal, this volume). '[T]heories must contain principles that provide a systematic integration of knowledge' (Botterill, this volume, p. 107).

2.2   The analogy with theoretical linguistics

Some friends of the theory-theory may abandon the analogy with professional science altogether, preferring a different analogy with theoretical linguistics. This analogy sees the theory-theory as adopting what Stich and Nichols (1992) call 'the dominant explanatory strategy' in cognitive science (1992, pp. 35–6):

the dominant explanatory strategy proceeds by positing an internally represented 'knowledge structure' – typically a body of rules or principles or propositions – which serves to guide the execution of the capacity to be explained. These rules or principles or propositions are often described as the agent's 'theory' of the domain in question. In some cases, the theory may be partly accessible to consciousness; the agent can tell us some of the rules or principles he is using. More often, however, the agent has no conscious access to the knowledge guiding his behaviour.

But, just as the analogy with professional science can be problematic, so also this analogy with linguistics raises some delicate questions.

The analogy prompts a host of questions about the notion of tacit knowledge, for example. The theory-theorist adopting this strategy needs to give some account of tacit knowledge that makes it clear just what attributions of tacit knowledge amount to – particularly, it must be clear that an attribution of tacit knowledge amounts to more than just a summary description of the practice or ability that is to be explained.

Furthermore, there may be an important disanalogy between tacit knowledge in the case of linguistics and tacit knowledge in the case of folk psychology. In the case of linguistics there is something to be said for the idea that the content of the tacit knowledge does not have to be conceptualised by the subject whose tacit knowledge it is. Ordinary language users do not grasp the concepts of linguistic theory, and so their tacit knowledge of linguistic principles does not constitute their mastery of those concepts. But in the case of folk psychology, ordinary practitioners do possess the concepts that will, presumably, be central in the tacitly known theory. Botterill (this volume) makes the related point that it would be natural for a theory-theorist to deny that the principles of the known folk psychological theory are completely inaccessible to consciousness, given that folk psychological practice includes providing explanations: '[W]hy should citing the psychological antecedents of action . . . appear to us to be explanatory, unless we have some sort of awareness of the principles involved?' (p. 114).

2.3   *The 'body of knowledge' strategy*

We turn now to a strategy that takes a relaxed view of the disanalogies between folk psychology and the theories that are characteristic of professional science. According to this version of the theory-theory, the key idea is that we can account for the explanatory abilities of human beings in the psychological domain by attributing to them possession of a body of knowledge about that domain. The body of knowledge might or might not be best thought of as structured in an especially theoretical way – as formulated in axioms and theorems, for example. But what is crucial is that it is an articulated body of knowledge that is specifically about the domain in question – here, the psychological domain. Stich and Nichols (1992) are the clearest advocates of this more relaxed (they say 'less restrictive') strategy.

The motivation for this strategy is clear. Stich and Nichols are attempting to provide a version of the theory-theory that is broad enough in its conception to withstand criticisms launched against specific forms that it might take. They are trying to provide a generic formulation of the theory-theory position (1995, p. 88):

If this [sc. the analogy with professional science] is correct, then folk psychology will bear a strong resemblance to the standard philosophical portrait of scientific theories in domains like physics and chemistry. But, of course, there are lots of domains of commonsense knowledge in which it is rather implausible to suppose that the mentally represented 'knowledge structure' includes theoretical constructs linked together in lawlike ways. Knowledge of cooking or of current affairs are likely candidates here, as is the knowledge that underlies our judgements about what is polite and impolite in our culture. And it is entirely possible that folk psychological knowledge will turn out to resemble the knowledge structures underlying cooking or politeness judgements rather than the knowledge structures that underlie the scientific predictions produced by a competent physicist or chemist.

Formulating the theory-theory in this more relaxed way has an important tactical role to play in the debate between the theory-theory and the simulation theory. As Stich and Nichols point out, taking the theory-theory in this way means that (1995, p. 90): '. . . even if it could be shown that people do not exploit lawlike generalisations in predicting and explaining other people's behaviour, this would not show that the theory-theory is wrong, and it would not provide any significant degree of support for the simulation theory'. Apart from this tactical advantage, adopting Stich and Nichols' strategy also provides us with the prospect of identifying a clear and fundamental area of disagreement between the theory-theorist and the simulation theorist.

On this more relaxed version of the theory-theory, the theory-theorist insists that my ability to predict and explain what my conspecifics will think and do will depend, *inter alia*, upon a body of psychological knowledge. If, in accordance with the more relaxed view, the theory-theorist is not going to put any great weight upon the precise way in which that body of knowledge is structured, then the theory-theory expands to fill a larger region of logical space, leaving only a rather restricted area for alternatives. A genuine disagreement between the theory-theory and an alternative view can be generated only if the alternative denies that our folk psychological ability depends upon our possession of a body of psychological knowledge, *simpliciter*. And this can seem like an untenable position for the imagined alternative since, surely, it cannot be denied that we do have psychological knowledge, and that, at least sometimes, it is deployed when we explain and predict other people's behaviour.

2.4   Folk psychology and folk physics

The apparent strength of the theory-theory position can be seen if we consider the comparison that Stich and Nichols (1992) draw between folk psychology and folk physics. The idea that we have a folk physics is the idea that our ability to move and act successfully in the physical world – to negotiate, for example, interactions with objects that we come into contact with – depends upon our possession of a body of information about, *inter alia*, the ways in which physical bodies generally tend to behave. Thus, it has been argued in the psychological literature that adult reasoning about physical objects is informed by knowledge of principles about continuity and solidity. Our possession of this knowledge explains why it is that (Spelke *et al.*, 1992, p. 607): '. . . no subject in any study of physical reasoning has ever judged that any part of a material object would move discontinuously or would coincide in space and time with a second material object'. The claim being made by those who think of our ability to negotiate the physical world as being dependent upon knowledge of a folk physical theory is not just that our practical abilities can be given a theoretical description. Rather, the claim is that knowledge of the principles about continuity and solidity is causally implicated in our abilities. Our possession of this knowledge explains why it is that we have those abilities with respect to physical bodies.

Against the background of this comparison, the theory-theorist of folk psychology says that, just as our ability to negotiate the physical world depends upon a body of knowledge about the ways in which physical objects tend to behave, so also our ability to negotiate the social world depends upon our possessing a body of knowledge about the way that people tend to behave. And now the dialectical position seems to be this. If the analogy with folk physics is a fair one, then any alternative to the theory-theory of folk psychology must give us grounds for supposing that our understanding of the social world proceeds on a quite different basis from our understanding of the physical world.

3   The simulation theory

The theory-theory involves a particular view of our epistemological relation to other people. According to that view, other people are objects in our environment, and the task of understanding them is no different, in principle, from the task of understanding the behaviour of other, more inert, objects ('stars, clouds or geological formations'). This view provides a clear rationale for the comparison between folk psychology and folk physics.

The simulation alternative sets out from a different starting point; namely, the thought that when we try to understand other people we are trying to understand objects of the same kind as ourselves. This renders our epistemological situation when confronted with the behaviour of our fellows radically different from the situation when we are confronted with the behaviour of other objects. The similarity between the understander and the to-be-understood creates the possibility of a distinctive methodology. As Heal (1986, p. 137) puts it: 'I can harness all my complex theoretical knowledge about the world and my ability to imagine to yield an insight into other people *without any further elaborate theorising about them*. Only one simple assumption is needed: that they are like me in being thinkers, that they possess the same fundamental cognitive capacities and propensities that I do.' It might be possible to employ something like this methodology while still regarding the explanatory and predictive tasks as proceeding in terms of 'how things generally tend to happen'. In that case, we would simply be using ourselves as measures of the way that things regularly occur: This is how things tend to happen with me; the other is much like me; so, this is how things will tend to happen with the other. But often, a simulation theory answer to our question (d) about the resources drawn upon in understanding other people is accompanied by a distinctive answer to question (c) about the key characteristics of our folk psychological practice.

According to this distinctive answer, what we are doing when we try to understand another person is not attempting to bring the other's behaviour under some law-like generalisation, nor even to assure ourselves that there is some generalisation that would subsume the events that confront us. Rather, we are trying to *make sense* of the other. Thus (Heal, 1986, p. 143): 'The difference between psychological explanation and explanation in the natural sciences is that in giving a psychological explanation we render the thought or behaviour of the other intelligible, we exhibit them as having some point, some reasons to be cited in their defence.' The simulation theorist's combined answer to questions (c) and (d) is then that the key characteristic of folk psychological practice is that it is a matter of rendering other people intelligible, and that the resources drawn upon include our knowledge of the world, and our ability to imagine, but not any body of distinctively psychological knowledge.

The role of imagining in this answer is important, since it cannot be taken for granted that simulation theory is the only way of developing the idea of folk psychological practice as involving a distinctive kind of explanation. The essential point is that the simulation theorist sees engagement in folk psychological practice as *re-enactment*.

Amongst philosophers working on the simulation approach to folk psychology, Robert Gordon (Gordon, 1986, 1992, 1995a, this volume) has done as much as anyone to spell out just exactly how the simulation strategy works. One of his examples (Gordon, 1992) has me walking along a trail with a friend when that friend suddenly turns and runs in the opposite direction. My job is to understand this piece of behaviour. In accordance with the simulation strategy, I first imagine how the world looks from his position (the position he was in immediately before he turned and ran). In imagination (or perhaps even in reality) I move myself to that position. Suppose that when I do this I can see what looks like a bear moving towards us. What am I – that is, I identified in imagination with my friend – to do?

Perhaps the answer is that I decide to run. (So far as the project of understanding my friend's action is concerned, this decision is still in imagination, though I may also take my own decision to run away as well.) In that case, I can explain my friend's running away; and if I had made the imaginative identification a few moments earlier, then I might have predicted his running away.

But perhaps that is not the answer. Maybe the answer is that I decide to 'play dead' – I have learned from hunting manuals that this is the thing to do if confronted by a bear. In that case, I am not yet in a position to explain what happened; as yet, I have not made sense of my friend's action. I have to take on board relevant differences between my companion and myself, and then re-run the decision process. Although the first case – 'total' projection – is the default strategy for simulation, most often what is required is a 'patched' projection, as illustrated by the second case.

3.1   The first-person case

The simulation strategy involves using imagination to cantilever out from our own theoretical and practical reasoning – leading to judgements and decisions – to an understanding of the beliefs and actions of another person. In imagination I go through some theoretical or practical reasoning and arrive at a judgement or a decision. If this is to yield a prediction about the beliefs or actions of another person then, of course, I need to be able to know about my own judgements and beliefs, decisions and intentions. But simulation theory itself does not, strictly speaking, provide an account of first-person knowledge of mental states. Rather, simulation theory takes some such account for granted.

In fact, there are two rather different approaches to first-person knowledge of mental states that have found favour with friends of simulation theory. Alvin Goldman (1989, 1993a) develops the idea that mental states like belief have intrinsic, introspectible qualities – in short, qualia. In apparent contrast, Gordon (1995a, this volume) sees first-person judgements as involving an 'ascent routine' (this volume, p. 15): '[I]f someone were to ask me, (Q1) "Do you believe Mickey Mouse has a tail?" I would ask myself, (Q2) "Does Mickey Mouse have a tail?" . . . If the answer to Q2 is Yes, then the presumptive answer to Q1 . . . is Yes.'

The issues between these two approaches are quite delicate. But, without entering upon a detailed comparison, we can make two remarks to suggest that the contrast might not be quite as stark as it initially appears. First, the idea that belief states have qualitative properties does not have to be coupled with the regressive idea of the subject having to match the properties of the belief with the properties of some mental 'colour card'. Second, engaging in an ascent routine clearly does not require possession of a concept of the mental state in question, if a concept is thought of as a mental template. But still, if an ascent routine is to yield a judgement to the effect that the subject believes that such-and-such, then the subject needs to possess the concept of belief that is deployed in that judgement.

Even if the idea that belief states have intrinsic, introspectible properties escapes a charge of regress, it is still apt to sound outlandish – as if belief states were being run together with sensations. But perhaps it is possible to make good sense of the idea by beginning from a thought about dispositional properties and their bases. A subject who (consciously) believes that, say, Mickey Mouse has a tail is in a position to judge that she has that belief. It is very natural to suppose that there is something about the belief state in virtue of which the subject is in a position to make that second-order judgement; and it is then quite natural to say that it is the belief's being a phenomenally conscious state that makes it accessible to the subject. What we do not need to say – what really would sound outlandish – is that the belief state's phenomenal properties are non-representational (or sensational) properties that are merely correlated with its representational (or semantic) properties. Rather, we should allow that representational properties can themselves be phenomenal properties.

This line of thought leaves unanswered important questions about the introspectible difference between different types of mental state with the same content – between believing and intending, for example. And there are important challenges for the idea of ascent routines, as well (see Carruthers, this volume). But, rather than pursue those questions and challenges, we turn to the point that the case of first-person knowledge of mental states is liable to seem problematic for the theory-theory too. Indeed, Goldman (1993a) uses this problem for the theory-theory approach to first-person attribution in order to motivate his own preference for cognitive qualia.

The problem for the theory-theory is that it does seem massively counterintuitive to suppose that first-person attributions require checking that a mental state stands in a particular network of causal relations before pronouncing it to be a belief, say, that Mickey Mouse has a tail. In response to this worry, Carruthers (this volume) makes the important point that it is open to a theory-theorist to adopt a perceptual – or more generally, non-inferential – account of our coming to make first-person judgements, while still holding that our grasp upon the contents of the judgements arrived at is constituted by our knowledge of a theory in which the mental concepts figure.

With this variation in place, the theory-theory is still offering two distinctive proposals. One proposal is an answer to our question (d) about the resources that are drawn upon in our folk psychological practice. Knowledge of a psychological theory is implicated in at least our third-person attributions, explanations, and predictions. The other proposal is an answer to our question (a) about concept mastery. Our mastery of mental concepts – whether they are deployed in third-person or in first-person judgements – is constituted by knowledge of a psychological theory.

The simulation theory also offers a distinctive answer to the question about resources that are drawn upon in third-personal folk psychological practice. The crucial ingredient is the capacity to engage in imaginative identification. But it is not so clear whether there is a distinctive simulation-theoretic answer to the question about concept mastery.

3.2   Simulation and mental concepts

Goldman (1989) is not optimistic about the prospects of the simulation approach yielding an account of our mastery of mental concepts, but Gordon's more ambitious ('radical') version of the simulation approach does seem to be intended as an answer to a question about concept mastery. In his first paper, Gordon speaks of simulation theory as offering 'a way of interpreting ordinary discourse about beliefs' (1986, p. 166), but does not address the concept mastery question in anything like the terms that we have posed it. However, in his more recent work, he moves closer to these issues, and in his paper in this volume he offers the beginnings of an account of what simulation contributes to mastery of mental concepts.

Gordon makes use of a spatial analogy according to which a person's being in a mental state is to be thought of as the state's being '*at a mental location*' or '*mentally* at a location'. Thus (Gordon, this volume, p. 18):

When an ascent routine is used within the context of a simulation, a new logical space is opened. One can understand the object-level question . . . 'Does Mickey Mouse have a tail?' to have answers *at* various locations in this space. For example, one child, Jane, might simulate another, Mary, and then ask herself, in the role of

Mary, the object level question, 'Does Mickey Mouse have a tail?' Simulation links the answer to the particular individual whose situation and behaviour constitute the evidence on which the simulation is based – the individual with whom one is identifying within the simulation. This, it seems to me, gives sense to the notion of something's being a fact *to* a particular individual.

Gordon's idea seems to be that our conception of Mary's believing that Mickey has a tail is a conception of the question 'Does Mickey have a tail?' having an affirmative answer at a particular point in a space, namely the point that Jane reaches in imagination by identifying with Mary. But the problem that is faced by any answer to the concept mastery question along these lines is that 'simulation is such a fallible procedure' (Goldman, 1989, p. 182).

Mary might not really believe that Mickey Mouse has a tail, even though Jane is indeed led to assert that Mickey Mouse has a tail within the scope of the best simulation of Mary that she can manage. In terms of the analogy with spatial location, the question might have an affirmative answer at the point that Jane reaches, but not at the point where Mary is really doxastically located. Because simulation is a fallible procedure, Jane may not reach the correct point.

If the simulation theorist is to make any further progress along these lines then, it seems, the analogy with spatial location needs to be coupled to a notion of idealised simulation. So, the revised proposal on behalf of Gordon's radical simulation theory is this. Our conception of Mary's believing that Mickey has a tail is a conception of the question 'Does Mickey have a tail?' having an affirmative answer at the point that would be reached in an *ideal* simulation of Mary. But, as Peacocke (1994, p. xxv) points out, this notion of idealised simulation is fraught with difficulties: 'Now consider a supposedly idealised simulator of another's attitudes. The . . . threat is that, in so far as we can make sense of the idea, we have to draw on some prior understanding of what it is for another to have particular propositional attitudes.' So, the prospects for the most radical kind of simulation theory are still unclear.

4   The shape of the debate

If we leave the concept mastery question to one side, and just focus on the question about the resources that are drawn upon, then the debate seems to come down to this. The theory-theory says that our ability to negotiate the social world depends upon our possessing a body of empirical knowledge about how people's situations, mental states, and behaviour are related. The simulation alternative needs to find a distinctive place for the ability to engage in imaginative identification while also denying that our folk psychological practice relies upon possession of a body of psychological knowledge.

There are then a number of ways in which the distinction between the two sides of this debate might be blurred. One particular kind of threat of collapse arises if the theory-theory makes use of the idea of tacit knowledge of a theory. For the notion of possessing tacit knowledge has to be defined, and once a definition is offered it is a substantive question whether someone who engages in mental simulation – as that is described by Goldman or Gordon, say – counts as having tacit knowledge of a psychological theory. If the notion of tacit knowledge is defined so thinly that a simulator also counts as a tacit knower of a psychological theory then, in a quite strict sense, the distinction between the two sides collapses (see Davies, 1994; Heal, 1994; Perner, 1994, this volume).

But, even supposing that the basic distinction between simulating or re-enacting and drawing upon a body of psychological knowledge remains intact, still there are ways in which the theory-theory approach and the simulation alternative might be argued to overlap.

4.1   *Opposed or complementary approaches?*

One line of argument that has been present from the outset of the debate is that a simulator needs to draw upon a body of psychological knowledge in order to carry through a simulation. Thus, Dennett (1981/1987, pp. 100–1):

How can it [sc. simulation] work without being a kind of theorising in the end? For the state I put myself in is not belief but make-believe belief. If I make believe I am a suspension bridge and wonder what I will do when the wind blows, what 'comes to me' in my make-believe state depends on how sophisticated my knowledge is of the physics and engineering of suspension bridges. Why should my making believe I have your beliefs be any different? In both cases, knowledge of the imitated object is needed to drive the make-believe 'simulation' and the knowledge must be organised into something rather like a theory.

Consider again Gordon's example in which my friend and I are walking along the trail. Surely, the theory-theorist will say, in order to explain or predict my friend's action of running away, I need to know something about the typical causal relations between recognising a bear, being afraid, and taking evasive action. In addition, I need to know something about my friend's psychological make-up, and that knowledge, too, will be dependent upon pieces of theory (about the attitude towards bears that tends to be produced by a certain kind of education, for example).

The simulation theorist has a number of responses to make at this point.

Particularly, the simulation theorist argues that the theory-theorist is making an unwarranted and unparsimonious assumption. This assumption is that, over and above any actual thinking (say, thinking about tracks, bears, and escape) that takes place – whether *in propria persona* or within the scope of a simulation – there are also general psychological principles, knowledge of which explains the movements of thought that occur during a period of thinking, or within some episode of simulation. The simulation alternative sees no need for these two layers of thought: a layer that is the actual episode of thinking about the world, and a layer of meta-thinking that brings about the movement of thought in the first layer. All that is needed, according to the simulation theorist, is that some thinking take place, in accordance with the canons of rational cognition. The dynamics of thought require no meta-cognitive engine.

This line of argument is used to reject the suggestion that mental simulation will inevitably be 'theory driven' rather than 'process driven' (Goldman, 1989). But it can also be used to undermine the theory-theory itself. For what the theory-theory appears to be committed to is not just knowledge of some general psychological principles, but also knowledge of indefinitely many indefinitely detailed principles about thought concerning specific subject matters (Heal, 1995, this volume). Botterill (this volume), Carruthers (this volume), and Perner (this volume) all concede, on behalf of the theory-theory, that the intrusion of something like simulation will be needed – what Carruthers calls 'simulation within a theory' and Perner calls 'content simulation'.

On the other side, advocates of the simulation theory typically acknowledge that inductively based generalisations play a role in real life use of mental simulation (Goldman, 1989, Harris, 1992), and Perner (this volume) presents empirical data that points in the same direction. So, to that extent, we seem to be moving towards a measure of agreement over the need for hybrid theories. Future research will need to address in detail the ways in which simulation and deployment of knowledge interact. As Perner says (this volume, p. 103): [S]ince any theory use involves an element of simulation and since simulation on its own cannot account for the data, the future must lie in a mixture of simulation and theory use. However, what this mixture is and how it operates must first be specified in some detail before any testable empirical predictions can be derived.'

4.2   Cognitive penetrability: The crucial test?

The point about the relative lack of economy involved in adoption of the theory-theory approach is made vivid by an example introduced by Paul Harris (1992). Suppose we are asked to predict the grammaticality judgements that a speaker of the same language would make when confronted with a range of sentences in the language. Harris reasonably claims that predictive success would be high, and offers this explanation (1992, p. 124):

The most plausible answer is that you read each sentence, asked yourself whether it sounded grammatical or not, and assumed that other English speakers would make the same judgements for the same reasons. The proposal that you have two distinct tacit representations of English grammar, a first-order representation that you deploy when making your own judgements, and a metarepresentation (i.e. a representation of other people's representations) that you deploy in predicting the judgements made by others, so designed as to yield equivalent judgements, strains both credulity and parsimony.

Furthermore, we might suppose, what goes for the prediction of grammaticality judgements goes also for the prediction of belief formation on the basis of inference and for the prediction of intentions and behaviour.

However, Stich and Nichols (1995) respond to Harris's example by distinguishing cases. They are inclined to make concessions to the simulation theory over the explanation and prediction of a person's judgements and beliefs in a particular perceptual situation, and perhaps also in the case of belief-formation on the basis of inference. But they argue strongly for the theory-theory as providing a better account of the prediction of behaviour. Given the role of theoretical inference in any decision-taking process, we are not convinced that different stances towards prediction of belief formation on the basis of inference and prediction of behaviour can be justified. But that is not our main concern here.

Stich and Nichols' argument hinges on the phenomenon of cognitive penetrability, introduced in an earlier paper (1992). The issue is this. If predictions are based upon deployment of a theory (a body of information or misinformation), then those predictions are liable to be false if the theory is incorrect in any way. Theory-based predictions are subject to error introduced by misinformation. But a flawed theory will obviously have no impact upon predictions that do not draw upon it. Even if I have deeply flawed psychological views, if I use mental simulation to generate predictions about what people will do given their beliefs and desires, then my flawed theory need introduce no error into my predictions.

So the crucial empirical question is, apparently, whether we are liable to make false predictions about other people's decisions, intentions, and actions. If we are then, according to Stich and Nichols (1992, 1995), this favours the theory-theory. And, as they point out, there are indeed examples where folk psychological prediction lets us down.

One of the examples used by Stich and Nichols (1992) involves predictions about what subjects will do when invited to select amongst items all of which are, unknown to them, identical in quality. Another example concerns predictions about the price for which subjects will sell back raffle tickets that were obtained in two different conditions. In both cases, predictors consistently give incorrect answers.

Goldman (1992) and Harris (1992) point out responses that are available to the defender of the simulation theory. The general idea of these responses is this. The simulation method will only arrive at correct answers if it begins from the correct inputs, and the inputs that the predictors use are very largely determined by the way that information about the original subjects' situation is presented to the predictors. Nichols, Stich, Leslie and Klein (this volume) report a more formal experiment, designed so as not to be open to the objections that Goldman and Harris raise. In this more tightly controlled setting, predictors still make errors.

However, there is a possible source of error in predictions that is still not addressed by these experimental findings. For, as Harris points out (1992, p. 134) there may be purely mechanical influences on decision taking that are not captured by mental simulation. Indeed, we can see how these influences might be relevant, even in the sort of case where Stich and Nichols (1995; and Nichols *et al.*, this volume) are inclined to make concessions to the simulation theory.

We are able to use our own perceptual abilities and our own inferential abilities in simulation mode in order to arrive at predictions about another's belief formation. But, if we learn that the other has just ingested a certain substance, then we cannot make allowances for that fact by imaginative identification alone. Unless we are prepared to ingest the same substance ourselves, we need to be told what effect it has upon the processes of perception and inference. What is needed, then, is a little piece of theory – some information about non-rational influences upon psychological processes.

Exactly the same goes for the processes of decision taking. Unless we are ready and able to subject ourselves to the same non-rational influences that affect those whose decisions we seek to predict, we shall need to augment our ability to simulate with some pieces of theory. This has always been accepted by the friends of mental simulation. As Heal says (1986, p. 139): 'Replication [simulation] theory must allow somewhere for the idea of different personalities, for different styles of thinking and for non-rational influences on thinking.' What the simulation theorist denies is that we need to draw upon an empirical theory about rational processes of belief formation or decision taking.

5   Conclusion

The mental simulation debate has reached a stage at which there is considerable agreement about the need to develop hybrid theories – theories that postulate both theory and simulation, and then spell out the way in which those two components interact. But the situation is complicated by the fact that there are several quite different versions of the theory-theory and of the simulation alternative. On the side of the theory-theory, we have already seen (Section 2 above) that there is a range of options, and certainly there are important differences between the approaches taken by, for example, Perner (1991a), Wellman (1990) and Leslie (1987). On the side of the simulation theory, Gordon (1986), Heal (1986) and Goldman (1989) each stress rather different ideas. Selective borrowing from these accounts would allow the development of a huge variety of hybrid theories.

We would like to draw attention to a type of theory that, on the one hand, does not belong in the theory-theory camp but, on the other hand, leaves out the key idea of at least Gordon's version of the simulation theory. This type of theory stresses both the importance of first-order thought about the world and the idea of a distinctive kind of explanation – making sense of another person – but does not regard either explanation or prediction as essentially involving imaginative identification with the other.

When I am considering how to act in a given situation, I bring to bear my knowledge about the world, and arrive at a judgement about what is *the thing to do*. Both knowledge and imagination are certainly drawn upon, but there need be no intrusion into my own decision taking of any body of empirical theory about psychology – about what people in certain situations and with certain propositional attitudes generally tend to do.

Then, when I turn to the task of explaining or understanding the actions of another person, just the same kind of normative judgement is relevant. Thus (McDowell, 1985, p. 389): '[T]he concepts of the propositional attitudes have their proper home in explanations of a special sort: explanations in which things are made intelligible by being revealed to be, or to approximate to being, as they rationally ought to be.' Once again, the imagination is liable to be involved. But there is no special role for imaginative identification in this transition from the first to the third-person, since the normative judgement about what is the thing to do is not an essentially first-person judgement.

The task of predicting the behaviour of another does require something more than just this kind of normative judgement. It requires the assumption – which might well operate as a kind of default – that the other will indeed do the thing that is the thing to do (Heal, 1986, p. 137): 'Only one simple assumption is needed: that they are like me in being thinkers, that they possess the same fundamental cognitive capacities and propensities that I do.' But there is still no special role for imaginative identification. So, this type of theory differs from at least Gordon's version of the simulation theory. It is also different, surely, from the theory-theory. The single empirical assumption that people will, on the whole, do the sensible thing scarcely amounts to the body of psychological knowledge that theory-theorists envisage.

There may well be some kind of theory involved in the process of arriving at a judgement as to what is the thing to do. Whether there is or not is not an obvious matter. But if there is, then it is not an empirical psychological theory about what people generally tend to do. As Simon Blackburn says (1992, p. 195): 'In one way or another the fact that we need to theorise under a "principle of rationality", or to see a proper point in people's doings in order to understand them, marks off this kind of theorising from anything found in the natural sciences'. We cannot now offer any evaluation of this alternative position, nor explore its extension to the explanation and prediction of another person's beliefs. We are not even sure whether it should be regarded as genuinely distinct from both the theory-theory and the simulation theory, or rather as a variation on the simulation theory theme. (It would appear to count as a version of the simulation theory on Stich and Nichols' (1992, p. 47) way of 'drawing the battle lines', though they assume that there are only two alternatives to be considered.) But we do think that it deserves consideration.

Part II

Modes of acquisition – theorising, learning, and modularity

Gabriel Segal

1   Introduction

Normal adult human beings are good psychologists. They can explain and, to an extent, predict their own and other people's actions on the basis of a battery of psychological concepts: perception, desire, belief, fear, wonder, doubt, and so on. Let us call the seat of these psychological abilities the 'psychology faculty'. The psychology faculty has been the focus of a great deal of research in experimental, theoretical and developmental cognitive psychology, as well as a fair amount of philosophy.

I believe that this investment of intellectual energy is well worthwhile, since the study of the psychology faculty relates in important ways to a variety of central interdisciplinary concerns. It intersects with questions in the philosophy of mind about eliminativism, knowledge of other minds and our conception of ourselves as human beings. It intersects in interesting and subtle ways with questions in philosophy of language about the semantics of sentences attributing propositional attitudes. And it relates to the most fundamental questions in psychology about concept acquisition and the structure of the mind. In this paper I'll address some aspects of the latter questions.

It is common practice among psychologists, linguists and some philosophers to talk of 'modules' of the mind. But there is a wide variety of quite different conceptions of modularity. In section 2, I will distinguish a few of these which I believe have a good chance of being genuine psychological, natural kinds. I will then go on to ask, in section 3, which ones, if any, apply to the psychology faculty.

2   Modularity

There are two different dimensions within which one can distinguish notions of modularity: synchronic and diachronic. The synchronic notions concern the capacity of a subject at a given time. A normal, adult human can, for example, see, use language, and psychologise. One can ask for an explanation of each of these capacities. And the explanations offered may invoke one or other kind of modularity. The diachronic notions concern the course of development of the capacity from birth (or before) through to maturity. I begin with synchronic notions.

2.1   Synchronic modularity

Suppose we are interested in a specific psychological competence, such as vision or language. A precondition of any kind of modular explanation of the competence is that we have a reasonably clear idea of its domain of application. Our visual competence enables us to gather information about the surface markings, shapes, orientations and locations of three-dimensional objects in space, from two-dimensional patterns of light on our retinas. Our linguistic competence concerns phonological, syntactic, and semantic properties of our language, and it underlies our ability to produce and understand the physical forms of sentences. These two domains of application are reasonably well demarcated and distinguishable from each other and from further cognitive domains.

There are probably many areas of cognitive competence that do not apply over a well demarcated domain. By contrast with vision and language, there is presumably no well demarcated domain for the competence to go shopping for Xmas presents or to execute a spying mission behind enemy lines. There are competent shoppers and competent spies. But there is not yet, and probably never could be, a detailed and precise theory of the domains of application of these competences. Or, to put the same point another way, the ability to shop and the ability to spy are not to be explained in terms of isolable competences at all.

Once we have reason to believe that there exists a genuine competence with a definite domain of application, we can ask for an explanation of the competence. And it is here that modularity enters the picture. A module is a component of the mind, or brain, a mechanism, a system or some such that explains the competence. To put it crudely: where there is something definite that we can do, we can ask if there is something definite within us that enables us to do it.

Different conceptions of modularity arise from different explanations of competences. I will distinguish four different notions of synchronic modularity. These almost certainly do not exhaust the field. But they are at least clear and clearly distinguishable, and will be enough to ground the discussion of the psychology faculty.

2.1.1   Intentional modularity

The first notion might well fall under the heading 'component of the mind'. Sometimes we can explain a competence in purely intentional terms by positing a specific body of psychological states that underlie it. I call the kind of modularity that arises from this, 'intentional modularity'. The idea of an intentional module is present in an early form in the work of Sigmund Freud, and has been further articulated and deployed by Noam Chomsky (see e.g. Chomsky, 1980, 1986). According to Chomsky, our linguistic competence consists in (largely unconscious) knowledge of a body of linguistic rules. The knowledge concerns a self-contained array of interrelated concepts (Phrase, Noun, Verb, Anaphor, Quantifier etc.) that fit together somewhat in the manner of a scientific theory, forming generalisations and so on.[1]

It would be pointless, however, to count any appropriately inter-related body of psychological states as an intentional module. Mere knowledge of a theory isn't likely to be a psychologically interesting category. But some of Freud's and Chomsky's theoretical posits have further interesting features. In particular, there may be a one- or two-way filter to information. In Jerry Fodor's (1983) terminology, intentional modules may be 'informationally encapsulated': some of the information in the subject's mind outside a given module may be unavailable to it. For example, information in the conscious mind is often not available to the Freudian unconscious. And, going the other way, intentional modules may exhibit 'limited accessibility': some of the information within a module may be unavailable to consciousness. For example, we are not conscious of most of the contents of the language faculty. As is often pointed out, that is one reason why linguistics isn't easy. Somewhat stipulatively, I suggest that if a set of appropriately related psychological states exhibits either informational encapsulation or limited accessibility, then they constitute an intentional module.[2]

2.1.2   Computational modularity

The second notion of module is that of a computational system, classically conceived. A computational system is a representation processor.[3] A representation is a physical configuration of some kind, with syntactic and semantic properties. A computer receives representations as inputs, produces representations as outputs and, usually, produces intermediate representations along the way. What makes a representation processor a computer is the role of syntax: which output representation it produces for any given input is entirely determined by the syntactic properties of that input. That is to say, there exists a function from the input representations to the output representations that is specifiable in purely syntactic terms.

A computer, in the relevant sense, is also a physical system. This means that it must be constructed so that the actual causal processes initiated by the input representation and culminating in an output representation do ensure that the syntactically defined function is instantiated. And a computer is also a semantic, or intentional system. The representations have meanings. If the computer is to do anything interesting, then the output representations must be reasonable in the light of the input representations. A genuine inference machine has the special property of being truth-preserving: if the inputs are true, then the outputs are true. But computers need not have that property. It may be that their inputs and outputs don't represent propositions, hence do not have truth values at all, as in a chess-playing computer. Or the computer may implement a heuristic: its outputs will usually be true, given true inputs, but not always.

It is very plausible that the early visual system is a computer. It takes pairs of representations as inputs, each one representing the pattern of light on one retina. And given an input pair it constructs a single output, representing the shapes, orientations etc. of objects in space. A complete theory of the visual system as a computer would specify all the relevant physical, syntactic and semantic properties of the representations, the processes that mediate them and the relations among the three kinds of properties. (See Marr 1982 for a detailed study of the computational theory of vision.)

It is likely that every computational module realises an intentional module. That is because there exists a self-contained and definite description of what it does in purely intentional terms. The only further requirement is that it exhibit either informational encapsulation or limited accessibility. The former is almost inevitable, since any computer will have a characteristic set of inputs. And it is unlikely that any computer in someone's head has a range of inputs that allows it access to all the information in that head.

By contrast, there is no reason to think that every intentional module is realised by a computational one. In understanding Chomsky it is very important to see that his account of linguistic competence is framed only in terms of an intentional module. It is true that he sometimes calls the language faculty a 'computational system'. But by that he doesn't mean 'computational system' in the sense I've just defined it. He just means that the rules we unconsciously know are recursive.

Purely intentional modules can co-exist with computational ones. For example, a number of linguists believe that a variety of computational modules have access to and deploy the information in the language faculty, the latter being conceived of as a purely intentional module, a body of knowledge. A parser, for instance, may be conceived of as a computational module that deploys the information in the language faculty to build up representations of the syntactic and semantic properties of physical sentence-forms.

It is also possible that at least some cognitive competencies are explained by intentional modules without the help of computational modules. There must, of course, be some explanation of how the contents of an intentional module (knowledge or whatever) are deployed in the execution of tasks. But this explanation might not invoke any computations, as I have defined them. Connectionist systems provide one alternative model. And there are surely others.

2.1.3   Fodor modularity

The third kind of module is also computational. But it has an array of further distinguishing properties. This notion is articulated by Jerry Fodor (1983). A 'Fodor module' is a computer which has the following properties: (1) Domain specificity (2) Informational encapsulation (3) Obligatory firing (4) Fast speed (5) Shallow outputs (6) Limited inaccessibility (7) Characteristic ontogeny (8) Dedicated neural architecture (9) Characteristic patterns of breakdown.

While every Fodor module is computational, there is no particular reason to suppose that every computational module is Fodor. As yet we do not have a well worked out theory of any computational module other than the early visual system, and this appears to fit Fodor's criteria rather well. But it is not unlikely that some other psychological competencies are explained by non-Fodor, computational modules. Acquired skills like driving or tennis, for example, may be computational while not having a characteristic ontogeny, though they do exhibit a number of other Fodor features. (Cp. Karmiloff-Smith, 1992.) And perhaps some acquired cognitive competencies, such as symbolic logic or chess are slow and have deep outputs.

2.1.4   Neural modules

The fourth kind of module is neural. A neural module is a functional component of the brain, describable in purely neurological terms.

A neural module need not also be intentional or computational. It may be, for example, that a specific competence, like the ability to construct and use cognitive maps, is fully explained by some neurological system (involving, say, sinusoidal waves in the dendrites of the hippocampus), without the system being a computer or containing (or realising) any body of knowledge. (See O'Keefe and Nadel, 1978.)

Evidently, though, a neural module can also realise any or all of a Fodor, computational and intentional module. Any of the other kinds of module might be realised in a neural module. But they needn't. It's at least *a priori* possible that distributed, global characteristics of the brain, rather than modular ones, realise computational or intentional modules.[4]

I think that, for present purposes, one might as well group distributed connectionist networks together with neural modules. The two could be distinguished. But they share the important properties of being able to realise the other types of module and of being able to stand alone, explaining a competence without realising another type of module.

2.2   Diachronic modularity

I move on, now, to the diachronic notion of modularity. This originates with Chomsky. Chomsky compares the development of the language faculty during an individual's maturation to the growth of an organ or limb. The idea is that there is a genetically determined pattern of growth. The language faculty develops – grows within an individual – along a definite and predetermined path. Like an organ, the faculty will only grow, or only grow normally, in an appropriate environment. If one's limbs and organs are to grow, or grow normally, one needs food, air, room to move and so on. The language faculty only grows given appropriate linguistic stimulation in an environment free of excessive trauma.

It is true that the mature state of different language faculties differs across individuals: people speak different languages. However, according to Chomsky, it does not vary very much. Different human languages are alike in deep structural respects and differ only in what might be considered peripheral details. Further, language only varies along specific dimensions (for example lexical items and word order). And the variation is confined within strict and definite limits. For each dimension of variation, there is a limited number of options available. To some extent, this is even true of the choice of lexical items.

Collecting these last two points: variation is parameterised. There is a specific parameter, one for each dimension of variation, and the number of settings a parameter may take is limited. Finally, the way the parameters get set according to experience is determined by species specific genes. Put two individuals in the same environment, however much they differ in other psychological respects, their language faculties will end up much the same.

Acquisition of language is task-specific. Children don't acquire language using general learning processes that can apply in various domains. Rather, the language faculty deploys very specific principles, suited only for learning language. In fact, this follows directly from the parameter approach. Parameters are options specifically for the alteration of Universal Grammar (UG). UG is a sort of language schema: it is what you get when you remove certain specifics from actual languages. Setting the parameters just specifies what UG leaves unspecified. Obviously, setting parameters of UG is not a process that would work in any other domain.

This is the modular conception of development. One can think of the module, as Chomsky sometimes does, in terms of a box that takes experience as input and produces knowledge of linguistic rules as output. The box is a diachronic intentional module. It has intentional contents (innate knowledge of language), and a set of language specific principles that restrict and determine the possible paths of development. And, importantly, the module has been genetically determined in its specifics. Just as we have specific genetic characteristics that determine that we grow hair and not horns, so we have specific genetic characteristics which ensure that we grow a language faculty.

There are, presumably, diachronic analogues of the computational and neural modules. But matters are complicated enough as it is, so I won't go into those.

3   The psychology faculty

I am going to assume a 'theory-theory' of the psychology faculty. Since the theory has been well articulated and well defended elsewhere (e.g. Josef Perner, 1991a; Henry Wellman, 1990) I will not discuss those issues here. Suffice it to say that psychological competence consists in knowledge of a psychological theory which deploys concepts like perception, desire, and belief within a network of causal-explanatory generalisations.[5]

3.1   Synchronic modularity

The psychology faculty certainly appears to be an intentional module. The faculty has a definite and self-contained body of knowledge that is framed in terms of a specific network of interrelated (and indeed, highly sophisticated and logically intriguing) concepts. Further, it appears to exhibit a degree of informational encapsulation. Watching a good actor can generate a sort of theory-of-mind illusion: even though one knows that he is not really in pain, or in love, or trying hard to solve a problem, it still seems to one that he is. It appears, then, that relevant information about the actor's real psychological states fails to influence the workings of the psychology faculty.[6]

Is the psychology faculty a computational module? Many of the theorists in the area offer purely intentional accounts of the faculty, with no explicit commitment to a computational theory: see for example, Perner (1991a), Wellman (1990), Gopnik and Wellman (1992), Meltzoff and Gopnik (1993). On the other hand, the accounts provided by Leslie (see e.g. Leslie and Roth, 1993; Leslie, 1994a) and Baron-Cohen (see e.g. Baron-Cohen and Ring, 1994a; Baron-Cohen, 1994) are at least proto-computational.

There is little direct evidence that bears on the question. Since we do not yet have any worked out computational theory of the psychology faculty, there are no specific tests that can be carried out to confirm or refute such a theory. However, there is a rather general argument that can be applied to this particular case. Fodor has argued that any systematic competence is almost certainly computational. I believe that when the argument is articulated with care and in depth, it is very powerful. It would take considerable space to spell it out properly. For that reason, and because it has been expressed in other places, (e.g. Fodor, 1975, 1987) and is reasonably well known, I will just provide a very quick sketch.

One paradigmatic group of systematic competences are those involving propositional attitudes themselves: competencies to form beliefs on the basis of evidence, to reason through practical syllogisms and so on. Such competencies have an open-ended character. There are infinitely many beliefs we might form, given only enough time, patience, memory and so on. The most attractive explanation of the open-ended character of the competences is that they are explained by possession of a finite stock of concepts that can be put together in a finite number of structures. Thus the concepts of lions, crocodiles and chasing can form the thought that lions chase crocodiles, by combining the two nominal concepts with the binary predicative one. Combining the same concepts in the same general structure but a different order gives one the thought that crocodiles chase lions. This thought can then be entertained, believed, doubted, desired-true, etc.

Given this general hypothesis, we can provide a powerful and elegant explanation of the open-ended nature of the competence. Any failures to form thoughts that are potentially determined by the competence are then explained by performance limitations: limited memory space and so on. Further, the hypothesis explains the systematic patterns we find among our thoughts: anyone who can think that lions chase crocodiles can also think that crocodiles chase lions. Why is this? Because once you have the concepts and can combine nominals with binary predicates, you can have both thoughts. Thus, what explains your capacity to have one thought, automatically explains your capacity to have the other.

Suppose, then, that each thought is made of isolable concepts that can recombine in different configurations. This already makes thought look rather like language: concepts are like words, thoughts are like sentences, modes of combining concepts into thoughts are like linguistic semantic structures. But now note that the actual production of thoughts is itself highly systematic: if you believe that p and you believe that if p then q, you will very likely be caused to believe q. If you desire q, and you believe that doing A is the best way to bring about q, and you believe you have no reason not to do A, then you will probably decide to do A. It looks, to put it simply, that the transitions among occurrent thoughts are rule-governed.

Computers come into the story when we ask how a physical system, such as a brain, could realise a systematic competence. To cut a long story short: if the concepts were syntactic objects, physically realised in the brain, then the brain could realise the competence. Moreover, as it seems, this is the only currently available precise and detailed theory that bears the explanatory burden. We know exactly what it means to say that a competence is realised by a computational system, and we can see exactly how the hypothesis explains the competence. No other theory or model has yet achieved this status. Obviously that doesn't mean the hypothesis is true. But it does mean that it is a good idea to pursue it in optimistic spirits until it is shown to be wrong, or until an alternative supplants it.

It is now obvious why one might think that the psychology faculty is a computational module. For our psychological competence is systematic in just the required sense. For each thought one can have, one can think that someone else believes, or doubts or entertains it. Hence it is open-ended. And the faculty's capacity to represent attitudes exhibits patterns, also mimicking those exhibited by the attitudes themselves. Finally, thoughts about desires, beliefs and so on, follow one another in systematic and apparently rule-governed ways: if you believe that Dee-Dee believes p, and that she believes that if p then q, then you will probably believe that Dee-Dee probably believes that q. All of this follows more or less directly from the theory-theory.

Is the psychology module also a Fodor module? At present it seems to fit the criteria reasonably well, but not entirely. It does appear to be domain specific, informationally encapsulated, to fire obligatorily, to be reasonably fast and to have a characteristic ontogeny (of which more below). It is not yet clear whether it has dedicated neural architecture (but see below). It's also not clear whether any of its contents are inaccessible to consciousness. On the whole, they seem to be accessible; but maybe there's more there than we know about. Further, the faculty's outputs are definitely deep, rather than shallow. But it may be that this last is not really an essential feature of Fodor modularity. Finally, it's also not clear whether it exhibits a characteristic pattern of breakdown. Autistic people are certainly impaired in their capacity to psychologise. But they seem to lack the faculty altogether, and so wouldn't provide evidence of characteristic breakdowns within it. See Baron-Cohen (1994) for further discussion.

Is the psychology faculty a neural module? At this stage the evidence is inconclusive. Baron-Cohen and Ring (1994a) cite some evidence, both from deficits and from SPECT scans, that the Orbito-Frontal Cortex is implicated in theory-of-mind tasks. This doesn't yet show neural modularity. However, the evidence is at least suggestive, and begins to point in that direction. Lacking any general arguments either for or against an expectation of neural modularity, we must await further developments before drawing a conclusion.

3.2   Diachronic modularity

Gopnik and Wellman (1994) present a carefully formulated version of the theory-theory, and argue that it is incompatible with the modularity of the psychology faculty.[7] They argue further that their version of the theory-theory provides the empirically more accurate account of the two.

Gopnik and Wellman operate with a single and very general notion of modularity. They mention Fodor, Chomsky and Leslie in one sentence. This runs together Fodor modules with diachronic and synchronic intentional modules (Chomsky) and computational modules (Leslie). However, they focus mainly on development, and their arguments bear directly on the issue of diachronic modularity. The arguments are subtle and stimulating, and deserve discussion.

The developmental aspect of their view holds that theory of mind is developed by a general theory-forming capacity, much like that deployed by adult scientists. They provide the following account of a fairly typical series of stages in theory change in science, and argue that it is mirrored in the child's developing theory of mind: (a) The theorist holds an initial theory which is confronted by counterevidence. When first presented with the counterevidence, the theorist may ignore it, treat it as noise. (b) Often the next stage is to bring in new theoretical apparatus, but use it only in auxiliary hypotheses, allowing the retention of the guts of the original theory. (c) The third stage is to use the new theoretical apparatus in other parts of the theory, but only apply it in limited contexts, still keeping the original theory on centre stage. (d) Finally the new apparatus becomes central, and a new theory is organised around it.

According to Gopnik and Wellman, the process of developing a theory of mind between the ages of two and five years follows that pattern. Very briefly: two-year-olds appear to use two basic mentalistic concepts, which are proto-concepts of perception and desire. These differ from the adult analogues in that they are not really representational. Desires are drives towards objects. Perceptions are rather simple causal relations between objects and persons. Crucially, two-year-olds don't have the idea of mis-perception: one cannot see an object yet be mistaken about some of its visual properties. At around three, an early concept of belief appears. But this also is non-representational: it is as if what one believes is just a copy of a real state of the world. The 'false-belief' tests pioneered by Wimmer and Perner show that three-year-olds typically cannot grasp the idea that one has a mistaken belief about an object. If one believes anything about it, then what one believes is true. By four or five, children have the adult conception of beliefs and other representational states and attitudes.

The development of a theory of mind exhibits the typical pattern of theoretical change. (a) Denial: three-year-olds do sometimes deny counterevidence: if a cup is blue and an adult says 'I think it is white', three-year-olds tend to insist that the adult thinks it is blue. (b) New theoretical concepts appear first in auxiliary hypotheses: three-year-olds do begin to show understanding of genuinely representational states. But this understanding first shows up only in relation to desires and perception, and doesn't extend to other core concepts of their theory. (c) New concepts used only in limited contexts: it appears that three-year-olds can come up with explanations in terms of false beliefs – hence a representational concept of belief – when there is enough pressure. If confronted with someone who has clearly acted in a way that fails to satisfy their desires, the children do sometimes explain this by false beliefs. However, they still tend to fail the standard false-belief tests, and don't seem to use the representational concept of belief in normal circumstances.

In fact it is not easy to see why there should be any conflict between the developmental theory-theory and diachronic modularity. The diachronic modularity thesis construes maturation of the psychology faculty as a process of setting parameters. Given certain stimulations from the environment, there automatically results an intentionally characterisable change in the faculty. Consider, for example, the much discussed change that typically occurs between the ages of three and four. At three children typically fail false belief tests, at four they pass them. Let us suppose, as Gopnik and Wellman do, that this change involves a genuine case of conceptual development.[8] They acquire a new concept, one that they lacked before. For convenience I'll adopt Perner's terminology. Thus the three-year-old begins with a concept of 'prelief' and ends up with a concept of belief.

According to the diachronic modularity theory, what has occurred is that there is, as it were, a switch in the diachronic module. The switch is labelled 'prelief-belief', and it moves from one setting to the other. This move may be caused by mostly exogenous factors. Or it may be caused more endogenously, by an internal clock or some such. One point of the switch metaphor (or the term 'parameter') is just to register the idea that there are a very limited number of conceptual changes that can occur at any moment in the developmental process.

The reason why it looks hard to find any incompatibility between these two accounts is that the latter could easily be seen as a model of the former.

The idea would be that the maturation of the psychology faculty is a cognitive process, rather like developing a theory on the basis of evidence. And, further, developing this theory is a matter of the setting of parameters in a diachronic module. Indeed one might even have much the same views about the development of scientific theories. Thus the process of conceptual change described by the developmental theory-theory, the move from a prelief theory to a belief theory, just is the setting of a parameter in the diachronic module.

But there is a genuine conflict. It concerns the specificity of the acquisition process. On the developmental theory-theory the processes involved in acquiring a theory of mind are general, the same ones that apply in other domains. On the diachronic modularity theory, the processes are specific to theory of mind and owed to a genetic programme that severely constrains the pattern and endpoint of development.

I think that the diachronic modularity view has a strong lead over the developmental theory-theory. There are at least four reasons for this.

First: as Leslie and Roth (1993) point out, the developmental theory-theory sees the child not just as a theorist, but as a quite brilliant theorist. The concepts of propositional attitudes are highly sophisticated and logically complex (as philosophers of psychology and language are painfully aware). And the theory is brilliant in its simplicity, explanatory power and breadth of application. In fact it is so good that its essential explanatory framework of states with causal powers mirrored by representational properties is retained in cognitive psychology. Children are good at developing theories in some other particular areas: e.g. some aspects of folk physics and folk biology. But they don't appear to be brilliant theorists across the board. For example, it takes them longer to come to grips with the intuitively rather simple concepts of preservation of magnitude and density than with the representational concept of belief. This suggests that specific areas of children's theory development, including psychology, involve special processes rather than general ones.

The point is not conclusive since there may be further factors that determine the rate of development. In particular there may be more pressure on children to learn about psychology than about preservation or density, in part because it's more important to them, in part because of the influence of adults. Nevertheless, it does seem to me that representational concepts of propositional attitudes are so sophisticated that unless children were pre-programmed to come up with them, it is hard to believe that they would do so within roughly their first four years.

Second: the pattern and end point of development do seem to be remarkably similar across individuals. As Gopnik and Wellman concede, the few cross-cultural studies that have been done suggest that the pattern is identical across the species. They respond to this by suggesting that if adults converge on the same theory in different cultures, then we would not expect much cross-cultural variation in children. But this is not a good response. First, we might ask how the adults happened to converge. The obvious answer is that they converged as children. And that brings us back to modularity. Secondly, it is not clear how large a role adults can play on Gopnik and Wellman's own theory. Their emphasis is precisely on the idea that children alter their earlier theories in the face of their inadequacies and failures. Adults would seem to be rather incidental to such a process.

If Gopnik and Wellman are to accord a greater role to adults as teachers, then they need to show how this role is to fit with their emphasis on the resemblance of the ontogeny of the psychology faculty to theory change in science. When people are taught theories, the pattern of change does not typically match that of development in science: there is no rejection of counterevidence, appearance of the new concept in auxiliary hypotheses and so on. Indeed, acquisition by teaching appears to be a possibility alternative to both modularity and Gopnik and Wellman's developmental theory-theory (see Astington, this volume).

Further, there does seem to be enough evidence from the many studies that have been done in the West, to show that development of a theory of mind has special characteristics that differentiate it from normal theorising. What is so striking is the similarity of development, after the starting point, across children. Most of them do come up with the same theory at roughly the same time. Moreover, at least as far as one can tell from anecdotal evidence, history, and literature, it appears that every normal human being from every culture, apart from very small children and genetically defective individuals, deploys some sort of belief-desire psychology.

By contrast, it is surely not the case that if one collected a few million scientists who started out with the same initial theory, then gave them the same counterevidence, that nearly all of them would arrive at the same revised theory – within roughly the same time span. And this is particularly so if they differ in general intelligence, in learning ability, in psychological well being and so on, the way children do. Indeed, we already know that psychologists disagree over the truth of the core aspects of belief-desire psychology. These points strongly suggests that acquiring a theory of mind involves a special acquisition process rather than a general one.[9]

Third: there is an important disanalogy between theory change in science and development of theory of mind in children. One of the processes driving theory change in science is explicit meta-theoretical reflection. Presumably, when a scientist is confronted by counterevidence, she begins to worry that her theory is false, and this causes her to look for alternatives. But very young infants do not appear to have the conceptual sophistication to formulate this worry: it is unlikely that they are aware that they hold a theory, that it is confronted by counterevidence and that it is therefore probably false. So it seems that at least one of the processes responsible for theory change in science does not play a role in acquisition of a theory of mind.[10]

The fourth, and most compelling reason to favour modularity is Williams Syndrome. This is a rare genetic disorder resulting in certain characteristic facial features and physical problems as well as a unique and particularly striking cognitive profile. Subjects are retarded, with an average IQ of around 50. They are also particularly impaired with respect to arithmetical and visual-spatial abilities. However they exhibit an unusually high level of linguistic ability, with a particular penchant for sophisticated and unusual vocabulary items. And, crucial to the present issue, they have often been noted for their relatively high degree of social skills.

A recent study conducted by Helen Tager-Flusberg, Kate Sullivan and Deborah Zaitchik presented a group of Williams Syndrome children (aged 4;4 to 11;2) with standard false-belief tests, as well as a series of simplified versions of the tests and a task that 'tapped children's ability to use mental states to *explain* action.'[11] They found that with the exception of the two youngest children, who lacked the linguistic ability or attention span to handle the tests, all the subjects passed the tests. These results indicate that children with Williams Syndrome have an intact psychology faculty.

By contrast, children with Williams Syndrome seem to suffer general impairments when it comes to the acquisition of theoretical, explanatory knowledge. Although this has not been researched in detail, as far as I know, at least one series of tests confirms the picture. Susan Carey, Susan Johnson and Karen Levine offer the hypothesis that there are at least two kinds of learning processes: 'enrichment processes' which are capable of 'accumulating and correlating information in something possibly like an associative network of knowledge', and 'conceptual change processes ... which actively reorganise knowledge and produce genuinely new conceptual structures'. They assembled tasks designed to diagnose the presence of each of the two kinds of process in the field of naive biology. They found that children with Williams Syndrome matched children of equivalent mental age on the tasks requiring only enrichment processes, but performed significantly worse on those requiring conceptual change processes.

If children with Williams Syndrome are able to acquire theories of mind but are severely impaired with respect to acquiring theories in all or most other areas (barring language), then it certainly appears that the acquisition processes involved in theory of mind are specialised in the way required by the modular conception of development. It is difficult to see how the developmental theory-theory could account for such a phenomenon.

There is a fifth consideration to prefer the modularity theory to Gopnik and Wellman's. This is not a consideration that favours the truth of the former, but rather its explanatory power. (Unfortunately, explanatory power doesn't argue for truth: they are just different virtues.) Gopnik and Wellman say this: 'the developmental data chart a succession of conceptions of mind each logically related to earlier conceptions'. This makes it look as though the revision of the theory, say, the move from prelief to belief, has the nature of an inductive or deductive rational process. If that were so, then it would indeed be easy to see the theoretical change as an instance of a general cognitive process that occurs in many other domains. But conceptual development is not like that: no deduction or induction can give one new concepts for old. The process of coming up with new concepts, whether in science or in maturation, is not a logical process. That is why it so hard to understand.

When a three-year-old is confronted by counterevidence to their current theory, and for the first time deploys a concept of a genuinely representational attitude (perception or desire), something very special has happened. They don't just use some kind of logic to reason through the problem. Rather, a new concept makes its first appearance. How does this happen? Why is it that concept that appears, rather than another, or no new concept at all? The developmental theory-theory does not really help answer these questions.

The modular approach does not fully answer them either. But it does give us a way of looking at them. The concept just grows under those circumstances. And the reason it does is that it is built into our genes. Specifically, just as we are specifically determined to grow hair but not horns. The modularity theory thus reduces conceptual development in childhood to a kind of process that is reasonably well understood in general terms, and applies across a very wide range of phenomena. The developmental theory-theory doesn't achieve anything parallel. One might say that there's no great mystery left on the modularity theory, while there is on the theory-theory.

Gopnik and Wellman point to two aspects of development of a theory of mind that seem hard to account for in terms of modularity. First, they point out that the early theory tends to produce false representations. I take it that they mean that the early non-representational concepts of attitudes are inaccurate, and feature in false claims about psychology. They argue: '[E]rroneous (as opposed to incomplete) representations, which are later modified and restructured, are ... difficult to explain on a purely modular account. Evolution might of course select for erroneous representation, the representation just has to be good enough to survive. But if the representational system is good enough, why, on a modularity account, would it be replaced in later development?'

The second aspect is the resemblance of the development of a theory of mind to typical cases of theory change:

It is, of course, logically possible that a maturational sequence of successive modules might just by accident parallel a theory-formation process, and that the triggering inputs just happen to bear the same relation to the privileged representations that evidence bears to theory. Such a view, however, seems unmotivated. It is easy to see how evolution might have selected for an (approximately) correct innately determined representation of the world. It is much more difficult to see how evolution would have selected for a series of representational systems, each maturing separately only to be replaced by another.

The modularist can meet these points. It is not implausible to suppose that the early theories of mind – the two-year-old's, three-year-old's and so on – are hangovers from phylogenetically prior stages. If this is right, then each new stage can be viewed as a case of what in systematics is called 'terminal addition'. A terminal addition occurs when the ontogenetic sequence of a descendant adds a final stage to the ontogenetic sequence of the ancestor (see Stephen Jay Gould, 1977, see also Povinelli, this volume, for related discussion). The false representations of, say, the three-year-old are a product of a relatively primitive system that was present in the species some while ago. The system was, indeed, good enough for survival. However, the new system, the one that humans now have, and that comes on-line at about four years of age, is a better one, and it was added on as a terminal stage of growth in the ontogenetic sequence.

Further, it is not implausible that the neural hardware underlying the earlier theories is a necessary developmental precursor of that underlying the later ones. Dendrites and axons are conditioned to grow in certain ways, given certain behavioural successes and failures. These behavioural successes and failures can only come about given the existence of an early theory that leads to them. There is no special reason not to suppose that the particular pattern of growth in these particular conditions is determined by specific genes. Ontogeny often doesn't recapitulate phylogeny. But we shouldn't be amazed if sometimes it does.

Of course the suggestion that the psychology faculty evolved by terminal addition is pure speculation. But at this stage that is all that anyone can provide. And that is all that is required to meet Gopnik and Wellman's challenge.

In conclusion, then, it does seem that as matters stand the diachronic modular theory has a significant lead over the developmental theory-theory.

ACKNOWLEDGEMENTS

Many thanks for comments and discussion to Simon Baron-Cohen, Ned Block, Sue Carey, Peter Carruthers, Noam Chomsky, Jerry Fodor, Alison Gopnik, Alan Leslie, David Papineau, Terry Parsons, Barry C. Smith, Peter K. Smith, Denis Walsh, members of the London Family, and of the Theories of Theories of Mind work-shop, and audiences at the philosophy departments of Amherst College, The University of Massachusetts at Amherst, The University of Madison-Wisconsin and Rutgers University.

NOTES

1 The notion of intentional modules is akin to James Higginbotham's (1987) notion of 'modules of understanding'.

2 The above should be considered only a very quick first sketch of intentional modularity. If one or more genuine psychological natural kinds fall under the concept then a lot of work remains to be done articulating it.

3 Unlike intentional modularity, computational modularity has already been well articulated by philosophers and cognitive scientists. See e.g. Haugeland, 1978 and 1982. Note that he commits himself to an account of intentionality that goes beyond anything I say here.

4 Technically, I should at this point revise my initial characterisation of modularity. I said that a module is a component of the mind, or brain . . . that explains a competence. Since explanation isn't transitive, a functional component of the brain that realises say, a computational module that explains a competence, might not itself explain a competence. I leave it to the reader to adjust the characterisation so that it covers such components of the brain. Thanks to Scott Sturgeon for the point.

5 In fact much of what I shall say is equally applicable to at least some versions of the simulation theory.

6 Baron-Cohen (1994) suggests that the psychology faculty is not informationally encapsulated. But I think his reason isn't adequate. See my comments in the same journal.

7 See also Gopnik and Wellman (1992) and Meltzoff and Gopnik (1993) for more on the same theme.

8 This is not a small concession. Leslie (1994a), argues that three-year-olds have the adult conception of belief, but they can't deploy it properly. If this is right, then the analogy with conceptual change in science is undermined.

9 Autism appears to be a genetic defect that results in a fairly specific theory of mind deficit. It might seem as though it therefore provides good evidence for modularity. But it doesn't really. Gopnik and Wellman allow that the child is born with an innate theory which is the starting point for subsequent development. Autism may be explained by lack of this initial theory, rather than lack of a module. See Meltzoff and Gopnik (1993) for a suggestion along roughly these lines.

10 I am indebted to Peter Carruthers for this point.

11 The work cited here and in the following paragraph was presented at the sixth international conference of the Williams Syndrome Association, at the University of California, San Diego, July 1994. The quotations are from Building Bridges Across Disciplines: Cognition to Gene, program and abstracts from that conference.

10   The relationship between SAM and ToMM: two hypotheses

Simon Baron-Cohen and John Swettenham

1   Introduction

One of the most important achievements of modern developmental psychology has been to draw attention to the universal and astonishing capacity of young children to mind-read: it appears incontrovertible that by four years of age, children interpret behaviour in terms of agents' mental states (Wellman, 1990; Astington *et al.*, 1988). In John Morton's (1989) chilling phrase, they *mentalise*: they convert the behaviour they see others perform, or that they perform themselves, into actions driven by beliefs, desires, intentions, hopes, knowledge, imagination, pretence, deceit, and so on. Behaviour is instantly, even automatically, interpreted in terms of what the agent might be thinking, or planning, or wanting. What makes this developmental achievement of such interest is that it raises a learnability problem: how on earth can young children master such abstract concepts as belief (and false belief) with such ease, and at roughly the same time the world over? After all, mental states are unobservable, and have complex logical properties, as Leslie (1987), following Frege (1892) points out. If anything, we should have expected that mental state concepts should be bafflingly difficult to acquire, and yet even the most unremarkable child seems to understand them – without any explicit teaching. Reading minds seems to come naturally, whilst reading words seems to require a considerable amount of instruction.

Chomsky's (1965) solution to a similar learnability problem in relation to the acquisition of syntax was to postulate an innate mechanism or set of mechanisms dedicated to syntactic development; and as Pinker (1994) points out, children with specific language impairment, which can be of genetic origin (Bishop *et al.*, in press), may be the tragic but important evidence that such mechanisms not only exist but can be selectively damaged. In a similar vein, Leslie's (1991) solution to the question of how mind-reading is universally acquired was to postulate an innate mechanism, called ToMM (or the Theory of Mind Mechanism). This proposal gains considerable credibility from the evidence that children with autism have selective impairments in the acquisition of mental state concepts, and in mind-reading (Baron-Cohen *et al.*, 1985; see Baron-Cohen *et al.*, 1993). They are in a real sense *mind-blind* (Baron-Cohen, 1990, 1995a). Given the innate basis of autism (Folstein and Rutter, 1988), one strong possibility is that genetic mechanisms normally enable neural structures or processes for mind-reading, and that in autism genetic abnormalities delay or prevent the development of such neurocognitive mechanisms. This genetic hypothesis is made more plausible by the evident adaptive value of mind-reading. Essentially, mind-reading allows flexible social interaction (based on shared plans), flexible communication (based on inferring a speaker's intentions, and sharing information that another individual might lack) and machiavellian deception (based on manipulating other's thoughts). As such, it is likely that mind-reading is a product of natural selection (Whiten, 1991).

In this chapter, we discuss ToMM in relation to an earlier developing mechanism: SAM, or the Shared Attention Mechanism. SAM is introduced in order to account for the developmental origins of ToMM. In particular, we examine the claim that SAM is a *necessary precursor* to ToMM. In doing so, we draw on two sorts of evidence: results from experimental investigations of autism, and results of a longitudinal study of infant behaviour predicting autism. Along the way, and following Gómez (1991), we unpack the precursor claim into two alternative hypotheses. But first we must introduce SAM.

2   SAM

SAM, or the Shared Attention Mechanism, is a special purpose neurocognitive mechanism, the function of which is to identify if you and another organism are both attending to the same object or event. SAM was first postulated by Baron-Cohen (1994),[1] as one component mechanism in the developing Mind-reading System in human beings. It is necessary to postulate a mechanism of this sort in order to explain how the infant transcends a purely solipsistic view of the world. SAM is quite a complicated but fundamental mechanism: it involves representing not only what another person sees (or wants), and not only what the self sees (or wants), but whether the self and the another person see (or want) *the very same thing*. We begin by briefly reviewing SAM's key features.

SAM develops in the normal human being at around 9–14 months of age. It builds 'triadic representations' which explicitly specify if you and another agent are attending to the same thing.[2] Triadic representations allow joint attention behaviours such as 'gaze monitoring' (when the child turns to look at the same object or event that another person is looking at

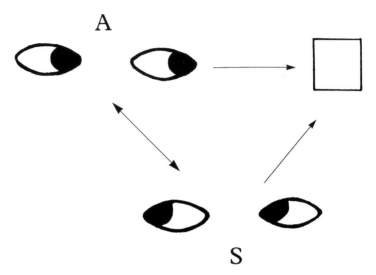

Figure 10.1 A triadic representation, expressed in pictorial format
(reproduced from Baron-Cohen 1994, with permission)

– Scaife and Bruner, 1975; Butterworth, 1991); and 'protodeclarative pointing' (when the child uses a gesture (typically the outstretched index finger)
to direct someone to attend to an object or event of interest, for its own sake
– Bates *et al.*, 1979).[3] Triadic representations have the following form,
expressed in a 'sentence'-like format: *[Agent/Self-Relation-(Agent/Self-
Relation-'Proposition')]*. For example, *[I-see-(Mummy-sees-'the cup is on
the table')]*.[4] An example of a triadic representation employed when the
infant produces the protodeclarative pointing gesture is *[Mummy-sees-(I-
see-'the cup is on the table')]*. Triadic representations, thus defined, are
pretty complex, but then so is shared attention itself.

The examples above relate only to shared *visual* attention. However,
SAM is amodal, meaning that it can build its triadic representations in any
modality (visual, auditory, tactile). An example of a triadic representation
built in the tactile modality would be *[I-touch-(Mummy-touching-'the cup
on the table')]*. In practice, since building triadic representations in the
visual modality is so much easier, and allows such a large number of potential objects or events to be shared in attention, SAM has a priority to be
used in the visual modality.

In 'pictorial' form, triadic representations (in the visual modality) resemble figure 10.1. The arrows in figure 10.1 represent the relation term, and
the two pairs of eyes represent the two agents (Self and another Agent).
Note that the relation terms between Agents are in principle bi-directional

(hence the use of the double-headed arrow), whereas the relation term between an agent and an object is unidirectional. This specifies that only agents (but not inanimate objects) are capable of having a perceptual relation with something else.

The notion is that SAM constructs triadic representations out of simpler, 'dyadic' representations. Dyadic representations have the form *[Agent-Relation-'Proposition']*, for example *[Mummy-sees-'the cup is on the table']*. Dyadic representations are built by other, more primitive mechanisms. (These are not discussed here, but see Baron-Cohen, 1994, or 1995a.) These allow the infant to represent perceptual and volitional states, for example *[Mummy-wants-'the cup on the table']*. SAM thus not only builds triadic representations using perception terms, but also using desire/goal terms. As such, it equips the child with an 'attention-goal' psychology (Baron-Cohen, 1993). This also allows the child to read gaze direction in terms of volition (Baron-Cohen *et al.*, in press). Note that the mental state concepts that SAM processes are not *fully* intentional. For example, when the normal toddler of eighteen months represents that s/he and another person are *looking* at the same object, they do not at the same time represent their own and the other's *knowledge* states.[5] Nevertheless, this enables the child to build a simple, limited, but usable theory of mind.

SAM's development appears to be universal/independent of culture: children the world over show gaze-monitoring and protodeclarative pointing (Bruner, 1983). This implies that its development is partly, if not completely, driven by individual, biological factors within the child. Finally, SAM is held to be necessary (though not sufficient) for the development of the normal child's mature theory of mind. To expand this last point, we need to review the mechanism thought to be responsible for this.

3   ToMM

Normal children show a remarkable ability to understand a range of mental states, and to use such mental state concepts in making sense of and predicting action (Wellman, 1990). For example, at two years old they clearly understand pretending (Leslie, 1987; Harris, this volume) and desire (Wellman, 1990); at three years old they clearly understand that people have thoughts and know things (Pratt and Bryant, 1990; Wellman and Estes, 1986); and at four years old they clearly understand that people can have different (and even false) beliefs about the same state of affairs (Wimmer and Perner, 1983). As mentioned earlier, Leslie (1987, 1994a) suggests that a special purpose neurocognitive mechanism is responsible for the normal child's rapid, fluent acquisition of this mental state knowledge. This is

ToMM, or the Theory of Mind Mechanism. Here we briefly review ToMM's key features.

ToMM develops in the normal child around 18–24 months. Its earliest manifestation is in the production of pretend play, which Leslie (1987) argues involves the child representing its own or someone else's attitude or 'informational relation' (pretending) to a proposition.[6] To achieve this, ToMM employs 'M-Representations' which explicitly specify an agent's informational relation towards a proposition.[7] For example, suppose we hear John say 'I have a nice new hat.' We need to compute his meaning. Was he being truthful, or was he intending to deceive? Might he have only intended it as a joke? Was he being sarcastic? Or was he just pretending? Maybe he was meaning none of these things: maybe he was simply suffering from a mistaken belief. M-Representations allow us to represent what we, as a listener or observer, think John's attitude towards the utterance was.

According to Leslie, M-Representations have the following form, expressed in a 'sentence'-like format: *[Agent-Attitude-'Proposition']*. For example, *[John-pretends-'I have a nice new hat']*. (He might be putting a book on his head as he utters this.) The attitude slot in M-Representations can be filled by any intentional term (think, know, believe, intend, hope, warn, promise, wish, dream, wonder, imagine, etc.).[8] ToMM's M-Representations allow for a special logical property of *fully* intentional terms, namely, their non-substitutability (Frege, 1892). That is, substitution of identical terms in a proposition preceded by a fully intentional mental state term is not guaranteed to preserve the truth-value of the sentence as a whole. For example, if 'A man was killed in Oxford Street today' is true, and the man that was killed was actually John's father, then 'John's father was killed in Oxford Street today' must also be true. However, if 'John knows a man was killed in Oxford Street today' is true, it does not follow that 'John knows his father was killed in Oxford Street today' is also true. That will depend on whether John knows his father was in Oxford Street at the time.[9] (This contrast with SAM's ability to represent mental state terms that are only partly intentional is important.)

ToMM not only builds M-Representations, but also integrates the child's knowledge about the relationship between mental states and action into a mature and usable 'theory', to make sense of and predict another's action. ToMM's development also appears to be universal/independent of culture: children and adults, the world over, interpret behaviour in terms of mental states (Wellman, 1990; Fodor, 1983). This implies that its development is partly, if not completely, driven by individual, biological factors within the child.

4   The relation between SAM and ToMM: two hypotheses

In the section on SAM above, the final claim made was that SAM is necessary for ToMM's development. Elsewhere this relationship has been discussed as a causal relationship (Baron-Cohen, 1994), as SAM being a 'precursor' to ToMM (Baron-Cohen, 1989b), and as SAM 'triggering' ToMM to function (Baron-Cohen and Cross, 1992). In this part of the chapter, we wish to flesh out this idea a bit further.

Historically, one key impetus for the idea that SAM might have anything to do with ToMM was the experimental evidence that children with autism appear to be severely impaired in both domains – joint attention and theory of mind. Thus, regarding joint attention, children with autism do not show spontaneous gaze-monitoring (Leekam *et al.*, 1994) or spontaneous protodeclarative pointing (Baron-Cohen, 1989b) – indeed, the whole range of joint attention behaviours is impaired in autism (Sigman *et al.*, 1986).

Regarding theory of mind, children with autism do not produce much (if any) spontaneous pretend play (Baron-Cohen, 1987), and have inordinate difficulty understanding false belief (Baron-Cohen *et al.*, 1985; Perner *et al.*, 1989). Nor do they easily understand knowledge formation (Baron-Cohen and Goodhart, 1994) or the appearance-reality distinction (Baron-Cohen, 1989c), or show a normal understanding of intentions (Phillips *et al.*, forthcoming). They also produce few mental state terms in their spontaneous speech, relative to both normally developing children and those with a mental handicap (Tager-Flusberg, 1993). Finally, they show poor understanding of deception (Sodian and Frith, 1992; Baron-Cohen, 1992), and many even fail to make the mental-physical distinction (Baron-Cohen, 1989c). This literature is reviewed more fully in Baron-Cohen (1993, 1995a) and discussed critically in the volume edited by Baron-Cohen, Tager-Flusberg, and Cohen (1993).

4.1   The lock and key hypothesis

Since SAM produces triadic representations, it follows that if SAM triggers ToMM in some way, it must be because triadic representations have some special property to enable this. Furthermore, given that ToMM builds M-Representations, it follows that if SAM triggers ToMM, it must be because triadic representations 'activate' M-Representations in some way, since producing triadic representations is all that SAM does. We will refer to this as the 'lock and key hypothesis'.

The lock and key hypothesis suggests that triadic representations are the key, and M-Representations are the lock.[10] To see how this might work we need to examine the different parts of these two types of representation,

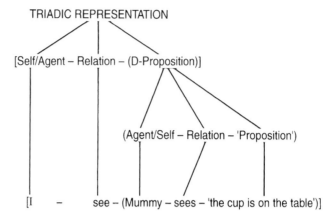

Figure 10.2 Tree structure of a triadic representation

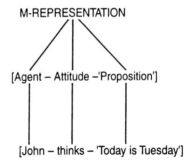

Figure 10.3 Tree structure of an M-representation

and identify in what way they may be 'naturally' compatible. The first thing to note is that triadic representations are like transitive-verb sentences: they have the unusual property of taking as their object an embedded proposition of an agent standing in a perceptual (or volitional) relation to a proposition. This is shown most clearly in a tree-structure analysis (fig 10.2). Here, we have called the special embedded proposition a D-Proposition, to mark that this is a proposition about an agent's *dyadic relation* to an object. It is not just any old proposition. The agent's dyadic relation may be perceptual or volitional. To continue with the tree-structure analysis, an M-Representation has the structure shown in figure 10.3, above.

If triadic representations are to be thought of as inputs to trigger M-

Representations, how might this happen? One possibility is that since both D-propositions (in triadic representations) and M-Representations are tripartite, they might have a special 'fit'. Another possibility is that cases where the triadic representation specifies that you and another agent are *not* attending to the same object/event may serve to distinguish the D-proposition in a triadic representation. For example, consider the triadic representation *[I-see-(Mummy-is not seeing-'the cup is on the table')]* (because I see she is looking in the opposite direction): such cases provide clear evidence that I and another agent can have different perceptual relations towards a state of affairs. D-propositions appear to have a compatible format to act as input for M-Representations (they have the virtually identical tripartite structure); and it may be that when they are within triadic representations they are clearly marked as belonging to one agent and not another, and can thus trigger M-Representations.

4.2   The metamorphosis hypothesis

An alternative to the lock and key hypothesis is that SAM and ToMM are not independent mechanisms; rather, SAM may be a developmentally earlier form of ToMM. We will refer to this as the 'metamorphosis hypothesis'. The metamorphosis hypothesis claims that, with development, SAM's triadic representations simply become more complex. For example, instead of only filling the Relation slot with *partially* intentional terms like *see*, *look*, *attend*, or *want*, the Relation slot can now be filled with *fully* intentional terms like *pretend*, *think*, *know*, *imagine*, and *believe*, etc., On this account, M-Representations are also triadic in structure, but use more complex mental state concepts.[11]

For this hypothesis to be plausible, we suggest that the definition of M-Representations be slightly revised, as follows: *(Self-Attitude-[Agent-Attitude-'Proposition'])*. An example of this would be *(I-think-[John-pretends-'the banana is a telephone'])*. This modified definition of an M-Representation allows the respective attitudes of Self and another Agent to be specified, in a parallel way to that seen in a triadic representation. Furthermore, this modified definition allows for the child to be aware that his or her own attitude might be different to that held by the other Agent.

Of course, saying that SAM's triadic representations have 'developed' into ToMM's M-Representations still begs the question as to how this has happened. Leaving this problem aside here, the key difference to bring out is that this alternative hypothesis suggests that there are not two independent mechanisms, but rather one mechanism changing in scope.

5   Testing between these two alternatives

In the previous section we have addressed the problem of analysing why triadic representations may be the right sort of input for activating M-Representations. To reiterate, the lock and key hypothesis is that SAM and ToMM are *independent* mechanisms which share a special developmental connection. The metamorphosis hypothesis is that SAM is a developmentally less mature form of ToMM. Both hypotheses predict that some children with autism may be impaired in SAM and therefore inevitably in ToMM, whilst late onset cases may have SAM intact but have an intrinsic impairment in ToMM. Yet other subgroups can be envisaged: those who are not impaired in these mechanisms in an all-or-none way, but who are significantly *delayed* in the functioning of one of them. Further research is needed to attempt to identify if such subgroups exist. As far as we can see, the only way of directly testing between these two hypotheses would be to examine cases of acquired damage (later in life) leading to double dissociations. Only the lock and key hypothesis would predict that double dissociations would be possible, and this would be strong evidence of the independence of these two mechanisms.

6   Evidence from early screening for autism

We wish now to switch to new evidence from our screening study of autism in infancy (Baron-Cohen, Cox, Baird, Swettenham, Nightingale, Morgan, Drew, and Charman, 1994). Whilst such evidence cannot test the two earlier hypotheses against each other, such evidence is relevant to the issue of whether SAM is necessary for the development of ToMM. This study is briefly reviewed next.

Between May 1992 and May 1993, 16,000 randomly selected children in the South East of England were screened at 18 months of age by their health visitors, using a specially designed checklist (called the *Checklist for Autism in Toddlers*, or the CHAT)[12]. Children with severe developmental delay were excluded from this population study. The key items in this checklist are protodeclarative pointing, gaze monitoring,[13] and pretend play. These are recorded by the parents and by the health visitor, separately. Protodeclarative pointing and gaze monitoring are of course joint attention behaviours, and thus should require SAM. Pretend play, according to Leslie, is an early manifestation of ToMM.

Of the 16,000 children screened, just twelve children failed all three items, on two administrations of the CHAT. Of these twelve cases, ten (or 83.3%) received a diagnosis of autism, using standardised diagnostic measures and established criteria. This is clear evidence that in autism there are severe impairments in SAM and ToMM, even by 18 months of age. Furthermore, it suggests that these are important indicators in the early diagnosis of autism. Of relevance to the precursor issue, there were no cases, in all the 16,000 children, of children who failed both of the joint attention items but who unambiguously passed pretend play. We take this as clear evidence that if SAM is impaired, then ToMM will inevitably be too.

From the population, we picked out for detailed study a comparison group of 22 children who were not producing protodeclarative pointing at 18 months, but who did show gaze-monitoring, implying that they did not lack joint-attention completely. We can therefore think of these cases as being delayed in aspects of joint attention, but not being severely impaired in SAM. From other work, we can predict that such children will be at risk not for autism but for forms of developmental delay (Tomasello, 1988). In our study, 15 of these 22 cases received a diagnosis of developmental delay, and none of these 22 children received a diagnosis of autism. This implies that if a child is simply slow in developing aspects of joint attention, this may be an indicator of language or general developmental delay. If however a child is severely impaired in SAM, an impairment in ToMM is an inevitable consequence, and this pattern carries a very high risk for autism.

ACKNOWLEDGEMENTS

The screening study reported here was supported by the MRC. We are grateful to Tony Cox, Gillian Baird, Auriol Drew, Kate Morgan, Natasha Nightingale, and Tony Charman – our colleagues on the screening study; and to Gabriel Segal and Peter Carruthers for valuable discussions.

NOTES

1 Its evolutionary history is also discussed by Baron-Cohen (1995a,b), and its neurological basis is discussed by Baron-Cohen and Ring (1994a).
2 The term 'triadic representation' is derived from Bakeman and Adamson's (1984) term 'triadic relation', which exists between two agents and a third object. They distinguish this from 'dyadic relations' which only involves a relation between two agents. Here, the focus is on *representing* these different kinds of social relations.
3 Povinelli and Eddy (1994) argue that simpler forms of gaze-monitoring may be possible without SAM (i.e., without any understanding of what I or you are *seeing*). Protodeclarative pointing, rather than gaze-monitoring, may therefore be the acid test of SAM. In humans, though, it is likely that both depend on SAM.
4 In Baron-Cohen (1994) a triadic representation was defined as [Self-Relation-(Agent-Relation-Object)]. We are grateful to Gabriel Segal for suggesting that

this representation should contain a proposition rather than simply an object, since infants appear to be able to represent propositions (Baillargeon, 1987).

5 Gabriel Segal and Peter Carruthers, our philosopher guides here, suggest the distinction we are groping for is that SAM's mental states can be thought of as *de re*, rather than *de dicto*. We are grateful to them for this suggestion, and return to this point later.

6 Note that others have argued this analysis of pretence is unnecessarily rich – e.g., Harris and Kavanaugh (1993), or Perner (1991a); but see Leslie (1994a) for a rejoinder to this criticism.

7 This is Leslie's term, which replaces his earlier term 'metarepresentations'. This change in terminology arose because of other authors also using the latter term (e.g., Pylyshyn, 1978; Perner, 1991a), but with a different definition. For the terminological wrangles, see Perner (1993) and Leslie and Roth (1993).

8 There remains an important question as to why, in normal development, some intentional terms (such as pretending) are understood before others (e.g., knowing) which in turn appear to be understood before yet others (e.g., believing). We do not address this issue here, but note it as an unresolved problem (see Leslie, 1994a, for one attempt at a resolution; or Harris, this volume, for another).

9 Another way of putting this, following Segal and Carruthers' suggestion, is that M-Representations represent mental state concepts that are *de dicto*, not just *de re*.

10 Lock and key hypotheses are of course widespread in biology: for example, DNA base pairs can only fit together in a specific way; antibodies can only fit on to the surface of specific antigens; certain hormones will trigger one mechanism to function but not another; etc.

11 We retain the terms *relation* within triadic representations, and *attitude* within M-Representations, to mark this distinction between the partially intentional nature of the former, and the fully intentional nature of the latter. However, in normal usage, these terms are obviously not mutually exclusive.

12 See Baron-Cohen, Allen, and Gillberg (1992), where the CHAT is fully described and its use in a genetic high-risk study of autism is reported.

13 In the CHAT, gaze monitoring involves following another person's pointing gesture and change of gaze direction. It could therefore more properly be called gaze-and-point-monitoring.

11　Theories and modules; creation myths, developmental realities, and Neurath's boat

Alison Gopnik

1　Modules and theories

I and others have made a case for the similarities between scientific knowledge and children's knowledge, and between scientific change and cognitive development (Gopnik and Wellman, 1992, 1994; Gopnik, 1988; Carey, 1986, 1988; Keil, 1989; Wellman, 1990). In the rest of this chapter I will call this general view of cognitive development the 'theory-formation theory'.[1]

However, it is important to say that not all knowledge is like science, and not all development is like scientific change. The analogy to science would be of little interest if it were. My claim is that there are quite distinctive and special cognitive processes that are responsible both for scientific progress and for particular kinds of development in children. Other kinds of cognition and cognitive development may be quite different. It is my further claim that theories and theory changes, in particular, are responsible for the changes in children's understanding of the mind. But this is an empirical claim and it only gains explanatory force if we can contrast it with other possible explanations. In previous work, I have outlined the distinctive features of a theory-formation account in some detail, and have contrasted it with the predictions of a simulation theory (Gopnik & Wellman, 1992). In this paper, I will focus instead on the contrast between this account and modularity accounts. These provide one contrast case to the theory-formation view. Moreover, I will suggest that when this contrast is clearly spelled out, the theory-formation view is the more likely candidate as an explanation for the child's developing theory of mind.

One serious alternative to the theory-formation theory is the idea that cognitive structures, including folk psychology, are the consequence of innate modules. According to modularity theories, representations of the world are not constructed from evidence in the course of development. Instead, innate structures create mandatory representations of input. In Fodor's (1983) analysis, for example, modules are not only innate, they are also encapsulated. On Fodor's view representations that are the outcome of modules, unlike those that are the result of more central knowledge and belief processes, cannot be overturned by new patterns of evidence. The encapsulation of modules means that they are indefeasible. Similarly, in Chomsky's theory of syntax acquisition, the initial innate structures mean that only a very limited set of possible grammars will be developed (Chomsky, 1980). They constrain the final form of the grammar in the strong sense that grammars that violate them will never be learned by human beings. On Fodor's view, as in Chomsky's view of syntax, the internal structure of the module cannot be reorganised as a result of input from other systems, though of course outputs from the module can be used by other systems.[2]

The classic examples of modules are supposed to be the specialised representations and rules of the visual or syntactic systems. Such modules map given perceptual inputs (retinal stimulation or strings of sounds) on to more abstract set of representations (2½d sketches or phrase-structures). They mandate certain 'inferences' or outputs and not others. Once the module has matured, certain representations of the input will result. Conversely, other representations simply could not be formulated, no matter how much evidence supported them.

Theory-formation views, like modularity views, propose that there are representations of input and rules that operate on them. On the theory view, however, the very patterns of representation that occur can alter the nature of the representational system itself, they can alter the nature of the relations between inputs and representations. As we get new inputs, and so new representations, the very rules that connect inputs and representations change. Eventually, we may end up with a system with a completely new set of representations and a completely different set of relations between inputs and representations than the system we started out with.

To borrow Neurath's philosophical metaphor, the theory-formation view sees knowledge as a boat that we perpetually rebuild as we sail in it. At each point in our journey there may be only a limited and constrained set of alterations we can make to the boat to keep it seaworthy. In the end, however, we may end up with not a single plank or rivet from the original structure, and the process may go on indefinitely

This kind of system may sound so open-ended as to be uninteresting. But in fact the theory-formation view proposes that representations will change in relatively orderly, predictable, and constrained ways. For example, the representational system may lead to a particular prediction about a new representation. The prediction turns out to be wrong, the new input, and so the new representation, is not what we predicted. Or the system may accumulate regularities, some representations consistently co-occur in ways that are not predicted by the representational system itself. Events like these cause the representational system to change, and do so in particular and predictable ways.

We don't, as yet, have a precise account of how such a system operates in detail, or exactly how such factors as counter-evidence or empirical generalisation play a role in the formation of new theories. (But then no one as yet has a precise account of exactly how a theory of mind module would operate in detail, let alone of how it could have evolved.) Still, there is nothing mystical or incoherent about the idea of a representational system that revises itself in this way. Indeed we have excellent evidence that just such a system exists in human minds already. Precisely this sort of system generates the representations of science. And we know at least something about how that system characteristically proceeds.

Often, the contrast between modularity accounts and theory-formation accounts is phrased in terms of a more general contrast between nativism and empiricism. But this general contrast does not capture the distinction accurately. First, while modules are innate, not all innate structures are modular. I have proposed a distinction between two types of nativism, modularity nativism and 'starting-state' nativism. On the 'starting-state' view the child is innately endowed with a particular set of representations of input and rules operating on those representations. According to the theory-formation theory, however, such initial structures, while innate, would be defeasible; any part of them could be, and indeed will be, altered by new evidence. We might propose that there are innate theories that are later modified and revised. The process of theory change and replacement might begin at birth. In fact, Andrew Meltzoff and I have suggested that there are specific innate conceptions of the mind, or, to be more exact, innate conceptions of persons, that form the basis on which more advanced theories of the mind are later constructed (1993). (For some alternative possibilities about the 'starting state' of theory of mind see, Baron-Cohen (1991c, this volume) and Hobson (1993a)). To continue Neurath's metaphor, innate theories are the boats that push off from the pier. The boat you start out in may have a considerable effect on the boat you end up in, even if no trace of the original remains.

Innate theories might be important in several ways. If children did not have these initial representations we might expect them to develop later theories in radically different ways, if they developed them at all. This may well be the case for children with autism. Moreover, the fact that the child begins with an initial theory-like structure, which is then revised and restructured in response to evidence, might help solve some underdetermination problems. Such problems have plagued accounts of conceptual change, both in cognitive psychology and in the philosophy of science. Certainly, this type of account seems more tractable than one in which theory-like conceptual structures are constructed from scratch from a disorganised flow of experience.

The combination of innate theories and innate theory-formation mechanisms also means that a theory-formation view will be quite different from classical empiricist accounts. The theory-formation view does not imply that representations are simply associations or rearrangements of sensory input. The representations of theories are highly abstract, and removed from the structure of the input itself. Theories, as much as modules, lead to representations that are far removed from immediate sensory experience.

2   Discriminating evidence

What kinds of evidence could differentiate between a modularity theory and the theory-formation theory? Many kinds of evidence that are commonly adduced to support modularity views actually can't discriminate between these views and the theory formation-view. The mere fact that there is some knowledge at birth or in very early infancy is compatible with either an innate initial theory or an innate module. So is the fact that innate neurological conditions such as autism lead to theory of mind deficits.

The fact that similar representations develop in different children at about the same age, also can't discriminate between the two views. The theory-formation theory proposes that there are powerful unconscious cognitive processes that revise already existing cognitive structures in response to evidence. The theory, then, would predict that if cognitive agents began with the same initial theory, tried to solve the same problems, and were presented with similar patterns of evidence they would, precisely, converge on the same theories at about the same time.

These assumptions are very likely to be true for children learning folk psychology. Children will certainly start with the same initial theory and the same theory-formation capacities. Moreover, they are surrounded by creatures with human minds, and these creatures interact extensively with the child; if they did not, the child would be unlikely to survive. Evidence of psychological states is ubiquitous and is also likely to be very similar for all children. Children the world over may develop similar representations at similar times because they are specified innately, or they may converge on the same conceptions because the crucial evidence is universally the same, and so are children's theory-formation capacities.

It might be objected that scientists do not always show this sort of uniform development, and that this weighs against the theory-formation view. Notice, however, that the assumptions of common initial theories and common ubiquitous patterns of evidence are generally not true for scientists. The relevant evidence, far from being ubiquitous, is rare and difficult to come by, and often must be taken on trust from others. Moreover, scientists also often begin with rather different theories, and quite typically approach different problems. Scientists are at a disadvantage in other ways, too. Children, by and large, live among others who hold the theory they will eventually converge upon, while scientists live among others who do not hold that theory. And an enormous amount of scientific time and energy is spent just obtaining the preconditions for cognitive work that children take for granted, protected leisure and an unlimited supply of experimental equipment.

In fact, however, in spite of these cognitive handicaps, scientists, like children, often do converge on a common account of the world. Indeed even the timing of scientific discoveries is often strikingly similar (see all those shared Nobel prizes), given independent labs working on the same problem with a similar initial theory and similar access to evidence. This convergence to the truth itself is the best reason for thinking that some common and general cognitive structures are at work in scientific theory change. Scientists working independently converge on similar accounts, not because evolutionary theory or the calculus or the structure of DNA (to take some famous examples) are innately given, but because similar minds approaching similar problems are presented with similar patterns of evidence. Whatever cognitive processes lead to this convergence in science may also be operating in children.

Evolutionary arguments also fail to support modularity views over theory-formation views. The view that cognition evolved has recently been associated with a particular, strongly modular account of cognition; as if the fact of evolution supported modularity (Barkow *et al.*, 1992). There is, however, no reason to identify the general claim that evolution is responsible for cognitive structure with a modularity view. In fact, the evolutionary arguments for modularity are typically of an extremely weak kind. They are, in fact, the very weakest kind of evolutionary argument, simply that a particular trait might be helpful to an organism in an environment, or, even worse, in a hypothetical past environment for which we have only the scantiest evidence. They are just-so stories. None of the evidence that typically is required to support evolutionary arguments in biology, for example, comparisons of closely related species in different environmental niches, or of distantly related species in similar niches, studies of differential reproduction or survival with or without the trait, or empirical evidence of the heritability of the trait, are ever presented. This is not too surprising, of course. Given the very uniqueness of most human cognitive abilities, this kind of evidence is, by and large, simply not available.

Ironically, moreover, modularity accounts may actually be in conflict with one of the best established findings in real evolutionary comparative psychology, a finding that is supported by such comparative studies. The finding concerns the correlates of relatively large brain size and complex cognition in a wide range of species. Several distinctive traits are found to correlate with large cortices across a wide range of species, including birds and mammals. Moreover, they are also correlated within variants of closely related species. The traits include variety of diet, polygamy, small clutch size, and, most significantly for our case, the relative lack of precocious specialised cognitive abilities in the young, that is a period of long immaturity (see e.g. Bennett and Harvey, 1985). Passing quickly over polygamy, human beings are, of course, at the extreme end of the distribution on all these other traits, and on relative cortical complexity. A serious evolutionary prediction about human beings would certainly not favour the idea that human babies have highly specialised innate cognitive structures, over the idea that they have more multi-purpose learning capacities which they employ in a period of protected immaturity.

Many writers have pointed out that from an evolutionary point of view, three of the most distinctive features of human beings are their long protected immaturity, the plasticity of their behaviour, and their ability to adapt to an extremely wide variety of environments. Equipping human children with particularly powerful and flexible cognitive devices, like theory-formation capacities, makes a great deal of sense as part of this evolutionary picture. We might indeed think of childhood as a period when many of the requirements for survival are suspended, so that children can concentrate on using their theory-formation capacities to acquire a veridical picture of the particular physical and social world in which they find themselves. Once they know where they are, as it were, they can figure out what to do. On this picture, it not so much that children are little scientists as that scientists are big children. Theory-formation capacities are precisely the evolutionary endowment that allows us to formulate theories of mind.

3   Modules and development

If these kinds of evidence cannot discriminate between theories and modules, what kinds of evidence can? The crucial evidence will be developmental. It is the dynamic features of theories, particularly their defeasibility in response to evidence, that allow us to discriminate them from modules.

Modular accounts of the acquisition of representational systems, are, in an important sense, anti-developmental (see for example, Pinker's discussion of 'the continuity assumption'; Pinker, 1984). Apparent changes in representation occurring over time, on these views, can only be accounted for by processes outside the representational system itself. For example, they may reflect the maturation of another module. Thus, in his latest position Leslie (1993) proposes several different modules that successively come on line in children's developing theory of mind. Baron-Cohen (1991c; this volume) proposes a different sequence of modules. Segal makes a similar proposal in this volume. Similarly, in modular linguistic theories it is sometimes proposed that early language, up until about age three or four when complex syntax appears, is not really language at all (Chomsky, 1980). It instead reflects the operation of a quite different representational system that is supplanted by the maturation of a 'real' language-acquisition device at about three.

Alternatively, modularity theories may invoke auxiliary hypotheses about information-processing developments to explain development. On this view, as well, however, development is not the result of endogenous conceptual changes, but rather the result of some external and non-conceptual changes in information-processing abilities. It is really Chomsky's competence vs. performance distinction, and the assumption is that performance rather than competence is what develops. (For a good recent example of this sort of argument applied to children's theory of mind, see Fodor, 1992.)

In some modular systems, of course, there are several alternative branching routes, so to speak, that determine the eventual form the module may take. These are often described as 'parameters' set by the input. 'Parameters' allow for a somewhat richer developmental story than one in which a module is simply turned on or off. The relation between input and the setting of the parameter is still, however, a relation of triggering. In contrast, in a theory-formation theory, by analogy with scientific theories, there should be indefinite scope for genuinely novel theories, not simply a choice of several options.[3]

In contrast, the theory-formation theory is inherently developmental. The picture I outlined above is of a representational system which is perpetually changing, and more significantly is changing because of processes within the system itself. It is a system for representing inputs, that changes precisely as a result of representing inputs. Theories change not because of external maturational or information-processing changes but because of the relations between the theories and evidence.

In fact, there is a simple crucial experiment that could adjudicate between the theory-formation theory and a modularity theory. Unfortunately, like nearly all the crucial experiments in psychology, it is immoral. Put the child in a situation that was the folk psychological equivalent of someone acquiring a Pidgin language. That is arrange for her to be surrounded and cared for by creatures with an equally complex but radically different psychological organisation than our own. Other things equal, the modularity view would predict that she would end up (eventually) with our folk psychology. The theory-formation theory would predict that she would instead end up (eventually) with a view of the mind that was at least approximately true of the creatures around her.

Lacking the crucial experiment there are other developmental data that are nevertheless relevant. First, we can consider the question of the complexity of conceptual change over time, and the relations between one point in conceptual development and another. Two general mechanisms seem particularly important in theory formation and change. One is the consideration of counter-evidence to the original theory. Another is the formulation of new conceptual schemes, often by adapting and revising ideas that are already understood in other contexts. In theory formation there are, quite typically, complex periods of transition between one theory and another that reflect the operation of these mechanisms. During these transitional periods we may see several kinds of behaviour that hint at conceptual change in action. For example, we may find that the theoriser initially develops auxiliary hypotheses that are specially tailored to deal with particular kinds of counter-evidence. Or the theoriser may accept a new theoretical idea in limited contexts that are close to the earlier theory, but resist wholesale revision of the old theory. Or the theoriser may be willing to accept the new theoretical idea when forced to do so by counter-evidence but not use the idea generatively, to make predictions. There is good evidence for all these transitional conceptual stages in the child's developing theory of mind (see Gopnik and Wellman, 1994; Gopnik, Slaughter, and Meltzoff, 1994).

As the number of representational stages increases, the transitional periods between them become increasingly complex, and the conceptual relations between them become increasingly clear, the maturational or information-processing view of development becomes increasingly implausible. Even Leslie would surely balk at proposing an 'Understand false-belief in the context of earlier perception and desire understanding, or when forced to by counter-evidence but not otherwise' module which matures at 3 years 3 months only to be replaced by a new module at 3 years 9 months. Similarly, it seems highly implausible that such transitions reflect some maturational recapitulation of phylogeny as Segal suggests (aside from the lack of evidence for such recapitulation in general). There is no reason to think that at any point in phylogeny creatures recognised false belief when forced to confront counter-evidence but not otherwise. And while we might propose information-processing explanations of a single transition, like the transition from three to four, it is much harder to see why an innate conceptual capacity would be successively masked by different performance constraints each leading to a different behaviour. The natural explanation for these transitions is that the child is creating and revising theories.

In addition to simply charting the complexity of these developmental transitions there is also some evidence in the literature that children's 'theory of mind' development can be accelerated or delayed by particular patterns of evidence. While still falling short of the crucial experiment, data like these also tend to support the theory-formation view. There are three particularly suggestive findings of this kind in the literature. First, there seems to be a robust and reliable sibling effect on false-belief performance (Perner and Ruffman, 1994). Children with more siblings do better on theory of mind tasks than those with fewer. This finding is particular noteworthy since it reverses the general effect of sibling position in the literature, in which children with fewer siblings do better on cognitive tasks than those with more. This effect is difficult to explain in terms of maturation or general information-processing skill. It is simply explained on a theory-formation theory account, however. Children with more siblings have substantially more evidence of differing desires and beliefs. Similarly, in a longitudinal study, Dunn found specific correlations between the degree to which parents explicitly discussed mental states early in the child's development and children's later understanding of false belief (Dunn, 1991). Most powerfully, in a longitudinal training study, we (Gopnik, Meltzoff and Slaughter, 1994) has found that by providing children with specific counter-evidence to their incorrect predictions it is possible to accelerate their understanding of false-belief. Moreover, the effect of this training seems to extend beyond simple false-belief tasks to other theory-of-mind tasks, such as appearance-reality tasks. Again, developmental evidence of this kind is most relevant in discriminating between the two theories, and it supports the theory-formation theory.

4 Modularity in peripheral and central processes: against underdetermination

Apart from these kinds of evidence, however, there are also other more general reasons for preferring the theory-formation theory. This is particularly true since many of the classical arguments used in support of modularity are not directly empirical, but instead are underdetermination arguments.

The canonical examples of modularity are relatively peripheral and in some sense non-conceptual systems, such as low-level visual and auditory perception, and syntax. It may make sense to think of these systems as indeed indefeasible. This is particularly the case for syntax, where modularity and innateness arguments have been made most strongly. The most distinctive thing about syntax is that it has no reality outside of the linguistic behaviour itself. There is no syntactic universe that we develop new and different ideas about. There is just the way we speak. If a child incorrectly infers the rules of a language it would be wrong to say that he or she has got the language wrong, she simply has created a new language. In fact, such cases as the development of Creoles, where the child develops into an adult who creates a new language rather than learning the old one, are often used to support the hypothesis that syntactic structures are innate. Similar phenomena would be epistemologically disastrous if we were dealing with real knowledge of the world. Objects and minds really do have distinctive properties, quite independent of our knowledge of them, and we have to find out about them. There is no language independent of our knowledge of language.

Chomsky himself has muddied the waters by saying that these structures constitute innate knowledge of language, rather than innate syntactic skill. If knowledge of language is innate, we might think, why not knowledge of other things as well? Chomsky sometimes talks as if he thinks the model of the acquisition of syntax may be quite widely applicable to areas of psychology that are more genuinely cognitive (such as our knowledge of the physical or psychological world). It is worth pointing out, however, that Chomsky himself has resisted applying the same sorts of theories to semantics that he has applied to syntax.

The relative success of modularity views in explaining these peripheral cognitive processes, has led, understandably enough, to a tendency to extend those views to all types of cognition. In particular, Spelke *et al.* (1992) have suggested such a model for at least some aspects of our ordinary knowledge of the physical world, and Leslie has, of course, argued strongly for such an account of our knowledge of the mind (Leslie, 1991). Spelke accurately describes these views as a kind of neo-Kantian view of epistemology.

There is, however, an important respect in which a modular account of high-level and central cognition, the kind of cognition involved in our ordinary understanding of the mind, for example, will be different from modular accounts of syntax or perception. The representations of syntax and perception are, at least plausibly, the end of the line. We may indeed have relatively fixed syntactic structures and perceptual experiences. We may not be able to overthrow these structures without abandoning syntax (as we do in scientific or formal languages) and perception themselves. In the case of concepts and beliefs, however, such structures cannot be the end of the line. Our beliefs and concepts can and do change all the time, and do so in radical ways in science. Historically, it was the very fact of these radical changes in science that led to the final abandonment of the Kantian view in philosophy. If we want a modularity view of conceptual structure to work, we must, at the very least, have some mechanism by which it feeds into a revisable, defeasible conceptual system, like the systems of science. Constraints must be overthrown, biases rejected, conceptual organs reshaped.

But if there is such a mechanism then the underdetermination arguments that are used in support of modularity in the first place become much weaker. The claim is that certain kinds of knowledge must be innate, since it is difficult to see how they could be learned. But the proposed learning mechanisms are not generally very powerful. A question we might ask is whether children could acquire certain kinds of knowledge, if they had a learning mechanism as powerful as that of science? Is a particular concept more underdetermined by evidence than scientific theories are? If we think that the knowledge in question could be acquired by the conceptual mechanisms of science, we would need some very clear and strong reasons for believing that children do not have such conceptual mechanisms. In fact, of course, there is considerable evidence for the operation of just such mechanisms in childhood. The underdetermination arguments will only seem plausible if we draw the line between science and ordinary cognition very high up, as it were, rather than quite low down. Moreover, in any particular case, it will then be an open empirical question whether the concept is the result of a module or a theory.

5   Interactions between theories and modules

So far we have been considering the epistemological relation between theories and modules. How could we tell when we have one or another? What kinds of evidence could discriminate between them? The developmental evidence seems crucial in this effort. Theories will have a distinctive developmental history and trajectory, and a distinctive relation to evidence. But there is another question to ask. Assuming that both theories and modules are logically possible structures, and assuming, as the developmental pluralists we are, that both types of structures can be found in development, we can try to understand the relations between the two types of structures.

There are several possibilities. First, both kinds of knowledge may exist in parallel. It is possible and indeed likely that modules and theories can coexist and conflict in adulthood. Certain perceptual illusions are, of course, the classic example of this. In something like the Muller-Lyre illusion our conceptual system overrides the perceptual system in the way we described above. Nevertheless the perceptual system seems to continue to generate its modularised representations. Notice however, that from the adult point of view the perceptual illusions that are generated by the modules only influence very small parts of our behaviour and language. We reach for the stick that we know is longer, and we need to construct a very special 'looks like' vocabulary to even express the perceptual phenomena at all. In contrast, our conceptual system centrally influences both our language and behaviour. It is an interesting question whether we can point to similar illusions in our understanding of the mind.

Another possibility, however, is that at some stages of development information from the originally modular perceptual systems becomes available to the central theory-formation system. Once in the theory-formation system the information guides action and language in a productive way and is subject to the same kinds of revision and restructuring as other kinds of information. Thus modules could serve two roles. First they could constrain representations in the proposed neo-Kantian way throughout life, as in the case of syntax and perception. But second, they could serve as the source of a particular class of innate theories. They could be an important source of information for theory-formation.

The most important point about all this, however, is that the question of which process is responsible for which aspects of our folk psychology is an empirical one. It is not a question that can be resolved a priori or by consultation with phenomenology and intuition. While I have made the case for the theory-formation theory, either theory formation or modularity might play a role in the ontogeny of a particular aspect of folk psychology. The question of how we know the minds of ourselves and others is an empirical question, and, in particular, a developmental question.

6   Folk psychology and scientific psychology

If the question of modularity versus theory-formation is an empirical question, does it have philosophical implications? The philosophical interest in the origins of folk psychology largely reflects a concern about its present and future. Both modularity and the theory-formation theory imply that there is nothing particularly privileged about the representations of folk psychology; this is why modularity theorists can be said to adopt 'the theory-theory' epistemologically. In this respect, both views stand in contrast to other accounts, such as simulation theory, introspectionist theories, or social constructivist theories. Both these views see folk psychology as a genuinely cognitive phenomenon, a set of representations that are about something in the world, whether these representations were forged by evolution or development. And both views suggest that ultimately folk psychology could be, indeed is likely to be, wrong in important ways.

The two views give quite a different picture, however, of the relation between folk psychology and scientific psychology. On the modularity view, there will be little relation between the representational processes that lead to folk and scientific psychology. Even as scientific psychologists, on this view, we will still be in the thrall of folk psychology, just as our perceptual and syntactic systems are in the thrall of their modules. On this view in particular, it would be very unlikely that developments in scientific psychology could influence our folk psychology, or that folk psychology could form a sound or useful basis for further elaboration in scientific psychology. Instead the two enterprises are profoundly different. Ironically, we might either exalt or despise folk psychology on this basis. We might see it as a Kantian imperative of our everyday lives, only to be defeated in the rarefied contexts of science investigation. Or we might see it as a primitive remnant of our evolutionary history to be eliminated and replaced by, for example, a scientific neuroscience.

The theory-formation view, on the other hand, proposes a deep continuity between folk psychology and scientific psychology. On this view the same powerful cognitive truth-finding processes are in play when the three-year-olds try to understand false belief and when we try to understand the three-year-olds. On the theory formation view, folk psychology ought to be considered the 'starting-state' theory for a scientific psychology, as the infant's innate theory of persons is the starting state for folk psychology. Indeed, folk psychology, on this view, would not be a separate kind of psychology at all, but simply the theory that most of us, most of the time, have arrived at when we get too old and stupid to do more theorising. Or, more optimistically, folk psychology is the theory we have arrived at when our period of protected immaturity, our cognitive Eden, has ended, and we are forced to take on the serious adult evolutionary chores of feeding, fighting, and reproducing. We might think of our enterprise as scientific psychologists as the further revision of the theory by the fortunate, or possibly just childish, few, who are given leisure to collect evidence and think about it.

Indeed, I think there is a good case to be made that the most significant advances in cognitive psychology and cognitive science have precisely taken folk psychology as their base and modified and expanded the conceptual schemes of folk psychology to apply to new kinds of evidence. The best functionalist cognitive psychology takes folk psychological notions like 'inferring' or 'reasoning' or 'following a rule' or 'believing' or 'desiring' and applies them in cases where no folk psychologist ever would. The great cognitive psychologists have used the vocabulary of belief, inference, rule-following and achieving goals, to explain phenomena like perceiving the moon on the horizon, uttering a grammatical sentence, or automatically and unconsciously reaching for a close object. Indeed it might be argued that the very idea of computation, the centrepiece of cognitive science, is itself derived from folk psychology. Turing begins, after all, with an account of what it is like to do a particular kind of conscious problem-solving, an account that would jibe with anyone's folk psychological intuitions.

The interesting thing about Turing and Chomskian linguistics and the modern theories of perception and motor control and the other great accomplishments of cognitive science is that rather than remaining content with folk psychological notions, they expanded, modified and formalised those notions. The new theories applied the old conceptual schemes of folk psychology to radically new kinds of domains and tested them with radically new kinds of evidence. In so doing, however, they were merely continuing the process we all engage in when as three-year-olds we apply our earlier conceptual understanding of desire and perception to the domain of belief, and modify and alter that understanding as a result (Gopnik, Slaughter, and Meltzoff, 1994; Wellman, 1990). These theoretical extensions of folk psychology, have, simply as a matter of historical fact, been consistently more scientifically productive than attempts to develop a scientific psychology by starting from the conceptual apparatus of physics or neurobiology.

If the theory-formation theory is right, all of us, three-year-olds and scientific psychologists alike, sail in Neurath's boat together. We all use the same basic cognitive tools with the same ingenuity and determination to piece together progressively more seaworthy vessels. Neurath doesn't mention of course, just what a messy, chilly, and damp business this is, or how very likely we are to feel that we are in over our heads. Still, there is a certain nobility about pursuing such a distinctively human enterprise.

ACKNOWLEDGEMENTS

I wish to thank all of the participants in the conference and also Henry Wellman, Andrew Meltzoff, John Campbell and Clark Glymour for helpful discussions about the ideas in this paper.

NOTES

1 Note that this is rather different from the use of the 'theory-theory' to describe a particular view of the nature of adult folk psychology.
2 The term 'module' is sometimes used in quite a different way in cognitive neuroscience, where it means little more than 'functional unit'. Some developmental psychologists have proposed similarly softened versions of modularity (see e.g., Karmiloff-Smith, 1992; Baron-Cohen, this volume). Baron-Cohen suggests a version of modularity without encapsulation. But these softenings rob the notion of any epistemological interest. If a 'module' just means a functional unit in a cognitive system then all knowledge is modular, and modularity claims are uninteresting
3 There is an interesting conceptual and formal question about whether an innate system with a sufficiently varied set of parameters and triggers would reduce to theory-formation, or vice-versa. The assumption of the theory-formation theory, after all, is that not all the logically possible theories will actually be con-

structed. Some of the possible theories will be constructed by human minds, given evidence, and some will not. Formally, this may not be profoundly different from the case of a module with many parameters differently triggered by evidence. Empirically, however, there is a world of difference between the degrees of freedom that seem to be available in syntactic or perceptual systems and those available in scientific theories as we know them. Theory formation is, presumably, a matter of some set of as yet unknown algorithms that take us from one set of representations to another. However, those algorithms must be deeply and radically different from those that have been proposed for modular systems.

12   What is theoretical about the child's theory of mind?: a Vygotskian view of its development

Janet Astington

1   Theory-of-mind development

1.1   *The only games in town*

Three different views, all well represented in this volume, have been prominent in the lively debate on the origins of children's theory of mind. They are the theory-theory, the simulation theory, and the modularity view, and they are, according to Gopnik (this volume) 'the only games in town'. Proponents of all three views agree that during their pre-school years children develop a theory of mind which underlies their ability to understand social interaction by the attribution of mental states to themselves and to others. But this 'theory of mind' is not the same for the theory-theorist, the simulation theorist, and the modularity theorist. Indeed, they may not even mean the same thing by the term 'theory'.

Samet (1993) distinguishes between taxonomic theories and postulational ones, relating the former to a weaker and the latter to a stronger sense of 'theory'. Taxonomic theories are conceptual systems which help to organise our experience within a domain. The concepts mediate our understanding of the domain in question, and can be used to explain phenomena in that domain. However, the concepts are not of unobservables which are postulated to exist in order to provide explanation of the phenomena. Although mental states may not be directly observable, we do have some experiential knowledge of their existence. Thus, in this sense, a theory of mind is a taxonomic set of concepts (of mental states) that allows us to interpret our own experience and others' behaviour in particular ways.

This sense of 'theory' is evident in the simulation theorist's assumption that although children's understanding is dependent on a system of mentalistic concepts, of belief, desire, intention, and so on, the system is not developed via some process of abstract theorising (Harris, 1991, 1992; Johnson, 1988). The concepts are derived from children's own direct experience of such states. On this view, even young children can introspect their own mental states and are intuitively aware of their own phenomenal

184

experience. They can then understand other people by a process of simula-tion, using their abilities for pretence which develop early in the pre-school years. That is, the child imagines herself having the beliefs and desires that the other person has, and imagines what she herself would do if she pos-sessed those imagined beliefs and desires. Harris (1989, p. 75) says that although children 'act like theoreticians rather than mere empiricists' in explaining people's behaviour by reference to beliefs and desires, these are not unobservable states which children have to posit in some way. Children are aware of these states in themselves and do not have to construct them as 'theoretical postulates'.

Theory-theorists, on the other hand, take 'theory' in its stronger sense and argue that children's development of social understanding is the result of their developing a theory of mind, like a scientific theory (Gopnik, 1990; 1993; Gopnik and Wellman, 1992; Perner, 1991a; Wellman, 1990). The view is part of a general stance to think of cognitive development in terms of theory construction and change (Carey, 1985; Karmiloff-Smith, 1988; Keil, 1989). According to this view, children's concepts of mental states are abstract and unobservable theoretical postulates used to explain and predict observable human behaviour. The concepts are coherent and inter-dependent, and the theory can interpret a wide range of evidence using a few concepts and laws. The theory is not static, but is open to defeat by new evidence, that is, it is subject to replacement by a new theory (Gopnik and Wellman, 1992). Or the theory is not replaced but extended, as scientific theories sometimes are, in order to cope with the new evidence (Perner, 1991a). On this view mental state concepts are theoretical entities that chil-dren postulate in order to explain and predict people's interactions. This view does not deny that children experience these states in themselves, but such experience is indirect and informed by the theory they currently hold (Gopnik, 1993).

Like theory-theorists, modularity theorists take the term 'theory' in its stronger sense and regard children's concepts of mental states as abstract theoretical postulated entities, organised into causal laws that can be used to interpret a wide range of evidence. However, the theory is not acquired through any process of *theorising*, rather it is innate and matures, in the same sort of way that a Chomskian language-faculty does (Fodor, 1987, 1992; Leslie, 1993, 1994b; Segal, this volume). Modularity theorists make the familiar argument that new concepts, such as that of misrepresentation which develops at about four years of age, cannot appear from nowhere. Because, on their view, the development of a concept cannot be explained by any deductive or inductive process, it must be there ab initio; that is, its development is genetically determined. The theory of mind module thus constrains development in a precise way – the theory is not subject to revision based on experience. Although experience might be required as a trigger, the module will not be modified in differential ways by different experiences, which predicts that the acquisition of a theory of mind will be a universal human achievement.

Certainly these three views have dominated debate within the municipal boundaries of children's theory of mind. There are, however, other possibilities. Case (1989) argues that children do not develop a domain-specific theory about the mind. Rather, the understanding that four-year-olds demonstrate in their successful performance on false belief tasks reflects a domain-general change in their cognitive abilities. In the final substage of the interrelational stage (Case, 1985) children become able to relate two mental representations to one another in an explicit fashion by means of some integrating scheme. This leads them to solve numerous social and non-social problems – including theory of mind tasks – all of which depend on their new ability to map one representation onto another. In a related vein, Frye, Zelazo and Palfai (unpublished manuscript) argue that performance on the false-belief task and other tasks assessing the development of a theory of mind require the ability to employ embedded rules, an ability that develops around four years of age. Undoubtedly children's cognitive abilities do increase over time in the ways Case and Frye *et al.* suggest. However, as Gopnik (this volume) points out, although increased resources will allow children to cope with increased cognitive complexity, they cannot in and of themselves account for theory of mind development. Children may be able to deal with more complex embeddings and integrations of mental states, but the mental state concepts themselves must come from somewhere.

1.2   Origins of mental state concepts

Other than saying they are 'postulated' theory-theorists say very little about where mental state concepts come from. They develop within a network of interdependent concepts on the basis of data from the world, including the social world. But the social world does not give the concepts to the child – it just provides the child with data for concept building. At earlier stages of development the child might possess concepts quite unlike the adult ones. The concept of 'prelief' for example, that Perner ascribes to three-year-olds, does not allow the child to distinguish between counterfactual action based on pretence or that based on false belief (Perner, Baker, and Hutton, 1994). In contrast, Woodfield's (1994) model of the slow-dawning of a theory of mind suggests that if a child has any mental state concept at all, it is the adult concept but the child may use it only in some situations and not in others.

Modularity theorists assume that concepts are innate and do not develop over time – the child has the adult concepts from the beginning. What develops is the child's ability to employ the concepts, which may partly depend on some linguistic triggering from the social environment, and partly depend on maturation of the child's cognitive capacities. Fodor's (1992) proposal, for example, assumes that three-year-olds already have adult concepts of belief and desire but that processing limitations restrict the child's ability to integrate information about a character's desire and his belief, which is required in standard false-belief tasks. Fodor does not consider the possibility that Olson (1993) puts forward, that it is the processing limitations themselves that limit the formation of the concept.

On the simulation view concepts come from introspection, although it is somewhat unclear how children come to think of their own mental states in terms of beliefs and desires – that is, how conceptual understanding is derived from phenomenal experience. Johnson (1991) considers the role of social experience, particularly the role parental talk plays, in transforming children's pre-reflective experience of mental states into reflective understanding of them. For example, young children are often frustrated by the conflict they experience between their own desires and intentions and those of others; parents may try to defuse such conflict by explaining it to the child using mental state terminology: 'He didn't know you wanted it,' and so on.

Such considerations – that the child's social world provides data, or triggering, or linguistic terms – not only make quite different assumptions about how the child's theory of mind develops, but in addition lead us to seek a fuller account of socialisation practices within a child's culture. In the process of enculturation during their early years children acquire language and come to understand the social rules within their culture.

An alternative view to those considered so far is that enculturation is itself the source of the child's mental state concepts. From this perspective, children would never come up with concepts of mental states except by encountering them in the culture. Bruner (1983) proposes that parents treat infants' spontaneous gestures as intentional communications and thus infants come to see themselves as having intentions and start to communicate intentionally. In a similar way, parents talk to toddlers about their thoughts, feelings, and desires, and the children come to see themselves as holding such states. Parents also use the same linguistic terms to talk about other people. That is to say, the children's own experience is construed in the same terms that are applied to others, and they come to see that others have similar experiences to their own. Thus, linguistic development is fundamental to the acquisition of mental state concepts because without language the child would not learn about these concepts, which are in the speech practices of the culture. In this sense the theory of mind, perhaps even mind itself, is a cultural invention. Olson (1994) traces the origin and development of the Western theory of mind, involving concepts of subjectivity, intentionality, and individual responsibility, from the time of the Homeric Greeks to the time of Descartes. During this time, mental states came to be seen as privately held within individuals but subject to interpretation and open to discussion by others.

The theory-theory, the simulation theory, and the modularity theory are alike in their emphasis on development within the individual. On all of these views children are constructing or employing a conceptual structure, a theory of mind. An alternative view is that children do not really acquire any theory of mind of their own but, through participation in cultural activities, they come to share their culture's way of regarding and talking about people's relations to one another and to the world. The contrast is between autonomous individual development which is facilitated by the social world, and interdependent activity within a communal world.

In the debate over how children develop a theory of mind, such social constructivist views have not been ignored but they have been less centrally represented (Bruner, 1990; Feldman, 1992; Hobson, 1991; Tomasello, Kruger, and Ratner, 1993). Sociocultural views are playing an increasingly important role in developmental theorising generally (Miller, 1993). Proponents of such views draw, directly or indirectly, on the legacy of Vygotsky.

2   A Vygotskian view of theory-of-mind development

2.1   *The Vygotskian perspective*

Vygotsky entered the debate going on in Russia in the years following the Revolution, concerning the influence of society and culture on individual consciousness. His theory was influenced by Marxism, not out of political expediency, but from a sincere belief in the relevance of dialectical and historical materialism to the investigation of psychological processes (Cole and Scribner, 1978). A fundamental tenet of dialectical materialism is that everything must be investigated in terms of its history. Although later states are not reducible to former ones, they can only be understood in terms of the changes that have occurred. From this perspective, all development must be studied in its socio-historical context. That is to say, we cannot abstract from context and separately investigate the universal aspects of the child's development, but only children's development within particular social contexts.

This point is of great importance when the subject of investigation is the development of a theory of mind because it leads us to ask to what extent folk psychologies vary across cultures. Is the Western theory of mind a universal feature of humankind? There are few data that address this question directly. The answer can be informed by anthropological research on language development and the development of emotion understanding in different cultures (Heelas and Lock, 1981; Holland and Quinn, 1987; Scheiffelin and Ochs, 1986). This research suggests, unsurprisingly, that there are both similarities and differences amongst cultures. The similarities presumably rest on the fact that physical and biological environments are fundamentally the same across cultures, whereas very different languages and social structures are built on these foundations. The expression and recognition of basic emotions is universal, but the proprieties of emotional expression and the type of more complex emotions developed and understood, varies with culture (Lutz, 1987). All cultures recognise the self, distinct from other persons and from the physical world, but the self's responsibility for action is differently conceptualised across cultures, as is the onset of perceived personhood. Similarly, the extent to which subjective states are open to interpretation and public discussion varies across cultures (Scheiffelin and Ochs, 1986).

This suggests that the universality of the theory of mind, as described in Western culture, is an open question. What few data currently exist are equivocal; for example, Baka children of the Cameroon understand false belief at the same age as Western children do (Avis and Harris, 1991), whereas Quechua children of Peru and Tainae children of New Guinea appear not to, even as they approach adolescence (McCormick, 1994). Of course, one would not want to claim from these data that the Quechua or the Tainae have no theory of mind, or a theory of mind fundamentally different from ours. Perhaps Western theory-of-mind tasks, or even testing itself, are not an appropriate way to assess their understanding – I say this whilst acknowledging the immense care McCormick took to use native speakers and culturally appropriate materials in her test situations. At this stage we do not know how universal the Western theory of mind is. All people have some way of interpreting social interaction, but it may not be *our* way. There are many open questions in the sociocultural view – the theory of mind may turn out to be much more relative than we imagine.

Vygotsky believed that everything must be investigated in terms of its social context and also in terms of its history. He was a true developmentalist who recognised the importance of understanding current competencies by examining their origin and evolution. Vygotsky was interested in more than child development, however. He applied the developmental approach not only to ontogenesis, but also to phylogenesis and sociocultural history (Wertsch, 1985). He believed that an understanding of human psychology depends on investigating development in each of these domains. He intended that this developmental approach would put the focus onto causal explanations of development, not just on descriptions of current states. In his view, development comes about through dialectical change, that is, a resolution of conflicting forces. Is there more than an analogy here with theory change, which comes about when predictions and evidence come into conflict? A fundamental difference is that, for Vygotsky, the conflicting forces are not just within the individual. Two concepts – mediation and internalisation – are fundamental to Vygotsky's theory of dialectical change.

Vygotsky elaborated Engel's idea, that in using tools to transform nature, humans are distinguished from other animals; tools mediate human interaction with the environment. He extended this idea to include signs as a sort of tool, and argued that signs or tools are used in indirect, or mediated, behaviour. Thus, for Vygotsky, language is vitally important because it mediates behaviour. Although he said that tools and signs are analogous because they both function as mediators in indirect activity, he made an important distinction between them. The tool's mediating function is externally oriented, towards changing objects and mastering the physical world; while the sign's mediating function is internally oriented, towards changing behaviour and mastering the self. Furthermore, the use of signs is a social process at first, which is gradually internalised, becoming an individual process. Vygotsky postulated that the internalisation of sign systems produces a qualitative change in the development of thought (Vygotsky, 1978).

Indeed, Vygotsky placed great emphasis on the importance of social processes, and of investigating the origins of an individual's competencies within his or her social group. This is one of the best known tenets of Vygotskian theory, which is elaborated in his theory of egocentric speech (Vygotsky, 1962). Vygotsky regarded egocentric speech as an intermediate stage in the transition from social speech to verbal thought. For him, the primary function of language is social communication, and it only later acquires an internal mental function. Initially, an adult's speech directs the child's behaviour and then later, the child talks to herself – egocentric speech – directing her own behaviour. Gradually, this egocentric speech ceases to be expressed aloud, becoming inner speech, or verbal thought. 'Language thus takes on an *intrapersonal function* in addition to its *interpersonal use*' (Vygotsky, 1978; p. 27, his emphasis).

In general, Vygotsky's argument is that any mental functioning is a kind of activity which can be performed by individuals or by groups (Wertsch, 1985). That is, cognitive processes can occur between individuals on the *inter*-mental plane, or within an individual on the *intra*-mental plane. This may seem strange if we think of the mind as within an individual, not between individuals. However, the idea that an individual's first experience of higher cognitive processes is social, not personal, is most important in Vygotsky's theory. This is clear in an often quoted passage: 'Any function in the child's cultural development appears twice, or on two planes. First it appears between people as an interpsychological category, and then within the child as an intrapsychological category' (Vygotsky, 1981, p. 163). The idea is fundamental to one of Vygotsky's best-known concepts: the zone of proximal development. This is essentially the intermental plane – where a mental function may occur between the child and another person, before it has been seen within the child as an intrapsychological category. Vygotsky defined this zone as 'the distance between the actual developmental level as determined by independent problem solving and the level of potential development as determined through problem solving under adult guidance or in collaboration with more capable peers' (Vygotsky, 1978, p. 86). The child is a genuine participant in the activity but would be unable to perform it alone. A frequently cited example is prompted remembering, where toddler and parent together construct a shared memory (e.g. Hudson, 1990).

2.2   Theory-of-mind tasks and the zone of proximal development

We might consider three-year-olds' precocious performance on theory-of-mind tasks as instances of shared mental activity within the zone of proximal development. For example, children are able to explain actions premised on false beliefs before they are able to predict a puppet's or story character's action as in the standard task (Bartsch and Wellman, 1989). In the prediction task, the child is shown two boxes: for instance, an empty Band-Aid box, and a plain box with band-aids inside. A puppet appears with a cut on his hand, the child is told he wants a band-aid, and then is asked where the puppet will look for band-aids. The typical response from three-year-olds is to predict that the puppet will look in the plain box where the band-aids are. However, in the explanation task, rather than asking the child where the puppet will look, the adult experimenter makes the puppet go towards the empty Band-Aid box and start to open it, and then asks the child why the puppet is looking in there. Some three-year-olds say that the puppet thinks the box has got band-aids in it. Of course, some three-year-olds perform correctly on the prediction task, and in fact in Bartsch and Wellman's data there appears to be little difference between the percentage of children who can predict actions based on false beliefs and who spontaneously explain mistaken actions by referring to false beliefs. That is, the production of explanations citing a false belief is relatively rare; children are more likely to cite desires to explain actions – 'He wants a band-aid.'

However, if the experimenter then asks, 'What does he think?', a fair proportion of three-year-olds reply, 'He thinks it's got band-aids in.' Of twelve children who passed only one type of task, eleven passed explanation but not prediction (the passing criterion was at least three out of four correct predictions, and at least four out of five appropriate explanations, prompted or unprompted).

To some hard-nosed experimentalists such prompted performance means very little. True, it does not tell us much about the individual child's understanding of false belief, but it is a clear example of false-belief understanding on the intermental plane, that is, within the zone of proximal development, where the child is guided by the adult's leading questions. For example:

ADULT: Look, here's Bill. Bill has a cut, see? And he wants a band-aid. Why do you think he's looking in there?
CHILD: He wants a band-aid.
ADULT: What does Bill think?
CHILD: There's band-aids in there.

Fodor cites Bartsch and Wellman's data, amongst others, as 'reasonably persuasive evidence that the young child does have a concept of false belief after all' (Fodor, 1992, p. 289). However, in examples like the one above it is unclear whether the concept of false belief is the child's concept, or a shared concept that exists in the dialogue, or the adult's concept that the child piggybacks on in some way.

We can give other examples of theory-of-mind task performance in the zone of proximal development: three-year-olds generally do not remember their own earlier false belief, after they have discovered that a familiar box does not hold its usual contents (Gopnik and Astington, 1988). However, they can be helped to remember what they mistakenly thought, if they put a picture of the usual contents into a mailbox before they see the unexpected contents, and then the experimenter reminds them of this when they are asked what they thought was in the box at the beginning (Mitchell and Lacohée, 1991). Again, from a Vygotskian perspective, the activity of remembering is socially shared; the child's performance is 'scaffolded' by the adult's reminders and control of the child's attention (Wood *et al.*, 1976).

Similarly, Sullivan and Winner (1993) found that three-year-olds were more likely correctly to predict another person's false belief in a modified version of the standard 'smarties' task where the child herself plays a trick on another person. In the standard task the child discovers that there are pencils in a smarties box and then is asked what a friend who does not see inside the box will think is inside it. Generally, three-year-olds predict that the friend will think it has pencils inside. In the 'trick' condition, the child and an adult are first tricked by an experimenter who asks them to guess (for example) what is in a smarties box that turns out to contain pencils. Then the experimenter leaves the room and the other adult suggests that she and the child play a trick on the experimenter, like the one just played on them. The adult makes a great performance of what fun it will be, how tricky they are, and so on. She then finds a crayon box in her bag and helps the child take the crayons out and think of something else to put into the box – all the time keeping up the fun of the game. Then, while the experimenter is still out of the room, the adult asks the child (in a 'very conspiratorial' tone) 'What will she [the absent experimenter] think is in here?' Approximately 75% of three-year-olds were correct on two trials in the trick condition compared with 25% of three-year-olds in the standard condition.

Again, one might argue that children's performance is scaffolded by joining in a game with the adult. They are active participants in a real-life social situation. Children may be able to predict the other person's false belief in this situation because people are usually wrong when they are tricked – that is the point of a trick. I am not arguing that the child has no understanding of false belief, just that false beliefs are inherent to that particular type of social situation, and so the understanding is in a sense between the child and the adult, supported by the usual expectations in that kind of situation.

One further example, and doubtless there could be more: children's pretend play and their understanding of pretence are often discussed in relation to their developing theory of mind (e.g. Harris and Kavanagh, 1993). Many issues are involved which I will not venture into, but one puzzle is how three-year-olds can understand that another person may entertain a 'pretend' representation but not a false belief. However, in the case of pretence, the representations, although they are different from reality, are shared by the participants in the pretend game. In this sense, they are *inter*mental, not *intra*mental. Perhaps this is why children understand pretend/real distinctions before they understand the distinction between appearance and reality (Flavell *et al.*, 1987), and how three-year-olds can predict a puppet's actions based on his pretence but not on his false belief (Peskin, 1993). Vygotsky (1967) himself suggested that play, including pretend play, creates a zone of proximal development for the child. Participation in pretend play may, as some have suggested, help children come to understand false belief. Perhaps participating in pretend situations, where representations different from reality are socially shared, helps children understand situations where representations are not only different from reality, but are not shared in a social pretend domain.

It is easy enough to give Vygotskian interpretations of children's performance on theory-of-mind tasks. However, it is a different matter to determine whether such descriptions really provide an explanation of theory of mind development. From a Vygotskian perspective, scaffolding a three-year-old's performance in the sort of ways I have described not only promotes earlier success, but is the mechanism whereby change comes about. We do not presently know whether such shared activity is a necessary precursor to false-belief understanding – obviously not by participation in experimental situations, but in similar conversations with parents or others. Certainly young children do have much experience of this nature. Parents talk to their children about feelings, thoughts, and desires from a very young age (Brown and Dunn, 1991; Dunn, 1988) and the extent to which they do this is related to the extent to which children talk about such states at a later point in time (Dunn, Brown, and Beardsall, 1991; Moore *et al.*, 1994). Children are also exposed to mentalistic talk in stories that are read to them and in their conversations about stories (Astington, 1990; Paley, 1984). And they are often audience to narratives in adult conversations (Heath, 1983).

From a Vygotskian perspective, these sort of experiences are essential. Children would never develop a theory of mind without them. For Vygotsky, all individual development originates in interpersonal activity; a shared activity becomes an individual one. Vygotsky argued that the individual's competence originates in the interpersonal zone. The child would not come to understand false belief, for example, without the necessary social experience. What sort of data might address this issue?

2.3   *Predictions from a Vygotskian viewpoint*

Dunn and her colleagues have investigated antecedents to false-belief understanding and shown that some aspects of family interaction and discourse, assessed when children were 2;9, are associated with the children's false-belief task performance at age 3;4 (Dunn *et al.*, 1991). Children who were better able to explain a puppet's action based on a false belief, had, seven months earlier, talked more about feeling states, participated in more talk with their mother about causal relations, co-operated more with their older sibling, and witnessed more controlling talk from mother to sibling. Moreover, the correlations were independent of the child's general verbal ability and the general amount of talk in the family. Dunn *et al.* argue that their results support the view that children's development of a theory of mind is mediated by talk and interaction within the family.

Perner, Ruffman, and Leekam (1994), reasoning from this finding, argue that children who have more opportunity for the sort of sibling social interaction that Dunn describes, will be more likely to perform correctly on false-belief tasks. Perner *et al.* showed that in a sample of seventy-six three- to four-year-olds, children with two siblings were almost twice as likely to pass a standard false-belief prediction task than only children were. However, it is not clear from Perner *et al*'s data whether other factors, such as language ability, may be mediating the relationship. We (Jenkins and Astington, in press) confirmed their finding, and showed that it was independent of the child's linguistic competence. Sixty-eight three- to five-year-olds were given four standard false-belief tasks: two change in location stories (Wimmer and Perner, 1983) and two 'unexpected contents' tasks (Perner *et al.*, 1987). They were also given a standard language test: the Test of Early Language Development (TELD) (Hresko *et al.*, 1981). Using hierarchical multiple regression analysis we found that age accounts for 41% of the variance in children's false-belief task scores, and language a further 7%. Adding family size to the equation accounts for a further 10% of the variance. That is, children from larger families do better on false-belief tasks, even after taking account of their age and linguistic competence.

Perner *et al.* (1994) argue that the effect that they found may come about because children in larger families have a larger data base on which to construct a theory of mind. They acknowledge that the effect of family size may be mediated by parental intervention in sibling interactions, but their emphasis is on the siblings' co-operative social interaction, especially in pretend play. In support of this argument they cite Dunn *et al*'s (1991) finding that the children who better understood false belief had earlier co-operated more with their older sibling. However, one could argue that the family size effect may be more directly due to parental intervention than to family size per se, and cite Dunn *et al*'s finding that the children who better understood false belief had witnessed more controlling talk from mother to sibling. If false-belief understanding is more related to parental style than family size, that is, if socialisation practices are more important than the size of the child's data base, this would support the enculturation view over the theory view. How might we investigate this?

A contrast is often made between two styles of parenting: authoritarian and authoritative (Baumrind, 1971). Authoritarian parents punish bad behaviour and demand obedience, whereas authoritative parents reason with the child and explain decisions and rules with reference to people's different points of view of the situation. Talking about different viewpoints may well help children understand that people have beliefs about the world, that their beliefs may be different from those of others, and that beliefs may change when a person acquires new information. There is evidence in the social development literature that children of authoritative parents are more socially competent than children of authoritarian ones. However, it may be the case that parental style is influenced by the nature of the particular child. It is also the case that authoritarian parenting is more prevalent under conditions of high stress and is associated with lower socio-economic status (SES). Delayed false-belief task performance amongst such children has been reported (Holmes *et al.*, 1994), although perhaps this is a function of language development. We know that there is a relation between false-belief understanding and linguistic competence, and that language development is delayed in low SES children. The Holmes *et al.* study did not assess the children's language competence.

Nonetheless, an important factor in Perner *et al*'s finding may not be family size so much as parental talk about mental states, which we might expect to be associated with a particular style of parenting. Thus, we might hypothesise that there would be a relation between parental style and children's false-belief scores. How might we test this? We could bring two siblings and their parent into the lab and set up a situation in which it is likely that the parent would have to intervene, such as having the family play a competitive board game, or having the children play together but providing scarce or unequally nice resources. We could then look for a relation between the target child's false-belief score and the way in which the parent intervenes in such situations, controlling for age and language. Alternatively (and more simply) we might set up such scenarios in a training study; that is, we would expose children who did not pass false-belief tasks to vignettes in which children quarrel and a parent intervenes, mediating the conflict by giving explanations of the participants' viewpoints with reference to their mental states. We would compare the later false belief task performance of these children with those in a matched control group who were exposed to the same situations in which mediation and reparation is made at a physical level.

Dunn *et al.* (1991) argue that their data suggest that children's theory of mind development is mediated by family talk and interaction, which is a Vygotskian view, although they do not explicitly call it such. For Vygotsky, individuals' competence originates in their social interactions and is then internalised, with language as the most important mediator. This suggests that children with greater language skills, who are better able to participate in linguistic interactions, will benefit more from such social interaction. Indeed, Gopnik (1990) has pointed out that the period during which there is the greatest development in the child's theory of mind is also the period during which the child acquires language. As mentioned, hierarchical multiple regression analysis of our data shows that age accounts for 41% of the variance in children's false-belief task scores, and language a further 7% (Jenkins and Astington, in press). However, age and language covary so strongly ($r = .69$) that this underestimates the effect of language. If language is entered into the regression equation before age, it accounts for 41% of the variance in false-belief understanding and a further 8% is accounted for by age. This leads to two questions: what aspects of language are important? And what role does language play?

The Test of Early Language Development (Hresko *et al.*, 1981) that we used is a standard measure of syntactic and semantic competence. In order to give us a measure of their pragmatic competence, the children in our study played a 'communication game' with the experimenter (Krauss and Glucksberg, 1969; Robinson, 1986). Child and experimenter each have an identical set of pictures, and there is a screen between them so that they can each see only their own set. The pictures differ from one another in small details. The game is to choose a picture without showing it to the other person and describe it so that she can pick exactly the same one from her set. The task measures children's pragmatic competence because they have to realise that the experimenter cannot see the picture and so will not know how to make a match unless given a precise description. Children received a composite score which took account of how informative they were and how much prompting they needed, over three trials. Performance on this task was significantly related to false-belief task scores, but unfortunately the task was too easy for many of the children and the ceiling on the measure reduces the correlation to the extent that it is not significant when age and syntactic/semantic competence are controlled for. However, if we exclude the children who perform at ceiling, 51 children remain and their pragmatic competence is significantly related to false-belief understanding ($r = .28$) controlling for both age and syntactic/semantic competence.

Work with children with autism has already shown the important relation between pragmatics and theory-of-mind (Baron-Cohen, 1988). But it is not just the pragmatics of language that is important; syntactic and semantic competence are important too. There are relations between syntactic tasks using complement-taking verbs and theory-of-mind tasks (de Villiers, 1995, March; Tager-Flusberg, 1995, March). There are also relations between the semantic understanding of *think* and *know* and tests of false belief understanding (Moore *et al.*, 1990). However, the relation between theory-of-mind development and linguistic competence may be dependent on more than the syntax of recursion and the semantics of mental verbs. The test that we used was a general standardised measure that involved many aspects of linguistic competence.

My second question, concerning the role that language might play in theory of mind development, cannot be answered from such cross-sectional, correlational data. We need to study children's development longitudinally, assessing their language competence and theory-of-mind development over the period of time during which they acquire understanding of false belief. We are conducting such an investigation in a current study (Astington and Jenkins, 1995, March). A Vygotskian perspective would predict that children's language scores at an earlier point in time would be related to their theory-of-mind tasks scores later on. So far the data support this prediction. Language competence appears to boost false-belief understanding.

3   Towards a multilateral view of theory-of-mind development

It is perhaps rather ambitious at this stage to propose a 'multilateral view' of theory-of-mind development. The aim would be to integrate different explanations of its development into a socially situated interactionist position. This is not a defeatist stance, but one that reflects the complexity of the child's development. We may not be able to give a solely internalist, nor solely externalist explanation of development. One view is not a substitute for the other, but we have to be clear what is explained by each and how they are related. There is obviously a two-way interaction between the child and the social world. Children come to understand the social world while at the same time that world itself provides the stuff on which they operate (Feldman, 1992). If we take this view, we have to be prepared to say what cognitive abilities allow children to engage in social interaction and to internalise the folk concepts of their culture, and to say whether these abilities are innate or are themselves constructed. Obviously something is innate; the important question is how much is innate and how specialised it is. Even if we take the strong theory view that children construct their theory of mind by postulating mental state concepts, we must allow some role for an innate component, and also for knowledge acquired from linguistic interactions in the culture.

Indeed, all the games in town acknowledge the importance of social interaction to some extent or another. The modularity view gives the least role to the social world, but even there it provides for triggering of innate concepts. In the simulation theory, the adult language plays a role in how the child construes her phenomenal experience and relates her own experiences to those of others. In the theory-theory the social world provides data that are used in the construction of concepts, or it lays out analogies for the child's benefit. If theory-of-mind development is likened to science we can think of the child as a scientist or as a science student – as a student, socialisation is vastly important. Thus, the issue is not whether social interaction is important, because it is of some importance in everybody's view.

The debate may concern more than the relative importance of social influence on development and its mode of interaction with biological and cognitive factors. Perhaps the theory-theory, the simulation theory and the modularity view are not complementary perspectives to one another and to Vygotskian ones after all, that taken together can enrich our understanding of the child's development. Perhaps the two sets of views are incommensurable theoretical perspectives, which are impossible to integrate. Indeed, impossible to evaluate on any comparable scale. One paradigm investigates the development of a theory of mind within the individual child. The other assumes that the child comes to share or appropriate the theory of mind of the culture (Raver and Leadbeater, 1993; Rogoff *et al.*, 1993).

Vygotsky himself was concerned to explain development in the individual. On his view, two separate lines contribute to development – the biological and the cultural – becoming integrated in the child's early years. Certainly Vygotsky focused on the contribution of the cultural line, assuming rather than extensively discussing the contribution of biology (Wertsch and Tulviste, 1992). Perhaps now is the time to make these assumptions explicit. This will bring us closer to a view of theory-of-mind development that integrates cognition and culture, and gives an active role to individuals as well as to their societies.

ACKNOWLEDGEMENTS

I thank David Olson for his helpful comments on this chapter, Jenny Jenkins for our research collaborations, and the Natural Sciences and Engineering Research Council of Canada for its support.

13   Desires, beliefs, and language

Paul Harris

1   Introduction

Young children find desires easier to understand than beliefs and may understand desires with little or no understanding of beliefs. In this chapter, I review evidence and explanations for that lag. I conclude by offering a novel explanation, arguing that children's conception of other people undergoes an important shift when they begin to engage in conversation. Initially young children conceive of other people primarily as agents with goals, but around three years of age they start to construe people as epistemic subjects capable of exchanging information for the formation and updating of beliefs. Hence, they shift from a desire psychology to a belief-desire psychology.

2   Evidence for the lag

Evidence for the lag between desire and belief understanding has emerged from research with autistic as well as normal children. Autistic children are poor at understanding false beliefs (Baron-Cohen, 1991b; Baron-Cohen, Leslie, and Frith, 1985; Leslie and Frith, 1988), especially second-order beliefs (i.e., beliefs about beliefs) (Ozonoff, Pennington, and Rogers, 1991a). There is no published evidence of an equivalent impairment in their understanding of desires.[1] They can remember and re-assert a previously-stated desire (Tan and Harris, 1991). Although they rarely talk about thoughts and beliefs, they do talk about desires (Tager-Flusberg, 1992; 1993). Such talk is, admittedly, mostly about their own desires rather than those of other people (Tager-Flusberg, 1994) but young normal children show a similar bias. Finally, despite their difficulty in understanding belief-based emotions, autistic children understand desire-based emotions (Baron-Cohen, 1991b).

Normal children also understand desires more easily than beliefs. In predicting what emotion someone will feel, they take account of variation between people in their desires before taking account of variation in their

200

beliefs (Harris *et al.*, 1989). When asked why someone has engaged in a particular action, they are more likely to mention desires than beliefs, even when desires provide only a partial explanation, as in the case of unsuccessful actions guided by a false belief (Bartsch and Wellman, 1989).

Perhaps the comprehensive documentation of the lag is provided by Bartsch and Wellman (1995). Their study of the spontaneous conversation of ten English-speaking children studied between the ages of approximately two and five years shows convincingly that children talk informatively about desires throughout much of the third year. By contrast, talk about thoughts and beliefs starts around the third birthday and only becomes as frequent as talk about desires around the fifth birthday.

Both desires and beliefs are usually assumed to be critical components of our folk psychology. Next, I consider several initially plausible explanations of the fact that they are not understood equally well by young children.

3   Explanations of the lag

3.1   Mentalising ability

A popular interpretation of the difficulties shown by autistic children is that they lack a 'theory of mind' or cannot 'mentalise'. Noting that autistic children talk about desires but rarely about thoughts and beliefs (Tager-Flusberg, 1993), Frith and Happé (1994) claim that this fits into a wider pattern of strengths and weaknesses that can be explained by a difficulty in mentalising. However, they do not explain why less mentalising ability – or none – is needed to understand desires as compared with thoughts and beliefs.

Perhaps when autistic children talk about desires, they do not conceive of them as mental states. They might learn to use the verb 'want' as a marker for their own requests without understanding that desires are mental states.[2] Alternatively, they might describe other people as wanting something only when they are currently engaged in some goal-directed action. Further research may shed light on these possibilities. Meantime, two points are worth noting. First, autistic children's talk about desires is, prima facie, an embarrassment and not a support for the alleged difficulty in mentalising because desires, just as much as beliefs, are central to our everyday conception of mind. Second, the suggestion that autistic children might have a non-mentalistic conception of desire is not likely to explain the development of normal children. As discussed later, there is persuasive evidence that normal children do have a mentalistic conception of desire in the third year of life – before they start to talk about thoughts and beliefs.

3.2   Modular accounts

Until recently, modular theorists have tended to ignore the lag between desire and belief understanding. For example, Leslie's account (1994) appears to be pan-attitudinal: it offers no basis for a distinction between desires and beliefs. It claims that during the second year a new processing device emerges (TOMM, system 2) that enables a shift from processing actions per se to the processing of mental attitudes, including wanting, pretending, and believing. On this account, one might expect an understanding of pretence, desire, and belief to emerge more or less simultaneously.

Existing data already contradict this prediction with respect to pretence and belief. For example, two-year-olds can make sense of another person's pretend initiatives (Harris and Kavanaugh, 1993; Harris, Kavanaugh, and Meredith, 1994; Leslie, 1994), whereas an understanding of belief does not emerge until later. Leslie and Roth (1993) explain this lag by introducing an additional piece of processing machinery, the selection processor. They argue that understanding pretence requires minimal input from the selection processor, whereas understanding false beliefs requires considerably more input (and particular variants of the false-belief task differ in precisely how much is needed). Such an account might be extended to explain the lag between desire and belief, but Leslie has not explicitly done so.[3]

Fodor (1992) attributes to two-year-olds a Very Simple Theory of Mind (VSTM) – simple in that it includes fewer psychological objects than the full-blown adult version. It does not include yens or suspicions but it does include desires and beliefs. This account, like Leslie's, implies the early availability of a belief-desire psychology. However, acknowledging that children display difficulties on belief tasks, Fodor postulates the operation of a default heuristic. Young children assume that agents act to satisfy their desires. By implication two- and three-year-olds appreciate what beliefs the agent holds but not their role in the guidance of action even when false. Although this account offers a reasonable explanation of data on the false-belief task and its variants (Perner, submitted) with some important exceptions (Wimmer and Weichbold, 1994), it fares poorly when evaluated against new data on children's talk about mental states (Bartsch and Wellman, 1995), described below. Specifically, on Fodor's account one would expect two-year-olds to talk about people's beliefs, including their false beliefs, even if they fail to realise the role of beliefs in the guidance of action. However, such talk emerges only at around three years of age even though talk about desires is widespread before that age.

In principle, a modularist could argue that separate modules, one dedicated to the processing of desires, and one to beliefs, become available at

different points in development. In discussing diachronic modularity, Segal (this volume) speculates about such a staggered set of modules. However, without some specification of why the processing requirements for understanding the two attitudes are different such staggered modularity offers only a post hoc account.[4]

3.3   The child as theoretician

In contrast to modularists, advocates of the theory-theory claim that the lag between desire and belief understanding marks a major shift in the child's theory of mind. I consider two such accounts.

Perner (1991a) allows that the two-year-old has an understanding of mental states such as wanting, but denies that the two-year-old conceives of someone who wants a particular state of affairs as mentally representing it. He proposes instead that the two-year-old is a situation theorist who conceives of an agent as directing his or her mental attitude of wanting at an actual or possible situation. A situation theorist appreciates that the agent will act to maintain or bring about the desired situation, and will feel happy or sad depending on whether it is realised.

The shift toward a representational theory of mind is marked by the child's understanding of false belief according to Perner (1991a). At that point, the child understands that the agent has a mental model of the state of affairs that is (mistakenly) taken to be true. In particular, the child realises that the agent still treats the representation as referring to, and correctly describing, an actual state of affairs, even though the child knows that the representation mis-describes the state of affairs to which it refers.

Given the centrality of false belief to Perner's theory, we might expect a lag between children's understanding of true beliefs and ignorance on the one hand, and false beliefs on the other. True beliefs and ignorance might be handled by a situation theory because the child can again conceive of an agent directing an attitude of knowing or believing to an actual or possible situation. Indeed, children do understand that people may or may not know about a situation (Pratt and Bryant, 1990; Pillow, 1989; Hogrefe, Wimmer, and Perner, 1986) before they solve the standard false belief task.

However, Bartsch and Wellman (1995) call this particular lag into question. They report that when three-year-olds start to talk about beliefs, they start to talk more or less concurrently about false belief, true beliefs and ignorance. Admittedly, at this stage children do not *explain* actions in terms of false beliefs – but they do grasp that someone's belief may be false. This finding implies that the initial emergence of an understanding of belief is

not closely linked to an understanding of false belief in particular, and not obviously underpinned by any insight into the paradoxical way that a representation (including a mental representation) can simultaneously refer to a given referent or situation while mis-describing it.

However, to understand beliefs in general, whether true, false, or as yet untested, children might need a concept of mental representation, and such a concept might be unnecessary for an understanding of desire. Bartsch and Wellman advocate this position (1995). They offer a different rationale from Perner (1991a) for attributing a representational theory of mind, one that is less closely tied to an understanding of *false* belief. They claim that: 'When children understand that mental contents exist as distinct from real world contents and appropriately consider both, then they have moved beyond a simple connections construal of a mental state to a representational construal' (ch. 3, p. 22). They acknowledge that the clearest evidence of children's grasp of this distinction comes from remarks about false beliefs. Nevertheless, they emphasise that children mark the distinction between thought and reality in other ways. In so-called Advance Belief contrastives, the child mentions what someone currently thinks but also admits that, as yet, it is not clear whether reality coincides with what that person thinks. More generally, Bartsch and Wellman argue that comments about false beliefs are only one part of a more pervasive change in which children comment on the content of people's thoughts as being distinct from, albeit sometimes coincident with, the way that the world actually is.

In my view, there are two problems in Bartsch and Wellman's account. One is centrally concerned with the rationale for attributing to children a representational theory of mind. The second concerns the contexts in which children start to understand thoughts and beliefs.

In a very informative analysis, Bartsch and Wellman compare Advanced Desire and Advanced Belief contrastives. In Advanced Desire contrastives, the child comments on a current desire, but one whose satisfaction is not afforded by current reality. Rather, the child comments on his or her desire for a future possibility, that, hopefully will be realised. For example, Abe (aged 3;0 years) says: '...When mommy gets home, her's going to put me in bed and read to me.' His father replies: 'I'll read to you tonight.' But Abe insists: 'How come? I want mommy to.' In Advanced Belief contrastives, the child states a current belief, but one whose corroboration is not afforded by current reality. For example, Abe (aged 3;9 years) is looking for his plastic canteen. He says that he didn't play with it outside, and an adult suggests: 'It must be inside then.' Abe replies: 'I think it's upstairs in my bedroom somewhere.'

Bartsch and Wellman report that Advanced Desire contrastives emerge

before Advanced Belief contrastives. However, this finding shows that an analysis of the difference between desires and beliefs in terms of their representational content is problematic. In each case, children can envisage a possible state of affairs, one whose existence is not ordained by reality as currently known, and they can comment on someone's desire for or belief in that possible state of affairs. Despite this parallel, children comment earlier on Advanced Desires than on Advanced Beliefs: an average lag of approximately six months is apparent for the four children for whom the most data are available. More generally, this conceptual parallel between the way that children talk about desires and beliefs undermines Bartsch and Wellman's attempt to tie the emergence of a representational theory of mind to the emergence of talk about beliefs. If children engage in parallel talk for desires, one should conclude instead that children have a representational theory with respect to both desires and beliefs. Alternatively, one should conclude that the ability to differentiate between reality and the mental content of a propositional attitude is too loose a criterion for attributing a representational theory of mind.

The second problem concerns the way that talk about thoughts and beliefs gets underway. Bartsch and Wellman propose that the child, armed with a simple desire theory, encounters certain mental phenomena that are puzzling unless thoughts and beliefs are invoked to explain them: 'The child's own experience of confronting unexpected circumstances, surprising states of affairs that do not accord with his or her own desires or expectations about the world, must push for a way to describe that sort of mental state' (Chapter 8, p. 54). However, a large body of research on infants implies that even three- or four-month-olds encounter events that violate their expectations. Hence, this line of argument implies that talk about expectations and beliefs ought to emerge just as early as talk about desires, if not before.

To sum up, neither of the two main theory-theory accounts of the lag between desire and belief are completely satisfactory. Perner (1991a) argues that in contrast to desires, an understanding of false beliefs requires an appreciation of how a representation can both refer to and mis-describe a situation. However, the later emergence of belief understanding does not appear to be narrowly tied to children's insight into false beliefs per se.

Bartsch and Wellman propose a more wide-ranging revolution in which children become increasingly sensitive to the gap between mental content and reality. However, children appear to be aware of a similar gap when they talk about desires. Second, it is not clear why children should begin to articulate the gap between expectation and reality only at three years of age if, as behavioural indices suggest, they are sensitive to that distinction much earlier.

3.4   Simulation theory

If, so far, I have been critical of existing explanations of the lag between desire and belief understanding, it is not because the theoretical approach that I favour immediately offers a satisfactory explanation. Indeed, as Bartsch and Wellman have cogently argued, their data on children's talk about the mind undermine existing formulations of simulation theory, including my own.

One problem is particularly acute. I argued that children should be equally competent at reporting their current beliefs and their current desires (Harris, 1991; 1992). The data analysed by Bartsch and Wellman (1995) show, however, that talk about beliefs, whether current or non-current, whether belonging to the self or to another, does not begin to emerge until around the third birthday, well after children talk cogently about their desires.

There is a second problem, unremarked by Bartsch and Wellman (1995), but evident nonetheless. Like Perner (1991a), I focused on children's difficulties in understanding how someone might *misconstrue* a situation. Hence, I made a distinction between those mental states that are directed at existing or possible situations, and those (such as false beliefs, or nonveridical perceptions) that are directed at counterfactual situations. The data analysed by Bartsch and Wellman (1995) suggest a different type of contrast, namely the contrast between desires, on the one hand, and beliefs on the other, whether those beliefs are directed at possible situations (as in Advanced Belief contrastives) or at known counterfactual situations (as in False Belief contrastives).

4   Is the lag illusory?

In conversation, we frequently collapse the distinction between our knowing something and what is the case. Indeed, questions about whether we know something (e.g. 'Do you know his name?') are not normally taken as enquiries about our knowing, but as requests for information about what is the case. Accordingly, we supply real-world information (the person's name) in reply. We would not normally specify any propositional attitude information (e.g. 'Yes, I do know') or even preface the real-world information that we supply with such a propositional attitude (e.g. 'Yes, I know his name is Henry.')

Admittedly, cases do arise when we comment on our propositional attitude. If we do not know the name, or we are unsure, we specify our propositional attitude (e.g. 'Sorry, I don't (know)' or 'I think it's Henry but I am not sure.') Thus, we cite our propositional attitude in those cases where we judge that we cannot reliably supply the requested information.

Conceivably, then, children's references to knowing and thinking provide a limited index of their understanding of those attitudes. Consider the following hypothetical exchange between an adult and a child. Adult: 'Do you know where Teddy is?' Child: 'In my room.' The child's reply is appropriate although there is no explicit marking that she or he *knows* the location. Now, consider a data-sampling strategy in which children's utterances that include mental verbs such as *know* or *think* are analysed, but utterances that do not contain those verbs, even though they are offered in reply to adult queries containing *know* or *think*, are ignored. Such an analytic strategy might underestimate the extent to which children comment suitably on what they know. Yet this is the analytic strategy that Bartsch and Wellman (1995) adopt. A different picture might emerge if adult input (containing verbs such as *know* and *think*) were taken as the starting point. Two-year-olds may supply appropriate answers to questions about what they know, even if they rarely mark that knowledge by saying: 'I know that . . .'

Nevertheless, even using the search strategy adopted by Bartsch and Wellman, children should still display uses of *know* and *think* where their knowledge falls short. As noted earlier, it is customary to mark ignorance of a fact by saying: 'I don't know'; or to mark uncertainty by saying: 'I think that . . .' At this point, however, another analytic strategy adopted by Bartsch and Wellman (1995) needs to be considered. Understandably, they sought to exclude phrases that serve a conversational function but do not obviously illuminate the child's understanding of mental states. For example, phrases such as: 'You know what?' were excluded as were 'short, unembellished or idiomatic phrases' (ch.2, p. 22) (e.g. 'Don't know' or 'I think so'). These exclusions can be justified in terms of the conservative strategy of including only genuine references to beliefs and desires, but they run the risk of excluding certain genuine, albeit unembellished, references. The exclusion of the responses 'Don't know' and 'I think so' is noteworthy. These are precisely the phrases that a child might use to mark ignorance or uncertainty.

In sum, the argument so far has been that in conversation, the propositional attitudes of knowing and thinking will often remain unmarked. A data-analytic strategy that ignores this conversational rule, and which also excludes unadorned markers of ignorance and uncertainty, is in danger of characterising the child as operating more or less exclusively with a desire psychology, and little or no understanding of belief. This corresponds, of course, to the portrait of the 2-year-old that is offered by Bartsch and Wellman (1995) and indeed by Perner (1991a). A more liberal, and encompassing analytic strategy might yield a different picture.

Despite these cautionary remarks, I doubt whether such a change of strategy would eliminate the lag between desire and belief talk that is so thoroughly documented by Bartsch and Wellman. In fact, I suspect that our conversational focus on information rather than propositional attitudes toward such information is a major component of that lag, and not simply a methodological trap. Two further pieces of evidence support this conclusion. Bartsch and Wellman offer a partial analogue of the more liberal strategy sketched above. Children's uses of terms such as *right, wrong, so, true,* and so forth also lagged behind the use of desire terms (ch. 6, pp. 15–17). Second, they analysed all uses of the verbs *think* and *know,* including those that appeared in stock phrases such as 'I don't know.' Again, this more encompassing strategy failed to eliminate the observed lag (ch. 5, pp. 4–5).

Finally, it is important to remember the evidence reviewed in section 2. In particular, several experiments have been conducted in which children are asked to make a similar sort of judgement (e.g. will a protagonist feel happy or sad?) in the context of two different scenarios one calling for an understanding of the protagonist's desire, and the other calling for an understanding of the protagonist's mistaken belief. In these experiments, children perform better on the desire task than the belief task (Baron-Cohen, 1991b; Hadwin and Perner, 1991a; Harris *et al.,* 1989).

5   A proposal

I speculate as follows. Children are involved in two overlapping but distinct forms of human activity. Together with their caretakers and siblings, they are involved in planful actions. They are also involved in communication, primarily through language. These two modes of human activity pull for different forms of psychological understanding. Specifically, action can be understood by construing other people as agents who want to achieve certain goals. By contrast, communication, especially when an exchange of information is involved (rather than the expression of requests or rejections), can only be successfully undertaken if people are construed as epistemic subjects. More precisely, communication partners must take one another's knowledge states into account if information is to be exchanged with the aim of forming new beliefs and revising old ones. My central claim is that children's understanding of other people as epistemic subjects develops in the context of their increasing proficiency at conversation involving the deliberate exchange of such information. Hence, my explanation for the lag is that a critical precondition for understanding beliefs but not desires – participation in the exchange of information through conversation – is not attained by most children until the third year.

5.1   Understanding people as goal-directed agents

For a planful, rational agent, it is important to be able to (1) identify the status quo (2) hold possible situations in mind (3) adopt pro or con attitudes toward those situations (4) select between actions in terms of whether they increase the likelihood of situations for which the agent has a pro attitude and/or reduce the likelihood of situations for which the agent has a con attitude. Thus, the execution of deliberate, planful action presumes an agent with some awareness of his or her pro or con attitudes toward possible situations. At the same time, such an agent can operate effectively without any awareness of holding beliefs about those situations. Representations of the current situation, and of what would ensue from various courses of action need not be marked by the agent as beliefs for planning to take place. The representations can be retrieved and used in planning without any specification of their origin, fallibility, or even their probability.[5]

In a social context it would also be useful for an agent to be able to (1) identify the pro or con attitudes of other agents and (2) have a communicative repertoire of gestures, facial expressions, and eventually words with which to communicate the desires of the self to prospective collaborators. Again, there is little call for the child to identify the beliefs of the other or to communicate his or her own beliefs. This will be especially true if the child and his or her prospective collaborator have some mechanism for jointly establishing which particular section of the world they are currently representing.

The implication of this speculation is that children's initial focus on desires combined with a neglect of beliefs, is part of the inbuilt machinery for engaging in planning including joint planning. In formulating and negotiating a plan, an agent must be aware not just of what it is that is desired but also of whether it is desired or not. By contrast, plans can be formulated on the basis of what is believed or known but the agent need not reflect on whether it is known or not, and with what certainty.

This focus on desires, with beliefs left 'transparent', reveals itself nicely in the two-year-olds' talk about the mind as described by Bartsch and Wellman (1995). Talk about desires is frequent, and occurs before talk about beliefs takes place. Moreover, the same pattern emerges whether the child is engaged in talk about other people or in talk about the self.

5.2   Understanding people as epistemic subjects

What eventually pushes the child toward an acknowledgement of the role of thoughts and beliefs? My proposal is that the child's growing experience, not as an agent, but as a conversationalist plays a critical role. In the course of the third year, children increasingly engage in conversations where information is exchanged. This exchange reveals itself in several different ways, including reports, questions, repairs, and denials. Children aged two and a half years can accurately recall and discuss past events including those that occurred more than three months earlier (Fivush *et al.*, 1987) and they can even do so with non-specific ('and . . . ?') prompting from adults (Peterson, 1990). They are also selectively informative; they provide more verbal information about an object's location if their interlocutor was absent rather than present during its placement (O'Neill, 1993). At this same age, children are also able to seek information by asking questions. Most of their questions are of the yes-no variety but *what* and *where* also occur together with occasional *why* questions (Hood and Bloom, 1979; Savic, 1975; Tyack and Ingram, 1977). Although information is sometimes requested to facilitate the child's ongoing plan of action, children also seek information independent of any ongoing plan; they pose questions about things that they happen to see or hear (Lewis, 1938; Przetacznik-Gierowska and Likeza, 1990). Children of two and a half years also respond appropriately when the exchange of information misfires and a repair is needed: if an adult asks for clarification of a child's assertion, the child responds in most cases, and offers the type of clarification that is sought. For example, children offer confirmatory responses most often following an adult's request for confirmation (e.g. 'Two?') and they provide specific information most often following an adult's specific query (e.g. 'Put it where?') (Anselmi *et al.*, 1986; Shatz and O'Reilly, 1990). Finally, at two and a half years, most children can use *no* not just to refuse parental requests but to reply negatively to an adult's question (Hummer *et al.*, 1993) or to dissent from an adult's assertion (Pea, 1982; Vaidyanathan, 1991).

From these various indices, it is reasonable to conclude that children of this age can use conversation as a means for information-exchange with no immediate practical aim in mind. Information is passed on from one person to another, as when someone is told about a past event that they did not witness. Information gaps are identified and resolved, as in the case of questions and repairs. Finally, information is challenged, as in the case of dissent or denial. Such information-bearing conversations should serve as a constant demonstration that partners in a conversation differ in what they know and believe about a shared topic. Indeed, conversation is effective to the extent that such gaps in shared knowledge and belief are taken into account and resolved or reduced. Even in verbal disputes, there is an acknowledgement that the interlocutor asserts something different from the self. Hence, in the course of conversation, the default assumption that is operative in the context of desire psychology – namely that agents share the same knowledge base with respect to a given situation – will be repeatedly undermined. Instead, children will be confronted by the fact that people differ in what they know and think.

It is important to distinguish my claim from superficially similar claims. It has sometimes been suggested that children's participation in conversations about psychological states including their exposure to terms such as *know* and *think* might help them to conceptualise mental states (Olson, 1988; Dunn, 1994; Smith, this volume). However, I am not making a claim about the effect of a particular topic of conversation or the use of particular lexical items in conversation. Instead, I propose that the structure of well-formed conversation alerts children to a hitherto transparent set of human capacities. According to my account, children could learn from conversation that people are recipients and providers of information irrespective of whether that conversation includes any explicit talk about *knowing* and *thinking* or psychological states in general.

I also do not wish to suggest that verbal ability per se (as indexed by verbal mental age) is a critical tool for belief understanding. Admittedly, conversational competence is likely to be correlated with verbal ability. Hence, to the extent that it indexes conversational competence, it would not be surprising if some minimal level of verbal ability appeared to be necessary for belief understanding. Still, if my argument is correct, it is conversational competence, and not verbal ability that is the key prerequisite.

6   Predictions

The claim that children learn about thoughts and beliefs in the context of conversation predicts that: (1) a minimal level of conversational competence is a precondition for belief understanding; (2) early references to *know* and *think* will be couched in terms of their conversational function rather than in terms of mental states in the strict sense (3) non-human primates – who lack the relevant conversational competence – will not understand beliefs, even though they may have some understanding of desires (4) non-human primates who gain some conversational competence might, in principle, make progress in belief understanding; (5) children who have a readily available conversation partner will be more likely to understand the role of beliefs than children who lack such a partner; and (6) belief understanding will not, at first, be closely linked to the child's explanation and prediction of action, but rather to the child's understanding of information exchange. I review evidence for these predictions below.

6.1   *Conversational competence and belief understanding*

If conversational competence is a precondition for false-belief understand-ing, we might expect a relationship between measures of the two abilities. There is evidence that the performance of normal children on false-belief tasks is correlated with general language competence (Bowler and Norris, 1993; Jenkins and Astington, 1994). However, my proposal focuses on con-versational competence in particular, not language competence in general. Studies of autistic children who may or may not possess the necessary con-versational competence help to evaluate this more specific claim. Two studies have shown that autistic children who pass the false-belief task perform better on standardised assessments of communication skills than those who fail (Eisenmajer and Prior, 1991; Frith, Happé, and Siddons, 1994). Indeed, Eisenmajer and Prior (1991) report that a measure of con-versational competence (which assessed various communicative intentions, including requesting information, rejecting or denying, informing, etc. in a contextually appropriate fashion) was a better discriminator of perfor-mance on the false-belief task than several other related measures such as Verbal Comprehension, Similarities, and Vocabulary (measures based on the Wechsler tests for children), Verbal MA and chronological age.

Evidence from other groups with disabilities also fits my proposal. Leslie and Frith (1988) report that although a group of autistic children mostly failed a test of false belief, a group of twelve children with specific language impairment responded correctly on the same task (with the exception of one child). Children with specific language impairment have difficulties mainly with the syntax of language, and not with its conversational func-tion. Similarly, children with Williams syndrome – who display consider-able skill in conversation despite severe visual-spatial deficits – perform quite well on standard tasks of belief (Tager-Flusberg *et al.*, 1994).

In sum, the study of children with disabilities shows that difficulty in the use of language for communicative purposes is strongly correlated with dif-ficulties on the false-belief task whereas other types of specific impairment show no such relationship. Moreover, non-pragmatic aspects of language ability – notably vocabulary size, and syntactic ability – show a weaker rela-tionship. This evidence supports the claim that information exchange via conversation is a prerequisite for the child's appreciation of knowledge and belief.[6]

6.2   *Learning to use the words* know *and* think

Existing studies confirm that the words *know* and *think* are the most fre-quently used cognitive verbs (Bartsch and Wellman, 1995; Furrow *et al.*,

1992). How do children start to use those verbs? If my account is correct, we might expect children to use the terms initially with a fairly narrow conversational function. Subsequently, usage would expand to include more evidently mentalistic references. Thus, at first a term like *know* would be frequently used to mark the speaker's ignorance in response to a question ('I don't know'), to seek information and/or action from an interlocutor ('Do you know what that is?' or 'Do you know where that goes?') or to introduce information ('Know what?') Similarly, a term like *think* would be used to exchange information ('Do you think that's a garage?') Such terms would rarely be used to make genuine reference to a mental state of the speaker, listener or a third party (e.g. 'Think about it in your head' or 'She doesn't know all this').

The three main studies of children's use of cognitive verbs confirm that this is indeed the pattern that is seen in the third year (Bartsch and Wellman, 1995; Furrow *et al.*, 1992; Shatz *et al.*, 1983). At the beginning of this period, genuine mental references are extremely rare, whereas conversational references that orchestrate the flow of information and interaction are much more common. At around three years, the frequency of genuine mental reference has increased, and as discussed in section 2, genuine references to mental states become increasingly frequent in the fourth and fifth year.

6.3   *Understanding of belief and desire by non-human primates*

Chimpanzees show signs of desire understanding. Premack and Woodruff (1978) provided evidence that a chimpanzee can understand what another agent wants to do (and predict the agent's next move). Chimpanzees can also collaborate with a partner – and exchange roles – in pursuit of a common goal (Povinelli, Nelson, and Boysen, 1992).

On the other hand, there is little persuasive evidence of belief understanding. Although primates engage in tactical ploys to secure various gains, while simultaneously blocking intervention, punishment or competition from other members of their immediate group (Byrne and Whiten, 1991; Cheney and Seyfarth, 1991), such ploys are not necessarily aimed at altering the beliefs of other agents (Premack and Dasser, 1991; Whiten and Byrne, 1991). In line with the assertion that primates do not understand informational states, emerging evidence confirms that rhesus monkeys (Povinelli *et al.*, 1991) and young chimpanzees (Povinelli, this volume; Povinelli, Rulf, and Bierschwale, 1994) are poor at selectively using information provided by someone who has had the opportunity for informative visual access as compared with someone who has not. There is some evidence that chimpanzees older than six years are more selective, suggesting that they have a rudimentary grasp of the role of visual access (Povinelli *et al.*, 1990). However, as Povinelli (1994) notes, this selective performance did not immediately emerge on a transfer test but only after repeated trials. Thus, there is no unequivocal evidence that older chimpanzees understand the link between seeing and knowing, and considerable evidence that younger chimpanzees find that link very hard to grasp.

6.4   Chimpanzee conversation?

Does the chimpanzees' acquisition of sign language permit them to engage in conversation and thereby understand informational states? In fact, chimpanzees rarely use signs for purely conversational purposes. They use them mostly for making demands or requests. The most loquacious chimpanzee studied to date, Kanzi, a male bonobo, is reported to devote more than 90% of his utterances to requests (Greenfield and Savage-Rumbaugh, 1990). Even in the case of repetition – one of the simplest forms of communication – chimpanzees, unlike children, do not use it to make a query, to issue a denial, or to keep a conversation going (Greenfield and Savage-Rumbaugh, 1993). Thus, even chimpanzees who are proficient in signing, do not appear to have the conversational competence to learn about informational exchange.

Admittedly, there is intriguing evidence that enculturation in a human environment can bring about notable cognitive changes. For example, Tomasello, Savage-Rumbaugh, and Kruger (1993) report that three enculturated chimpanzees (one common chimpanzee, and two bonobos all exposed to a lexigram communication system) performed much better on tests of immediate and delayed imitation as compared with mother-reared chimpanzees. The performance of the enculturated chimpanzees was equivalent to, or even exceeded (on delay trials) the performance of children aged two and a half years. However, such superior imitation is unlikely to call for an understanding of belief. Instead, it may depend upon the cultivation of joint attention to objects and events that is so frequent in a human environment (Tomasello, in press).

I know of no comparable investigations of the understanding of informational states by enculturated chimpanzees. Recent evidence of language comprehension by Kanzi (Savage-Rumbaugh *et al.*, 1993) suggests that such tests might be feasible. Two complimentary research techniques might be employed. First, it is possible to ask whether Kanzi supplies and seeks information in accordance with the knowledge or ignorance of an interlocutor. Suppose that Kanzi wants to retrieve an object, knows where it is, but needs human assistance. Will he supply more location information to an ignorant helper than an informed one as do two and a half year old children (O'Neill, 1993)? Reciprocally, suppose that Kanzi is seeking information. Will he seek information from an informed listener rather than an ignorant one? Granted Kanzi's limited participation in conversation, as noted earlier, he might well fail such tests notwithstanding his linguistic abilities.

6.5   The availability of a conversation partner

Two recent studies have shown that children with siblings display a more precocious understanding of false-belief tasks than only children (Jenkins and Astington, 1994; Perner, Ruffman and Leekam, 1994). The exact explanation for this link is not yet clear. Certain possibilities can already be ruled out, however. The effect does not appear to be due to the experience of 'teaching' a younger sibling; children with an older sibling also benefit. Conversely, the effect does not appear to be due to the experience of 'learning' from an older sibling; children with a younger sibling also benefit. A plausible explanation of this pattern of results, therefore, is that children with siblings engage in more conversation.[7] In particular, they have more opportunities to discover how information may be exchanged via conversation. Children with siblings will have repeated opportunities to discover that conversation partners differ in whether they know what you tell them and in whether they can tell you what you ask. Such differences between conversation partners may be especially evident in the context of triadic conversations in which a parent and a sibling differ in their reply to the child's assertion or question.

6.6   The relation between desire and belief understanding

In their monograph, Bartsch and Wellman (1995) examine various possible links between desire and belief understanding. For example, they correlate the frequency with which desires are mentioned with the age of onset for belief references. No correlation was found. Similarly, when the frequency of desire talk was correlated with the frequency of belief references, no correlation was found. Bartsch and Wellman did find that age of onset of desire explanations was correlated to age of onset of belief references, but this kind of continuity might simply reflect linguistic precocity that shows up across independent domains. Thus, contrary to what one might expect on the basis of the theory-theory, there is no persuasive evidence that desire talk is a launching pad for belief talk. Rather, when children start to refer to thinking and knowing, they do so in a descriptive fashion, disconnected from the explanation of action.

7   Relationship to theoretical accounts

How does my proposal relate to existing theoretical accounts of the child's theory of mind? It is distinct from them because the possibility that language, especially conversational competence, might push for a different conception of mind has been ignored. Recall that it was experiments on chimpanzees (Premack and Woodruff, 1978; Woodruff and Premack, 1979) together with subsequent commentary and refinement (Bennett, 1978; Dennett, 1978; Harman, 1978) that inspired research with children. Although it has proved easier to make empirical headway with children, the questions posed – regarding the understanding of seeing, knowing, beliefs and deception – are also applicable to non-verbal primates (see chapters by Povinelli, Gómez and Whiten, this volume), even if they are harder to settle.

Nonetheless, existing theoretical accounts can be drawn upon both to attack or elaborate the proposal as it stands:

7.1   Modular accounts

Advocates of modularity might re-work the proposal as follows: conversational competence and an understanding of informational states are indeed linked but not in the manner suggested. Conversation does not provide a context for the child's developing understanding of knowing and thinking. Instead, it is the activation of a module dedicated to the understanding of knowing and thinking – perhaps at some point in the third year – that provides a basis for engaging in conversation. By extension, this argument implies that autistic children are poor conversationalists because that module malfunctions. Similarly attempts to turn chimpanzees into conversationalists are doomed to fail because they lack such a module. This counter-proposal has considerable force, but I believe my account is simpler and more parsimonious.

To explain why, I need to sketch an account of the emergence of conversation. From 18–24 months, a great deal of talk is about here-and-now objects or events. For that talk to get underway, children need to have a capacity for joint attention (with their conversation partner) to a common topic in the immediate environment. The evidence suggests that autistic children, and also chimpanzees, diverge from normal children even at this point. In each case, their capacity for joint attention is deficient. From 24–36 months, the child's conversational horizon expands: increasingly, there is 'displaced' talk about topics that are not immediately present. Even in the context of talk about such 'displaced' topics, an equivalent joint focus of attention – mediated by language – is still needed (Tomasello,

1988). However, as such displacement increases, there is an increasing like-lihood that the two partners will diverge in their knowledge of the topic under discussion; one partner may have witnessed the event being discussed but not the other. This divergence is less likely for a topic in the here-and-now because both partners can concurrently observe or explore it.

Thus, my argument is that during this later period of displaced conversation the child is increasingly exposed to differences in knowledge and belief, and such exposure is a prerequisite for explicit talk about knowing and thinking. Thus, I suggest that more simple competencies, notably the capacity for joint attention, rather than a module dedicated to an understanding of knowing and thinking, serve as a prerequisite for conversation about shared topics. Once conversation is underway, and becomes increasingly displaced from the here-and-now, then an understanding of information states can be initiated. Without a capacity for joint attention, even rudimentary conversation about the here and now is problematic.

7.2   Theory-theory accounts

Theory-theorists, as discussed earlier, have emphasised children's emerging insight into the nature of mental representation. My proposal suggests an obvious but plausible context for the emergence of that insight. Language is the representational medium through which we learn most directly about the content of other people's thoughts and beliefs, the congruence of those thoughts and beliefs with our own, their congruence with reality, and the conviction with which they are held. Admittedly, we can sometimes infer that content (and even infer that it is false) by tracing its history. Thus, we can infer whether someone knows about a current situation by checking whether they witnessed its realisation, but that type of inference is both sophisticated and limited. It has to be motivated by a prior understanding of the link between informational access and belief; it gives us no direct clues about someone's commitment to a belief; it will not help us to work out what someone believes about a situation that they witnessed but we did not; and it will not help us to work out what beliefs they hold about future situations. Conversation does not suffer from any of these restrictions. It can inform us of what someone believes about actual as well as possible situations, and how firmly they believe it, irrespective of whether we appreciate the source of their belief, and irrespective of whether we have witnessed or can witness the situation that is the referent of their belief.

In sum, if children do learn something about the fundamental nature of representation in the pre-school years, language is the medium of representation that is likely to be most instructive.[8]

7.3   Simulation accounts

Simulation accounts, in common with other approaches, have been developed mainly to explain children's increasing accuracy in predicting what people will do or feel in the context of goal-directed action. They have not been especially concerned with the kind of anticipatory skill that is needed for conducting connected and informative conversation. However, such an elaboration seems feasible. Two points, in particular, stand out.

First, theory-theory accounts have stressed the child's growing understanding of propositional attitudes, independent of any given point-of-view. Indeed, theory-theorists have seen it as a virtue that their account credits the child with such a person-neutral stance. Yet conversation constantly underlines the centrality of point-of-view. Pronouns and deictic terms must be produced and understood with respect to a given point-of-view. In this context, the simulation metaphor of the child being increasingly capable of setting aside his or her current point-of-view so as to imaginatively share another's perspective seems appropriate. Conversation demands this constant shuttling back and forth between our actual stance – which we voice as speaker – and the stance of our interlocutor – which we temporarily take on as we listen and comprehend.

The second point concerns the content of conversation. As several commentators have noted (including its critics) simulation theory offers a plausible explanation of our ability to anticipate the linguistic and inferential performance that other people will display. Especially when that performance applies to a specific content, we surely base our expectations of what the other will say, understand, or infer, not on a theory of the other but on what we might say, understand, or infer, were we facing similar circumstances (Harris, 1992; Heal, this volume; Stich and Nichols, 1995, this volume). Conversation is unusual in that it provides rapid feedback regarding the success of our predictions. If we misjudge what the other will understand, the conversation will falter, and repairs and clarifications will be needed. As noted earlier, this feedback process is already underway in the third year. One plausible outcome is that it helps children to fine-tune their simulation of a conversation partner. As a result, we might expect individual children to master an increasingly diverse set of conversational styles as they become sensitive to variations among their conversation partners, in presuppositions, knowledge and status.

8   Conclusions

From around two years of age, and increasingly during the third year, normal children have the opportunity to discover and enjoy one of the unique abilities of our species – to use language to exchange information. It would be surprising if this new horizon did not lead children to a different perspective on the way that the human mind works. If I am right, idle conversation reveals the human capacity for knowing and thinking, independent of any immediate plan of action.[9]

ACKNOWLEDGEMENTS

I thank Janet Astington, Dermot Bowler, Peter Carruthers, Tim German, Daniela O'Neill, Daniel Povinelli, Michael Tomasello, and Henry Wellman for helpful commentary and discussion. I am particularly grateful to Karen Bartsch and Henry Wellman for the opportunity to read their forthcoming monograph (*Children talk about the mind*). Some of the research described was supported by grants from the ESRC, United Kingdom (R 000 23 3543 and R 000 22 1174).

NOTES

1 Phillips *et al.* (1994) report that autistic children perform worse than normal and mentally handicapped children on more complex tasks involving desire satisfaction and desire change. Nonetheless, the autistic children tend to perform better on such tasks than on standard tests of false belief.
2 In his chapter in this volume, Gordon argues that first-person attributions might be initially learned in the context of such pragmatic contexts. If his developmental account is valid, we might conceive of autistic children as arrested at this early stage.
3 In fact, he has offered two inconsistent accounts of desire understanding, linking it to the earlier-appearing action processor (TOMM, system 1) in Leslie and Roth (1993, p. 105) but to the attitudinal processor (TOMM, system 2) in Leslie (1994, p.122). In neither case, however, is the role of the selection processor discussed in relation to desire.
4 Carruthers (personal communication) defends staggered modularity on evolutionary grounds. He argues that a desire psychology – even without a belief component – would confer an evolutionary advantage because it would enable desire-based predictions of action with a fairly high success rate. By contrast, a belief psychology – with no desire component – would have a poor success rate. Thus, a module for desire psychology would evolve first followed by a more complex module for belief-desire psychology.

    However, whatever the plausibility of this evolutionary argument, it tacitly assumes that modularised capacities that emerge late ontogenetically also emerged late in our evolutionary history. This assumption seems dubious, however. Should we assume that those psychological processes that regulate sexual interest in the opposite sex, processes that normally become active around only puberty, developed late in evolutionary time?
5 Carruthers (personal communication) points out that planful action might not require an agent to be aware of desiring or not desiring a particular situation.

Instead, the agent might review possible situations and adopt a plan of action that will increase the likelihood of the situation that emerges top in some metric of goodness or attractiveness. According to this argument agents need only be aware of the value that they place upon an object not of the fact that they desire or value it.

However, even this argument tacitly grants the child both an awareness of the particular situation that is desired and also an awareness of the desirability of that situation. Thus, it amounts to a crude desire psychology – but one that takes an anti-subjective stance toward desire by locating desirability in the object rather than the subject. Conceivably, children do start off with this sort of stance. Still, it is not obvious that they could hold onto it. They would presumably discover that situations are constantly changing in their rank-order of attractiveness (e.g. the object that seemed so attractive to play with a moment ago seems dull now).

6 Doherty (1994) reports that children's performance on a synonym detection task in which they judged whether someone had named an item (e.g. 'bunny') appropriately, without using the same name as they themselves used (e.g. 'rabbit') was strongly correlated with their performance on a false-belief task. This evidence supports Perner's (1991a) claim that understanding (false) belief calls for a differentiation between the sense and the referent of a representation. However, a grasp of synonymy may be part of a much wider appreciation of the way that different people can represent the same referent differently. Again, sustained conversation, rather than synonymy in particular is likely repeatedly to show that people can represent the same situation differently even though it is the joint topic of their conversation. For example, in the following exchange, both partners refer to the same person, but represent that person differently: 'He's left'; 'Who?'; 'Josef'?

7 Carruthers (personal communication) makes the important point that children with limited or delayed exposure to conversation (e.g. deaf children) should show difficulties on tests of belief understanding if my proposal is correct.

8 Gopnik, Slaughter, and Meltzoff (1994) suggest that children initially acquire an understanding of representation, particularly misrepresentation, in the context of perception, and then use that as a model for misrepresentation in the context of belief. They offer evidence that the two types of understanding emerge in succession and that the first can facilitate the second. However, this proposal does not offer a detailed explanation of the timetable documented by Bartsch and Wellman (1995). Two-year-olds use the word 'see' appropriately and often in their spontaneous speech (Bretherton and Beeghly, 1982). Why does it take them so long to start using 'think' and 'know'? More generally, why is perception a model for understanding belief rather than vice versa?

9 Whiten (this volume) points out that in the case of non-verbal creatures, their psychological predictions can often be (conservatively) interpreted as predictions about behaviour. By contrast, conversation permits, and indeed calls for, the exchange of information about informational attitudes independent of any immediate behaviour based on that information.

Part III

Failures of acquisition – explaining autism

14   What could possibly explain autism?

Jill Boucher

1   Introduction

Autism has proved remarkably difficult to describe and explain, rather in the way that schizophrenia has resisted clear description and explanation. This is easily overlooked. My first aim is therefore to set a context within which people who are not specialists in autism may place mind-reading explanations of autism.

A second aim of the chapter is to suggest some logical constraints on psychological explanations of autism in general. Some of these constraints are well recognised and have been discussed with relevance to autism by other writers (Happé, 1994a; Ozonoff *et al.*, 1991a). Other constraints are more specific and have not, I think, been paid much attention. I argue that paying attention to these constraints should help to narrow the field of tenable psychological explanations of autism.

The third aim of the chapter is to assess mind-reading theories of autism against these constraints. I will use the term 'mind-reading' to cover what is thought by some to be achieved by simulation (e.g. Currie, this volume; Harris, 1993) and by others as utilising a theory of mind based on a 'mind-reading module' (e.g. Baron-Cohen and Swettenham, this volume; Carruthers, ch.16 this volume; Leslie and Roth, 1993). I will not discuss the relative merits of these two types of mind-reading theory in the case of autism.

This chapter is concerned with explanations of autism at the level of psychological processes underlying manifest behaviour. However, neurobiology is increasingly being used to construct and constrain psychological explanations of autism, and possible links between behaviour and brain function will be touched on. It is therefore relevant to point out that a number of structural, functional, and biochemical brain abnormalities have been found in individuals with autism or in group comparison studies, but no consistent abnormalities have been found across all cases (Minshew, 1992). It is known, however, that autism can result from a number of different etiological factors, including genetic vulnerability, infectious diseases in the mother during pregnancy, metabolic disorders, and certain diseases which affect the child's brain. It is usual to suggest that different etiological factors converge on a 'final common pathway' to produce whatever brain damage or dysfunction is necessary and sufficient to cause autistic behaviour.

2   What has to be explained: behaviour, definitions and concepts of autism

2.1   *Behaviour in people with autism and current definitions*

It is widely agreed that people whom it is appropriate to describe as autistic have the following 'triad' of impairments (Wing and Gould, 1979; American Psychiatric Association, 1987; World Health Organisation, 1987):

(1) Specific abnormalities of social behaviour, affecting in particular reciprocal relating and empathy;
(2) Communication difficulties affecting non-verbal communication, conversational skills (pragmatics) and prosody;
(3) Lack of creativity and imagination as evident in, for example, a paucity of creative pretend play and an inability to role play, this lack of creativity being accompanied by a characteristic rigidity and repetitiveness of behaviour.

A fourth type of impairment which some claim to be universally present is:
(4) Sensory and perceptual abnormalities of various kinds.

Additional problems which are frequently but not universally present in people with (1), (2) and (3) include: (5) Nonmodality-specific language learning difficulties. This abnormality formed a part of Kanner's original definition (Kanner, 1943) and was included in all definitions of autism up until the 1980s. (6) Ritualistic, obsessional, and compulsive behaviour and marked resistance to change: this abnormality was also stressed in earlier definitions. (7) Generalised learning difficulties (mental retardation). (8) Spoken-language-specific disorders (e.g. difficulty in establishing a phonological system or in learning to use grammatical sentences).

Many other abnormalities may also occur, some of which have more of a physiological than a psychological basis, for example, pica, or the tendency to eat inappropriate substances; floppy muscles; clumsiness; visual impairments; excessive thirst.

It has been shown by Bolton and Rutter (1990) that non-autistic relatives of people with autism (especially in the case of identical twins one of whom is autistic and one not) frequently have *either* social relating difficulties *or* developmental difficulties related in some way to language. Individuals who have one or other of these abnormalities but who are not autistic

according to current definitions are said to fall within the broader phenotype for autism.

2.2   Concepts of autism

Autism was originally described as a *syndrome*. A syndrome is a medical
condition in which a disparate set of physical and/or behavioural abnormalities regularly occur together as a result of a single common cause at a
physical level (e.g. as in Down's syndrome). To the extent that a syndrome
stems from a single cause it may be conceptualised as a unitary condition.
That is to say that the symptoms which define the syndrome will not be dis-
sociated: individual symptoms will not occur on their own, and the severity
of criterial symptoms will tend to be correlated in each individual. Symptom
severity will of course reflect interactions with other factors (intelligence,
personality, life experiences) in addition to the initial given 'dose' of the
symptom. Some variation in symptom severity will therefore occur, but significant correlations between symptoms will remain despite this variation.

The original definition of autism as a syndrome (Kanner, 1943) was nar-
rower than the definition currently in use. Kanner defined autism in terms
of language learning difficulties and ritualistic and obsessional behaviour
in addition to the impairments of social relating, communication and cre-
ativity/perseveration which are emphasised currently. Not surprisingly, the
incidence of what may be referred to as Kanner's syndrome (KS) is much
lower than the incidence of autism as currently defined. Autism as currently
defined is in fact nearly four times as common as KS, or 'classic autism'
(Wing, 1988).

Abnormalities (1), (2) and (3) alone fit well with definitions of Asperger's
syndrome (AS) (Asperger, 1944, Wing, 1981; Frith, 1991), although clumsiness is also included in some definitions of AS. However, AS is not usually
diagnosed in people with general learning difficulties, and approximately 75%
of people with the triad of impairments have general learning difficulties.

If we want to include KS under the umbrella term 'autism', we are forced
to move away from the syndrome concept of autism, since a single syndrome cannot itself contain two distinct syndromes, KS and AS. There are
two ways out of the difficulty. First 'autism' can be conceptualised as consisting of a set of *distinct but related subtypes*, including AS, KS and also
possibly including other suggested subtypes, such as semantic and pragmatic language disorders (Bishop and Rosenbloom, 1987). A second way
out of the difficulty is that suggested by Wing, which is to conceptualise
autism as a *continuum* or *spectrum* of developmental disorders in which
three core social abnormalities (the triad of impairments) plus or minus
other disabilities all occur and vary independently of each other. The term

'continuum' specifically describes the independent variation which, it is claimed, can occur across the criterial and concomitant symptoms.

The distinction between the concept of autism as a syndrome, and the concept of autism as a continuum rests on whether or not the triad of impairments are dissociable from one another: if they are not, we have a syndrome; if they are, we have a continuum. The distinction between the concept of autism as a set of distinct but related subtypes and the concept of autism as a continuum rests on the randomness or otherwise of the co-occurrence of impairments along the various dimensions of behaviour: if co-occurrence is not random, in other words if clusters of symptoms regularly occur together more often than would be predicted by chance, then the concept of a continuum collapses into a concept of related subtypes.

2.3   Why definitions and concepts matter to psychological theories

Definitions of autism are obviously important in that they determine what has to be explained. Definitions are also important in that they determine the group of individuals who are studied in psychological or other research into autism. For example, if we want to study KS we will select our participants from the 1 in 2,200 individuals who conform to earlier definitions of autism (e.g. Kanner,1943; Rutter, 1978). If we want to study autism as currently defined we will select subjects from the much larger group of 1 in 500–600 individuals who conform to post-1980s definitions.

Concepts of autism as a syndrome, as a pair or group of related but diagnostically distinct subtypes, or as a multidimensional continuum, require different models of explanation. The fit between different concepts and different explanatory models is outlined and discussed below in the section on psychological theories.

Criterion A: An initial criterion for a satisfactory theory of autism is that it should state clearly what definition of autism is being used, which set of individuals are being studied, and what concept of autism is assumed.

2.4   Criterion A and mind-reading theories

Psychologists such as Baron-Cohen, Leslie, or Harris who have proposed and tested mind-reading-deficit hypotheses of autism use the DSM III (American Psychiatric Association, 1987) definition of autism, outlined above. Baron-Cohen and Leslie seek to explain impaired social relating, impaired communication and lack of pretend play ((1), (2), and (3) above) in terms of deficient mind-reading. They explain behavioural rigidity and repetitiveness in terms of the secondary effects of anxiety and disorientation. Baron-Cohen *et al.* do not attempt to explain what are, on the DSM

III definition, concomitant or noncriterial features of autism, such as language learning difficulty or mental retardation. Nor of course do they attempt to explain physiologically determined abnormalities such as floppy muscles or excessive thirst.

A problem for these psychologists is that the DSM III definition selects for study a broad group of individuals including cases of AS as well as cases of KS, i.e. individuals with good verbal skills as well as individuals with poor verbal skills. Ozonoff *et al.* (1991b) found that only people with KS (and poor verbal skills) fail on standard theory of mind (ToM) tasks. People with AS (and good verbal skills) perform successfully on these tasks. This could explain why failure on ToM tasks has not been consistently demonstrated in groups of individuals selected on DSM III criteria. More importantly, it strongly suggests that failure on ToM tasks is related to verbal abilities rather than to the social relating, communication and creativity deficits which ToM deficits are hypothesised to explain. It may be the case, therefore, that proponents of the modular mind-reading theory of autism need to rethink the definition of autism which they are using and the precise group, or groups, of subjects to whom their theory relates. Happé (1994b) discusses this issue fully.

Psychologists who have proposed defective mind-reading as (part) explanations of autism are, I think, working on the assumption that autism is a syndrome (plus or minus concomitant disorders), rather than a set of subtypes or a continuum. In working with the concept of a syndrome rather than with a concept of subtypes they are consistent with the majority view concerning this much-discussed issue, namely that there is insufficient evidence at present to prove the existence of diagnostically distinct subtypes. In seeking to explain social relating, communication and creativity deficits by a single mechanism the modular mind-reading theorists cannot be allying themselves to a continuum concept of autism, since the essence of this concept is that impairments along all affected dimensions of behaviour are dissociable (i.e. could not be explained by a single psychological – or physical – mechanism). If we were to pursue the suggestion that theory of mind deficits are associated with verbal disabilities, we might wish to abandon a syndrome concept in favour of a subtypes concept.

3   Psychological explanations of autism

3.1   A brief history

In setting a context within which simulation and modular mind-reading theories of autism may take their place it is probably useful to describe a small selection of alternative theories, past and present.

Kanner originally suggested that autism, conceptualised as a syndrome, resulted from 'an innate inability to form the usual biologically provided affective contact with people'. He then flirted with the psychodynamic hypothesis that autism was caused by 'refrigerator mothers', but quickly returned to his original hypothesis. However, various other psychodynamic explanations of autism were proposed during the 1950s and 1960s, despite increasing evidence of organic brain abnormalities in children with autism. Psychodynamic explanations remain influential in Europe, and still have their English language proponents.

Kanner's theory and psychodynamic theories are similar in that they place socio-affective abnormalities at the core of autism. They differ in that Kanner saw the cause of the socio-affective deficits as endogenous whereas psychodynamic theories see the cause as environmental. In the 1960s a different type of environmental explanation was proposed in terms of abnormal learning experiences.

As the evidence of organic brain abnormalities increased, there was a rejection not only of psychodynamic and learning theories (which assumed environmental causes of autism) but also of the assumption that social deficits are at the core of autism. Instead there was a succession of theories from the late 1960s through to the early 1980s arguing first that linguistic/symbolic deficits are primary, and then that various types of cognitive deficit are primary (see for example Rutter, 1968; Hermelin and O'Connor, 1970; Ricks and Wing, 1976; Hoffman and Prior, 1982). In 1985, Baron-Cohen, Leslie, and Frith proposed that children with autism lack a theory of mind.

Cognitively oriented mind-reading theories have dominated autism research in the United Kingdom in the last ten years. However, in the States over that period there has been a general return to considering endogenous social deficits as primary (see for example Fein *et al.*, 1986; Sigman *et al.*, 1987). Hobson (1993a) in the UK has also argued for the primacy of socio-affective deficits. As mind-reading theories have increasingly moved back from seeing lack of a theory of mind, or of metarepresentational processes, as the primary cause of autism, identifying, rather, the precursors of a theory of mind, they have increasingly converged with socio-affective theories (Hobson, 1993b).

Recently demonstrations of deficits in high-level planning and attention switching have led some researchers to suggest that central executive dysfunction is central to autism (Ozonoff *et al.*, 1991a; Hughes and Russell, 1993). Attentional abnormalities originating more peripherally within the system have for many years been hypothesised to be a primary cause of autism (Ornitz and Ritvo, 1968; Courschesne, 1987; Dawson and Lewy, 1989).

As is clear from the above, theories of autism proposed over the years have been extremely varied (and would have appeared even more varied had more of the very many published hypotheses been described). The range of possible primary psychological deficits which have been proposed reflects not only the many different ways in which behaviour in people with autism differs from normal behaviour. It also reflects the difficulty of assigning roles of cause and effect to psychological processes which interact with each other over time, so that any primary deficit will lead to secondary deficits which may themselves exacerbate the primary deficit as well as leading on to yet further deficits. In addition, the able individual with autism (the most usual subject of research) will compensate at least to some extent for his or her early difficulties, which will then be wholly or partially masked.

It is noticeable that psychological explanations of autism are, not surprisingly, 'of their time'. Thus, for example, the successive influence on psychology of psychoanalysis, learning theory, Chomskian linguistics, the information processing model, and the growth of understanding of prelinguistic social interaction have all been reflected in successive theories about autism. The influence of cognitive science on psychology in the 1980s is reflected in mind-reading theories of autism. Neuroscience seems likely to be the next significant influence. And when the neural substrates and brain-behaviour links underlying autism have been understood, perhaps there will be a revival of interest in the psychodynamics of development in people with autism, and we will have come full circle.

The long history of attempts to explain autism at a psychological level, the variety of such attempts, and the range of theories currently proposed should be taken into account by anyone proposing their own explanatory theory of autism, or, in fact, anyone using the case of autism to argue for one or other particular theory concerning mentalising and the development of mind. This comment should, however, be taken as a caveat rather than a criterion for a good psychological explanation of autism.

3.2   Explanatory models

3.2.1   The single primary deficit model

So long as autism was considered to be a unitary syndrome, most psychological theories of autism assumed that the criterial features of the syndrome were caused by a single underlying primary psychological deficit. By 'primary', or 'fundamental', is meant a deficit stemming directly from brain pathology, i.e. a deficit which is irreducible in psychological terms (Rutter, 1968). It is parsimonious to assume a single primary deficit. In addition, a single primary deficit may appear to be indicated by the selective nature of the social, linguistic, and repetitive behaviour abnormalities which characterise autism. In a minority of cases of autism, individuals can function at high levels in almost all areas, good language may be acquired, and many of the forms of social competence. Nevertheless the individual is autistic. This has challenged researchers to look for a single 'missing ingredient' (Frith, 1989; Happé, 1994b).

3.2.2   The single critical deficit model

An interesting variant of the single primary deficit model has been proposed by Hobson (1993a). He maintains that a single psychological deficit underlies the criterial features of autistic behaviour, but suggests that the crucial deficit may arise in a number of different ways and is not necessarily primary in all cases. Hobson, like Kanner, proposes that the critical underlying deficit in autism is an inability to make normal socio-affective contact with others. He argues that this can either be primary in that it arises directly from brain pathology, or secondary to, for example, blindness or severe sensory deprivation.

3.2.3   The dual or multiple deficits model

There is no reason why autism, even if conceived of as a unitary *syndrome*, should be explicable in terms of a single primary or critical psychological deficit from which all the criterial features of behaviour stem. Goodman (1989) and Ozonoff, *et al.* (1991a) point out that syndromes characterised by apparently disparate behaviour are usually explained by a single underlying cause at a physical, rather than at a psychological, level. The example of Down's syndrome has already been cited. Goodman cites the further example of Wilson's disease, in which a multiplicity of abnormalities are explicable in terms of an isolated genetic deficit affecting copper metabolism. He suggests that multiple primary deficits at a psychological level might co-occur in autism as a result of a shared vulnerability of different brain systems to genetic or environmental effects, shared vulnerability arising from proximity, shared blood supply, shared sensitivity to an environmental toxin, shared susceptibility to nutrient deficiency, shared neurotransmitters, shared viral receptors, or shared developmental periods of maximum vulnerability. Thus, if autism is conceptualised as a syndrome, the criterial features of behaviour may well turn out to be explicable in terms of two or more primary psychological deficits with a common physical cause.

If autism is conceptualised as a *group of discrete subtypes*, then it cannot be explained by a single primary or critical deficit, and the number of primary deficits hypothesised must relate to the number of subgroups hypothesised. For example, Bishop (1989) hypothesised that KS, AS, and semantic pragmatic language disorder (another suggested subtype of autism) could be explained by different combinations of a primary language learning deficit and a primary social interaction deficit. Bishop suggested that both primary deficits are present in KS, or classic autism; that the social interaction deficit alone is present in AS; and that the language deficit alone underlies semantic and pragmatic language learning disorder. Bolton and Rutter's (1990) demonstration that social relating difficulties and language-learning related difficulties occur independently of each other in non-autistic relatives of people with autism is consistent with Bishop's hypothesis.

If autism is conceptualised as a *continuum* of a minimum of three independent impairments, usually accompanied by other dissociable impairments, then a minimum of three specific primary psychological deficits must underlie the continuum.

In conclusion, the only concept of autism which is consistent with a single primary (or critical) psychological deficit model is the syndrome concept, and Goodman has argued powerfully that most syndromes stem from a common physical cause rather than a single psychological cause. The subtypes model has, logically, to be explained in terms of more than one primary psychological cause. And the continuum concept must be explained in terms of at least three primary psychological causes. The continued search for a single primary, or critical, psychological deficit therefore appears to be unjustified in terms of its capacity to explain autism. It also appears to be unjustified on the grounds that the search for a single primary deficit has proved unproductive over many decades of research.

Criterion B for a well articulated theory of autism is that there should be an appropriate fit between the concept of autism assumed and the explanatory model offered.

3.3   Criterion B and mind-reading theories of autism

Mind-reading theories are single primary deficit theories. Thus Baron-Cohen and Leslie claim to explain all the definitional features of autism in terms of a defect somewhere or other within a mind-reading module, or, in the case of repetitive behaviour, as secondary or 'knock-on' effects caused by disorientation and anxiety. Since Baron-Cohen and Leslie appear to assume the concept of autism as a syndrome, hypothesising a single primary deficit as the cause of core features of autism is not logically untenable, though unlikely, as argued above. Both Carruthers and Currie (this volume) go further, attempting to explain in terms of a mind-reading deficit not only the 'classic triad of impairments' but also the repetitive behaviour and lack of creativity which characterise autism.

Baron-Cohen has recently argued for a subgroups model of autism in Baron-Cohen and Ring (1994a). Subscribing to a subgroups model would of course commit him to at least a dual deficit explanatory model. However, the two deficits hypothesised by Baron-Cohen and Ring are defective functioning of a shared attention mechanism (SAM) and defective functioning of a theory of mind mechanism (ToMM). Both these proposed mechanisms lie within the mind-reading module and produce similar symptoms, though with different onset times. Baron-Cohen's hypothesis therefore remains a single (mind-reading) deficit explanation of autism as a syndrome (with varying time of onset). If he went on to relate primary dysfunction of SAM to one qualitatively distinct subtype of autism and dysfunction of ToMM to another, then an interesting dual deficit hypothesis relating to a subtypes concept might emerge.

3.4   Theory types

Rogers and Pennington (1991) argue that 'We do not expect to find specific deficits in young autistic children that are maintained throughout development. Rather, we expect to see some signs of a deeper underlying deficit specific to autism stand out during a specific developmental stage, only to be accomplished to some degree at a later developmental stage and replaced by other symptoms of the underlying deficit . . . Ours is a theory of heterotypic, rather than homotypic, continuity.'

Defined in this way, homotypic and heterotypic continuity are not greatly different from each other. If I understand Rogers and Pennington correctly, they claim that homotypic continuity consists of a persistent primary deficit which remains causally operative with *unchanging* manifestations, whereas heterotypic continuity consists of a persistent primary deficit with *changing* manifestations. It is difficult, however, to envisage a persistent, causally operative deficit with unchanging manifestations which does not also produce changing secondary effects. For example, an intractable hearing loss will persist with certain unchanging effects, such as inability to respond to environmental sounds. However, intractable hearing loss may also produce a cascade of secondary effects, such as reduced mobility, over protectedness, reading delay, under achievement at school and so on. This blurs any distinction made in terms of changing as against unchanging effects of persistent primary deficits.

I propose, therefore, to use the term heterotypic continuity to describe conditions in which the primary deficit does not itself persist as an active cause (which is an alternative interpretation of Pennington and Rogers' use of the term). On this definition, heterotypic continuity becomes synonymous with the familiar concept of developmental delay, though with an emphasis on the successive results of an initial delay. For example, delayed myelinisation of nerve fibres can cause delayed speech and language which (as the myelinisation problem resolves) can cause reading difficulties which (as the speech and language normalises) can cause loss of self esteem and so on. On this definition of heterotypic continuity the psychological causes of developmental disorders change over time, each successively giving way to others.

Criterion C: Heterotypic, or delay, theories of autism must be able to specify the chain, or chains, of cause and effect which maintain the criterial features of autistic behaviour. Delay theories must also be able to explain why the chain of cause and effect maintains the criterial features of autistic behaviour in a rather consistent way, rather than leading to increasing divergence between individuals, with a return to normalcy in some.

3.5   Criterion C and mind-reading theories

Leslie argues that unimpaired performance by some people with autism on some mind-reading tasks can be explained in terms of compensatory mechanisms masking an underlying persistent primary deficit (Frith, Morton and Leslie, 1991). His theory is therefore clearly homotypic. Baron-Cohen, on the other hand, has sometimes suggested that autism results from developmental delays in the acquisition of mind-reading skills, and that the unimpaired performance of some people with autism on mind-reading tasks can be explained in terms of their having overcome an initial delay (Baron-Cohen, 1989a; 1991a). In one version, therefore, his theory is heterotypic.

With regard to the requirement that delay theories identify a chain of factors capable of maintaining autism, one supposes that to do this Baron-Cohen would traverse back up the successive stages of the mind-reading module from goal directedness to joint attention to metarepresentation to theory of mind. With regard to the requirement that delay theories explain the consistency of the effects of successive developmental delays, Baron-Cohen would, I think, do this in terms of pre-programmed staged developments within a mind-reading module. However, there are severe problems in proposing that inability to metarepresent, or lack of a theory-of-mind (with all its precursors in place), can maintain autism. In the first place, small children and many learning disabled people cannot metarepresent and do not have a theory of mind but are not autistic (see below for further discussion of this point). In the second place, people with AS can succeed on theory of mind tasks but are nevertheless autistic, and to date no deficit further down the line has been suggested to explain the persistence of autism in these people.

4   Further criteria for assessing psychological theories of autism

4.1   Explanatory power

Criterion D: A satisfactory and full psychological explanation of autism must be able to explain the unique set of criterial features of behaviour which defines autism as a syndrome or, possibly, as a continuum; or the unique sets of criterial features of behaviour which are eventually used to define subtypes of autism. A psychological explanation must also be consistent with characteristic behaviour within the broader autistic phenotype (see above).

The *range* of abnormal behaviour to be explained is broad, especially if, as I believe will be the case, the presence or absence of verbal learning difficulties and, possibly, other deficits currently seen as concomitant rather than definitional, are eventually included in definitions of subtypes. In addition to explaining the broad range of behavioural abnormalities, tenable hypotheses of the psychological origins of autism must be able to explain the *specificity* of the impairments: i.e. the fact that many aspects of behaviour are left either completely unimpaired (in cases of 'pure' autism, where mental retardation is not present), or less impaired than other aspects of behaviour (in cases of autism associated with mental retardation).

4.2   Criterion D and mind-reading theories

Bishop (1992) and Happé (1994a; 1994b) have discussed the explanatory power of mind-reading theories of autism and both authors conclude that deficits in the acquisition of a theory of mind and its precursors can explain much but not all of the broad range of autistic behaviour. Bishop argues that ToM theories are not well able to explain the full range of social deficits which characterise autism (see also Klin and Volkmar, 1993). Both Bishop and Happé argue that mind-reading theories have difficulty in explaining the problems of planning and executive control which appear to be a consistent feature of autism (but see Carruthers, ch.16 this volume). Both Bishop and Happé accept that mind-reading theories may be able to explain the specificity of social and communicative impairments.

4.3   Causal precedence

Criterion E: Homotypic theories must argue convincingly that the deficits which they propose as primary, or critical, predate all the manifestations of autism which they seek to explain. Delay theories must be able to do this for the succession of deficits which are claimed to maintain autism.

4.4   Criterion E and mind-reading theories

Both Leslie and Baron-Cohen were initially criticised for hypothesising primary deficits at too high a developmental level to have been operative from the normal age of onset of autism (before 30 months in almost all cases). Baron-Cohen has been rigorous in hypothesising and investigating increasingly primitive mechanisms as the primary deficit. Leslie's most recent suggestion that the primary deficit lies in an early activated subsystem of the ToMM is also more able than earlier versions of his theory to satisfy the criterion of causal precedence. Whether or not the mechanisms currently identified by Baron-Cohen and by Leslie as primary are activated sufficiently early in development to explain the very earliest occurring signs of autism is controversial (Klin and Volkmar, 1993).

4.5   Universality

Criterion F(i): If a single persistent psychological deficit is proposed as both necessary and sufficient for the development of an autistic syndrome, then that impairment must be present in all autistic individuals for as long as they are described as autistic. Similarly, if it is proposed that a linked pair or set of primary and persistent deficits are jointly necessary and sufficient to cause an autistic syndrome, or an autistic continuum, or any one identifiable subtype of autism, then the proposed combination of deficits must be universal to all people within the syndrome, continuum, or subtype of autism, so long as they are described as autistic.

By the same reasoning, a deaf person has a hearing loss for as long as they are described as being deaf, and a deaf-blind person has hearing and visual impairments for as long as they are described as being deaf-blind. Their deficits will be apparent in comparison with the visual and auditory abilities of normal people of any age above infancy (since normal visual and sensory acuity is achieved within the period of infancy). The primary deficits which underlie autism will be apparent in comparison with the abilities of normal individuals at or above the age at which the abilities in question normally come on stream.

Criterion F(ii): In the case of delay theories it must be shown that one or more of the successive deficits, or successive pairs/sets of deficits, hypothesised to be capable of causing or maintaining autism (as a syndrome, continuum, or set of subtypes) is present in all autistic individuals at any one stage of their lives. The deficit or deficits must be apparent in comparison with the abilities of normal individuals at or above the ages at which each of the successive abilities normally come on stream.

4.6   Criteria F(i) and (ii) and mind-reading theories

A homotypic version of the modular mind-reading theory must be able to show that goal directedness, shared attention (Baron-Cohen) or ability to ascribe agency (Leslie) is more impaired in *all* people with autism than in normal toddlers. An intelligent twenty-year-old autistic person may of course have compensated for his or her underlying deficit, achieving at least some of the manifest behaviour associated with shared attention or the ascription of agency without using an underlying shared attention mechanism. However, this does not destroy the logical points (a) that the hypothetical deficit must still be present (and active) since it is claimed to cause autism and (b) that the onus to demonstrate its presence is on the theorists.

Joint attention deficits are in fact present in the large majority of young children diagnosed as autistic (Mundy *et al.*, 1986). This is encouraging for Baron-Cohen's current theory. However, failure on standard tests of theory of mind is present in only around 75% of older children and adults with autism. This is worrying for the theory, which claims that the operation of ToMM is dependent on intact inputs from SAM. The good performance of many autistic people on ToMM tasks is worrying for Leslie's version of the theory for the same reason (see Happé, 1994b for a fuller discussion of these issues).

Baron-Cohen has attempted to explain the fact that some people with autism pass ToM tasks by appealing to the notion of a developmental delay. The suggestion here is that those people with autism who pass standard ToM tasks pass them in the normal way, utilising the ToMM mechanism, rather than passing the tasks using compensatory strategies. But if this is the case it must be asked what deficit is hypothesised to supersede a defective ToMM as the cause of autism. Without an answer to this question it is not possible to test Baron-Cohen's delay theory against the universality criterion.

4.7   Uniqueness

Criterion G: Hypotheses concerning the psychological origins of autism must be consistent with the fact that most individuals, including very young children and people with severe learning difficulties, are not autistic. In other words, the primary psychological deficit(s) which cause autism must be unique to autism.

Many years ago I argued that severe language learning difficulties (then hypothesised to be the cause of autism) could not by themselves cause autism since there exists a group of children who have language learning difficulties which are so severe that they are effectively unable to learn spoken language, but who are not autistic (Boucher, 1976). This is a simple and obvious bit of reasoning. Just as obviously, the fact that most congenitally deaf-blind people are not autistic indicates that sensory impairments are not themselves the *primary* cause of autism (though they might in some cases be primary causes of *critical* deficits which might cause autism, as argued by Hobson).

Similarly, the fact that the majority of profoundly or severely learning disabled people are not autistic indicates that the psychological deficits underlying autism cannot be in the area of higher cognitive functions, such as the ability to metarepresent. Inability to metarepresent may be one of the consequences of the underlying deficit, and a consequence which can only manifest itself in people whose mental age is above a certain level. However, inability to metarepresent cannot itself be the cause of autism.

4.8 Criterion G and mind-reading theories

The uniqueness criterion has been accepted by mind-reading theorists in the case of a comparison between young children and people with autism, and was one of the reasons why both Baron-Cohen and Leslie have focused of late on precursors of mind-reading, such as shared attention, which young children do have. It would be very interesting to find out whether severely learning disabled people show joint attention/understanding of agency: Baron-Cohen/Leslie must predict that they do, and this could well be the case. However, if they did not, then the onus would be on the mind-reading theorists to demonstrate what mind-reading abilities severely learning disabled people do have which people with autism do not have. If such abilities cannot be demonstrated then it is reasonable to doubt their existence. If mind-reading theorists argue that it may be difficult to demonstrate the existence of mind-reading abilities in people with severe learning difficulties, I would argue that if these abilities are never manifested in overt behaviour (i.e. demonstrable) they are of no functional use to the individual, and therefore as good as non-existent.

Baron-Cohen and Ring's recent reinstatement of the hypothesis that autism can be caused, at least in some late developing cases, by defective ToMM, rather than by defective SAM, is not consistent with the uniqueness criterion: children below the age of about three and a half, and also severely learning disabled people, lack a functional ToMM, but they are not autistic. As has been argued above, lack of a functional ToMM cannot, therefore, cause autism. This is not, of course, to say that lack of a functional ToMM in people with autism is uninteresting: it is extremely interesting at the level of the analysis and description of autistic behaviour. However, it is not interesting as a possible primary cause of autism.

4.9 Continuity with acquired disorders

Criterion H: This criterion states that any persistent primary impairment of organic origin which is sufficient to cause and maintain autism will have its counterpart in some identifiable form of acquired neurological disorder.

Continuity clearly exists across very broad domains of behaviour which may be affected by brain pathology. Thus sensory, motor, perceptual, linguistic, cognitive, social, emotional and motivational impairments are all represented in both developmental and acquired neurological disorders. Equally the brain systems implicated in these broadly defined functions are, again generally speaking, the same in developmental and acquired neurological disorders. It appears that this continuity derives from the fact that the human brain is innately predisposed to subserve specific functions within specific brain areas or systems. There is, it is true, some degree of plasticity in brain development. For example, in cases of unilateral brain damage in children the undamaged hemisphere may take over certain functions which are normally subserved by the damaged hemisphere. In children with profound hearing loss that part of the brain which normally subserves spoken language comes to subserve signed language. However, these examples actually underline the fact that certain brain areas (whether in the left or the right hemisphere) are predisposed to subserve certain types of function (even in the event of receiving non-standard input).

It seems likely that continuity across developmental and acquired disorders also exists at a more detailed level. This is suggested by evidence that some types of behaviour and related brain function are organised on a modular basis which includes micromodules, or dissociable subcomponents. For example, on the basis of studies of individuals with acquired disorders it has been suggested by cognitive neuropsychologists that complex functions such as language processing, reading and writing, or face recognition can be broken down into subsidiary functions which are consistent across individuals and also dissociable i.e. they can be impaired independently of each other. The boundaries of modules and micromodules seem likely to be determined by innate and therefore universal constraints on development (Karmiloff-Smith, 1992).

The implication of this line of argument is that brain pathology which disturbs these predispositions in children will cause effects within the detailed functional domains which have been identified in adults. This supposition is borne out by, for example, studies of individuals with congenital or early acquired prosopagnosia (impaired ability to recognise faces) and studies of correspondences between developmental and acquired aphasia. I would therefore argue that theories of autism which specify a primary deficit in an innately determined biological mechanism such as a mind-reading module must be able to identify an acquired disorder affecting the psychological function(s) underpinned by that innate mechanism.

To argue for continuity of domains, or behaviour functions, which may be affected in developmental and acquired disorders is not to argue that the effects within domains are the same in developmental and acquired disorders. Clearly they are not, since in the one case a deficit will disrupt development, whereas in the other it will disrupt established behaviour.

4.10   Criterion H and mind-reading theories

Leslie, Baron-Cohen and their colleagues propose the existence of a pre-programmed mind-reading module. If they are correct about the innate and modular nature of mind-reading, then it should be possible to identify an *acquired* disorder of mind-reading caused by the breakdown of function within this module. Neither Leslie nor Baron-Cohen have, I believe, speculated about a possible acquired or later developing disorder affecting mind-reading. Frith (1992) has argued that autism is related to schizophrenia, in that both involve a defective mentalising mechanism. However, this is speculative, and Karmiloff-Smith (1992) sees the lack of clear cases of specific *loss* of a theory of mind as a possible argument against the ToMM theory of autism.

5   Summary and conclusion

The theory that a deficit in mind-reading causes autism has produced a body of research which has greatly illuminated our understanding of autism over the last ten years. However, the theory in its various current forms (e.g. Baron-Cohen and Swettenham, this volume; Leslie and Roth, 1993; Harris, 1993; Currie, this volume) faces a number of difficulties as an explanation of autism.

Definition and concepts of autism. Evidence that failure on theory-of-mind tasks occurs in cases of Kanner's syndrome but not in cases of Asperger's syndrome suggests that a subgroups concept (rather than a syndrome concept) and separate definitions of KS and AS (rather than the broad-based definition of autism provided by DSM III) could be useful in future mind-reading-autism research.

Explanatory models. In as far as Baron-Cohen and Leslie are attempting to explain the social, communication, and pretend play deficits of autism in terms of a primary deficit of mind-reading, and in as far as they argue that the repetitive behaviour which also defines autism is secondary to the other symptoms, a single primary deficit explanation of autism is being proposed. A single primary (or critical) deficit model seems increasingly unlikely to be able to explain autism and the behaviour which occurs within the broader phenotype. Investigation of two possible subgroups (KS and AS) would necessitate hypothesising at least two primary deficits. Explaining the existence of two subtypes of autism and two distinct dissociable autism-related behaviour traits within the broader phenotype (see Section 2.1) would necessitate hypothesising at least three primary deficits.

The delay version of the theory. This has been proposed by Baron-Cohen from time to time, but not fully developed. It runs into a number of difficulties which appear to make it untenable.

Explanatory power. The explanatory power of the mind-reading theory is considerable. In particular it goes a significant way towards explaining the specificity of characteristically autistic behaviour. It has, however, been argued in three recent reviews that a mind-reading deficit can probably not explain the broad range of behaviour which occurs within the criterial behavioural areas of impaired social relating, impaired communication, and impaired behavioural flexibility (Bishop, 1992; Happé, 1994b; Klin and Volkmar, 1993).

Causal precedence. Recent versions of Baron-Cohen's and Leslie's theories are better able to satisfy this criterion than previously. However it is still a matter of dispute as to whether the primary deficits identified by Baron-Cohen and by Leslie predate the very earliest signs and symptoms of autism.

Universality. Deficits in shared attention appear to be quite pervasive in autistic children. However, failure on theory-of-mind tasks is not pervasive in older children and adults with autism, and especially not in cases of AS. A defective SAM might, therefore, if it were found to persist, satisfy the universality criterion, whereas a defective ToMM could not.

Uniqueness. Similarly, defective shared attention may be unique to autism (if non-autistic people with profound or severe learning disabilities show evidence of shared attention); but failure on theory-of-mind tasks is not unique to autism and therefore cannot explain it.

Continuity with acquired disorders. It is not immediately clear that mind-reading theories satisfy this criterion, although it has been suggested that schizophrenia represents an acquired form of ToMM deficit.

The mind-reading theory, especially as it has been developed by Baron-Cohen over the years, but also in the form in which it has recently been restated by Leslie, is increasingly and encouragingly convergent with other important theories. In particular, theories of autism as fundamentally a cognitive disorder and theories of autism as fundamentally a socio-affective disorder are now converging onto the common ground of the very early occurring, innate or pre-programmed pre-requisites for the normal development of social cognition. It remains to be seen whether or not the theories completely converge onto a single deficit in this area.

If they do it may be necessary to posit a second (dissociable) primary deficit in the area of verbal learning and metarepresentation, and perhaps a third (dissociable) primary deficit in the area of behavioural flexibility. Non-autistic individuals within the broader phenotype might have either the first or the second of these (or deficits closely associated with them, genetically). High functioning individuals with KS would have all three primary deficits. High functioning individuals with AS would have only deficits one and three.

This, however, is speculation, and speculation is quite the easiest part of the business.

ACKNOWLEDGEMENTS

I would like to thank Peter Carruthers and Simon Baron-Cohen for their stimulating comments on earlier drafts of this chapter. I incorporated many of their suggestions, but we agreed to differ on other points. So any errors of fact or logic are all mine.

15 Simulation-theory, theory-theory and the evidence from autism

Gregory Currie

I want to compare two explanations of autism. Both these explanations are suggested by the apparent fact that people with autism have difficulty in understanding the mental states of others, though both seek to explain a great deal more about autism than this. Each derives from a hypothesis about what it is that enables normally developing children to understand those mental states. So I shall begin by explaining, very briefly, what those two hypotheses are and what is at stake between them.

1 Knowing that and knowing how

According to one view, I understand the minds of others – and, incidentally, my own mind as well – by virtue of possessing a theory of mind: a theory either acquired by observation and hypothesis formation, or a theory innately given (see, respectively, the contributions by Alison Gopnik and Gabriel Segal to this volume). This view is generally known as the 'theory-theory'. The other view says that I understand the minds of others by imaginatively projecting myself into their situations and using my own mind as a model of theirs. Running my own mental states 'off-line', I am able to *simulate* the mental processes of another, and thereby to learn, for example, what decision he will make. This is the simulation-theory; it is a version of the idea that our access to the minds of others is partly through empathetic contact with them (Heal, 1986 and Gordon, 1986).

Advocates of this second view emphasize that simulation offers us a relatively 'information poor' method of coming to conclusions about other minds. By using my mind as a model of yours, I can draw predictions about what you will decide without having a theory of the psychology of decision-making. An analogy may make that clearer. You and I have the same type of car. In order to find out how fast yours will go I don't need a theory about how cars of that kind work; instead I just see how fast my car will go, and assume that yours will go just that fast as well. Whether mental simulation can take place in the absence of *any* prior understanding of mind is a question simulationists themselves do not agree on. For example, Robert

Gordon (this volume) argues that we can undertake successful simulations without having to make inferences from our own case to the case of the agent we are trying to comprehend. Other simulationists hold that simulation requires a grasp of mentalistic concepts, and an ability to make first-person attributions of those concepts (see e.g. Goldman, 1993a). But this is an issue I am going to bypass in the present essay. Even if the simulation-and-theory-go-hand-in-hand approach is right, the debate over autism might remain quite a sharply defined one. You may think that normal mentalistic understanding is the product of both simulation and theory, but hold that the absence of either one would be disastrous for the development of that understanding, and hold that the peculiar conjunction of deficits in autism is caused exclusively by a failure of theory – or of simulation. That, anyway, is how I shall read the debate over autism and I shall consider only pure strategies according to which autism is exclusively a failure of theory, or exclusively a failure of simulation. The truth might be more complicated than this, but we ought to consider the simpler hypothesis first.

'Theory-theory' and 'simulation-theory' are names that have most often been used for general theories about how we normally understand mental states and processes. But I shall use them here as names for theories about what it is that people with autism *lack*. According to theory-theory, as I use the term, autism is centrally a deficiency of knowledge, or at any rate of belief. Simulation-theory says that autism is a deficiency of imaginative capacity – the capacity to project the self imaginatively into a situation other than its own current, actual position. So the debate, as I set it up, is a kind of knowing that/knowing how dispute. According to theory-theory, there are some propositions the autistic person doesn't know – and perhaps could not even formulate. On the simulation view, the autistic person doesn't know how to project himself into situations other than his own current, actual situation. But my high-jacking of these labels should not lead us to suppose that someone who thinks that we normally acquire understanding of mental states by way of theory, and who therefore counts as a theory-theorist in the ordinary sense, will automatically be a theory-theorist in my sense. You might be a theory-theorist who holds that the primary deficit in autism is nothing to do with mentalistic understanding, and that issues about how normal folk understand the minds of others sheds little or no light on autism – perhaps not a very likely hypothesis on current evidence, but the data is equivocal enough not to rule it out entirely. Or you might simply have no opinion on the matter. The same goes for the relation between simulation-theory as generally conceived and as I am using it here: to be an enthusiast for the hypothesis that simulation plays an important part in normal understanding of mental states is not automatically to take the view that simulation is the key to understanding autism. On the other hand, the debate about autism may have important implications for the broader debate about what underwrites the normal understanding of mind. Suppose, for example, that people with autism are strikingly deficient on a certain task, T. And suppose we find strong empirical support for the hypothesis that this deficiency is caused by difficulties with simulation. Then we have evidence for the hypothesis that the performance of normal subjects on T is to be explained in part by simulative competence.

2   Explaining autism

The most highly developed version of the theory-theory, and the version which has received the most attention, is the so-called 'metarepresentational theory' of Alan Leslie (1988, 1991, 1994a). Accordingly, I shall say something about the explanatory power of Leslie's theory from time to time throughout this essay. However, other versions of the theory-theory are beginning to emerge and some of them seem rather better supported by the evidence than Leslie's theory is (see e.g. Peter Carruthers, ch.16). In connection with Leslie's theory, one other point is worth mentioning. I concentrate in this paper on the question of empirical support for various versions of simulation-theory and theory-theory. I believe there are also difficulties of a purely conceptual kind with Leslie's theory, which I have addressed elsewhere (Currie, 1995).

Explaining autism is, of course, a matter of the most pressing practical significance, though an explanation of it might not initially bring us very much closer to a cure. It is also of deep theoretical interest, given its relation to the issue of how mind is normally comprehended. But for me, the issue has another kind of importance. I have argued elsewhere that the idea of simulation is a very helpful one if we are trying to understand the nature of the imagination. Indeed, I have suggested that simulation may stand to imagination much as the concept of H_2O stands to the concept of water: something on which the phenomenologically accessible features of imagination supervene, but which is itself discoverable only a posteriori (Currie, 1995). One way to test this suggestion would be to see how far the range of human capacities at least partly dependent on the ability to simulate coincides with the range of capacities which we intuitively count as 'imaginative'. On the view about imagination I have just described, we would expect there to be a systematic correlation between what we pre-theoretically count as 'imagination-driven' competencies and simulative competencies, though this correlation probably would not be perfect – we are notoriously prone, after all, to count samples of XYZ as water when we apply intuitive criteria rather than strict scientific ones. One way to test the imagination-is-simulation hypothesis would be to see how far the range of autistic deficits, or at least those which can safely be counted as 'central' deficits, correspond to intuitive failures of imagination. If it turns out that there is such a correspondence, and if there is also good evidence that autistic deficits are caused by problems with simulation, the imagination-is-simulation hypothesis gets corroboration.

In what follows it will be important to bear in mind the sharp distinctions I am drawing here between three things: having a theory of mind, engaging in simulative or empathetic role-taking, and understanding other minds. The first two of these categories are distinct proposals about how we implement the third category; the first two thus correspond, respectively, to theory-theory and simulation-theory. I make this point because some authors speak as if having a theory of mind just *is* having whatever it takes to understand other minds (Premack and Woodruff, 1978, Baron-Cohen *et al.*, 1985), while others identify empathy with understanding other minds (Cunningham, 1968) or even with theory of mind (Gillberg, 1992). And there is another, related, source of confusion I should like to identify. Theory-theory is a theory about autistic understanding of the mind, or of mental concepts. In order to explain autistic deficits on tasks which do not obviously require understanding of mind – executive function deficits, for example – the theory-theorist has either to claim that these deficits do, appearances to the contrary, require understanding of mind, or that the deficit is some sort of secondary effect of the failure to understand mind (both strategies are evident in Peter Carruthers' contribution to this volume). Thus the explanatory options available to the theory-theorist are rather tightly constrained. But simulation-theory is not in that position. The simulation-theorist is not bound to hold that any autistic deficit explained by her theory is thereby the product of a failure to understand mind. The reason is that the idea of simulation is not itself essentially tied to the understanding of mind: understanding of mind is just one of the functions of simulation, it is not part of the definition of simulation. Simulation, as I have defined it here, is a process whereby we run our mental processes off-line, taking pretend or *ersatz* inputs. Simulation is defined in terms of the nature of the process itself and not in terms of the function of the process. It is true that the idea of simulation was first bruited in connection with the understanding of mind (Heal, 1986; Gordon, 1986), but that is an accident of history. Simulation might have been introduced first of all to explain the psychology of games of imaginative pretence, the idea being that in such situations we run our mental machinery on pretend inputs like 'I am a pirate', or whatever it is the game dictates (see Currie, 1995). So while it might be a criticism of the theory-theory that it assigns a more central role to autistic deficits on mentalistic understanding than the data warrants, this is not a criticism to be levelled against the simulation-theory.

Yet there is a noticeable tendency in the literature to suppose that simulation-theory is like theory-theory in centring attention on the issue of understanding mind. Jill Boucher (this volume) for example, explicitly uses the term 'mind-reading explanations of autism' as a generic term to cover both theory-theory and simulation-theory. This is a misleading description. The simulation theorist is not automatically bound to give a greater emphasis to so-called mind-reading tasks in explaining autism than to any other aspects of the condition she proposes to explain.

There are other explanations of autism besides the two I shall consider here. There is the hypothesis that 'the communicative problem in autism is due to a weak or absent impulse to rework life experiences into narratives' (Bruner and Feldman, 1993, p. 285); that autism consists in a lack of drive for 'central coherence' (Frith, 1989); that autism is an affective disorder (Kanner, 1943; Hobson, 1991). I shall not discuss Bruner and Feldman's theory here, nor will I discuss the affective theory. It is necessary, however, briefly to mention the coherence theory, because it has been argued (Frith and Happé, 1994, especially p. 126) that the coherence theory should be combined with the theory-theory to explain certain features of autism – such as executive function deficits and peculiarities of autistic perception – not explained by theory-theory. Whether this combination of theories can be given a unified formulation is presently unclear. And Frith herself has said that the coherence/theory alliance would not explain the *variability* of autistic understanding of other minds (Frith and Happé, 1994, p. 126). But I shall not examine Frith's proposal in detail, for the following reason. Frith assumes that Leslie's theory adequately explains certain aspects of autism – notably deficits in pretence and mentalistic understanding. In suggesting that Leslie's theory be combined with her own she seeks to compensate for what she sees as failures of Leslie's theory in other areas. But I shall be arguing, in conflict with Frith's presupposition, that Leslie's theory does *not* provide good explanations for autistic performance on tests of mentalistic understanding and pretence, in which case the combination she proposes would not be empirically adequate.

So I shall concentrate on the debate between theory-theory and simulation-theory. The contrast between these two is sharp, and has important consequences for our view of normal psychological development, our understanding of other minds, and the status of folk-psychology. Both simulation-theory and theory-theory offer a general perspective on human cognitive development and claim to say something fundamental about how human beings understand one another. The starting point for both these views is autistic failure on tests of comprehension of mental states, sometimes called theory-of-mind tests, though that is not a description a simulationist will like. Instead I shall call them 'tests of mentalistic understanding'. This is not an attractive phrase, but it has the virtue of not pre-supposing that what is at stake is comprehension of a theory. I shall start by saying something about autistic performance on such tests. Then I shall look at autistic deficits in other areas, notably pretence and executive function. There are other important features of autism to be considered, such as the issue of early affect sharing and peculiarities of autistic perception. These will be considered elsewhere (Currie, in preparation).

3   Mentalistic understanding and Wing's Triad

It is generally agreed that people with autism typically have difficulty understanding that someone may have false beliefs – or rather beliefs different from the subject's own – and be caused thereby to behave differently (Baron-Cohen *et al.*, 1985). However, about 25% of people with autism regularly pass so-called 'first-order' false-belief tests. And in a study by Ozonoff and colleagues, individuals with Asperger syndrome – who are like those in the high-functioning autistic group in respect of social and communicative difficulty, absence of spontaneous pretend play and executive function deficits – have been found to perform well on these false-belief tasks: their performance on the first-order false-belief task was exactly the same as that of the normal control group, and their performance on a second-order false-belief task was not significantly below that of controls (Ozonoff *et al.*, 1991b. See also Bowler, 1992. On the relation of Asperger syndrome to autism see Frith (ed.), 1991.) I do not see how this is to be squared with at least one version of theory-theory: Leslie's theory that autism is an inability to produce metarepresentations. On this view, people with autism are not able to form mental representations (thoughts) which have as parts of their contents that someone is in a representational state (see e.g. Leslie, 1988). It would seem, from the false-belief test results, that quite a lot of people with autism can metarepresent. But still they suffer, to varying degrees, the symptoms we associate with autism. The explanation for this given by Leslie and colleagues is that success on false belief tasks is to be found only in older autistic children who have learned various rules of thumb, for example that people who haven't seen something don't know about it (Frith, Morton, and Leslie, 1991, p.436). This seems to me not to address the difficulty. The rule as stated refers to the mental state of knowing, and anyone who represents that rule to himself is, in effect, representing to himself a rule which says something about the mental states of others: he is, in other words, metarepresenting. But if autism is a failure to metarepresent, how have older autistic children acquired a rule, comprehension of which requires metarepresentation?

Other versions of theory-theory according to which autistic difficulties arise from a fragmented or incomplete theoretical network, but one which is not so incomplete as to deny the agent access to mentalistic concepts, have less of a problem here. They can allow that autistic failures to understand other minds admit of degrees (see Carruthers, this volume. A similar theory was suggested to me in discussion by Louise Anthony). Such theories need not hold that people with autism have a problem with metarepresentations, but theories of this kind do most naturally go along with a 'modularist' approach to theories of mind rather than with the view that a theory of mind is normally developed by way of general observation and hypothesis-formation skills. For if theory of mind is part of general-purpose, inductively acquired knowledge, how is it that people with autism are so selectively impaired on mentalistic understanding? Autistic performance on false-belief tasks cannot be explained by saying that they are stuck at the general level of comprehension of three and a half year-olds, because they perform near ceiling on the so-called 'false photograph' and 'false map' analogues of the false-belief tests, whereas normal four and a half year-olds do worse on these tests than they do on the false-belief test (in the case of the false map, they do much worse: 80% pass the false-belief test, only 33% pass the false map task) (Leslie and Thaiss, 1992). People with autism also perform better than normal four and a half year-olds on understanding behavioural and mechanical tasks (Baron-Cohen *et al.*, 1986).

Simulation-theory explains failure on false-belief tasks in terms of simulative incompetence; the child cannot understand that Sally (the puppet in Wimmer and Perner's original experiment) will look in the wrong place for her sweet because she has an impaired capacity to simulate Sally, whose epistemic situation differs from the child's own in so far as she lacks knowledge the child possesses. When it comes to explaining the variability of autistic performance on these tests, the simulationist seems to have two options. The first would be to explain cases of autistic success by saying that, in such cases, which typically involve older and more able subjects, the child is not able to simulate, but is able to bypass the simulationist route and to use a (perhaps rudimentary) theory of mind to predict the outcome. This option is not available to a simulationist like Robert Gordon (this volume) according to whom we rely on simulation for mentalistic concepts, for without simulation there would in that case be no possibility of theory. The other option would be to say that people with autism have a greater or lesser degree of difficulty with simulation and that those less severely affected are able to make the kinds of perspective shifts required for the first-order, and in some cases even for the second-order, false-belief tasks.

Here it is important to realize that a mechanism of simulation is likely to have many components, defects in any of which might be responsible for an observed simulative deficit. The capacity to simulate plausibly requires (at least) four things. First of all it requires an input identifier, which chooses particular states (beliefs and desires) to be run off-line. The input identifier will be adequate to the extent that it successfully identifies appropriate inputs for the task in hand, which might be to mirror the mental state of another, or to engage in a pretence as dictated by a certain game of make-believe. The second requirement will be a feeder mechanism, which ensures that the chosen input is fed into the appropriate part of the mental machinery. The third is an output detector, which will enable the subject running the simulation to detect the *ersatz* decision, or whatever is the output of the simulation. Fourthly, functional simulation requires a motivational component: the mechanisms of simulation might be intact, but they will do no work if the subject is not motivated to run the system.

Not all of these four components are equally plausible as candidates for explaining variability in autistic performance. For example, it is easy to see that a selection mechanism might work well or at least adequately when it comes to selecting certain kinds of inputs and less well with others. We might, for example, order candidate inputs on a metric of 'epistemic distance' from the subject's actual and current beliefs and desires, it being more difficult for the input mechanism to access more distant candidates. It might also be that the effectiveness of the accessing procedure, especially for epistemically distant candidate inputs, is dependent to some degree on external cues, and that a certain kind of damage to the accessing system makes it more than usually dependent on such cues. And a motivational deficit might also be one that differentially affected certain kinds of inputs: ones which lacked a certain kind of salience for the subject, for example. On the other hand, damage to the feeder mechanism or to the output detector does not seem so obviously helpful in explaining variability of performance; if you can feed in and read out states with one kind of content, why not all kinds? On current evidence, we are not in a position to opt for any particular hypothesis about exactly what kind of simulative damage, if any, is involved in autism, or to say whether different patterns of autistic deficit might correspond to damage at different simulative sub-mechanisms. But certainly, simulation-theory cannot be judged as inconsistent with the observed range of autistic competencies on a priori grounds alone.

However, the following seems to be a problem for the simulation-theory. Understanding other people's beliefs and desires is one aspect of mentalistic understanding; another is understanding other people's perceptual states – what they can and can't see. Autistic children seem to be able to tell whether another person, whose visual perspective is different from that of the child, can see something. But on the simulation view, surely autistic children should do badly on such tests, because passing the test seems to require that the subject simulate the other's visual perspective. One possible response was suggested to me by Simon Blackburn: knowing where another creature is looking has such significance for survival that it is plausible that there is a dedicated mechanism hard-wired to solve line-of-sight problems. And indeed, Simon Baron-Cohen and Pippa Cross have pointed to some neurological evidence concerning both humans and animals which suggests that this is the case (Baron-Cohen and Cross, 1992, p.175).

What of the classic triad of autism: impairments of social competence, communication skills, and pretending (Wing and Gould, 1979)? Theory-theory and simulation-theory do about equally well on the first two, since both can plausibly derive social incompetence and communicative difficulties from lack of understanding of mental states: if you don't understand other people's beliefs, desires and intentions you won't relate to them well, since that requires co-ordinating your mental states with theirs, and you won't be able to communicate with them to the extent that you won't be able to figure out speaker's meaning as distinct from semantic meaning. Indeed, a recent study by Francesca Happé (1993) indicates that autistic performance on communicative tasks is poor exactly in areas where pragmatic competence comes most strongly into play, e.g. metaphor and irony. One important index of social competence would be the ability successfully to deceive; the successful deceiver knows what others believe and knows how to encourage and to exploit their false beliefs. Both theory-theory and simulation-theory predict that people with autism, because of their difficulties with understanding the beliefs of others, will be incompetent at deception, which in fact they are (see Oswald and Ollendick, 1989; Baron-Cohen, 1992; Sodian and Frith, 1992).

What of the third: lack of interest in pretend play? Let us here distinguish between pretence in behaviour and an inner, mental pretending which I shall call *imagining*. I believe it is this inner mental process of imagining which theory-theorists like Alan Leslie have been trying to characterize and explain, and that, consequently, is what I shall focus on here also. The assumption is that autistic children have some sort of deficit of imagining, exhibited in the poverty of their pretend behaviour. How is this to be explained by the theory-theorist? Leslie has argued that autistic failure with pretence is itself due to an inability to deploy 'metarepresentations' (see e.g. Leslie, 1988, pp. 28–29); the autistic child's problem is that she cannot attribute imaginings to others. However, despite it's having been claimed that 'one distinctive feature of Leslie's account is that it explicitly shows how pretending is but a special case of understanding pretence in others' (Leslie and Frith, 1990, p.122), it remains unclear to me *why* competence with the notion of imagining should depend on an ability to attribute imaginings to others. After all, being able to *believe* things does not seem to depend on the ability to attribute beliefs to others. Also, while normal children engage in pretence from age two, they do not engage in what is called complex social pretend play – the earliest unambiguous indicator of their understanding of imagining in others – until around the age of three and a half, suggesting that the capacity for imagining *precedes* understanding of imagining in others (Jarrold, Carruthers, Smith, and Boucher, 1994, citing the evidence of Howes and Matheson, 1992).

A friend of the metarepresentational theory might take a somewhat different line from that adopted by Leslie, saying that imagining is a peculiar mental state in that one can be in a state of imagining only if one is aware of being in that state. In that case, the capacity to imagine would require the capacity to attribute imagining to *one's self*, and would therefore require the ability to represent yourself as being in a certain kind of representational state, or in other words to metarepresent. Many people who have written on pretence and imagination seem to hold that one of the things which distinguishes imagining is that you cannot imagine something unless you are aware of imagining it. I happen not to believe this, but my reasons are largely based on premises available only to someone who already accepts simulation-theory rather than theory-theory, and so it would be inappropriate to argue for that here (but see my 1994). The real difficulty for this proposal is that there is a growing body of evidence which suggests that children with autism do understand the notion of imagining and are capable of a limited range of pretend play. Lewis and Boucher (1988) have shown that autistic children's pretence is unimpaired relative to controls when the play is 'instructed', that is, when the children are told what to pretend. And Jarrold, Smith, Boucher, and Harris (1994) have shown that the ability of autistic children to identify the pretend objects and outcomes involved in a game of make-believe and to reflect on the pretend nature of the actions involved does not differ significantly from that of controls. In that case a theory which explains autistic problems with pretence as due to an incompetence with the concept of imagining must be wrong.

Simulation-theorists have a plausible account of autistic deficits on pretence. It is natural to think that childhood games of pretence in which the actors play at being pirates or bears are driven by the actors mentally taking on these roles and imagining being pirates or bears. In doing these things, the children simulate, to the best of their ability and within the compass of their relevant knowledge, the experience of being pirates or bears (perhaps with children these acts of simulation fall so far short of their targets that it is merely by courtesy that we describe them in terms of 'imagining being a bear', but I take it we are resigned to the massive doses of charity that interpreting our children's actions requires). We would expect autistic children to show a lack of pretend play, if as I have suggested, imaginative pretence is a simulative operation. That autistic children are apparently capable of instructed pretend play once again raises the question of exactly what kind of damage to the simulative capacity is involved in autism. The capacity for instructed play might be explained by saying that the autistic person's difficulty is with accessing the relevant inputs, and that instruction can function to locate inputs which the input-identifier cannot locate on its own; alternatively, the instruction may compensate for inadequate motivation.

Is there evidence relevant to the hypothesis that autistic children suffer a motivational deficiency when it comes to pretend play? Hardly any, according to a recent review (Jarrold, Smith, Boucher, and Harris, 1994). The authors do note the suggestion that 'play therapy designed to increase symbolic play in autistic children is accompanied, when therapy is successful, by increased positive affect during play' (p. 299), suggesting that the difficulty might be a motivational one. But the same review finds some degree of corroboration for a claim which seems to be a difficulty for simulation-theory, and for theory-theory also: that spontaneous functional play in autistic children is impaired in a way similar to that in which spontaneous symbolic play is impaired (p. 303). The difficulty is that symbolic play, but not functional play, is said to involve pretence, and so a deficiency on both would suggest that low levels of autistic play cannot be explained in terms of pretence and its mentalistic correlate, imagination. While I agree that this may turn out to be a problem, my current view is that the functional/symbolic distinction needs a much better elaboration than it has so far received. I do not, in particular, believe that the use of an object for purposes of pretence requires the agent to see the object as a symbol for something else (see Currie, 1995).

It is widely accepted that autistic children, as they grow older, have little enthusiasm for fiction. How is this to be explained? There is a good case, I believe, for saying that works of fiction are simply the more sophisticated descendants of children's games of pretence: such games ask us to imagine doing and being things we are not. Fictions ask of us the same thing: they ask us to imagine being people who learn truths from reliable texts, images or whatever the fictional medium in question is. In reality we are not such people, and the texts or images we imagine ourselves learning from are not really reliable guides to truth. But we imagine these things, just as children imagine being pirates or bears in the games they play (see Walton, 1990 and Currie, 1990). If that is right, then the simulationist account of autistic play easily extends to cover the lack of enthusiasm for fiction.

4   Executive function deficits

There are symptoms of autism, some of them apparently rather significant, which fall outside the classic triad. There is a pattern of disabilities which seems to reflect deficits of what is called *executive function:* 'the ability to maintain an appropriate problem-solving set for attainment of a future goal. It includes behaviours such as planning, impulse control, inhibition of pre-potent but irrelevant responses, set maintenance, organised search and flexibility of thought and action' (Ozonoff *et al.*, 1991a, p.1083). Ozonoff and her colleagues offer the following as evidence of executive function deficits: that people with autism are upset by apparently trivial changes in their surroundings, wish to adhere rigidly to the details of famil-iar routines, have narrowly focused, fact-based interests, and engage in stereotyped behaviour. Also, their behaviour does not seem to be future oriented; they don't anticipate the consequences of behaviour, are un-self-reflective, impulsive and appear unable to delay or inhibit responses. There are several tests which have been devised to measure executive func-tion performance, notably the Tower of Hanoi problem and the Wisconsin Card Sorting Test. A recent study found that performance on these tests was the factor which most strongly differentiated the autistic group from controls: much more strongly than performance on first-order false-belief tasks, and more strongly than performance on second-order false-belief tasks (Ozonoff *et al.*, 1991a, p.1091. See also Rumsey, 1985; Rumsey and Hamburger, 1988; Steel *et al.*, 1984; Bishop, 1993).

Theory-theorists might explain at least some of these features – depen-dence on routines, insistence on environmental sameness, narrow focusing on fact-based topics – as 'side-effects' of the intentionalistic deficit, saying that insistence on sameness, routine, repetitive, and stereotypic behaviour are responses to a world which is alarming and unpredictable. Impulsiveness and lack of self-reflection might also be explained in terms of failure to deploy intentionalistic notions, since such a failure might plau-sibly result in an inability on the autistic person's part to monitor his or her own mental states. Peter Carruthers (this volume) has emphasized the importance of this. I'm not sure, however, that this approach would explain, say poor performance on the Tower of Hanoi problem. It seems to me that what I need to do, in order to perform well on this task, is to review various strategies: to think about taking off and putting on the rings in a certain order, and then to see whether that strategy gets stuck at a certain point, in which case I discard that strategy. In other words, what I need to attend to is strategies and how they work, and not to my own strategy-testing mental processes.

How should a simulationist approach the problem of executive function deficits? One approach would be to say that, while people with autism have difficulty with simulation, that difficulty is itself to be explained in terms of executive function difficulties. On this view, executive function would be a deeper explanatory notion than simulation, at least relative to the problem currently under review; the idea would be that while autistic failures on, say, pretence and other mind problems are due to an inability to carry out certain kinds of simulations, simulative incompetence is itself due to an inability to set aside the current, actual situation (the subject's own beliefs and desires, for instance) in favour of a hypothetical situation (the make-believe situation of the pretence, for instance). Paul Harris, one of the developers of the simulation-theory, has offered a suggestion along these lines (Harris, 1993).

I shall call this approach weak simulationism, because, while it appeals to the idea of simulation as explanatory of autistic deficits in pretence and other mind tasks, it does not hold simulative incompetence to be the fundamental difficulty in autism; rather, executive function deficits are held to play that role. A strong version of simulationism, on the other hand, would say that autistic problems with pretence, other mind tasks and executive functions are to be explained by reference to deficits of simulation. (Such a hypothesis would not, of course, rule out some further, deeper, explanation of autistic deficits of simulation.) Notice that 'weak' and 'strong' modify 'simulation', not 'hypothesis'. I am not claiming that we have two hypotheses, a weaker and a stronger in the logical sense, with the weaker entailed by but not entailing the stronger. In the logical sense, the two hypotheses are independent.

Unfortunately, there is not a great deal of evidence currently available which bears on the question whether strong simulationism is a better explanation than weak simulationism. One recent study, however, sheds doubt on the weak hypothesis. Jarrold and colleagues carried out an object-substitution test on four groups, including a group of autistic children. The test was designed to show what objects would be preferred substitutes for a given, functional, object. If the difficulties of autistic children with pretence were, as Harris suggested, caused by an inability to set aside real-world default settings, then, so it was reasoned, autistic children would have difficulty, relative to controls, in substituting an object with a known function for another object with a different, known function, and they would tend to prefer as a substitute an object without any clear function. However, the outcome of the experiment indicated that the autistic group had no greater difficulty selecting the 'counterfunctional prop' than did the control groups (Jarrold *et al.*, forthcoming).

Jarrold and colleagues point out that their result is not a conclusive refutation of what I am here calling weak simulationism. Still, in the light of the result, it is worth considering the prospects for strong simulationism. According to this hypothesis, autistic problems with pretence, other minds and executive function are all to be explained in terms of simulative incompetence. I have outlined simulative explanations for pretence and mentalistic comprehension; it remains to consider executive function deficits.

The Tower of Hanoi problem illustrates, I believe, the role of simulation in problem solving. If you face a task which could be tackled in a number of ways, and it is hard to see straight off which way would be successful, it may help if you can perform the task in a certain way *in imagination*. That way, you get to find out which potential strategies to discard without incurring the costs of failing the task because you actually used a poor strategy. Now suppose, in line with a suggestion I made at the beginning of this paper, that to imagine doing something is to simulate the experience of doing it. As we perform a task, our beliefs and desires change; as I complete part of the task, I acquire a new belief: that I have completed that sub-task. And my desire to perform that sub-task dissipates, since a desire satisfied is a desire I no longer have. Now the changing pattern of beliefs and desires which corresponds to a certain performance is something I can simulate: I run my decision-making mechanism off-line, using as inputs *ersatz* versions of those very beliefs and desires. It might also be important, in order to simulate performance on a task like the Tower of Hanoi, to be able to *imagine seeing* – that is, to visualize – the apparatus as I remove and re-stack the rings. I have argued elsewhere that visual mental imagery is itself a simulative operation: an operation whereby the central processing parts of the visual system are run off-line (Currie, 1995). If that is right, a simulation-based approach to solving a Tower of Hanoi problem would involve the simulation of belief, desire, and perceptual states as well. If people with autism have difficulties with all or any of these simulative operations, they can be expected to perform poorly on tests such as this. We would also and for the same reason expect that they would have general difficulties in planning strategies for practical, everyday action, would find it difficult to anticipate the consequences of their actions, and would find it difficult to substitute a new strategy for an old one where changed circumstances make the old one unsuccessful, as exemplified in the Wisconsin Card Sorting Test.

How will the strong simulationist explain autistic preferences for narrowly focused fact-based topics which seem boring and pointless to the rest of us? These topics – the addresses of institutions, train timetables, the constitution of sewage pipes – are tedious for most people (except where the information serves some further, functional, goal) because they do not allow for any exercise of the imagination. If autism is, at bottom, a failure of imagination, the activities most of us find interesting are simply not available to autistic people.

We can also tell a plausible simulationist story about why disruption to routine and change in the environment are so disturbing to people with autism. Simulationists say that simulating being in a certain situation is a bit like having the experience of being in that situation: it has the same kinds of internal, affective, and cognitive effects, but is disconnected from behaviour. So if you have the capacity to simulate, you have the capacity to rehearse, in advance, some of the various possible changes which might take place. That is one way we might become habituated to change. People who can't simulate change can therefore be expected to find change more difficult to cope with than the rest of us do.

5   Conclusion

Here I have reviewed, in no great detail, some of the strategies available to theory-theory and to simulation-theory for explaining some of the deficits we associate with autism. My sense is that simulation-theory is slightly better supported by the available evidence than is theory-theory, but that this superiority is far from decisive. The evidence, particularly as it relates to mentalistic comprehension, pretence and executive functions, is presently somewhat fluid and confused, and new evidence might radically change the degree of corroboration that accrues to each theory. Also, what I have been calling 'theories' here might better be described as *research programs*: rather unspecific propositions which are capable of being embodied in different theories which would then constitute different testable versions of the program (Lakatos, 1978). The history of science commonly reveals a pattern whereby a research program well supported at one time and seemingly superior to its rival is eventually discarded because new evidence, or old evidence reassessed, is better explained by the rival. That may well be the ultimate fate of the simulation-theoretic program. Also, a fully satisfactory assessment of the simulation-versus-theory debate, even as confined to the present state of the evidence, would have to take into account the whole vast and bewildering range of autistic symptoms. Here I have focused on just a few of them.

ACKNOWLEDGEMENTS

Earlier versions of this paper were read at the University of North Carolina, Chapel Hill and at the Theories of Theories of Mind Conference at Sheffield University in 1994. On both occasions members of the audience made important suggestions which I have tried to take account of in this version. Special thanks go to Jill Boucher, Alvin Goldman, Paul Harris, and Roy Sorensen for discussion of these issues.

16 Autism as mind-blindness: an elaboration and partial defence

Peter Carruthers

In this chapter I shall be defending the mind-blindness theory of autism, by showing how it can accommodate data which might otherwise appear problematic for it. Specifically, I shall show how it can explain the fact that autistic children rarely engage in spontaneous pretend-play, and also how it can explain the executive-function deficits which are characteristic of the syndrome. I shall do this by emphasising what I take to be an entailment of the mind-blindness theory, that autistic people have difficulties of access to their own mental states, as well as to the mental states of other people.

1 Introduction

In a series of publications since 1985 Alan Leslie, Simon Baron-Cohen and others have argued that autism should be identified with *mind-blindness* – that is, with damage to an innate theory of mind module, leading to an inability to understand the mental states of other people. (See Baron-Cohen *et al.*, 1985; Leslie, 1987, 1988, 1991; Leslie and Roth, 1993; Baron-Cohen, 1989a, 1990, 1991a, 1993; and Baron-Cohen and Ring, 1994b.) I shall be concerned to elaborate and defend this proposal, showing that it has the resources to handle rather more of the relevant data, and rather more elegantly, than even its originators have realised.

There is widespread agreement that autism at least *involves* a kind of mind-blindness. That is, it is generally agreed that people with autism have considerable difficulty in appreciating the mental states of others – well-documented in their difficulties with false-belief tasks, for example – resulting in impaired social interaction and poor communicative skills. Where there is very considerable disagreement, concerns the explanation of this phenomenon, and also the question of how *central* it is in the aetiology of the syndrome as a whole.

Both Leslie and Baron-Cohen believe that mind-blindness lies at the very heart of the autistic syndrome. They maintain that autism results from damage to a specialised theory of mind module, which underlies the mind-reading abilities of normal subjects. This module is held to contain an implicit theory of the structure and functioning of the human mind, which is accessed whenever a normal subject ascribes a mental state to another person, or seeks a mentalistic explanation of their behaviour. It is possible that this module is organised into a number of distinct sub-systems (see Baron-Cohen and Ring, 1994b; Baron-Cohen and Swettenham, this volume), and that it may develop in the normal individual through a number of different stages, perhaps corresponding to the different theory-stages postulated by some developmental psychologists (e.g. simple desire psychology; perception-desire psychology; belief-desire psychology; as postulated by Wellman, 1990 – see Segal, this volume). But the two crucial claims made by those adopting this position are firstly, that the theory of mind module is an innate, isolable, component of the mind which embodies a *theory* of the nature and mode of operation of minds. (This is then a version of the so-called 'theory-theory' of our understanding of other minds, defended by many writers, including Lewis, 1966; Churchland, 1981; Stich, 1983; Fodor, 1987; Wellman, 1990; and others.) And secondly, that it is this module which is distinctively damaged in the case of autism.

Others (for example Frith, 1989; Harris, 1989, 1991, 1993; Hobson, 1993a; and Melzoff and Gopnik, 1993) take a different view, arguing, in various different ways and for various different reasons, that the mind-blindness of autistic people is a *consequence of* some more basic deficit. I shall make no attempt at a systematic survey of these competitor theories here, focusing only on one which seems to have been gaining ground lately. This is the proposal put forward by Harris (1989, 1991, 1993) and elaborated more recently by Gordon and Barker (1994) and by Currie (this volume), that the mind-blindness of autistic people is an effect of a deeper inability to engage in imaginative thinking.

According to this alternative proposal, the fundamental deficit involved in autism is an inability (or at least a reduced ability) to engage in imaginative, counterfactual, suppositional thinking. It is for this reason, it is supposed, that autistic children rarely engage in spontaneous pretend play, and tend to display behaviours that are stereotyped and rigidly routinised. It is also held that the difficulties autistic people have in reading the minds of others results from this same underlying deficit, since mind-reading abilities are claimed to require the ability to identify oneself imaginatively with the other person. (This is the so-called 'simulation-theory' of our understanding of the minds of others, notably defended by Gordon, 1986, 1992a, 1995; Harris, 1989; and Goldman, 1989, 1992b, 1993a.)

These competing explanations of autism involve us in wider disputes about the nature and origins of our conception of the mental states of other people in the normal case. I believe that in general there are powerful reasons for preferring the theory-theory to simulation-theory as an account of these matters (see Carruthers, ch.3 this volume). I believe that there are convincing reasons, also, for preferring a modularised, nativistic, version of the former to the child-as-little-scientist versions of theory-theory proposed by Gopnik and Wellman (Wellman, 1990; Gopnik and Wellman, 1992; Gopnik, 1993 – see Carruthers, ch.3 this volume and 1992 ch. 8; and Segal, this volume). But it has to be admitted that simulation-theory currently provides a rather more convincing account of some aspects of the autistic syndrome – specifically, the absence of pretend-play, and the inflexibility and lack of creativity of autistic thought. To the extent that this is so, to that extent we have *some* reason to prefer simulationism to any form of theory-theory.

I should stress at this point that in order to provide a viable alternative to the mind-blindness account of autism, the simulationist explanation must involve commitment to the sorts of radical simulationism defended by Gordon and Goldman. This is because the more limited form of content-simulation canvassed by a number of writers in this volume (see Carruthers; Heal; Perner; Botterill) is incapable of accounting for the data. For autistic subjects have problems across a whole range of theory of mind tasks, not just with those that involve predicting people's thoughts on the basis of other things that they are already known to think. When I speak of 'simulation' in this chapter, therefore, I should be understood as referring to its more radical variants.

What I propose to do, is not to mount any general defence of nativistic theory-theory, but only to show that an account of autism as mind-blindness can surmount the particular hurdle sketched above, being capable of providing explanations of the data that are just as convincing and elegant as can be given by simulationism. The core of my proposal will be that the mind-blindness theory has only *appeared* to be losing out in the above respects, because its proponents have paid insufficient attention to the consequences of their view for the access (or rather lack of access) that autistic people will have to their *own* mental states. It is here that I shall begin.

2   Mind-blindness and blindness to self

What account is the theory-theorist to provide of our knowledge of our own mental states? Here I shall help myself to the view elaborated briefly in Carruthers (ch.3 this volume). (See also Gopnik, 1993, for a variant on the approach.) I claim that a theory-theorist should regard self-knowledge as analogous to the theory-laden perception of theoretical entities in science. Just as a physicist can sometimes (in context, and given a background of theoretical knowledge) *see* that electrons are being emitted by the substance under study; and just as a diagnostician can sometimes *see* a

cancer in the blur of an x-ray photograph; so, too, we can each of us sometimes see (that is, know intuitively and non-inferentially) that we are in a
state accorded such-and-such a role by folk-psychological theory.

It is, I claim, part of the normal functioning of the human mind that a
mental state, M, if conscious, will automatically give rise to the belief that
one has M – where what one will recognise M *as*, is a state having a particular folk-psychological characterisation. This is not to say that all of the
principles of folk-psychology which play a part in generating that belief
will necessarily be accessible to us. But although the process of acquiring
self-knowledge may involve theories that are only implicitly (and innately)
known by the subject, still the upshot of that process – the knowledge that
I am in M – will nevertheless be theory-involving. On the theory-theory
account, what I recognise my own mental states *as*, are states having a particular folk-psychological role, even if I am unable to provide, consciously,
a complete characterisation of that role.

Now, what would this account predict, concerning the self-knowledge of
someone who has suffered damage to their theory of mind module? The
answer is plain – either such a person will be incapable of recognising their
own mental states as such at all, or they will, at best, only be able to do so
laboriously and unreliably. For, by hypothesis, it will be an innate theory of
mind module which provides, in the normal case, the network of theoretical concepts and principles which enables us to individuate our mental
states as such, as and when they occur. Anyone who lacks such a module,
or in whom such a module is damaged, will either lack those concepts and
principles altogether (and so be incapable of self-knowledge), or will have
only a fragmentary grasp of them (in which case knowledge of self will be
equally fragmentary), or will perhaps have acquired those concepts and
principles laboriously, through general learning mechanisms (in which case
self-attribution will, almost certainly, be slow and laborious also).

How do these predictions match up against the few empirical findings
which are available? They are certainly consistent with the data reported
by Baron-Cohen (1989c, 1991a), who found that autistic children have as
much trouble remembering their own recent false beliefs as they do in
attributing false beliefs to other people, and that autistic children also have
trouble drawing the appearance-reality distinction. The former result is
exactly what the mind-blindness theory would predict: if autistic people
have difficulty in understanding the notion of *belief*, then they should be
incapable of (or at least poor at) ascribing false beliefs at all, whether to
another agent or to themselves. Similarly, the mind-blindness theory
would predict that autistic people will lack adequate access to their own
experiences, as such (as opposed to access to the states which their experiences are *of*), and hence that they should have difficulty in negotiating the

contrast between *experience* (appearance) and *what it is an experience of* (reality).

The above predictions are also consistent with the data recently reported by Hurlburt *et al.* (1994), who tested three Asperger syndrome adults using the descriptive experience sampling method. This technique involves the subject wearing a small device that produces a beep at random intervals through the day, which the subject hears through an earphone. Subjects are instructed that their task is to 'freeze the contents of their awareness' at the moment when the beep began, and then to write down some notes about the details of the experience. Normal subjects report inner experiences in four major categories: inner verbalisation, visual images, unsymbolised thinking, and emotional feelings. All three of the subjects tested by Hurlburt *et al.* using this method were high-functioning autistics, who appeared able to understand the experimental instructions – two were capable of passing second-order false-belief tasks, and the third could pass first-order tasks, but not second-order tasks. Hurlburt *et al.* found that the first two subjects reported visual images only – no inner verbalisation, no unsymbolised thinking, and no emotional feelings. The third subject could report no inner experience at all.

Of course this is a very small sample of subjects, and the results are perhaps not easy to interpret. But they do suggest that autistic people might have severe difficulties of access to their own occurrent thought processes and emotions. For of course no one would want to deny that these subjects *have* thoughts and emotions. While autistic subjects surely must have propositional thoughts and emotional feelings, they do seem to have difficulty in knowing introspectively what their current thoughts and emotions are. (Why visual images should be any easier to self-attribute is something of a puzzle. Perhaps because perception-desire psychology is easier to acquire than belief-desire psychology – see Wellman 1990 – and because visual images are closely related to visual perception.)

Data apparently problematic for the predictions of the mind-blindness theory of autism are presented by Naito *et al.* (1995), who claim to find that autistic children who are incapable of attributing false beliefs to other people, in standard false-belief tasks, can nevertheless remember their own recent false beliefs without difficulty. (See also Leslie and Thaiss, 1992.) But in fact this data is easily explained away. For the experimental set-up was such that subjects were asked to remember what they had earlier *said* an object was (Naito *et al.* used deceptive-appearance tasks), and likewise to predict what another person would *say* that the object was. It is no surprise at all that autistic people should pass the first task but fail in the second. For, in fact, no theory of mind abilities are required in order for you to remember what you have just said. Whereas in order to predict what someone else will say, you first have to predict what they will *think*, and then generate a sentence appropriate to express that thought; which of course requires theory of mind ability.

If the mind-blindness account of autism is correct, then, we should expect, and we appear to find, that autistic people are as blind to their own mental states as they are to the mental states of others. It is this consequence of the theory which will shortly be put to good work in the main body of this chapter: explaining why autistic children do not engage in spontaneous pretend-play, and explaining why the thought and behaviour of autistic people should be so rigid and inflexible. But first, it may be worth noting briefly, here, that such an account seems capable of explaining, also, the many reports of disordered and fragmentary sensations amongst autistic people (see Frith, 1989). For one of the normal functions of the theory of mind module will be to classify and identify our own sensations for us. If that module is damaged, precisely what one would expect is that the subject's inner life would seem chaotic, fragmentary, and confused.

3   The problem of pretence

The mind-blindness hypothesis has no difficulty in accounting for two of the triad of autistic impairments identified by Wing and Gould in their classic Camberwell study (1979) – namely, impairment in social relationships, and in verbal and non-verbal communication. For these deficits are exactly what one would predict of someone who has severe difficulty in reading the minds of others. On the other hand, the third element of the triad – the absence of pretend-play – is, on the face of it, much more problematic. For why should mind-blindness interfere with pretence? One would expect it to interfere with social, or shared, pretence, of course, since this may require children to read the minds of their co-pretenders. And one would also expect a mind-blind child not to engage in the sort of play which involves attributing mental states to dolls or other pretend agents. But it is far from clear why mind-blindness should lead to any *general* deficit in pretend-play, such as is found in autism.

Leslie has boldly grasped this nettle, proposing that the very same cognitive mechanisms which are involved in theory of mind tasks also underlie the child's capacity for pretence (1987, 1988). He postulates the existence, in normal subjects, of a special-purpose mechanism, the *decoupler*, whose function is to uncouple a given representation – 'banana', say – from its normal input-output relations, so as to enable that representation to be manipulated freely without affecting those relations (as when the child pretends that the banana is a telephone while retaining the knowledge that it is still a banana *really*). Crucial to this account, for present purposes, is Leslie's claim that the de-coupler functions by forming a *second-order* representation of the de-coupled representation. For he can then go on to claim (with some plausibility, given that assumption) that this very same mechanism is employed when the child turns to mind-reading tasks, forming a representation of the mental state of another person (also a second-order representation). If such a de-coupler were to form a crucial component of the theory of mind module, then it is only to be expected that mind-blind subjects would also display deficits in pretend-play.

Leslie's proposal is deeply unsatisfying, however. For there is nothing to motivate the claim that solitary pretence requires the capacity to form second-order representations of one's own representations, beyond the need to save the mind-blindness theory of autism. Rather, what is required for pretence is the capacity to entertain a representation in a different *mode*, or as the content of a different mental *attitude* (as different from belief as belief is from desire) – namely, in the mode of *supposition*, or of *imagination*. To pretend that the banana is a telephone, the child does not have to represent its own representation of the banana, it just has to *suppose* that the banana is a telephone, and then think and act on that supposition. (See Perner, 1991a, where this criticism is developed at length; see also Jarrold *et al.*, 1994; Currie, 1995.)

In addition to the major criticism just sketched, Leslie's proposal faces a number of other problems, in response to which his account has been forced to become increasingly baroque (see Leslie, 1993). One is to explain why, if the very same de-coupling mechanism is employed in both pretence and theory of mind tasks, normal children should show competence in pretending so much earlier (age two) than they are able to pass false-belief tasks (age four). Another is to explain why properly social, co-operative, pretence should emerge so much later than solitary pretence (see Jarrold *et al.*, 1994). And yet another problem is raised by the data, replicated in a number of different studies, suggesting that while autistic children do not often pretend spontaneously, they do have the *capacity* for pretence if prompted (see, for example, Lewis and Boucher, 1988). I shall not pursue these problems here. Instead, I shall show how the mind-blindness theory of autism can explain the absence of spontaneous pretence in autistic children without having to have recourse to the hypothesis of the de-coupler.

4   Resolution of the problem of pretence

In a nutshell, my suggestion is that because autistic children are, through mind-blindness, deprived of ready access to their own mental states, they are at the same time deprived of the main source of enjoyment present in normal pretending. So the reason why autistic children do not engage in spontaneous pretence is not because they cannot do so, but rather because they do not find the activity rewarding. The problem is one of motivation, not of incapacity. However, this idea will require some setting up.

Why do children pretend? What is enjoyable about the activity of pretending? Plainly what is pleasurable are not, in general, the physical actions by means of which the child carries out the pretence. True enough, the enjoyment of pretend-fighting, and of the sorts of rough-and-tumble wrestling engaged in by the young of most other species of mammal as well as human children, probably does lie in the physical exertion involved, and in the attempt to dominate an opponent. But the same can hardly be true of the kinds of symbolic pretending distinctive of human beings. There can be nothing enjoyable about the activities of putting a banana to one's ear and talking to it *as such*. Rather, what is enjoyable about pretence, I suggest, is basically the sense of being able to manipulate one's own mental representations in imagination; which then requires, of course, that one should have ready access to the states containing those representations.

The young of all species of mammal engage in play of some sort, the function of which seems to be to prepare them for adult activities. (See Smith, 1982.) Thus young springbok will practise the leaps which will one day be necessary to keep them out of reach of predators; young stag deer will engage in the kind of pretend-fighting and head-butting which will later be employed in the competition for mates in the rut; and the kittens of all species of cat will, in the course of their wresting with their siblings, practise just the kinds of stalking, leaping, biting, and holding which will form an essential part of adult hunting. It seems reasonable to suppose that the young of each species are programmed to find intrinsically rewarding, in play, just those activities (or those that are sufficiently similar to them, at least) which will form crucial components of their adult behavioural repertoire.

Now, for which adult activities are young children practising, when they engage in pretend-play? At one level you might be tempted to say: for those very activities that they are pretending to perform. The little girl pretending to be a mother bathing a baby is practising to become a mother who will bath a baby, the little boy pretending to be an airline pilot is practising to become an airline pilot, and so on. But it would be absurd to suggest that children are programmed to find *these* activities, described at this level, intrinsically rewarding. For most of the activities that children pretend to perform would not have existed at the time when human cognitive and motivational systems were evolving (*mothering*, of course, is one of the exceptions). Indeed, many of the things that children may pretend to do or be may actually be impossible to do or be in reality. The child who is pretending to turn objects to gold through a Midas-touch can hardly be practising to turn objects to gold as an adult! And the child who is pretending to *be* an aeroplane can hardly be practising to *become* an aeroplane in adulthood!

It is much more plausible to claim that children find rewarding that feature which is common to *all* forms of pretend-play, namely the manipulation of the child's own mental states, through *supposing* or *imagining*. (Hence, of course, the interest that normal children also take in fiction and story-telling – an interest notably absent amongst autistics.) Then, just as you cannot enjoy running or jumping without being conscious of (or being aware that you are) running and jumping, so, too, I suggest, you cannot enjoy supposing or imagining without being conscious of your (mental) activity. In general, *enjoying Xing* presupposes *awareness of Xing* – which is why you cannot enjoy digestion, sleepwalking, or subliminal perception.

It is surely incontrovertible that supposing, or imagining, is one of the distinguishing marks of the human species. It is the human capacity to *suppose* that such-and-such were the case and reason from there, or to *imagine* performing some activity and work out the consequences in advance, that underlies much of the success of our species. It has often been said that humans are distinctively *rational* animals. It may be closer to the truth to say that they are uniquely *imaginative* animals, since many other species seem to share our capacity to act intelligently in the light of desires, but none (excepting perhaps chimpanzees) share our ability to reason from supposed premises or to explore the consequences of imagined scenarios – and certainly none has this ability to such a high degree. Small wonder, then, if much of human childhood should be devoted to forms of play whose function is to practise this very activity.

However, if the enjoyment of pretence requires a child to have access to its own mental state of pretending, then am I not committed, just as Leslie is, to saying that even a two-year-old must be capable of meta-representing its own mental representations? There are two factors distinguishing my proposal from Leslie's, however, in a way that renders it substantially more plausible. First, on my account, unlike Leslie's, there need be no necessity for the child who is pretending that the banana is a telephone to meta-represent its own representation of the banana. Rather, it need only – at most – meta-represent *that it is now pretending*. That is, the meta-representation involved may only extend to the *attitude* of pretending, without also embracing the *content* of what is pretended. Put differently, one might suggest that children are wired up to detect and represent, and find intrinsically rewarding, the mental state of pretending, without having to form a meta-representation of any other aspects (including the content) of that state. The second factor follows on naturally from the first. It is that young children may only have meta-*awareness* of their states of pretence, without yet being capable of meta-*representing* – that is, conceptualising or thinking about – those states. It may be that young children can *detect* their own pretence, and find it rewarding, without yet having the capacity to *think that* they are pretending.

A comparison with another proposed modular system may be of help at this point. Consider the face-recognition module, which has been hypothesised by many different researchers. It is highly plausible that it is this very module (at an early stage of growth and development) which is implicated in the neonate's well-documented discriminations of, and responses to, faces and face-like shapes. But it is highly *im*plausible, of course, to maintain that the infant is, at that stage, capable of entertaining *thoughts about* faces. Rather, the early development of the face-recognition module enables an infant to *detect* faces without yet conceptualising them *as* faces. This early non-conceptualised awareness of faces may be one of the crucial inputs upon which later development of the module depends. So, too, then, in the case of the mind-reading module – it may be that in early stages of its development it enables a young child to detect, and be aware of, its own mental state of pretending, among others (which is necessary if the child is to find that state rewarding), but without the child being capable, as yet, of entertaining thoughts about the pretence of itself, or of other people. Here, too, I suggest, the child's unconceptualised (introspective) awareness of its own mental states may be one of the crucial inputs to the normal growth and development of the theory of mind module.

I have suggested that what is *basically* enjoyable about pretend-play is the activity of supposing or imagining itself, which then presupposes that the child has ready access to its own mental states, particularly its own acts of imagining. This should not be taken as denying that there can be *some* forms of satisfaction to be derived from imagination which do *not* presuppose meta-awareness of one's own mental activity (or not immediately, anyway). In particular, it seems to be part of the functioning of the imagination that imagined scenarios should engage directly with the appetitive system, and with the emotions – and this can be fun. Imagining a juicy steak can make you hungry, imagining an act of sexual intercourse can make you sexually aroused, imagining a free-fall from an aeroplane can make you frightened, and so on. It is easy to see why this should be so, if the main function of the imagination lies, not in fantasy, but in practical reasoning. (Here I am in agreement with Currie, 1995 and this volume; and Harris, 1991, 1993.) If the imagined result of the plan under consideration, of going to the kitchen and doing some cooking – namely, a juicy steak – had no tendency to engage with the appetitive system, it could have no tendency to set me in motion, either.

Although sometimes it is the imagined object, rather than the activity of imagining itself, which gives rise to enjoyment, it is arguable that even this enjoyment presupposes meta-awareness of one's own mental states. It is not (unassuaged) sexual arousal in itself which is enjoyable, but rather the bodily sensations distinctive of that state, of which one is aware. Similarly, it is not the fear of falling from an aeroplane which is itself enjoyable, but rather the thrill of this combined with the knowledge that I am only imagining, and really sitting safe in my arm-chair at home. So the conclusion stands undamaged: the enjoyment of pretence presupposes that subjects have ready introspective access to their own mental states. Small wonder, then – if it is true that autism is a form of mind-blindness – that autistic people should rarely be found to engage in pretence.

5   Stereotyped behaviour, inflexible thought

Properly understood, then – as entailing its introspective corollary – the mind-blindness account of autism can provide a smooth and elegant explanation for the fact that autistic children are distinguished by their absence of pretend-play. The explanation is that such children *can* pretend but do not particularly enjoy it. The question remains, however, as to why, when autistic children are prompted to pretend, their pretence is often so stereotyped and unimaginative. For example, if asked to pretend, with or without the aid of props, to do as many different things as they can think of (e.g. wear a hat, read a book, etc.) autistic children generate far fewer activities than do normal controls (see Jarrold *et al.*, in preparation). Why should this be so, if autistic children really do have an undamaged capacity for imagination, as the mind-blindness theory of autism would predict, and contrary to what the simulationist account would propose?

The answer, in this instance, is easy – it may be because *they have had less practice at imagining*. If the function of pretend-play is to exercise the imagination, then it is small wonder that those who have exercised little should perform less well. The autistic child who is prompted to engage in pretence is like a bird capable of flight who has never or rarely flown. Although the innate cognitive basis for pretence is present, just as the innate basis of flight is present in the bird, one would expect that it would be rusty and slow through ill-use.

In reality, however, the body of data provided by Jarrold *et al.* (in preparation) is only the tip of a very large and well-established ice-berg, which may threaten yet to sink the mind-blindness theory of autism. This is the aspect of autism which is perhaps the best well-known, namely the tendency of autistic people to engage in repetitive activity, to be obsessed with order and ritual, to have very narrowly focused interests, and to be generally very uncreative and unimaginative in their thought and behaviour. How is this to be explained, if autism is to be identified with mind-blindness? Are these features not better explained by the simulationist account? My strategy, here, will be to divide and conquer, offering differing explanations of different aspects of the phenomena.

The obsessive side of autism seems best explained as a by-product of social alienation, as has traditionally been proposed. Autistic children live in a world that is at once puzzling and threatening. To see this, think how much of the child's environment is social in nature, and how much of the time of a normal child will be occupied with social interactions of one sort or another – interactions with peers or siblings, story-tellings with parents, negotiations with carers over foods and bed-times, and so on. Much of this would seem utterly opaque to a mind-blind child, and most of the behaviour of the people around such a child would seem wholly unpredictable. It would not be entirely surprising, then, if some autistic children should respond by isolating themselves still further from the puzzling social world around them, seeking refuge, out of loneliness and distress, in repetitive activity. And small wonder, also, if some autistic children should try to gain a measure of control over their world by imposing arbitrary, but orderly and predictable, rituals.

The narrowly focused interests of many autistic people, too, may be explained as resulting, partly from loneliness, partly as a further reaction to the opaque nature of the social world. (Yet another proposal will be made in section 6 below.) I can well remember, myself, as an unusually lonely adolescent, spending hours absorbed in the play of light in the dew-drops on a bud or leaf, trying to persuade myself that this was a matter of the deepest metaphysical significance. And when one reflects on just how many of the normal objects of childhood and adolescent interest – fiction, films, sex, and competitive sports, for example – presuppose a good deal in the way of social awareness and mind-reading ability, it is not so surprising that autistic people might be happy to discover an area of interest – albeit bus time-tables, or the calendar dates of days of the week – which they can understand, and at which they can excel.

There remains, however, a good deal of evidence of lack of flexibility of thought amongst autistic individuals, which is not so easily explained as a mere by-product of social alienation and loneliness. In particular, a number of studies have tested autistic people on problem-solving and planning tasks, and found that they perform much less well than controls. For example, Ozonoff *et al.* (1991a) tested autistic individuals on the Tower of Hanoi problem, finding that success or failure in this task successfully classified 80% of the children in both the normal and the autistic groups. The autistic children tended to persevere with unsuccessful strategies, despite repeated failure; whereas normal children were much more ready to try new strategies as old ones failed.

Such findings have led both Leslie and Roth (1993) and Baron-Cohen and Ring (1994b) to accept that autistic people, in addition to mind-blindness, *also* suffer from a separate executive-function deficit, caused by collateral damage to areas in the frontal cortex close to those that appear to be involved in theory of mind tasks. While this by no means refutes their position – after all, every theory of autism must accept that there are *some* phenomena (for example, the excessive thirst experienced by many autistic children) that are caused, not by the syndrome itself, but by collateral brain-damage – nevertheless, it is good scientific practice to try to minimise accidents. I believe it is possible for the mind-blindness theory of autism to do better.

6   Practical reasoning and second-order thought

In philosophical circles it has been widely accepted, at least since Frankfurt's classic 1971 paper, that the normal operation of the human practical reasoning system routinely involves second-order evaluations of first-order thoughts and desires. In deciding what to do on a free afternoon while the family are away – whether to stay in with a novel or go out into the garden to cut the grass – I may consider such things as: how much I *want* that the grass should be cut, as opposed to how much I want to read my novel; whether there will be later opportunities to satisfy these desires if they are not satisfied now; how *likely* it is that I will be able to read free of interruptions if I stay in, and how likely it is that it will remain dry enough to garden if I go out; and so on. In all this I am both evaluating my own desires and determining the degree of credence which I am prepared to place in my own beliefs – which presupposes (in many cases, at least) that I have *access to* my desires and beliefs.

Admittedly, it may sometimes be possible to weigh up one desire against another without raising, explicitly, any meta-representational question. I may, for example, ask myself simply *how good the novel is*, or how important reading would be as against neatly mown grass. In this I should be reflecting on the *goals* of my prospective actions, rather than on my desires for those goals as such. But even here, it is hard to see how such a process of reasoning could work, except through introspective access to my *appetitive response to the thought of those goals*. Similarly in the case of belief – I may, sometimes, ask myself simply *how likely it is that it will rain*, without explicitly evaluating (that is, meta-representing) my *belief* that it will. But in many cases, at least, degrees of credence cannot rationally be assigned without an element of second-order reflection. For example, in answering the question concerning the likelihood of rain, I may have to recall the source of my belief (whether a weather-forecast, or 'red sky at morning', or whatever) and evaluate its reliability. Such a procedure can only be possible if I know that I have (and so meta-represent) that belief.

Not only does human practical reasoning routinely involve access to our own beliefs and desires, it also involves something much stronger, I believe. For it is obvious, on reflection, that our practical reasoning systems routinely employ a kind of reflexive, introspective, access to our own recent sequences of occurrent conscious thinkings. (See my 1996 where this idea is developed in some detail.) Having recently been thinking about a problem in a particular way, I can then think about the thoughts that I have just entertained, and think about the problem-solving strategy I have just been employing. Or having been weighing up carefully the pros and cons of a number of different courses of action, I can then think, 'I shouldn't be so cautious and rational in my thinking – spontaneity has its value too!' All of which again presupposes, of course, that I have regular second-order access to my own occurrent thought-processes.

According to the modular hypothesis being defended here, the capacity for these sorts of swift and reliable forms of meta-access to our own beliefs, desires, and sequences of thinking and reasoning will be mediated, in the normal case, by the operation of the theory of mind module. It is therefore to be predicted that someone who is mind-blind, or whose theory of mind module is damaged, will experience considerable difficulty in tasks which involve the more complex (second-order) forms of practical reasoning. This is because such a subject's access to their own mental states will be relatively difficult, slow, and unreliable. We should therefore expect such a person to perform poorly on tasks that require them to evaluate their own desires or beliefs. And we should also expect them to perform equally poorly in tasks that require them to evaluate their own recent problem-solving strategies.

So here we have an explanation of the poor performance of autistic people in the Tower of Hanoi problem. (This is in addition to the partial explanation already sketched in section 5 above, that the suppositional reasoning of autistic people may suffer for lack of practice, because of the rarity of pretend-play in childhood.) The explanation is: they do poorly because solving such problems requires reflection on one's own problem-solving strategies. One must try out a strategy, either in imagination or on the board, and then when it fails, think about that strategy itself and how it might be modified and improved. It is no surprise, then, to find that autistic people mostly fail by perseverance, continuing with unsuccessful strategies despite repeated failures. For the mind-blindness theory of autism predicts that such people would experience difficulties of access to their own sequences of thinking and reasoning.

Here we also have a further explanation, I think, of the narrow and often idiosyncratic interests of many autistic adolescents and adults. (Again, this is in addition to the explanation given in 5 above, that autistic people will seek areas of interest which do not require mind-reading abilities, and where they can find, or impose, a measure of order and control.) For it is a reasonable hypothesis that regular second-order evaluation of our first-order desires and interests is one of the major engines driving the diversification of our value-systems. It is (at least in part) by reflecting on our desires and interests, and comparing them in imagination with alternatives, that our values diversify. We ask ourselves, 'Is my interest in stamp-collecting really that rewarding? Would it be a good idea if I got myself interested in nineteenth-century novels instead?' And it is by regular reflection on our projects and values that we attain, and retain, a sense of proportion. We ask ourselves, 'Is this project really worth all the time I am devoting to it? Do I care about it *that* much? Would I not rather be doing something else instead?' By hypothesis, autistic people will find such second-order reflection difficult. So it is only to be expected that their range of interests might remain narrow, and that they should invest a degree of commitment in their projects which appears, to an outsider, to be out of all proportion to the true value of those activities.

My proposal has been that the executive-function deficits of autistic individuals are a consequence of their mind-blindness. An apparent problem for this proposal, however, is the finding that Asperger's syndrome subjects *pass* false-belief tasks while still failing at problem-solving tasks such as the Tower of Hanoi. (See Ozonoff *et al.*, 1991b.) Does this not seem to show that it is problems of reasoning or imagining which are the more fundamental? Does the data not lend support, indeed, to the simulationists' view that it is, rather, a defective imagination which causes mind-blindness when sufficiently severe? (See Harris, 1993.) I do not believe, in fact, that these data raise any particular problem for the explanations offered above. For the proposal is not that the blindness of autistic individuals to the minds of themselves and others will necessarily be total. On the contrary, the proposal is that the theory of mind module may be partially intact in some cases of autism; and in other cases, that subjects may use alternative – general learning – strategies to gain at least a rudimentary grasp on the theory of mind. The prediction is only that all autistic people will find mind-reading, of themselves or others, relatively difficult, slow, and unreliable.

Now, the point to notice about the false-belief tasks is that they only require, for their solution, a limited number of mental-state attributions. The subject must recognise what the other person has and has not *seen*, for example, and use this to underpin the attribution of a *false belief*, before putting this together with the other's supposed *desire*, to generate a prediction about what they will do. And this is a problem that the subject is normally given, altogether, some minutes to solve. In the case of the sorts of problem-solving tasks that require regular second-order monitoring of one's own problem-solving strategies, in contrast, a whole myriad of mental states will need to be self-ascribed in a matter of seconds. Small wonder, then, that there might be particularly able autistic people whose grip on theory of mind is good enough to enable them to succeed in false-belief tasks, but still not good enough for them to keep reliable track of their own problem-solving strategies, and so still not good enough for them to succeed in tasks like the Tower of Hanoi.

(Note that it is an empirical prediction of the line being pushed here, that those autistic people who succeed in false-belief tasks will nevertheless take considerably longer to solve them than do controls. I find it surprising that amongst all the studies that have been conducted on the theory of mind abilities of autistics and normals, no one seems to have thought of gathering data on *speed* of theory of mind problem-solving.)

I have claimed that the mind-blindness theory of autism can explain the executive-function deficits common amongst autistic individuals. But let me stress that this is not, in any sense, to *identify* autism with failure of executive function. I have only claimed that an intact theory of mind module, giving the subject swift and reliable access to their own thought-processes, may be a *necessary condition for* success in complex practical reasoning tasks. There is, of course, a good deal more to practical reasoning than mere success in accessing one's own mental states. So it is only to be expected that there may be executive-function deficits which do *not* involve failure in theory of mind tasks. And, indeed, that is exactly what we find. Executive-function deficits occur in many clinical populations – for example, obsessive-compulsive disorder, schizophrenia, hyperactivity, etc. – who do not have theory of mind deficits. (I owe this point to Simon Baron-Cohen.)

In this connection, too, it may be worth noting some recent data which causes severe problems for the simulationist explanation of autism (or which will do so, at least, if it proves to be replicable and robust). This data relates to Williams syndrome children, who suffer from a rare genetic disorder giving them a distinctive, and highly uneven, cognitive profile. The crucial finding is that Williams syndrome children suffer severe difficulties in practical reasoning and problem-solving tasks (for example, performing very poorly in a modified version of the Tower of Hanoi – modified to become a verbal rather than a visual task, since Williams syndrome children have notorious problems with visuo-spatial reasoning); but that they have no difficulty whatever with theory of mind tasks – on the contrary, their social and communication skills are precocious (Annette Karmiloff-Smith, personal communication).

This data may prove extremely important. For it is very hard to see how hypothetical, imaginative, thinking can be a presupposition of theory of mind ability, as simulationists maintain, if there exist individuals who lack the former but possess the latter. According to the mind-blindness proposal, in contrast, there can be (at least) two quite distinct ways in which problem-solving abilities can be damaged: one is by damage to the hypothetical reasoning faculty itself (which, one might suppose, is what happens in the case of Williams syndrome); the other is by damage to the theory of mind module which gives normal subjects regular access to their own problem-solving thinking, serving to make the latter more efficient and reliable.

Conclusion

I have argued that the crucial implication of the autism-as-mind-blindness hypothesis, hitherto not sufficiently noticed, is that autistic individuals will not only experience difficulties in ascribing mental states to other people, but will equally have problems in achieving second-order awareness of their own mental processes. This is because the theory of mind module will be just as much implicated in self-attribution as in other-attribution. This implication then enables the mind-blindness hypothesis to provide a simple and elegant explanation of the fact that autistic children rarely engage in spontaneous pretend-play – it is because, lacking easy self-awareness of their own mental states, they do not find the sorts of intrinsic satisfaction in pretence that normal children do. The same implication also enables us to explain the narrow interests and problem-solving deficits associated with autism, again because autistic people lack regular second-order awareness of their own desires and thought-processes.

ACKNOWLEDGEMENTS

I am grateful to the following for many valuable comments on earlier drafts of this chapter: Simon Baron-Cohen, George Botterill, Jill Boucher, Jack Copeland, Paul Harris, Chris Jarrold, Shaun Nichols, Peter J. Smith, and Peter K. Smith.

Part IV

Wider perspectives – evolution and theory of mind

17   When does smart behaviour-reading become mind-reading?

Andrew Whiten

1   Introduction

The question of whether or not an individual is discriminating between others' states of mind is commonly addressed through a contrast with the alternative that it is merely discriminating between others' behaviour patterns. This is a frequent point of debate in the case of pre-verbal infants (e.g. Perner, 1991a, p. 128) and non-verbal animals (e.g. Cheney and Seyfarth, 1990b, p. 235), where it is usually assumed that mind-reading is a more advanced cognitive achievement than behaviour-reading, and that the latter will precede the former in either evolutionary or ontogenetic mental change.

However, mind-reading is not telepathy. So, the recognition of another's state of mind must somehow rest on observation of certain components within the complex of others' *behaviour patterns* together with their *environmental context:* that's all we can see – we can't see their minds in the direct way suggested by the idea of telepathy. This means that the contrast of mind-reading with behaviour-reading is not so straightforward as it may first appear: mind-reading, one might say, must be some sort of 'behaviourism'! At least, it must reflect some special form of behaviour analysis – special because it must differ from what we typically consider to be the mere perception of behaviour patterns (Whiten, 1993; 1994). Thus, rather than ask where mind-reading differs from behaviour reading, I shall tackle the question of when behaviour-reading *becomes* mind-reading, regarding the latter as some sort of sub-category of the former.

The question of what shall count as making this transition is surely a profound one. It underlies the debates which have occupied so much of the present century over whether the academic/scientific version of psychology (as opposed to folk psychology) should be mentalist or behaviourist, and how it can, in the mentalist case, be objective. The question is of fundamental importance in our attempts to specify both the development of human mentalism from its origins in infancy and its evolutionary origins as inferred from comparative studies of other species. It is also of relevance to a much wider range of disciplines including philosophy of mind, social anthropology, psychiatry, and law, which are concerned with issues like recognising deception, or intent to harm, in an individual's actions.

2   What would non-verbal mentalism look like?

In the case of verbal humans, the mental states which are the 'building bricks' of folk psychology are neatly labelled (beliefs, wants, and so on) and conventionally defined well enough in each linguistic culture that we can tell each other about our mental states, and the mental states we may assign to others. Mental verbs like *think* can be shown to be a special class, distinguishable from action verbs like *hit* in logical aspects of the way they relate to their referents (referential or logical opacity). We need not delve into the technicalities of this here (see Dennett, 1988, for a clear exposition) because, although the exercise helps to delineate a list of mental states humans have found it useful to label, it does not in itself help us to recognise the *non-verbal* mentalist in any direct way.

What the discovery of referential opacity has done, perhaps, is to demonstrate the possibility of a sharp mental/behavioural divide: a point of view which according to Preston (1993) 'appears to be tacitly and nearly universally accepted among philosophers of mind and psychology', and which is summed up in a quotation from Fodor (1968b, p. 55): 'The distinction between mentalism and behaviourism is both exclusive and exhaustive. You must be either a mentalist or a behaviourist.' But Preston goes on to show the senses in which the two are in fact neither mutually exclusive nor conjunctively exhaustive. With respect to exclusivity, she argues that each approach, as applied by psychologists, tends in practice to incorporate some element of the other.

When we turn to the case of potential non-verbal mind-readers, like preverbal infants (Trevarthen, 1977, 1993; Reddy, 1991) and non-verbal apes (Premack and Woodruff, 1978; Whiten, 1993), the blurring of the distinction becomes more acute. We cannot appeal to the analysis of language which in the case of referential opacity appears so elegantly to pick out 'the mental'. In a group of chimpanzees there is no conversation about what Flo thought Fifi wanted, just individuals behaviourally interacting with each other. If they are mentalists, how would their behaviour look, compared to if they are behaviourists? Where we are tempted to say *A responded to the mental state of B* (the state of B *wanting* A's banana, for example), shall we not always be faced with the problem that A responded directly to whatever was the evidential basis for the mental state (probably B's behaviour and/or the situation it faced)? And when, to look at the reverse causal pathway, we are tempted to say *A attempted to change the mental state of B so it would perform act X*, shall we not have to concede that A was just as likely to be attempting *to get B to do X*? More fundamentally, what makes the mental and non-mental alternatives really different in practice? The same issues arise in the case of pre-verbal infants.

These dilemmas remain in the case of experimental tests. Thus, when Premack and Woodruff (1978) showed that a chimpanzee would choose a photograph depicting the correct behavioural solution to a problem faced by another individual, the criticism was made that perhaps the chimpanzee simply knew, not the individual's *purpose*, but rather just what was the next thing to be *done* by such an individual in those circumstances (Bennett, 1978).

When, then, would it become valid to say that a non-verbal creature was reading behaviour in a way which made it of real interest to say they were mind-reading? Below I shall consider several alternatives. They do not allow us simply to say, *that's mentalism* or *that's not*: rather, there are grades of mind-reading (Whiten, 1994). The point is that some grades are non-trivially, interestingly different from others which are more easily thought of as 'just behaviour-reading'.

3   Implicit mind-reading

In our language of mental terms, we *explicitly* recognise and differentiate states of mind: states have specific labels, like *belief* and *desire*. But perhaps one could investigate whether mental states must be acknowledged as *implicit* in certain patterns of action in others which some non-verbal animals respond to. This point of view has been elegantly expressed by Gómez (1991). Gómez studied a young gorilla faced with the problem of shifting a door-latch which was out of her reach. Initially, she used a human caretaker as an object, pulling them to the door and then climbing on them to reach the latch. Later, a more interesting strategy developed in which she gently led the human towards the door, alternating her gaze between his eyes and the latch, and then taking his hand a little way in the direction of the latch. Humans easily interpret this as a request.

In this second strategy, Gómez remarks, 'she seemed to use eye contact to monitor if the human was *attending* to her request that he *acted*. Thus, she seemed to understand that in subjects, perceiving is causally related to acting. And here is where the mind appears, since the co-ordination between perceptions and actions is carried out by the mind' (p. 201). This phenomenon may be important as a potential precursor of the more sophisticated discriminations which develop in children, between states of ignorance, knowledge, and false belief, for in all of these the observer translates from observed relationships between an individual's perceptual access in relation to environmental circumstances, to their later, causally linked, actions. From this perspective, then, it is an important insight to recognise the ape as performing a certain grade of (implicit) mind-reading. However, we must acknowledge that what the ape apparently recognises can be economically described in terms of direct observables: i.e. the relationship between the human's gaze behaviour and the latch, and the later, contingent action of opening the latch.

This appears similar to the 'behaviour-reading' interpretation of the experiment of Premack and Woodruff mentioned earlier. It also appears to be compatible with a conception of mind-reading which has been developed by ethologists, who have noted the usefulness to one animal of being able to predict the future behaviour of others with whom it must to do business, whether this be mating, fighting, or a host of other interactions where the outcome bears on survival and reproductive success. Krebs and Dawkins (1984) noted that: 'Animals can, in principle, forecast the behaviour of other animals, because sequences of behaviour follow statistical rules. Ethologists discover the rules systematically by recording long sequences of behaviour and then analysing them statistically, for example by transition matrices, and in the same way an animal can behave as if it is predicting another individual's future behaviour.' And they go on to suggest that:

we may use the term mind-reading as a catch-word to describe what we are doing when we use statistical laws to predict what an animal will do next. For an animal, the equivalent of the data-collection and statistical analysis is performed either by natural selection acting on the mind-reader's ancestors over a long period, or by some process of learning during its own lifetime (Lorenz 1966). In both cases, 'experience' of the lawfulness of the behaviour of victims becomes internalised in the brain of the mind-reader. In both cases its mind-reading ability enables it to exploit its victim's behaviour by being 'one jump ahead of it'. The mind-reader is able to optimise its own behavioural choices in the light of the probable future responses of its victim. A dog with its teeth bared is statistically more likely to bite than a dog with its teeth covered. This being a fact, natural selection or learning will shape the behaviour of other dogs in such a way as to take advantage of future probabilities, for example by fleeing from rivals with bared teeth . . . mind-reading refers to a role that an individual can assume' (pp. 386–7).

I quote this fully, first, because it is important that all readers interested in mind-reading understand the breadth of meaning of the term as it is used in this literature, and Krebs and Dawkins' review represents an authoritative view in ethology. Second, it well expresses a hypothesis about the functional utility of mind-reading in predicting others' future actions, which is often put forward as the power and raison-d'etre of human mentalism (e.g. Premack and Woodruff, 1978; Wellman, 1991).

However, the quite direct sense in which mind-reading as defined by Krebs and Dawkins is a form of behaviour-reading is clear from the quotation above. Notwithstanding my earlier comment about the positive value of Gómez's interpretation of his gorilla as evidencing an implicit theory of mind, the gorilla's action might also, and as easily, be accounted for as 'using statistical laws to predict what an animal will do next', these laws referring to linkages between the human's gaze and actions on the latch.

At an even more general level, it could be argued that mind is implicit in much, or even (according to how broadly we define mind, as the causal mechanism for animals' behaviour) most animal behaviour: so to respond to another's threat behaviour, for example, is to respond implicitly to their aggressive state of mind. In this sense, implicit mind-reading is common, but this approach to mind-reading would not take us interestingly beyond behaviour-reading. Gómez's handling of the idea of implicit mind-reading in the particular case he discusses is important for the reasons discussed earlier, but we need to look further afield for a more general solution to identifying non-verbal mind-reading.

Before moving on, however, we should note what appears to be a rather different sense of 'implicit mind-reading' which has recently been applied by Clements and Perner (1994). Clements and Perner have shown that children may fail a standard test of false belief attribution (in which they are required to predict where a person will search for an object moved without their knowledge), yet their eye gaze indicated a correct prediction. They suggest the latter shows an 'implicit understanding of belief', contrasting it with a lack of 'explicit' understanding as revealed in verbal responses. This may be a useful measure to apply in experiments with non-verbal subjects like non-human primates. However, it would appear to be equivalent to any other measures one could use with such subjects: since they cannot give an explicit response in the form of speech, non-verbal measures like gaze *must* be used to record the distinctions they make. It is not obvious that gaze is any different to other behaviours which have been used to this effect, such as pointing (Povinelli *et al.,* 1990) or vocalising (Cheney and Seyfarth, 1990b). Thus, Clements and Perner are distinguishing 'implicit' by reference to how the putative *mind-reader* demonstrates behaviourally that they are indeed mind-reading; whereas in the earlier discussion of this section I have been concerned with whether the distinctions the putative mind-reader makes are about *others'* behaviour patterns, or mental states. Whether the subject uses gaze or speech to indicate where she thinks a subject in the situation used by Clements and Perner will search is a different question from what she is discriminating: is she discriminating states of mind, or does she just know how individuals will behave in these circumstances (e.g. will search where they last saw the object)?

Thus, whichever sense of 'implicit' versus 'explicit' is applied, the behaviour-reading versus mind-reading distinction has not been satisfactorily cracked.

4   Recognising deception

Arguably the more interesting aspect of the Krebs and Dawkins analysis outlined here lies in their reasoning about the nature of communication, which they suggest may explain the *evolution* of mind-reading. In an earlier paper, Dawkins and Krebs (1978) questioned the conventional ethological wisdom which stated that animals' communication signals have evolved to transmit to others good information, particularly about their internal motivational state (motivation to attack, or court, and so on). Dawkins and Krebs argued that this idea is fundamentally flawed because animals are not expected to evolve actions merely for the benefit of others: rather, signals should evolve which most successfully manipulate others to the genetic benefit of the sender (but note that this more general formulation incorporates the possibility that if such benefits *do* arise through helping others, this will be selected for too). The deception and other forms of manipulation which thus evolve, in turn provide the selection pressure for mind-reading: because it now becomes important for animals to read not just the surface behaviour (which may be misleading), but to distinguish from this the underlying 'true' state of mind – the other animal's real intentions, such as the intent to attack while appearing friendly (Krebs and Dawkins, 1984).

This analysis seems to me to offer an important conceptual basis for what it could be for an animal to be 'really mind-reading': viz., the situation in which it identifies the true state of the mind of its protagonist, discounting the surface behaviour which on a particular occasion is at variance with that state. An appreciation of teasing, whether in apes (Kohler, 1927) or human infants (Reddy, 1991) may also fall into this category. Ironically perhaps, this essential contrast which appears to necessitate reference to a mind/behaviour distinction, is lost in Krebs and Dawkins' 'behaviourist' definition of mind-reading cited in the previous section.

However, consider how an animal *could* come to see through deceptive ploys to the true state of the protagonist's mind. One way ('history') would be that it learned by experience that under certain conditions a different interpretation was warranted: for example, a particular individual might come to be recognised as untrustworthy because they so often cry wolf. A second way ('leakage') would be to recognise tell-tale cues in the protagonist, such as the equivalent of blushing in humans. And a third ('contradiction') would be to recognise other inconsistent cues, such as when A acts as if seeing some interesting object, the non-existence of which B has independent grounds for recognising. Records of primate behaviour exist which appear to correspond to each of these three criteria (Whiten and Byrne, 1988; Byrne and Whiten, 1990; 1991). However, each of these ways of discounting can be re-described as an observational analysis, with the mind-reader succeeding at its task because it discounts certain conventional signals in favour of some other observable criteria which are given more weight.

As in the case of the implicit mind-reading described for Gómez's gorilla, we must acknowledge that such phenomena are of great interest with respect to the emergence of the mature mentalism humans come to apply, because even though they *may* be adequately characterised as sophisticated behaviour-analyses, they require the mind-reader to tap into cues which represent likely important observational foundation stones even for the adult human mentalist. Thus when the latter is dealing with another's intent to deceive them, they must surely do this on the basis of discerning one or more of the three types of 'give-away' sketched above – history, leakage or contradiction.

However, in the human mentalist, we assume there must be a brain state which corresponds specifically to (encodes) the state of mind in the protagonist – 'deceptive intent'. It is not apparent that this is necessary in the case of the animal counter-deceiver described above: they may just know to distrust certain behavioural and contextual signs in favour of others, and we need say only that their brain encodes these signs. In the next section, we consider what is additionally required to diagnose encoding of others' *states of mind* by a non-verbal mind-reader.

5   Mental states as intervening variables

I have explained the concept of mental states as intervening variables quite fully elsewhere (Whiten, 1993; 1994), and so provide a concise description here. My starting point has been the usage of the idea of intervening variables in an earlier phase of animal psychology. It was shown that a number of different aspects of rats' drinking behaviour (the amount they would drink, how hard they would work to get water, and so on) could each be caused by any one of a number of conditions (eating dry food, going long without a drink, and so on). This could be represented as a large number of S-R (stimulus-response) links, joining each of these inputs to each of the behavioural outputs (fig. 17.1a). But alternatively, an intervening variable can be posited which underlies the pattern of

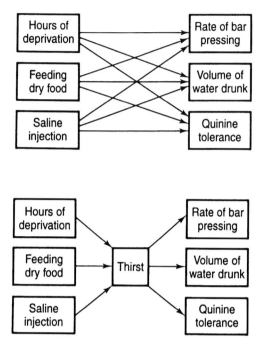

Figure 17.1 A simple example of an intervening variable.
(a) The relationships between three independent and three dependent variables in the case of rats' drinking; (b) Recognising an intervening variable (here called 'thirst') permits a more economic representation of the causal linkages, in this case reduced from the nine shown in (a), to six (after Miller, 1959; Hinde, 1970; Whiten, 1993).

results: this variable is not directly observable, and is thus an 'intervening variable' the value of which can be affected by any or all of the input variables, and having changed, can itself affect each of the outputs (Miller, 1959) (fig. 17.1b). It does not really matter what we call the intervening variable, but in this case 'thirst' would not be unreasonable. We now have a representation of these phenomena which is more *economic of representational resources*, because the multitude of S-R links no longer need to be coded. The observer needs only to know that the 'Ss' can each lead to the state (thirst, in this case) and that for an organism in this state certain 'Rs' can be forecasted. The more different conditions which can affect the intervening variable, and the more outputs it can affect in turn, the more efficiency of representation can be gained by its replacing a profusion of specific S-R links.

The suggestion is that recognising a state of mind in another follows this

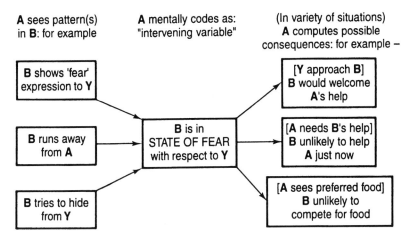

Figure 17.2 The recognition of a mental state as an intervening variable: fear.

Here, a hypothetical primate, A, reads the mental state of fear in an individual B, coding this state as an intervening variable generated on different occasions by a variety of circumstances like those shown on the left, and in turn giving rise to various predictions appropriate to different circumstances such as those shown on the right. Such mentalising gains the same economy of representation expressed in Figure 1(b) contrasted with 1(a) (after Whiten, in press).

general pattern: for the folk mind-reader, attributing a mental state is in important respects the same as recognition of intervening variables by the professional psychologist. Any specific state, such as B *knowing* a certain thing, may be recognised by A on the basis of a number of different observable conditions which can cause this knowledge: and once the knowledge is attributed, that state itself could lead to a multitude of outcomes predictable according to circumstance. Thus recognition of such states in others can be a powerful way of representing and predicting their behaviour patterns, economic of neural resources. Figures 17.2–4 illustrate hypothetical examples for different mental states.

A number of points should be made about the significance of the intervening variables conception:

(1) *Power*. As outlined in the previous paragraph, the intervening variables conception suggests why we or other mentalist creatures might be mentalists, in terms of that same cognitive power or efficiency obtained by crediting the rat with 'thirst'.

(2) *Nature of mentalism*. It also proposes what it can *be* to be a mentalist, as opposed to a behaviourist who instead learned all the specific S-R rules of

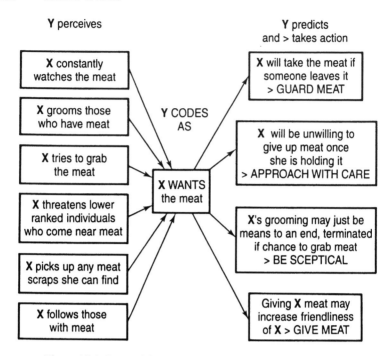

Figure 17.3 Recognising another individual's state of desire as an intervening variable.
This hypothetical example concerns a baboon Y, who recognises a state of wanting in another baboon X, with respect to competition over a desirable food source. The general scheme is as for Figure 2. As the number of eliciting circumstances on the left rises (and so too for the relevant consequences on the right) so the gains in economy of recognising such intervening states rises (after Whiten, 1994).

others' behaviour patterns. In other words, it provides perhaps the most defensible definition of mentalism, compared to other approaches outlined earlier. However, mentalism is still a term which grades into behaviourism, because it is applied on the basis of *how complex* webs such as those shown in Fig. 17.1b and 17.2–4 are. If such a web had only one line of links (for example, if fig. 17.2 only included the link between (on the left, input side) X putting something in a location and (on the right, output side) X's ability to recover it, we would have nothing distinguishable from a behavioural rule).

(3) *Abstraction.* Intervening variables constitute *states which others are classed as being in*: it is not necessary that they are seen as 'internal' to others, even less that they are seen as being 'in the head'. But see point 5, below.

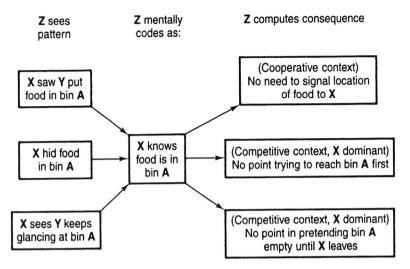

Figure 17.4 Recognising another individual's state of knowledge as an intervening variable.
Here Z reads X's state of knowledge, portrayed in the scheme developed in Figures 17.2–17.3 (after Whiten, 1993).

(4) *Cleverness.* If mentalism conceived in this way owes its existence to cognitive economy, it may appear a paradox if our current working hypothesis that it is refined only in particularly clever species like apes (Whiten, 1993; Povinelli, 1993) is confirmed. The answer may depend on distinguishing the process of *acquisition* of mental state discrimination from the *application* of mentalism on subsequent particular occasions.

Thus, the capacity to recognise in the first place the complex pattern which is covered by an intervening variable (see figs. 17.1–4) may require considerable neural resources, of a level we see only in apes. It is once this recognition has taken place that application in behavioural analysis can become efficient on any one occasion, facilitating fast and sophisticated tactics to be deployed in, for example, what has been described as political manoeuvring in chimpanzees (de Waal, 1982; Byrne and Whiten, 1988).

(5) *Insight.* I have remarked before that the recognition phase may be likened to an insight into the underlying pattern (Whiten, 1993). This would suggest that experience could play an important part in the acquisition of a theory of mind, however much guided by innate preparedness. Although the idea of innateness rests on evolutionary theory, the fact of evolution itself presents a difficulty if innateness is thought of as a sort of pre-formation which solves the problem of recognising certain complex patterns in the world, like language structure, or mental states: would not

some recognition have been necessary before natural selection could operate to shape a special-purpose mechanism to facilitate such recognition (a 'theory of mind' module – Leslie and Thaiss, 1992)? At a more specific level, I suggest it is plausible that mental states must have been recognised in ancestral populations before words (names) came to be designated for them, and thus before children were raised in an environment suffused with mental state names.

(6) *Explicit mentalism.* Continuing this line of argument, there is a sense in which mental states as intervening variables could be said to be *explicitly* recognised by the mind-reader, even if the mind-reader is itself non-verbal. Explicit here means that in the brain of the mind-reader, there is a state which uniquely codes for the state (i.e. the intervening variable) of the mind that they are reading, this latter being an inclusion class which could be identical to the one which you and I name with a word like *knowing* or *wanting* (see Bennett, 1976). If the mind-reader picks out this phenomenon in the same way we do, even though they cannot name it, they are doing something more than the implicit mind-reading discussed earlier, where no such corresponding inclusion class is recognised.

(7) *Methodology.* An implication of this analysis is that mentalism cannot be diagnosed using a one-shot test, like the standard Sally-Anne 'false-belief' task, which could be solved by applying a single behavioural rule, such as that people search for things where they last watched them put. According to the analysis above, mentalism is diagnosed only when the mind-reader classes different situations as leading to the same mental state, and puts this classification to different uses according to context. Few animal experiments approach this (see Whiten, 1993, 1994; Heyes, 1993). Ironically, it *may* be our ability to recognise this complex of evidence in large batches of everyday situations which permits us to assign our children to different levels of mind-reading competence with some confidence, without performing any experiments at all. It is interesting that at this stage of our science, we do not know for sure how we *do* do this!

6   Experience projection

Povinelli and his colleagues have performed experiments on role reversal with both monkeys and apes. Each subject first played one of two roles. In one, their task was to indicate gesturally to an ignorant human which of several containers was baited with food: if successful, they received a share of the food. Other subjects played the role of the ignorant partner, and thus had to learn to make use of the helpful gestures of a human in order to choose the correct container. When performance had reached a high criterion of success, the roles of the non-human and the human were in each case reversed. Povinelli, Nelson, and Boysen (1992) found that three of four chimpanzees showed evidence of role reversal, whereas Povinelli, Parks, and Novak (1992) found that rhesus monkeys did not, having to learn their new role afresh. The behaviour of the chimpanzees is consonant with a report by Savage-Rumbaugh (1986), that chimpanzees did not begin to use lexigrams to indicate the identity of the specific food in a container of which their partner was ignorant, until they had themselves been in that role of being ignorant, yet needing to know in order to obtain a reward.

It is not obvious how the chimpanzees would succeed in such a task by behaviour analysis. In the condition of Povinelli *et al.* where they are initially the ignorant partner, we might suppose that after reversal, they are showing (delayed) imitation of the behaviour of the human, who earlier pointed: and this sounds like an explanation resting only on behaviour analysis. However, given that chimpanzees do not mimic everything humans do, it is not obvious why the chimpanzees would point unless they recognised the other as being in a state where this could influence their behaviour, and apparently their only basis for doing this would be their own previous experience of ignorance, which had made the gesture of pointing helpful to them. In the other condition, where the chimpanzee initially pointed, an ability after role reversal to benefit from the pointing of the human is more difficult to see as (delayed) imitation of the human's behaviour, since the human had only selected a container, as indicated by their partner's gesture. The alternative explanation is along the lines of the chimpanzee 'understanding what the gesture means'; or (relating this more directly to mentalism) extrapolating to the human their own earlier communicative intent, perhaps of encouraging a correct choice in the partner.

Heyes (1993) has argued that in the experiments of Povinelli *et al.*, the chimpanzees may merely have learned what to do on reversal *more quickly* because they had learned most of what they need to know during the pre-training and previously (see Povinelli, 1994a; Heyes, 1994b). However my point here is one of principle rather than problems in the practice or reporting of one particular experiment. What I am suggesting is that one can envisage situations in which a subject adopts a reversed role which is novel for them and not explicable as a copy merely of the behaviour of their partner before reversal: the alternative explanation remaining is that they are using their own past experience in one of the roles as the basis for constructing appropriate actions towards another individual in that role. That would appear to be one further valid sense in which such a non-verbal subject would be acting as a mentalist rather than behaviour analyst.

This, one might argue, would be a case of the working of the simulation theory, discussed in chapters 2–8. This is probably true, but I have chosen to talk about 'experience projection' here to emphasise a difference in agenda. 'Simulation-theory' is now commonly discussed in contrast with 'theory-theory' as a rival explanation for some demonstrated competence in mentalism. Here, my emphasis has been on isolating mentalism in the first place, and I am suggesting that where a novel action can be explained only through some process of experience projection, one has a basis for regarding the subject as showing one sense of mentalism, rather than anything easily interpretable as behaviour analysis.

7   Conclusion

I have reviewed four candidate bases on which it might become genuinely informative to talk of a non-verbal creature being a mentalist, as opposed to a behaviour analyst. The first two – implicit mentalism and counter deception-have limited power to the extent that their claims on mentalism too easily appear to collapse to behaviour analysis. The phenomena to which they draw our attention are, however, important in the study of the origins of mentalism, for they are concerned with likely precursors of mature human mentalism.

The other two candidates – intervening variables and experience projection – received more positive appraisal. In the previous section, I acknowledged the last of these as what has come to be called simulation. Is the other, then, just a version of the other well-worn alternative, a theory-theory? It may sound like it: I emphasised earlier that recognising mental states as intervening variables was in the nature of an insight into the causal patterns existing with respect to the elements in the left and right columns of figures 17.2–4: a little theory, one might say, about what can unify those elements, *viz.* the intervening variable. However, that is not all there is to it. I see no reason why, in principle, one could not gain the same insights into one's *own* patterns of behaviour, and apply that insight then to others. So, the intervening variables conception is agnostic on theory-theory versus simulation-theory. Nor do I see any strong reason to rule out the possibility that sophisticated mental state recognition arises through an interplay of insights gained with respect to the mental perspective of either self or other, each one of these providing hypotheses for testing against their predictive utility from the alternative perspective.

My discussion of these bases for discriminating mentalism and behaviour analysis has focused on what we might regard as merely the basic building bricks of any theory of mind – *states of mind* as recognised by the mind-reader. I have suggested elsewhere that we should perhaps reserve the expression 'theory of mind' (ToM) for the ascription and integration of two or more such states to explain or predict action (Whiten, 1994). If one wishes to equate 'mentalism' only with the complexity achieved in this conception of ToM, then the recognition of any *single* mental state as portrayed in figures 17.2–4 will not count as mentalism. I think such an equation of ToM and mentalism is best avoided. It is surely not implausible that there is one stage at which the child recognises its first mental state (and thus becomes a ground-level mentalist), and a later stage at which it recognises more states and starts to apply them combinatorially in a simple ToM. An analogy in language acquisition might be learning the first words, and later combining them to achieve more complex ends. The same two-stage argument applies to evolution, where initial recognition of a mental state like *wanting* would likely have been followed only later by a wider 'vocabulary' of mental states and the beginnings of a combinatorial 'syntax' for analysing action in these terms.

How would a mind-reader capable of reading only one mental state operate? Philosophical analyses have tended to focus on what can be achieved by reading two or more states and integrating them, and particular attention has been given to 'belief-desire reasoning', in which others' actions can be explained or predicted powerfully through the conjunction of these two motivational and epistemic states, if accurately read (e.g. Davidson, 1980; Bennett, 1991). Where only one state is read, however, prediction/explanation would clearly have to rest on interpreting the mental state recognised not in conjunction with another mental state, but in its relation to behavioural dispositions and surrounding circumstances. Thus in the case of recognising and utilising a recognition that X *wants* the meat (Fig. 17.1b), Y could proceed to predict that X's action will be to *take the meat* if no barriers intervene, just by knowing that this is an expected action under such circumstances.

P. Carruthers (personal communication) has raised the interesting issue of whether the attribution of some mental states could *not* be used in this way, because by their nature they must operate in conjunction with other states. In figure 17.1c, for example, the outcomes on the right are predictable given not only X's state of *knowledge*, but also X's *want* of the food, which is implicit in the scenarios represented. In the case of child development, Wellman (1990, 1991) has characterised two-year-olds as 'simple desire psychologists', consistent with the one-state level of operation sketched in the previous paragraph: the older child, however, eventually becomes a 'belief-desire psychologist'. Since the recognition of belief appears to be a more advanced achievement than recognition of desire, it is possible that if any non-human species is shown to recognise belief, it will also recognise desire and thus potentially be a belief-desire psychologist.

But would it *have to be* a belief-desire psychologist? Or could an attribution of belief, like that of desire, be used in conjunction with information on behavioural dispositions and circumstances to make predictions? One way in which this could work would be where the desire can always be assumed, as some sort of default; in the scenario of figure 17.1c, for example, the food may be one which X will always want if it can get it (clearly, if sometimes X does not want the food, recognising beliefs but ignoring this motivational variability will be useless for prediction). One might object that a reliance on such default desires means that Z is really a belief-desire reasoner because desire is implicit in all the computations. However, one might equally argue that beliefs are implicit in Y's model of X in Fig.1b, where Y is just a desire-psychologist: in this case it is implicit that X *believes* the object to be a piece of edible meat, that it *believes* approaching it is a good first step to getting it, and so on. What is really at stake is whether the desire element in such reasoning could be handled by a behavioural analysis, and it seems to me that in principle it could. Thus, instead of Y coding X's state of desire as an intervening variable of the sort shown in figure 17.1b, it might utilise a straightforward S-R rule that (for example) if X has once tried to grab the meat, it will try to grab the meat again: and this in conjunction with a diagnosis of X's beliefs about the location of the meat will lead to novel and appropriate predictions of X's actions.

This may appear to be a merely academic issue if the earlier suggestion is true, that recognition of belief will tend to emerge only after recognition of desire is in place. However, it may be of more relevance to what happens in practice, insofar as it raises the possibility that a number of mental states might be recognised, with each used somewhat in isolation from each other, and in conjunction with more obviously behavioural variables and circumstances, to predict and explain actions. A theory of mind, in which multiple mental states are manipulated, may be worth distinguishing as an additional achievement: the analogy with language acquisition alluded to earlier would be that child or chimp might have a significant vocabulary of mental states it recognises before starting to combine them predictively and syntactically *as* mental states, in the 'intervening variables' sense described earlier.

ACKNOWLEDGEMENTS

I am grateful to the following for discussions which have been particularly helpful in thinking through some of the issues discussed in this paper: Jonathan Bennett, Peter Carruthers, Daniel Dennett, Juan-Carlos Gómez, Paul Harris, and Annette Karmiloff-Smith.

18   Chimpanzee theory of mind? the long road to strong inference.

Daniel Povinelli

1   Timing of the evolution of theory of mind

Here is an extreme view of the evolution of theory of mind:[1] prior to about four million years ago no organism ever paused to consider its own mental experiences or the mental experiences of others. This view carries with it the implication that the reproductive payoffs that led to the selection for theory of mind began to be realised only during the course of human evolution. It also implies that for some (as-yet-unknown) reason the complex social groups common to many mammals had not produced the right mixture of social or physical problems sufficient to drive the evolution of neural material capable of representing mental states. In short, this view implies that it was something about the unique history of human evolution that led to our pervasive and unshakeable folk psychology of mind. Of course, there are even more extreme views than this. For example, it has been maintained by some that theory of mind emerged coincident with the evolution of human language or that it is merely an illusion created by linguistic conventions (e.g., Wittgenstein, 1953; Langer, 1942; Lutz, 1992). Still more extreme would be the view espoused by some cultural anthropologists that beliefs about the mind are relative constructs peculiar to the cultures in which they are formed (e.g., Geertz, 1973; Mauss, 1984; La Fontaine, 1984).

The extremity of the views described above are in one direction only. It is possible to construct equally extreme views about the antiquity of theory of mind. For example, one could argue that theory-of-mind-like abilities are innovations that emerged during the evolution of the last common ancestor of the great apes and humans, that they were primitive mammalian innovations, or even that it was an innovation primitive to all vertebrates (for different views on the antiquity of consciousness and theory of mind see Fox, 1982; Gallup, 1982; Griffin, 1976; Rollin, 1989; Harris, this volume). Central to these views is the common denominator that knowledge about the mind is not restricted to the human species.

Some investigators will find some of the possibilities outlined above difficult to accept. They will argue that good science should not give space to what does not cohere well with the rest of our beliefs: thus, we should reject the extreme positions regarding the widespread distribution for theory of mind on *a priori* grounds (Peter Carruthers, personal communication). After all, is it not absurd to suppose that birds and snakes have access to some of their own mental states? Conversely, do humans from diverse cultures really possess fundamentally different theories of mind? Unfortunately, as long as we leave it up to our intuitions to decide, almost any position concerning the evolutionary history of theory of mind can be justified. The reason that this state of affairs continues to exist is because views about the minds of other species have largely been driven by what particular theorists view as plausible, not by what is testable. Indeed, some commentators chastised our early empirical attempts to compare chimpanzees and rhesus monkeys' understanding of mental states on the grounds that the results merely supported widely held beliefs 'that chimpanzees are smarter than monkeys in almost all ways' (Mitchell *et al.*, 1994, p. 762)! Ironically, one result of this emphasis on intuition is that the current data set remains far too impoverished to allow an easy rejection of any of these positions.

In contrast to the view described above, this essay starts from the assumption that good science is about strong inference, and that strong inference is best arrived at by using the method of multiple working hypotheses (Chamberlin, 1897). In this fashion, various alternative hypotheses are outlined up front, and each are used to generate a set of predictions. Hypotheses which generate the most useful predictions ascend as the most viable until new alternatives are proposed and evaluated. Accordingly, in this chapter I stake out no *a priori* claims about which species (or cultures) possess (or possessed) a theory of mind. My aim is to provide theoretical justification for the conceptual and methodological sensibility of a research agenda which in the long run can answer a very basic question: do any species other than humans possess some kind of appreciation of the mental world? In short, do other species represent mental states, and if so, which species and which states?

2   Species that might have a theory of mind

I begin by examining some theoretical reasons why at least one group of organisms – the great apes – might be a reasonable place to begin to search for theory of mind in other species. Evolutionary biologists might think that I am about to commit an egregious error by selecting one representative of the great ape/human clade, *Pan troglodytes*, and then using them to make a general claim about the group in question. However, I focus on chimpanzees for strictly practical reasons, and I fully acknowledge the striking species differences among the living great apes in social organisation, ecology, and perhaps even cognitive abilities. My purpose is to show that there is a set of plausible reasons why chimpanzees (at least) might have a theory of mind. Thus, I set aside worries about other species[2] and merely note that if chimpanzees possess some kind of theory of mind, then depending upon one's assumptions about the ancestry (polarity) of the trait and the exact phylogeny of the great ape/human clade, then there might be reasons for suspecting that other species in this clade – or even most species in the primate order – might as well. However, in examining these logical possibilities I neither take as obvious the claim that chimpanzees have a theory of mind, nor do I view the claim as a straw man to be immediately refuted. Instead, I see the examination of the possibilities as a crucial first step in outlining a theoretical and methodological framework for a long-term research program designed to determine if theory-of-mind skills are a uniquely derived feature of the human lineage, or if other species possess at least some portions of a common epigenetic[3] program governing the construction of representations of the mental states.

2.1   Control of the timing of cognitive developments

There are several facts which could lead one to suspect that chimpanzees have at least some understanding of the mind. But in order to appreciate them, it is necessary to consider two constructivist views of the timing of cognitive developments (see fig. 18.1). One reasonable view of cognitive development is that abilities which emerge at later ontogenetic time-points build in some fundamental manner upon earlier ones, and that most new cognitive structures emerge from domain-general shifts in representational abilities (fig. 18.1a). Thus, detectable differences in task performances across a seemingly wide range of domains (spatial, temporal, verbal) could be treated as being linked to underlying shifts in representational abilities. One particular version of this approach was Piaget's monolithic theory of intellectual development. A second variant of this constructivist approach to cognition is to assume that many skills are domain-specific, but within these domains the representational changes build upon earlier ones. The fundamental difference between this view and the first is that the domain-specific view argues that in many cases there may be little relation between shifts in one domain and shifts in others (fig. 18.1b). From an evolutionary point of view, this would imply the presence of different control mechanisms across domains, allowing for evolution to proceed at different rates across domains.

These two views are clearly artificial. For when it comes to specifying

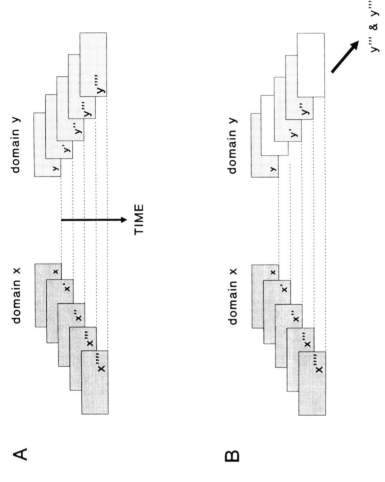

.Figure 18.1 Two views of the relation among cognitive developments in 'separate' domains. In (a) changes across apparently distinct cognitive domains are necessarily yoked to fundamental core shifts in representational abilities or processing abilities, in (b) epigenetic interactions which determine the rate (and perhaps even ordering) of cognitive developments are specific to each domain.

exactly what we mean by a given 'domain' it becomes obvious that these views really just represent extreme ends on a spectrum of possibilities. As long as we set aside extreme cases of modularity, each domain will at best refer to a psychological territory with sketchy borders. This vagueness will arise precisely because although the concept of a domain may have heuristic value, precise neural boundaries within the brain may be as difficult to define as are the boundaries of other heuristically useful, but difficult to define biological constructs such as species (e.g., Mayr, 1957; Burma, 1954; Ghiselin, 1975). Thus, I proceed cautiously using the distinction, but I do not abandon it because depending on which end of the spectrum one falls, the same data set may give rise to very different interpretations.

2.2   Reasons for suspecting that chimpanzees harbour a theory of mind

If we were to accept some version of the domain-general argument advanced above, then existing evidence concerning general cognitive development in chimpanzees might provide support for the possibility that they have some ability to represent mental states. For example, suppose that we could demonstrate that in some domains these apes possessed clusters of abilities which young children develop at the same time they are beginning to attribute certain mental states. If so, then a domain-general view of cognitive development might lead one to suspect that chimpanzees also possess the ability to represent mental states. If theory of mind is just another arena in which general transitions in representational abilities manifest themselves, and if chimpanzees display clear evidence of such transitions through their performance on standardised tasks, then we would have a coherent reason for suspecting that they may also possess theory of mind.

In order to move beyond theoretical claims, let us consider two possibilities concerning the onset of theory of mind in human development. First, it is possible that infants as young as 12 months form representations of mental states, albeit simple ones. For example, Baldwin and Moses (1994) have proposed an early understanding of attentional focus through studies which have investigated the capacity of 12- to 13-month-olds to understand that others refer to things in the external world. Baron-Cohen (1994) interprets joint attention behaviours (proto-declarative pointing, gaze-following) as evidence of a similar kind of goal-desire psychology of infants by 12 to 14 months. A second possibility is that the capacity for genuine representations of mental states does not emerge until 18-24 months (Gallup and Suarez, 1986; Barresi and Moore, in press). Indeed, 18-24 months seems to represent an especially striking turning point in human development. As noted in figure 18.2, a wide range of behaviours emerge at this

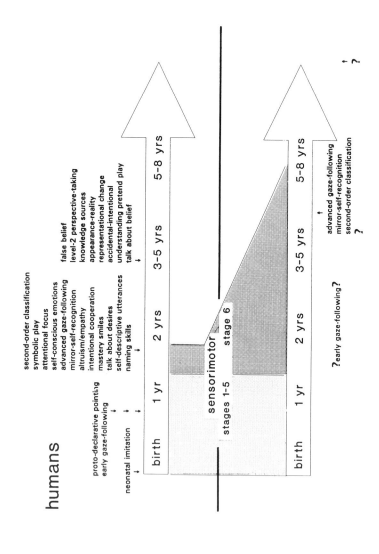

Figure 18.2 Comparison of selected cognitive developmental pathways in humans and chimpanzees

point: pretend play, self-recognition in mirrors, correct personal pronoun use, an explosion in naming skills, co-operative play, simple acts of altruism, level-1 perspective-taking, mastery smiles, self-descriptive utterances, closure of stage 6 object permanence, directives to adults, along with several others. Thus, in addition to an emphasis on interesting cognitive changes which may be occurring between three and five years of age (Wimmer and Perner, 1983; Perner, 1991a; Wellman, 1990), two additional periods may be of special interest in looking for early theory-of-mind skills: one is between 12 and 16 months and the other is between 18 and 24 months.

With these two periods of human development in mind, we can now ask if chimpanzees display any behaviours akin to those which are emerging in infants during these two time periods. In terms of general development, there is clear evidence that chimpanzees display some *behaviours* which typically emerge in young children in both of these time-frames. For example, great apes (including chimpanzees) and humans are clearly travelling along a similar developmental trajectory (although at different rates) in terms of general development and sensorimotor intelligence up until the complexity of behaviours shown by 18 to 24-month-old human infants (Chevalier-Skolnikov, 1983; Parker and Gibson, 1977; Mathieu and Bergeron, 1981; Vauclair and Bard, 1983; Mignault, 1985; Hallock *et al.,* 1989; Bard *et al.,* 1992; Poti and Spinozzi, 1994). However, by the eighteenth month or so in human development, we reach a point at which the typical human and chimpanzee pattern are beginning to diverge – although perhaps not completely. For example, there is some evidence that chimpanzees reach some of the same landmarks typically achieved by the 18 to 24-month-old child, such as stage 6 aspects of sensorimotor intelligence, spontaneous second-order classification skills, language comprehension skills similar to 12 to 18-month-old human infants, and self-recognition in mirrors, although many may not be achieved until four to eight years of age (Mathieu and Bergeron, 1981; Spinozzi, 1993; Savage-Rumbaugh *et al.,* 1993; Gallup, 1970; Povinelli, Rulf, Landau, and Bierschwale, 1993). The point of this cursory review is to point out that if chimpanzees and humans are displaying similar developmental transitions along these general lines, then there is evidence for substantial commonality in the cognitive-developmental pathways of the two species.

But what does the picture look like if we narrow our search to behaviours which may have a relationship to theory of mind in human development? Here the chimpanzee data set become thinner and less compelling. Although there have been some direct attempts to test for theory of mind in non-human primates, it is not necessary to infer from these data that chimpanzees possess theory-of-mind capacities comparable to three to five-year-old human children (see 2.3 below). However, chimpanzees do clearly display two behavioural patterns which have been theorised to have a possible relation to human theory-of-mind development: joint visual attention (gaze-following) and mirror self-recognition. To begin, joint visual attention is present in some form by 6 months of age in human infants, and apparently undergoes several developmental changes throughout infancy (Scaife and Bruner, 1975; Butterworth and Cochran, 1980; Butterworth and Jarrett, 1991; Corkum and Moore, 1994). However, one important finding is that although gaze-following is present quite early, it is not until about 18 months that infants will track another's line-of-regard into space outside their immediate visual field (Butterworth and Cochran, 1980; Butterworth and Jarrett, 1991). Baron-Cohen (1994) has proposed that joint visual attention is evidence of a 'shared attention mechanism' which is a precursor to theory of mind development in normal humans. He has recently bolstered this claim by providing preliminary evidence that the absence of gaze-following (together with pretend play and proto-declarative pointing) at 18 months predicts a diagnosis of autism, a syndrome which has been held to be at least partly characterised by theory-of-mind impairments (Baron-Cohen and Swettenham, this volume).

We have recently documented that chimpanzees display the gaze-following response, and have now replicated this finding several times. Our results indicate that chimpanzees will track another's line-of-regard under the following conditions: (a) the subject sees an experimenter orient their head and eyes (or just their eyes alone) to a point above and behind them, and (b) an experimenter is already positioned in an unusual visual orientation before they enter (fig. 18.3; Povinelli and Eddy, in press a; Povinelli and Eddy, in press b). The general phenomena has also been independently experimentally documented by Sanjida O'Connell (personal communication). Indeed, we have extended the finding by demonstrating that chimpanzees even understand how line-of-sight can be impeded by the opaqueness of objects (fig. 18.4; Povinelli and Eddy, in press b). I am especially confident about the replicability of these findings because they require no training, and the results are derived from dependent measures which are not differentially reinforced. However, unlike Baron-Cohen (1994) I am not confident that gaze-following is tapping into a mentalistic appreciation of the attention of others. Indeed, there are good theoretical and empirical reasons for thinking that the early appearance of gaze-following may have nothing to do with a subjective understanding of attention, even though at later ontogenetic time-points it may be imbued with such meaning by organisms with a theory of mind (Povinelli and Eddy, 1994). Nonetheless, it is critical to note that our findings reveal that in terms of the complexity of their gaze-following behaviour, chimpanzees are probably displaying the level of sophistication shown by 18-month-old human infants (Butterworth and Cochran, 1980).

In addition to gaze-following, I am also quite confident that chimpanzees are also capable of self-recognition in mirrors. This phenomenon emerges by about 18–24 months in human infants (Amsterdam, 1972; Lewis and Brooks-Gunn, 1979). By this age, many young children demonstrate an understanding of the correspondence between the physical appearance of their image in a mirror and their actual appearance. Thus, when confronted with a mirror after having been marked on the nose or forehead they will reach up to touch the mark. Chimpanzees also recognise themselves in mirrors (Gallup, 1970; Povinelli, Rulf, Landau, and Bierschwale 1993; Gallup, *et al.*, in press). Mirror-naive chimpanzees initially respond socially to their mirror images, but the best available evidence now indicates that within several minutes to an hour of continuous mirror exposure many chimpanzees display self-exploratory behaviours which entail orienting to the mirror and using their hands to manipulate parts of the body difficult or impossible to see otherwise (the eyes, nose, ears, teeth, ano-genital region; see fig. 18.5). However, there are debates about the distribution, ontogeny, patterns of emergence, and underlying meaning and cause of this phenomenon (see Lin *et al.*, 1992; Swartz and Evans, 1991; Povinelli, Rulf, Landau, and Bierschwale, 1993; Mitchell, 1993). Nonetheless, the fundamental phenomenon of chimpanzee self-recognition in mirrors is comparable to that displayed by 8- to 24-month-old children, and I do not believe that this fact can be seriously questioned at this point, despite attempts by some to do so (Heyes, 1994a; see reply by Gallup *et al.*, in press).

Gallup (1982; Gallup and Suarez, 1986) has argued for a strong relation between mirror self-recognition and theory of mind both across and within species. Although I cannot do his hypothesis justice here, suffice it to say that he has interpreted self-recognition in mirrors as reflecting an underlying capacity for self-conception, and that such self-knowledge can be used to generate limited inferences about minds of others. Lewis and colleagues have also argued for the relation between the emergence of self-recognition in mirrors and the development of an understanding of certain mental aspects of self and other (Lewis *et al.*, 1989). Some tentative support for this view has come from two directions. First, some researchers have reported significant correlations between self-recognition in human infants and other behaviours which may have a link to early theory of mind (synchronic play: Asendorpf and Baudonniere, 1993; early altruism: Johnson, 1982, Bishof-Kohler, 1988; self-conscious emotions: Lewis *et al.*, 1989). Second, early research suggested a correlation between those species which have shown evidence for self-recognition and successful performance

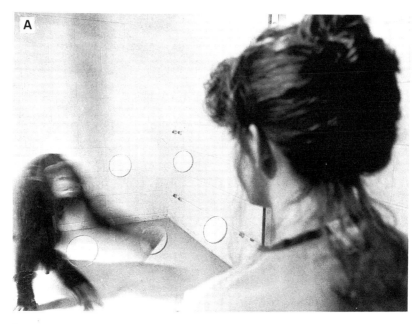

Figure 18.3 Setting and procedure for gaze-following studies in chimpanzees. (a) chimpanzee enters test unit and gestures in front of the experimenter, (b–d) experimenter shifts gaze to predetermined location above

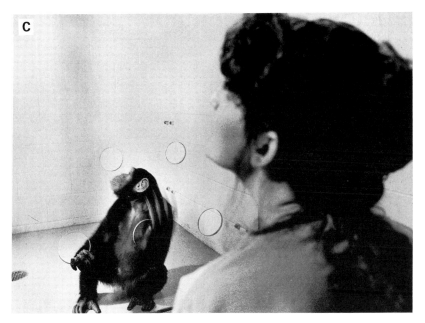

and behind the subject and chimpanzee turns head to follow experimenter's gaze. Various control treatments demonstrate that the subject's head-turning is triggered by the experimenter's gaze.

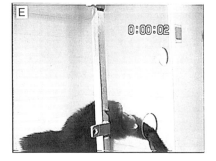

Figure 18.4 Two views of a chimpanzee demonstrating an ability to appreciate the interaction between an experimenter's line-of-regard and an opaque surface. In (a)–(c) the experimenter looks at a target on an opaque partition so that her line-of-sight (if projected straight ahead strikes the back wall of the test unit. The subject leans forward and sideways to attempt to look at the surface of the partition facing the experimenter. In (d)–(e) the same trial is shown but from the videotapes used by naive raters who were told to note whether the subject attempted to look at the square target. Various control treatments ensured that the subjects' responses were controlled by the gaze of the experimenter.

Figure 18.5 Contingent (a) and self-exploratory (b–d) behaviours in chimpanzees viewing themselves in mirrors. Chimpanzees in (e)–(f) displaying self-exploratory behaviours as observed through a one-way mirror. – (for c–f see next spread)

E

F

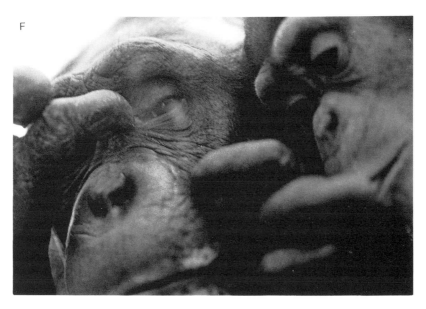

on theory-of-mind tasks (Povinelli, 1993). This latter data, however, deserves close scrutiny (see section 2.3 below).

Let us assume for the moment that some version of the domain-general argument is correct; further let us assume that the sophisticated form of gaze-following and mirror self-recognition are observable behaviours which follow from domain-general shifts in the representational system of human infants at around 18 months. If true, and if apes display both, then there would be reason to suspect that they also are able to form representations which take as their content mental states such as desires, goals, and attention – e.g., the same kinds of simple representations of which either infants (on the early view) and/or toddlers (on the late view) are capable. I am not claiming that this must be the case – indeed, there are good a priori arguments against such a view, some of which I review below – rather, I am simply claiming that it might be the case. To summarise, evidence that chimpanzees are travelling along the same general developmental track as 12 to 18-month-olds provides a clear rationale for taking seriously the possibility that chimpanzees form the same kinds of representations of mental states (probably non-epistemic ones) of which young infants and children are capable.

2.3   Reasons for doubt

Let me now return to the domain-specific view which argues that theory of mind represents a relatively isolated domain of cognitive development, proceeding with only superficial connections to changes in other cognitive domains.[4] This domain-specific view does not exclude the interpretation that apes have a theory of mind, on the other hand it would find no particularly compelling reason to see chimpanzees' successful performances on non-theory-of-mind tasks as indicating that they represent mental states. Indeed, even if we restrict our focus to the behaviours that (a) chimpanzees clearly display and (b) have possible theoretical links or empirical correlations with theory of mind (self-recognition in mirrors and advanced gaze-following), a domain-specific interpretation of these behaviours could still be advanced. For example, these abilities might develop with little or no interaction with representations of mental states either within or across species. Of course, correlations in human development between self-recognition and other behaviours which also seemed linked to theory of mind such as those described above would need to be explained in non-causal terms, as would significant associations between the absence of gaze-following and pretend play in autism on the one hand, and theory-of-mind deficits in autism on the other (Baron-Cohen and Swettenham, this volume).

Given that different starting assumptions about cognitive development yield different conclusions about the plausibility of theory of mind in chimpanzees, it might be useful to shelve theory for the moment and examine the evidence for theory of mind in chimpanzees. Several reviews of this area of research are already available (Premack, 1988; Cheney and Seyfarth, 1990; Povinelli, 1991, 1993; Whiten, 1993; Heyes, 1993; Tomasello and Call, 1994). Thus, instead of reviewing each of the (relatively few) investigations of theory of mind in non-human primates, I shall summarise the evidence to date as falling into two classes. First, we can examine the research strategies which have used spontaneously occurring behaviour, typically involving some kind of social manipulation of one animal by another, for evidence of an understanding of mental states on the part of various species (de Waal, 1982; Whiten and Byrne, 1988). Although the kinds of approaches to studying theory of mind using anecdotal evidence ranges from the causal to the systematic, all fall prey to similar problems. In particular, where a theory-of-mind interpretation suggests itself, a learning theory interpretation (or the deployment of some more tightly canalised, 'hard-wired' algorithms) cannot be ruled out by systematic manipulations of independent variables. In addition, there are several other classes of spontaneously occurring behaviour which may be central to theory of mind which are strikingly absent in chimpanzee culture: proto-declarative pointing, pretend play, and teaching (Premack, 1984; Cheney and Seyfarth, 1990; Povinelli and Godfrey, 1993).

The second class of data has emerged from laboratory-based studies in which experiments were designed for the purpose of testing hypotheses about the presence of theory of mind in non-human primates. To date, there have been only a handful of such studies, restricted to macaques and chimpanzees (Premack and Woodruff, 1978; Woodruff and Premack, 1979; Silverman, 1986; Povinelli, Nelson, and Boysen, 1990, 1992; Cheney and Seyfarth, 1990; Povinelli, Parks, and Novak, 1991, 1992; Hess et al., 1993; Povinelli, Rulf, and Bierschwale, 1994). However, the experiments to date which have been offered as some evidence that chimpanzees may have a theory of mind suffer from methodological limitations related to the absence of attempts at replication, problems of learning, and difficulties in controlling for attention and motivation across species (Dennett, 1983; Premack, 1988; Whiten, 1991, 1993; Povinelli, 1991, 1993; Povinelli and Eddy, in press; Heyes, 1993).[5] Finally, what about experimental studies of phenomena such as imitation which have been posited to have a potential relation to theory-of-mind development (Meltzoff and Gopnik, 1993)? Unfortunately, the jury is still out with respect to the chimpanzee's capacity for true imitation (Tomasello, Kruger, and Ratner, 1993). Thus, careful examination of laboratory-based studies of theory of mind reveal that we have no effects that have been replicated, let alone replicated and extended.

It would be wrong to think that I am implying that gaze-following and self-recognition are the *only* two phenomena possibly related to theory of mind that chimpanzees possess. On the contrary, I am indicating that these are the only ones that have passed the test of experimental demonstration and replication.

To summarise, a domain-general view of cognitive development could see in the existing data base enough evidence to suggest that chimpanzee cognitive development (although extended) looks very similar to the cognitive development of human infants up to about 18 months. On such a view, this would provide strong circumstantial evidence that they also possess some theory-of-mind skills, especially those early ones which are in place in human infants at 18 months. In contrast, the domain-specific view of theory-of-mind development would see no reason to interpret similarity in other areas of cognitive development as evidence one way or the other for similarity in theory of mind.

3   A conceptual framework

I have hinted that a search for theory of mind in chimpanzees makes sense within an evolutionary frame of reference. But I have not yet outlined why this is so. Figure 18.6 provides two models of the great ape/human clade, both of which display the African ape/human clade as an unresolved trichotomy – meaning that it is still too early to decide who is most closely related to whom within this group (Marks, 1994). Figure 18.6 displays two alternate possibilities concerning the developmental pathway related to theory of mind in humans. In the early evolution model, theory-of-mind skills are shown as having been an innovation primitive to the great ape/human clade and as a result are shared (via common descent) in members of the group, with caveats concerning gorillas (see Povinelli, 1994b). Note, however, that the schematic I have chosen reflects the notion that various ontogenetic stages or conceptual transformations are conserved. Thus, each of the members of the group which today possess the genetic instructions for theory of mind share a common developmental program. Thus, the basic ontogenetic sequence of theory-of-mind deployment could be relatively constant across species (although the rates might be quite different). The second model treats theory of mind as primarily a human innovation, and as a result it is not present in other members of the clade.

The two models in Figure 18.6 thus represent two possibilities concerning the timing of the evolution of theory of mind. They do not represent the most extreme view of either position I outlined in the first section of

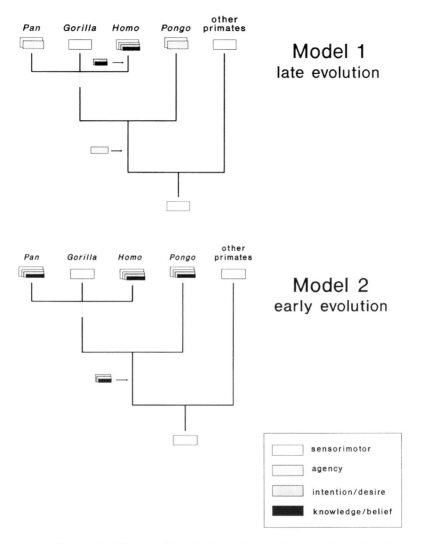

Figure 18.6 Two models of the timing of the evolution of arbitrary aspects of theory of mind. The African ape-human grouping is shown as an unresolved trichotomy to reflect controversies in the taxonomy of this group (Marks, 1992, 1994). The early evolution model posits that fundamental components of mental state attribution evolved before the differentiation of the great ape/human group. Note the secondary loss of some features by gorillas (see Povinelli, 1994). The late evolution model posits that most (if not all) aspects of mental state attribution evolved uniquely (and recently) in the human lineage.

this essay, but they do provide a solid set of alternative working hypotheses which can be tested by comparing theory-of-mind development in young children and young chimpanzees. The theoretical and methodological justification for these comparisons has been provided elsewhere (Povinelli and deBlois, 1992a, 1992b; Povinelli, 1993). In addition, the models should assist non-biologists in understanding that comparing the development of theory of mind (or any psychological capacity) across species does not assume some mysterious process of recapitulation. Recapitulation is a biological pattern which results from the inheritance of ancestral ontogenetic programs; generally speaking, the wider a time-span between the common ancestor of two species, the less 'recapitulationist' the ontogenies will appear. A better description is to dispense with the term 'recapitulation' altogether and to cast the inquiry in modern evolutionary terms – which portions of psychological ontogeny among the living great apes and humans are shared primitive traits inherited from a common ancestor, and which are most recently evolved aspects of psychological ontogeny, perhaps found only in humans?

4   Young chimpanzees' knowledge of seeing-as-attention: a case study

In order to demonstrate how the conceptual framework offered above can be practically implemented, I now describe a series of studies that we recently conducted on theory of mind in chimpanzees. The focus of these studies was a very simple question: do young chimpanzees understand the intentionality of visual perception? By intentionality we mean the following: do chimpanzees understand the 'aboutness' aspect of the perceptual act of seeing? We thus set out to ask if they understand that visual perception 'refers to' (or is about) objects or events in the external world. Note that such a narrow question eliminates many very interesting mentalistic questions about visual perception that one might ask. For instance, we explicitly did not wish to ask our apes if they understood the relation between seeing and knowing (that visual perception is a knowledge acquisition device; see 4.1 below). We had already done this, and obtained largely negative results (Povinelli *et al.*, 1994). Thus, we winnowed our interests in order to focus upon the simplest mentalistic aspect of visual perception of which we could think: that seeing subjectively connects organisms to other objects and events in the world (see Flavell, 1988). These studies were driven by the theoretical models outlined in the previous section concerning the timing and order of the evolution of theory of mind. The early evolution model predicts that chimpanzees should easily demonstrate such abilities, whereas the late evolution model predicts that they should not.

4.1   Knowledge about visual perception

Before I describe this recent research, it is necessary to draw a clear distinction between several kinds of information processing or knowledge that one might have about eyes. First, many organisms are extremely sensitive to the presence of eyes and eye-like stimuli (e.g., see Gallup *et al.,* 1971). There may be several reasons for this sensitivity including the fact that eyes are a useful stimuli for detecting the presence of a predator or social competitors. However, despite this general sensitivity to eyes, this kind of evidence alone is not sufficient to conclude that an organism understands anything at all about visual perception as a mental event.

There are two additional levels at which an organism might understand the eyes, and both of these involve an appreciation of the locus of the eyes as an interface between the private world of the mind and the shared external world. First, an organism may understand that visual perception subjectively connects organisms to the external world. In other words, an organism with the ability to form representations of mental states could equate the perceptual/geometric relation of 'seeing' with the internal mental state of 'attention'. In this sense, to see something is to be mentally or cognitively connected to that thing (Flavell, 1988). Flavell and his colleagues have demonstrated that by two and a half years of age human children have established this kind of understanding of the link between the eyes and the mind (Lempers *et al.,* 1977). There is some reason to believe that some species of non-human primates may also possess this kind of appreciation of seeing (Chance, 1967; Menzel and Johnson, 1975; Gómez, 1991). However, the kinds of evidence that have been brought to bear on the question of non-human primates' understanding of seeing are open to several different interpretations (Povinelli and Eddy, in press a).

The final kind of understanding of visual perception which we will consider here concerns the understanding that in addition to linking an individual's mental state of attention to the external world, visual perception also alters one's internal experiences, states of knowledge and beliefs. Flavell and colleagues have investigated the development of this understanding of visual perception in young children and have demonstrated that it is not until about four years of age that children realise that visual perception can give rise to unique mental experiences or states (Flavell *et al.,* 1981). Other lines of evidence also indicate that it is not until about this same age that children appreciate seeing as playing a causal role in knowledge acquisition (Wimmer, Hogrefe, and Perner, 1988; Gopnik and Graf, 1988; Ruffman and Olson, 1989; O'Neill and Gopnik, 1991; Povinelli and de Blois, 1992a). Collectively, these data suggest a marked developmental asynchrony between young children's understanding of seeing-as-attention and seeing-as-a-knowledge-acquisition-device.

4.2   *What young chimpanzees know about seeing: new evidence*

Timothy Eddy and I have recently investigated young chimpanzees' knowledge about seeing-as-attention. The reason for this selection was two-fold. First, human knowledge about visual perception begins in infancy with the appearance of the gaze-following response, although the extent to which this knowledge is embedded in representations of mental states (as opposed to geometric calculations) is not clear. Second, there is a further elaboration of that knowledge at some point in late infancy to the point at which this knowledge possesses genuinely mental content. These two facts led us to realise that an extensive series of studies of this phenomenon might reveal the commonalities and differences in human and chimpanzee understanding within a quintessential mental domain: the experience of seeing. We thus executed a number of studies with a group of seven young chimpanzees to determine if they understand visual perception as a mental event.

Our research strategy has been to pit two explanatory frameworks against each other and to then evaluate them by their ability to generate accurate predictions about what our young apes would do in various circumstances. One of these is a mentalistic framework which attributes a theory or folk psychology of seeing to the animals. This framework makes no commitment about the upper-level of complexity of that understanding, but minimally assumes that the apes understand how the physical relation to eye direction and orientation anchors an internal mental state of attention in an organism to the world. In contrast, our second framework is derived from learning theory and starts with the assumption that chimpanzees form no representations of the mental states of others (such as attention) and as a consequence have no mentalistic understanding of eye gaze. This does not mean that the animals cannot reason about eyes, but rather that their reasoning is limited to the observable contingencies between eyes, eye direction, and subsequent behaviour. Thus, from the very outset of these investigations we shelved (to the best of our ability) our preconceived beliefs about what chimpanzees ought to understand about seeing, and instead outlined the predictions that these two very different frameworks would make about an ape's reaction to the perception of the visual systems of others.

In order to set the stage for our studies, we trained the animals to use their natural begging gesture (arm outstretched, palm up) to request food from an experimenter. All of the animals rapidly learned to enter a testing lab, scan to see whether a trainer was standing or sitting on the right or left, approach a clear partition and stick their arm through a hole in front of the person in order to beg for food. Just to be sure the animals' performance on this task would be stable, we trained them to rigorous criteria whereby they were virtually flawless.

This initial training now allowed us to ask the apes if they understood seeing-as-attention. Whom would the chimpanzees approach and request food from if they entered the test lab and encountered two trainers standing or sitting in front of them, one of whom could see them, the other of whom could not? We designed several treatments to test the animals, some of which used familiar objects to prevent one of the trainers from seeing, and some of which involved more natural circumstances where one trainer could see the animal but the other could not. In one of the object treatments, one trainer placed a bucket over his head, the other held a bucket on her shoulder without obstructing her view. In the other object treatment, one trainer wore a blindfold over the eyes, the other wore it over the mouth. The two natural conditions were back-versus-front (one trainer facing forward, the other facing away) and hands-over-eyes (one trainer obscuring her eyes with her palms, the other looking forward while covering his ears). These initial set of treatments were all focused on a very specific question: which framework could better predict from whom the chimpanzees would beg for food when one of the experimenters was looking straight ahead with their eyes open and the other had their vision obscured? The mentalistic framework predicted excellent performance from trial 1 forward; the learning theory predicted poor performance initially, followed by improvement after repeated trials. To begin, however, we needed to assure ourselves that the chimpanzees could use their gesture to choose correctly between the two experimenters when an obvious cue was present that had nothing to do with understanding mental states. Thus, we created a treatment in which the apes were confronted with two trainers, one of whom held out a block of wood, the other of whom held out a piece of fruit or a small cookie.

In order to gain the maximum interpretative leverage possible, we used a combination of traditional small-N and group design features. First, within each session of ten trials only two were designated as probe trials ahead of time. Thus, the majority of trials within a session were simply spacing trials in which the subjects received the same treatment they had during training – a single experimenter positioned on either the right or left. This meant that we had within-session controls on whether or not the subjects were both (a) motivated to respond and (b) attending to the general features of the task. Second, the nature of the probe trials was alternated in an ABA design so that sessions containing block-versus-food probe trials surrounded the sessions which contained the various visual occlusion probe trials. This meant that we had temporal control across sessions for determining whether or not the subjects were motivated and attending on probe trials involving a discrimination between two experimenters. The final feature of the design was that very few probe trials were administered (only two per session, typically four per experiment per condition) and they were separated by spacing trials. Because we had six to seven subjects in all of the studies, this allowed us to look at the group's responses on trial 1 and trial 2 for a very sensitive diagnosis of whether they possessed an initial disposition to gesture to the one who could see them. In addition, the subjects typically only received four total trials on a given treatment within an experiment, thus further constraining the problem of learning. With these controls in place we were in a position to determine which framework could best predict the apes' actual performance.

In the initial sessions of block-versus-food, the chimpanzees performed excellently from trial 1 forward: all of the subjects entered the test unit and responded by begging in front of the trainer offering the food. This result meant that the subjects had no difficulty reorienting from spacing trials with only one experimenter present to block-versus-food probe trials involving two experimenters. This was encouraging, because if they had experienced trouble here, the logic of the experimental design would have collapsed. These preliminary results demonstrated that the chimpanzees could easily use their gesture to make a choice between two different experimenters in a situation that did not involve the deployment of a folk psychology of seeing.

In striking contrast to this excellent performance on the initial two sessions containing these non-mentalistic probes, the subjects' performances dropped to chance when we administered the two-object treatments. Thus, on blindfold and bucket-probe trials, the group responded by gesturing in front of the person who could *not* see them as often as they gestured to the person who could see them. Was it because their motivation had declined as the experiment had proceeded? Our within-session controls allowed us to reject this general motivational/attentional critique; the subjects responded at nearly 100% correct on the spacing trials surrounding the probe trials. Was it possible that their ability to choose between two experimenters had waned across repeated probe trials? When we re-administered sessions with block-versus-food probe trials the subjects' performance shot back up to near-perfect levels. The logic of the ABA design allowed us to conclude that it was something about the treatments themselves that had yielded the effects obtained.

The results for one of the natural treatments looked identical to those just described: excellent performance on surrounding probe trials of block-versus-food and excellent performance on the surrounding spacing trials, coupled with chance-level performance on the hands-over-eyes probe trials. However, we obtained completely different results with the back-versus-front probe trials. In this case, the subjects' performances were significantly above-chance and did not differ from surrounding probe and spacing trials. This effect was present from trial 1 forward, with 5/6 animals correct on trial 1 and 6/6 correct on trial 2. Thus, in direct contrast to the other treatments, the animals seemed to possess an immediate disposition to orient selectively in front of the trainer facing forward and execute a begging gesture (see fig. 18.7).

A direct comparison of the two frameworks indicated that the learning theory generated more accurate predictions about what the animals would do. In three out of four treatments the animals did not seem to appreciate that one of the experimenters was connected to them in a subjective manner. However, the results of the back-versus-front treatment caused us to probe the situation further. The learning theory's explanation for the subjects' immediate success on the back-versus-front treatment was that there was a stimulus configuration (the trainer facing forward) that was identical to the correct response on their hundreds of training trials. The mentalistic theory's explanation was that (for one reason or another) the front-versus-back treatment was simply the most ecologically relevant instantiation of seeing-versus-not-seeing, and hence the chimpanzees performed best in this situation. We realised that we could test these accounts by confronting the chimpanzees with an equally ecologically relevant treatment in which two trainers both faced away from the subject, but one of them looked back over his shoulder toward the test unit. If the mentalistic account of the back-versus-front performance was correct, the animals should respond well; if the learning theory account were correct the animals should respond at chance.

We carried out this experiment using all of the controls described earlier (see Experiment 3, Povinelli and Eddy, in press b). Exactly as the learning theory predicted, the subjects performed excellently on the spacing trials, the block-versus-food probes, and the back-versus-front probe trials. Yet in direct contrast to these results, the group's performance dropped to chance on the looking-over-the-shoulder probe trials. For the animals it did not seem to make a difference that one of the trainers could see them and the other could not; despite the fact that one of the trainer's faces was completely visible to the subjects and one was not, the animals had no preference for begging to one over the other. This finding removed any unique reason for favouring the mentalistic framework's interpretation of the back-versus-front performance.

Despite this rather impressive correct prediction by the learning theory,

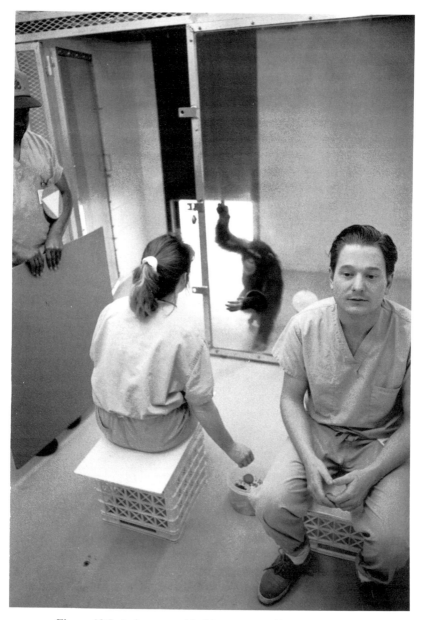

Figure 18.7 A five-year-old chimpanzee subject gestures in front of a trainer who can see her. This back-versus-front procedure was the only treatment in which the subjects gestured to the person who could see them from trial 1 forward.

we did not abandon the mentalistic framework. One of our hypotheses was that perhaps the apes did in fact understand that only one of the trainers was subjectively connected to them, but were startled by the unusual configurations of objects and body postures (especially given that for methodological reasons both experimenters were required to be associated with identical objects). In addition, perhaps the hesitations we detected on many of the probe trials were really startle reactions. Thus, the mentalistic framework could claim that our procedures masked an underlying appreciation of seeing-as-attention because introducing objects and unusual bodily postures on probe trials co-varied with the treatments under investigation. The framework could be interpreted as predicting that if the subjects were thoroughly habituated with the objects that were to be the ultimate cause of visual occlusion, then they should perform much better on the critical probe trials. We thus conducted a series of studies to test this interpretation (see Experiments 4-9, Povinelli and Eddy, in press b).

Here I will just describe one of these studies. First, circular cardboard screens were constructed that could hang around the experimenters' necks. The screens were large enough to obscure the entire head of the trainers. However, before we used these screens as a means of visual deprivation, we had the experimenters wear them on several sessions of standard trials, and then included them on block-versus-food trials, and on back-versus-front trials. In addition, we even had both trainers hold the screens up above their shoulder (without either face being obscured) in order to ensure that the subjects would associate successful performance with the presence of the screens being held up. At this point we were ready to pit the two frameworks against each by introducing the crucial probe trials; one of the trainers holding the screen in such a manner as to obscure the entire face, the other holding it above his or her shoulder. Despite these laborious efforts to rescue the mentalistic framework, we could not do so. The apes entered the test unit, scanned the trainers, and then proceeded to choose randomly. Indeed, there were even several striking trials where the animals looked straight at the screen obscuring the trainer's face, gestured, looked again, and finally extended the arm even further, apparently unaware that the trainer could not see what they were doing. Indeed, the learning theory implies that we cannot exclude an even lower-level interpretation of the apes' performance – perhaps they do not even understand that such a thing as 'seeing' exists.

Additional experiments manipulating the distance, height, and gaze orientation of the trainers generally had little or no effect on the subjects' performance. However, further experiments revealed a learning effect. Thus, across the eleven studies the subjects were beginning to perform at above-chance levels in several of the treatments. There were two possible ways of interpreting this result. One was to assume that the subjects had extracted some stimulus-based rule from all of the various visual deprivation treatments we had administered. The other possibility was that the subjects had finally understood the task at hand: select the trainer who can see (read: is mentally attending). We decided to test this issue by analysing the various stimulus configurations we had previously presented to the apes. There seemed to be two possible rules they might use: 'pick the person whose face is visible' or 'pick the person whose eyes are visible'. Fortunately, neither rule made exactly the same predictions about how the animals would perform under two novel treatments: attending-versus-distracted (one experimenter looks straight ahead, the other looks up into the corner of the ceiling) and eyes-open-versus-closed. The 'face' rule predicted chance performance in both of these situations: the 'eyes' rule predicted chance performance when both eyes are visible (attending-versus-distracted) but good performance in eyes-open-versus-closed. Finally, the mentalistic framework predicted a different pattern of results altogether. It predicted that the subjects should have performed well on both of these novel treatments.

The actual results of these studies (Experiments 12 and 13) provided clear support for the 'face rule' over the 'eye' rule, and provided no support for the mentalistic framework. For example, the subjects performed randomly on their initial trials of both of the attending-versus-distracted and eyes-open-versus-closed treatments, thus indicating the subjects were not able to use an 'eye' rule, at least not in the eyes-open-versus-closed context. In addition, when the subjects entered the test unit on the attending-versus-distracted trials, they followed the line-of-sight of the distracted experimenter by turning and looking behind them. A crucial aspect of this finding is that it established something of which we had not been certain previously: that the subjects were scanning the faces of the experimenters before making their choices. They had to be, otherwise they could not have turned and looked behind them selectively on the attending-versus-distracted probe trials. Finally, it is important to point out that the subjects continued to respond poorly on only one of the initial treatments: blindfolds. Interestingly, this was the only treatment in which the same amount of each of the two trainers' faces were visible. In all of the treatments on which they were now succeeding (buckets, looking-over-shoulder, screen-over-face, hands-over-eyes) one of the trainer's faces was virtually completely obscured, but the other was clearly visible. This discrepancy between the blindfold treatment and the other treatments provides even further evidence that the subjects were using a rule about whose face was visible, not who was seeing.

Finally, in order to be absolutely certain that our non-verbal test was really measuring what we thought it was measuring, we tested young three-year-olds and compared their performance to older three and four-year-old children. If our task was measuring seeing-as-attention (and not some higher-order understanding of visual perception) then young three-year-olds should perform at above-chance levels: a variety of lines of evidence indicate that young three-year-olds understand this aspect of seeing (e.g., Lempers *et al.,* 1977; see section 4.1). In contrast, if the task was measuring something more complicated (such as the seeing-knowing relation) then the young three-year-olds should display chance performance, with the older children performing above chance (see section 4.1). We trained them in a similar fashion to the chimpanzees and then tested them using three of the treatments we had administered to the chimpanzees. The results established that as a group even young three-year-olds performed at levels well exceeding chance on their first trial with several of the exact same treatments and procedures used with the chimpanzees (Experiment 15, Povinelli and Eddy, in press b). This finding matched our *a priori* prediction that the task could be solved by simply understanding seeing-as-attention, without understanding the more complicated notion of visual perception as a knowledge acquisition device.

5   Lingering conceptual worries

Despite the clear biological rationale for comparing the psychological development of closely related species, commentators frequently worry that tests such as the ones just described are unfair to the chimpanzees. The concerns raised take several forms, but at the core of these criticisms is an underlying concern that it just does not make sense to compare chimpanzees and human children. Below, I describe each of four different meanings of this claim that I have encountered, and I attempt to assess their strengths and weaknesses.

5.1   Do chimpanzees have a 'weak' theory of mind?

First, in response to theory-of-mind tasks on which chimpanzees perform poorly, some researchers reply that perhaps chimpanzees have a weak theory of mind, and the tasks we give the animals are too complicated for them. First, if the argument is to extend beyond a vacuous claim, the nature of this weakness must be specified. The most biologically plausible possibility I can think of is to assume that chimpanzee behaviour is largely governed by learned or evolved social algorithms but that their representational code can compress less information about social information, and hence ultimately their (presumably) image-based representational system for encoding mental states is less efficient than the additional linguistic-based system of humans. This alternative could make good biological sense if we viewed some human psychological innovations like language as providing a mechanism which allowed for more complex representations of mental states. To use a familiar example, perhaps desires and goals can be represented without a linguistic representational system, but perhaps representations of knowledge and beliefs requires the additional compressional power of a linguistic code. But if this (or something like it) is true, it does not mean that our tests are unfair. To the contrary, it would still be perfectly legitimate – indeed, essential! – to ask questions about common descent of those developmental programs. To ignore these differences would raise the spectre of a curious 'same-but-different' dilemma: on the one hand we would be deciding that we cannot compare chimpanzee and human psychology, but on the other hand we would maintain that chimpanzees do indeed have aspects of theory of mind. If the former were true, then the latter would remain an act of faith, not an inference of science. The general point is clear: if we believe that chimpanzees have less efficient representations of mental states than humans in particular domains, then we should revise our paradigms to investigate this possibility. Indeed, the tests described above were partly motivated for that very reason – it seemed to us that the non-epistemic mental aspects of seeing (attention) might be easier to compress into a visually based representational code than the epistemic aspect (seeing-as-knowing). Thus, our recent efforts to determine if chimpanzees understand seeing-as-attention were a strategic retreat from earlier attempts to ask chimpanzees if they understood the seeing-knowing relation.

Before we turn to other criticisms, it is important to note another variant of the weak theory-of-mind idea. It is possible to maintain that chimpanzees have some, most or all of the representations of mental states that humans do but that they only deploy them in particular ecological contexts. For example, perhaps chimpanzees do understand the seeing-knowing relation but only demonstrate it *when they are in a competitive social situation,* or perhaps a competitive social situation *with a member of their own species,* or perhaps a competitive situation with a member of their own species *in the wild.* This variant is related to the next criticism, and so I will explore it there instead.

5.2   *Is theory of mind anthropocentric?*

A second meaning of unfair is that the tests are anthropocentric. A charge is sometimes made that chimpanzees have a theory of mind, but it is a theory of the chimpanzee mind, not of the human one. Although it has an appealing biological ring to it, upon close inspection if this idea is intended to be distinct from the notion examined above, it becomes very difficult to define. At one level the challenge reduces to an acknowledgement that apes and humans both have an understanding of the mental world – that is, that they both form representations of mental states; at another level the content of the representations differ in some species-specific manner. But what, exactly, are the differences? Specifying them becomes of paramount importance because although as evolutionary biologists we must recognise the idea of the evolution of specialised traits and behaviours, we must also be psychologists and ask: what is the nature content of the representations that differs? To defer this question would be to concede that this objection to experiments of the kind we advocate has not been carefully thought out.

There are several possible arguments that could be made to shore up the charge of anthropocentrism. For example, it could be maintained that chimpanzees and humans begin along similar paths because of the inheritance of common epigenetic instructions related to an intentional understanding of behaviour, but begin to diverge as ontogeny proceeds, revealing innovations which uniquely evolved in the course of the separate evolution of each species. As I hinted above, it is possible that theory of mind first evolved as an ability which was deployed in limited circumstances such as social competition. On this view, later innovations, perhaps ones that occurred only during the course of human evolution, extended this disposition to apply in many contexts, either as the result of a new specific mechanism or a generalisation module. Such accounts are possible. However, there are implications of these views. First, and most importantly, it would not follow from this theoretical position that our tests are unfair. Rather, it would render them even more indispensable than before because we would need them in order to discover the commonality and differences in theory-of-mind development in the two species. Second, it would mean that certain fundamental, core attributes (or ancillary components) of common-sense psychology are in fact uniquely derived in the human lineage. That is, trying to explain away negative findings with chimpanzees on high-level theory-of-mind tasks by appealing to a different theory of mind in apes means giving over these differences as exclusively human innovations. All of this suggests that tests such as ours can precisely pinpoint where and when the chimpanzee's hypothesised theory of mind is deployed. And if the chimpanzee's theory of mind is really so circumscribed, our laboratory tests would clearly reveal that unlike our common-sense psychology, theirs does not engage more or less automatically across situations, but is restricted to specific contexts.

5.3   *Are laboratory tests ecologically valid?*

Another criticism is to remain silent about the exact differences in theory of mind between the two species, but to explain the current negative findings with chimpanzees by recourse to an argument that laboratory-based tests are ecologically irrelevant. There are two versions of this claim. One is that the logic of these tests is not relevant. In other words, it could be that chimpanzees only use their theory-of-mind skills in social manoeuvrings that are ecologically relevant to them. By itself, this argument reduces to the claim that we just examined. But a second version of the claim is that it is the captive setting itself, not the particular tests, which creates the ecological irrelevance. Thus, anecdotes from natural settings could be taken as evidence that in these settings the animals do, in fact, deploy a common-sense psychology, but lab-based tests fail to reveal this psychology because of the captive setting. The problem, of course, is that monkeys and apes display similar patterns of social manipulation in captivity and in the wild (Menzel, 1973; de Waal, 1982; Whiten and Byrne, 1988; Coussi-Korbel, 1994). Given that the argument cannot therefore be about the setting, it would have to be about the specific context; thus, we return to the claim that theory-of-mind skills cannot be easily found in chimpanzees outside of some as-of-yet-unspecified social circumstances.

5.4   *Reasoning about the mind of another species*

Another meaning of the fairness charge that I wish to explore is the claim that most theory-of-mind tasks given to animals involve situations in which the subjects are asked to make inferences about the mental states of humans, not the mental states of other members of their species. For example, Seyfarth and Cheney (1992) argued that our initial attempt to test chimpanzees for an understanding of the perception-knowledge relation was limited because the subjects observed human actors, not other chimpanzees (Povinelli, Nelson, and Boysen, 1990). This argument reduces to a claim that chimpanzees and humans share a similar theory of mind, but because of some combination of the morphological and behavioural differences between us they are not inclined to assume that we have mental states. Of course, there is no comparable evidence that human children are impaired when reasoning about dolls, adults, other children, imaginary characters instantiated by figurines or pictures in books, or, indeed, even animals themselves. A moment's reflection will allow us to see that we have returned to the same-but-different dilemma. This time the tests are unfair because chimpanzees really do understand the psychological relations in question, but fail to attribute them outside their own species. But why is the human anthropomorphism gradient so extensive as to cover nearly all animate (and even inanimate) objects, but the equally rich chimpanzee theory of mind is peculiarly restricted to other creatures with just the right combination of black hair, knuckle-walking, prognathism, large ears, and so on?

I am not claiming that it is impossible that this is the case, just that we understand what the implications of this claim would be. Indeed, even in humans there are very intriguing differences in the willingness of adult humans to attribute complex mental events to other organisms. Eddy *et al.* (1993) reported empirical evidence that humans do not attribute theory of mind to other creatures in a random or blanket fashion, but their attributions depend critically upon the degree to which (a) the animals resemble them physically (e.g., other primates), or (b) they have formed attachment bonds with the species in question (e.g., dogs and cats). It is interesting in the present context to note that very few (if any) of the human subjects participating in the Eddy *et al.* (1993) investigation had ever formed attachment bonds with another primate species, but this did not prevent them from attributing theory-of-mind skills to these species, presumably based on their physical similarity to humans. Conversely, dogs and cats, to which most of the subjects had probably at one time or another formed primary attachment bonds, were given high ratings as well – despite their dissimilar morphological appearance. It is perhaps not trivial therefore to note that in the case of captive chimpanzees reasoning about humans both conditions are met: chimpanzees have formed attachment bonds with humans and we resemble them physically. Finally, note that this is an empirical issue which can be tested in the laboratory.[6]

5.5   Are non-human primates a special case?

Finally, it is important to ask if the criticisms explored above present a unique burden to those of us who study non-human species. In other words, if it is not fair to compare chimpanzees to humans, is it any more or less fair to compare pre-school children to adult humans, or even older children? And if pre-school children do not drive the point home, what about pre-verbal human infants? Is it somehow unfair to attempt to ascertain if they have a pre-verbal theory of mind? I do not think so. And once this is granted we are forced to acknowledge that the exact same (and very real) conceptual fairness problems exist regardless of whether our subjects are human infants or children on the one hand, or chimpanzees on the other (Povinelli, 1993).

Some researchers wishing to retain the conceptual integrity of comparing theory of mind across ages within humans, but not across species, might retreat further and argue that in the case of developmental psychology at least the organism under study is a member of the same species as the adults to whom it is being compared – adults who we know develop a common-sense psychology. But for this argument to have force it would be necessary to assume that theory-of-mind evolution in the human species resulted from ancestral variants who possessed rudiments of common-sense psychology at birth (or that later occurring innovations were canalised backwards through existing developmental programs). If we did not make this assumption – that humans are born with some kind of theory of mind already activated – then we would never be sure when our between-age non-verbal comparisons were in the same logical position as across-species non-verbal comparisons; that is, comparing organisms with a particular theory-of-mind (older children, adults) to ones we are not sure about (12-month-olds). But there is no necessary reason to accept this position. It could be that fundamental human innovations in theory-of-mind psychology were created through innovations which occurred at relatively late points in existing developmental programs. Were this the case, there would be no particular reason to think that just because the infant is human it avoids the question of conceptual fairness. The general point is this: if the conceptual problems associated with asking another closely related species about what capacities they possess are insurmountable, then the inferences about ontogenetic transformations sought by developmental psychologists are crippled by the same problems.

At this point some observers might throw up their hands in despair and adopt the view that it is impossible to bridge the developmental and evolutionary transitions within human development, across human cultures, and across other species (for an example of this kind of despair as applied to the animal research, see Heyes, 1994b). I disagree. As long as we keep in mind that 'theory of mind', 'folk psychology', and 'mental state attribution' are heuristic constructs, then our research strategies can proceed on firm ground. Sets of predictions generated by each framework can be tested in a systematic manner. Theory construction and falsification can proceed as in any other science, avoiding the nihilism of the radical deconstructionist while simultaneously moving toward stronger and stronger inference about which aspects of the mind other species are capable (or incapable) of reasoning.

6   Do chimpanzees have a theory of mind?

Our research is not the final word on whether chimpanzees have a theory of mind. Indeed, it is not even the first sentence of the first chapter of the future volume, *Principles of the chimpanzee's theory of mind*. For example, there are multiple working hypotheses to account for our data, only one of which is that theory of mind is a unique feature of the human species. Without elaborating let me simply note that Povinelli and Eddy (in press b) have discussed in detail two other very real possibilities: one is that there is a marked asynchrony in the rate of development between chimpanzees and humans such that our apes are simply too young to show the abilities in question (see fig. 18.2); the other is that both young and mature chimpanzees have an amodal theory of attention such as that proposed by Baldwin and Moses (1994) for 14-month-old human infants. I present the recent round of studies to show that future research on chimpanzees' understanding of the mind can proceed with both methodological and conceptual rigor.

But already our data suggests (although not in a statistical way) that some aspects of the domain-specific versus general account of cognitive constructions can be evaluated. For example, one of our apes (Megan) has tested positive for mirror self-recognition since she was three years old, unlike most of her age-mates who have produced a negative diagnosis even to the present. Yet at about five and a half years she performed no better than her companions on the seeing-as-attention tasks described in section 4. This could be taken as hinting that the domain-general argument is wrong because self-recognition in mirrors in young children occurs at about the same time (18–24 months) as initial understanding of mental states (desires). Alas, however, tests of seeing-as-attention similar to ours may be difficult for children younger than about two and a half years (Lempers et al., 1977). Thus, a domain-general account could still prevail if there are necessary general cognitive achievements which must occur between these two time periods in young children before they can equate seeing as the mental state of attention. Clearly, we need better non-verbal tests of simple mental state attribution that are very sensitive to the 18-24 month age range in human children (Povinelli et al., 1991; Povinelli, 1993).

So do chimpanzees have a theory of mind? One participant at the conference on which this volume is based expressed understandable frustration after listening to the papers on this topic. To her, it seemed as if the debate about theory of mind in non-human primates has been a simplistic 'yes-they-have-it'-'no-they-don't' roller coaster ride. But I hope that this essay will help to clarify that it will require patience to achieve even minimal closure on the question of whether apes or other animals represent mental states. To be sure, there are those who wish a quick answer. Indeed, their impatience has allowed them to overlook important methodological caveats that have been laid out in the primary literature. For example, Smith (this volume) concludes that there has been a shift in views concerning chimpanzees' understanding of the mind, and believes that it is perhaps best to conclude that theory of mind cannot exist without language. Heyes (1994b) concludes that when it comes to theory-of-mind research in animals it is best to be a 'curmudgeon' (p. 242). I am willing to conclude that it is necessary continuously to upgrade our thinking about the relation between ontogeny and evolution and to use this theory to intelligently (and experimentally) challenge our intuitions about which species have a theory of mind. That, after all, is the long road to strong inference.

ACKNOWLEDGEMENTS

I thank Tim Eddy, Dare Baldwin, Radu Bogdan, Peter Carruthers, Lou Moses, the late Norton Nelkin, and Chris Prince for comments and thoughtful discussions that impacted upon the final text. Photographs are by Donna T. Bierschwale. This work was supported by National Institutes of Health Grant No RR-03583-05 to the New Iberia Research Center and a National Science Foundation Young Investigator Award to DJP.

NOTES

1   I use the term 'theory of mind' in the spirit in which Premack and Woodruff (1978) intended it. Thus, in this essay, I use the term to refer to any representation of unobservable mental states which serve the function of generating predictions about future behaviour or explanations for previous behaviour. I defer the issue of whether young children are young scientists-in-the-making to others (see Gopnik, this volume).
2   Those interested in the debate over potential differences in theory of mind among non-human primates are referred to other sources (Gallup, 1982; Whiten and Byrne, 1988; Cheney and Seyfarth, 1990; Povinelli, 1993; Whiten, 1993; Tomasello and Call, 1994).
3   I use the term epigenetic as opposed to developmental to emphasise the idea that the final path taken by developing neural systems depends upon both environmental feedback and genetic instructions. This is especially important in the current context given that several authors have argued for the possibility that abnormal environmental inputs in the form of contact with humans may potentially have dramatic effect upon great ape cognitive development in areas such as self-recognition in mirrors and imitation (Povinelli, 1994b; Tomasello, Savage-Rumbaugh, and Kruger, 1993).
4   To sustain this view plausibly, research showing significant correlations between pre-schoolers performance theory-of-mind tasks and other cognitive tasks would have to be explained in non-causal terms (e.g., Frye, Zelazo, and Palfai, unpublished manuscript).
5   Not all of the previous studies suffer from the general criticism that the critical trials are contaminated by 'learning'. Heyes (1993) has argued that our role-reversal studies, for example, may have involved learning in the critical reversal phase and complains that we did not report the trial-by-trial data in our original report. But a reading of the Povinelli, Nelson, and Boysen (1992) report reveals that this is not true. 'Additional support for Darrell, Sheba, and Sarah's

immediate comprehension comes from an examination of their first few trials within the initial role reversal session. As an informant on the first day of role reversal, Sarah produced accurate pointing to the correct location (from among four possibilities) on the first thirteen trials before making the first of her two errors... As an operator, Sheba's first six choices were all correct before she made her only error in twenty trials' (p. 637). In the context of Harris' (this volume) theory, it is of interest that this task performance was consistent with the hypothesis that the subjects saw their partner as performing specific actions to fulfil specific desires. Although it has not been replicated and suffers from some methodological drawbacks (Povinelli, 1991), it is possible evidence that chimpanzees understand others as intentional agents, even if they do not understand epistemic states. Similar task performance by 18- to 24-month-old humans has been demonstrated by Brownell and Carriger (1989).

6 We have explored two ways to attempt such investigations. One is to train chimpanzees as reliable enough actors to carry out our protocols. The second is to obtain convincing enough chimpanzee costumes for our undergraduate and graduate student actors to don during experimental trials. To date neither approach has met with much success.

19 Non-human primate theories of (non-human primate) minds: some issues concerning the origins of mind-reading

Juan-Carlos Gómez

This paper is about the kinds of theories of mind (ToM) that non-human primates can be supposed to possess. In relation to this topic I will consider three main issues: (1) What kinds of minds do non-human primates possess (e.g., do they 'know' or 'believe')? (2) Do non-human primates understand 'overt' mental states (e.g., attention) in others?; (3) Do non-human primates understand 'covert' mental states (e.g., knowledge) in others?

The question 'Do non-human primates have a theory of mind?' seems to be addressed with the implicit assumption that either they do or they don't. And if they don't have a genuine theory of mind (whatever this is), then their apparently mentalistic feats must be reduced to uninteresting trial-and-error learnings. I will argue that, to understand the problem of non-human ToMs, it is necessary to consider an intermediate possibility: the practical understanding of overt mental states as expressed in intelligent social actions. In arguing this I will resort to the notion of implicit understanding and implicit representations, especially as they have been recently treated by Karmiloff-Smith (1992). I will concentrate my discussion on the great apes (chimpanzees, gorillas, and orang-utans), our closest evolutionary relatives, and will, after a brief discussion of the overt mental state of attention, speak of epistemic mental states like knowing or believing.

1 The ape mind: do apes know and believe?

In this section of the book we are supposed to struggle with questions such as: does the chimpanzee have a theory of mind? Do apes believe that other people have beliefs? Do they know what others know or ignore? I will start, however, by asking a preliminary but often neglected question: do apes believe or know anything at all? If we are interested in the ToMs non-human primates may have evolved, a logically preliminary question is what kinds of minds non-human primates possess. Indeed the kind of ToM an ape is likely to have evolved must be a theory of the *ape* mind. If ToMs are an adaptation to the social behaviours generated by conspecifics, they must be theories of conspecifics' minds, i.e., in the case of chimpanzees, gorillas, and orang-utans, they can be expected to possess theories of the chimpanzee, gorilla, and orang-utan mind, respectively.

However, most attempts at addressing the ToM issue in primates seem to have assumed that ape minds are largely like human minds. Thus most experiments trying to assess apes' ToM (Premack and Woodruff, 1978; Woodruff and Premack, 1979; Premack, 1988; Povinelli *et al.*, 1990; Gómez and Teixidor, 1992) have used human beings as the subjects whose minds had to be understood by the ape. In all these tasks the apes had to react to a mental state that occurred in a human mind. In this sense, the apes are asked to show a theory of *human* minds.[1] Before addressing the question of apes' theories of mind we should, then, address the issue of apes' minds. Are really the ape and the human mind essentially similar in their most basic features, i.e., are both capable of forming representations that can be described as 'intentions', 'knowledge', 'ignorance' or 'beliefs'?

I shall approach this issue resorting to the well-known Piagetian object permanence task (Piaget, 1937). Object permanence is assessed by means of a simple test: an object is hidden under a cover while the subject watches the whole operation. If the subject looks for the now invisible object under the cover, he/she is said to know that objects continue to exist even if they are no longer visible. Apes are known to develop the Piagetian object concept (Doré and Mercier, 1992). Consider, for example, the following performance of an infant gorilla on a standard test: an infant gorilla is sitting on the lap of a person. A sweet is shown to him until he shows interest. The sweet is then put under a cloth while the gorilla is watching. The gorilla takes the cover apart and retrieves the sweet (personal observation).

When the ape looks for the object under the cover, is this evidence that he *knows* that the object is under that cover? Apparently the answer must be a positive one. However, perhaps we would not feel so confident about our answer if the question were: does the ape *believe* that the object is under the cover? 'Believing' implies knowing something with some degree of uncertainty, and this seems to imply the ability to entertain a 'belief attitude' towards our own knowledge (i.e., the ability to have a representation of our own belief with something like a tag specifying its degree of certainty). There is a sense of 'knowing' that also implies having an attitude towards the known content (this time, one implying certainty). It is this kind of knowledge that we can find difficult to impute to animals or preverbal children on the sole basis of their ability to retrieve hidden objects.

The sense in which we say a gorilla *knows* that the object is under the cover is rather that of its having somehow registered, represented, 'the object under the cover', and having this representation linked to a retrieval action. In a sense, what the animal knows is *how* to retrieve the object (i.e., a procedural representation), but implicit in this procedure must be some representation *that* the object is under the cover. Gorillas may 'know' in the sense of having a representation of 'X under Y' and by adjusting their intentional (goal-directed) actions to that representation. That representation need not be propositional, neither need it be a representation detachable from the executive part of the procedure in which it is integrated. Perhaps if we were able to have a look at this procedural representation, we would not actually find a part that could be glossed as 'X under Y'. Perhaps this is merely implicit in the procedure (e.g., something like 'If X is covered by Y, put Y aside to get X'). Thus, a representation may be said to be 'implicit' in at least two different senses: in one, it is knowledge embedded in a procedure and it cannot be taken outside of that procedure. For example, the procedure 'If object is under X, then remove X' would be based upon such a representation if the conditional clause could not exist without its consequent. But a second possibility is that a piece of knowledge is implicit when it is *implied* by the available representations. In the above example, 'X is covered by Y' *implies* that X is under Y, but this is not explicitly registered in the procedure – it is merely implied. Now, for an 'implied' representation to become explicit, it is necessary to develop the implication, i.e., to build a new representation in which something that was not originally represented is now represented. On the other hand, to make explicit an embedded representation, it could be enough to break the procedure into its component parts (and perhaps making a copy of it in a different representational format; see Karmiloff-Smith, 1992), which could also involve some sort of re-representation, but without having to *develop* anything new.

Whatever option we prefer, from the above ability to retrieve hidden objects we can at best conclude that apes (somehow) 'know', but not that they believe. However, there is a more complex object-search task, involving invisible displacements, that introduces the need to revise one's knowledge about the location of the object. For example, if a gorilla is shown a cake in my hand, I close the hand, move it under a cloth (where I covertly leave the cake), and then take out my closed hand, the gorilla will open my hand and look in it. He is puzzled for a second, then he looks at the cloth, extends his hand, withdraws the cloth and finds the cake (personal observation).

If the animal has a representation of 'the cake in the hand', what happens to his representation when he discovers that the cake is not in the hand? Apparently, some kind of inference occurs that activates a different representation – 'the cake under the cloth'. The gorilla must be capable of replacing a representation for another, i.e., somehow considering two alternative representations of reality. I propose that this representation is a sort of 'procedural belief', in that it somehow captures the possibility of misrepresentation or alternative representations of reality. The gorilla in the above example seems to accept the failure of his first representation and then acts according to a new one. This new, alternative representation can only be the result of some sort of inference. Interestingly, the ability to solve invisible-displacement problems seems not to be present in monkeys or cats (Doré and Mercier, 1992), which hints at the possibility that this is an important landmark in the evolution of representation.

In summary, there seems to be some justification to assume that apes form representations about the world that seem to guide their behaviours: they somehow *know* and even *believe* things about the world. Their ability to engage in object search tasks suggests that they can entertain representations of the world that go beyond the information given by perception. They can even revise their representations or hold alternative representations concerning the same object or event (which closely approaches having a 'belief'). We are uncertain about the status of these representations. Are they propositional? Are they explicit or implicit? If implicit, in what sense are they so? Pursuing these questions is an important task of cognitive primatology, but in the meantime we can tentatively assume that in apes there is a mind to build theories about (both by primatologists and by the apes themselves), one that can provisionally be characterised as entertaining some kind of knowledge. The available evidence seems to justify asking the question: do apes have a ToM? Do they understand that others may entertain representations of reality, for example that others may know or ignore the whereabouts of an object? However, we must remember that these representations may essentially consist of procedures and, therefore, an ape ToM may be a theory of the procedures available to others and the conditions of their applicability.

2   Ape theories of ape minds

Now to the ToM problem. Chimpanzees and gorillas can be said to 'know' and to 'believe' in some way. Even if we assume that their knowledge is procedural – *knowing how* to do things – we can still ask whether they attribute this ability to their conspecifics (for example, whether they anticipate that other apes will retrieve an object where they saw it was placed). Note that this formulation may lead us to a different way of posing the ToM problem. Attributing a mental state implies representing a representation that is in the mind of another person (and that, therefore, is unobservable), whereas attributing the ability to look for something where it was previously seen can be based upon the representation of observable behaviours. 'Seeing' can be said to be an 'overt' mental state, because it is usually accompanied by observable behaviours (the eyes and other body parts oriented to an object), and in this sense you can see another organism's seeing. An organism's knowledge of 'seeing' could be supported by first-order representations. However, 'knowing' and 'believing' are covert mental states, because they are not accompanied by external behaviours: one cannot 'see' somebody knowing or believing something. An organism's knowledge, in this case, has to be supported by second-order representations (Dennett, 1987).

Thus, when posing the ToM question we must clarify which mental states whose attribution we are asking about – overt or covert. In the following section I will concentrate upon the understanding of the overt mental state of visual attention.

3   Seeing seeing, and attending to attention: steps towards ToM

Most observational and informal reports suggesting some ToM abilities in great apes seem to involve overt mental states. For example, most deceptive behaviours collected by Byrne and Whiten (1990) imply the manipulation or avoidance of other animals' attention, mostly visual attention. For instance, an adult male chimpanzee capable of hiding his erected penis from the dominant male's view when spotted near a receptive female (de Waal, 1982), apparently with the aim of avoiding an aggressive reaction, seems to understand something about the role of visual attention in the behaviour of other animals. Understanding attention is manifested in two complementary kinds of patterns: following the attention of others and directing (or avoiding) other people's attention to particular targets. Following the line of regard of a person involves reacting to the eyes as a sort of pointer that highlights particular objects in the environment. Note that when we follow the line of regard of a person with the expectation of finding an object, we are inferring the existence of an object that we have not seen with our own eyes and that is somehow linked to that person. Perhaps the origins of understanding 'seeing' lie in this ability to follow the gaze of others with the expectation of finding an object. This can also be considered to be an early and simple way to know what is in the other's mind, because the contents of the other's mind – the object looked at – is in front of the beholder's eyes. No second-order representation is needed to impute this kind of knowledge. In fact, it is an ability that emerges very early in human infants (Scaife and Bruner, 1975; Butterworth, 1991).

The procedure of looking at the same object the other is looking at involves, then, some knowledge of what the other is seeing. Correspondingly, directing the eyes of people to particular objects involves some knowledge of how to make things perceptible to others – how to make them meet objects with their eyes. The latter is again something that human infants do very early – by the end of their first year of life (Schaffer, 1984). Finally, we must consider the special situation where the object of another's attention is a person. Many primate interactions have other primates as their targets (remember the above examples of deception). Avoiding the attention of others or managing to draw their attention upon oneself are important procedures in interaction. Let's have a look at some of the abilities of anthropoid apes in the realm of attention understanding.

4   Apes and visual attention

I have defended the existence of an implicit understanding of attention in anthropoid apes relying upon the results of a series of studies about the communicative abilities of hand-reared gorillas (Gómez, 1990, 1992). I found that a hand-reared gorilla would include visual attention-getting and -redirecting behaviours in her procedures to request actions or objects from people. For example, one subject's favourite way of making requests was to take people by their hands towards the objects they were expected to manipulate. Before doing this, she would typically approach the person, touch him on his knee, wait until he would look down, and then, after making eye contact, she would perform the requesting procedure of leading the person to the target (usually engaging in eye contact again while moving). Procedures like this seem to imply some understanding that objects and people's actions are not directly connected, but mediated by a special subset of behaviours – visual attention patterns. (See Gómez, 1991; Gómez *et al.*, 1993 for an extensive discussion of joint attention in pre-verbal requests and its ToM implications). Similar behaviours have been described in all species of great apes, both in nature and in captivity (although not always using this label) (Gómez, in press). To what extent (and how deeply) do apes understand the role of attention in interacting with others?

In an experimental study addressed at assessing several joint-attention competences in young chimpanzees (Gómez, Teixidor, and Laá, unpublished data), we tried, first, to confirm that chimpanzees do take into account other people's attentional states when interacting with them, and secondly, to determine the attentional cues to which chimpanzees are sensitive. The chimpanzees were offered the opportunity to request food from a human by means of reaching gestures. We systematically varied the attentional availability of the human: in normal trials she was looking at the chimpanzees waiting for their gestures, whereas experimental trials consisted of different forms of inattention from the human: (a) Human with back turned to chimpanzee and food, (b) Human with head oriented to chimp, but eyes closed, (c) Body oriented to chimp, but head turned to a corner, (d) Head oriented to chimp, eyes open, but oriented over chimp's head.

Addressee's inattentive condition	Mean % of trials evoking attention-getting responses (N = 6)	Individual hand-rearing (N = 3)	Poor hand-rearing (N = 3)
Back to the chimp	68	100	40
Eyes closed	48	70	27
Head to a corner	71	100	50
Eyes over chimp	84	100	73
All conditions	68	92.5	47.5

Table 19.1. Results of the experiment about the ability of young chimpanzees with different hand-rearing histories to call the attention of inattentive people when making requests.

Our hypothesis was that the chimpanzees would show their understanding of attention by using attention-getting procedures, such as touching the humans and trying to make eye contact with them in the conditions of inattention.

The results (Table 19.1) showed that overall the six chimpanzees called the human's attention in the appropriate situations in 68% of the trials. However, there were important individual differences. Three of the chimps called the attention of the inattentive human in only about 50% trials, whereas the other three did so in 86%, 92% and 94% of the trials in which the human was inattentive. When the experimenter turned her eyes to the chimpanzee in response to the latter's action, eye contact was generally established, i.e., the chimpanzees seemed to be waiting for the human's gaze to be directed at them.

The "eyes closed" situation proved to be the most difficult for all the animals, whereas the "eyes over head" situation was the simplest. Surprisingly, in what we had anticipated would be the easiest situation (that in which the human was sitting with her back to the animal), two of the chimpanzees kept making requests (extending their arms towards the food) despite the lack of response from the inattentive human and without trying to call her attention (in 6 out of 9 trials).

The individual differences found among the chimpanzees could be partly explained resorting to Tomasello *et al*'s (1993) concept of "enculturation". The three chimps who performed better were those who, without being fully enculturated in Tomasello *et al*.'s sense, nonetheless had had a more extensive and individualised hand-rearing history with humans.[2] The other three, though habituated to friendly and frequent contact with humans in a zoo setting, had not experienced "individualised" hand-rearing. (It is important to remember that the gorillas who developed attention-getting procedures, as described above, were hand-reared too.) Hand-rearing by humans could, therefore, promote the development of a better understanding of attention in infant apes. However, the nature of 'enculturation' is still unclear. Does hand-rearing create an understanding of attention that otherwise would not emerge in the apes? Does it simply accelerate the emergence in young apes of something that would nevertheless eventually appear? Or perhaps it just facilitates the learning of human-specific expressions of attention thereby making it easier for them to pass tests where they have to react to humans?

Other aspects of joint attention were explored in the same experiment. Three of the six chimpanzees followed the gaze of the experimenter in condition (c) when, after leaving a desirable object on the table, she would look away to a corner behind the animals. Interestingly, only one of the gaze-followers was a chimpanzee with individual handrearing; the other two were the ones who kept making requests despite the addressee being clearly inattentive with her back to the chimps or her eyes closed. Povinelli (this volume) found that six young (apparently not "enculturated" nor individually hand-reared) chimpanzees consistently followed a human's gaze in a situation similar to the one described above. Interestingly these same chimpanzees apparently failed to take into account the human's attention when making requests from them. It is difficult to ascertain whether these gaze-following behaviours are performed with the expectation of finding an object or whether they are a more primitive sort of response.

By and large, it can be said that young chimpanzees with a hand-rearing history demonstrate a good appreciation of the connection between 'seeing' and 'acting'. They are capable of catching and redirecting the visual attention of people towards the objects they want them to manipulate, and in this they seem to coincide with the abilities observed in hand-reared gorillas.

Now, what kinds of representations might support these joint-attention behaviours of chimpanzees and gorillas? Baron-Cohen (1994a, 1995, and this volume) has suggested a mechanism (SAM) specialised in computing joint-attention representations of the kind 'SELF sees (AGENT sees OBJECT)'. This notation could be used to describe the representations supporting behaviours like the non-verbal requests of gorillas and chimpanzees. In Baron-Cohen's proposal, 'see' is a relational term explicitly represented in the string, but it remains embedded between the terms it connects. My proposal is that, to support procedures like requesting, these strings would be further embedded into more complex sequences.[3] For example, the chimpanzee that calls the attention of an inattentive person and then requests a desired object is engaging in something like:

(SELF sees (AGENT sees not OBJECT)) >> (AGENT sees SELF) >> (SELF sees (AGENT sees OBJECT)) >> (AGENT gives OBJECT to SELF),

where the chimpanzee (SELF), after discovering that the human (AGENT) is not looking at the target (OBJECT), calls the human's attention upon himself and then makes her look at the target with the final aim of having the target given. 'Seeing' is embedded in subroutines involving Agents and Objects. It is a connecting link in a structure which, in turn, happens to be a connecting link in a more complex structure. In this sense, 'seeing' is deeply embedded and perhaps highly dependent upon the terms it connects.

In summary, there is evidence that the great apes include some representation of the overt mental states of seeing and/or attending in their procedures for social interaction. These representations seem to be implicit at least in the sense of being embedded in chains of actions interconnecting agents and objects.

5   Seeing leads to knowing: representing covert mental states

The crucial step towards ToM is the ability to infer 'knowledge' from the meeting of an object and the eyes of the other person – i.e., the ability to build a representation of what remains in the other's mind once the contemplated object has disappeared. Do apes understand that a person *knows* what he or she has *seen* – i.e., that 'seeing' leads to 'knowing'?

I will illustrate the discussion of this point with an experiment concerning an orang-utan's ability to adapt her actions to what a human knows or ignores (Gómez and Teixidor, 1992). This test was designed to assess non-verbally the reaction of an orang-utan to a false-belief situation similar to the ones used in the standard ToM tests (e.g., Wimmer and Perner, 1983; Baron-Cohen *et al.,* 1985). Unfortunately, these powerful tests depend upon language for their administration. Our test tried to overcome the problem of language by relying upon the non-verbal request strategies of a fifteen-year-old orang-utan named Dona.

Dona was in a cage in front of which there were two boxes locked with padlocks. The keys of the padlocks were kept inside a smaller box hanging at about 1.70 m above the floor. One person – the *Provider* – entered the room, took the keys from the small box, opened one of the big boxes on the floor and put food in it (without looking at the orang-utan and ignoring any requests). She locked the box again, returned the keys to the small box and left. Then, a second person – the *Giver* – entered and sat in front of the boxes attending to the orang-utan. If Dona pointed with her extended arm to one of the boxes, the Giver would take the keys, open the selected box and give the food to the orang-utan. Throughout the experiment a *Camera person* remained inside the cage videotaping the trials.

These were the normal trials – a simple request task Dona carried out without difficulty. Interspersed with them, the experimental trials were administered: in these the location of the keys was changed before the Giver entered the room. The change could be done by one of three persons: the Provider (after baiting the box), the Camera person, or a Stranger who entered the room immediately after the Provider had left. The point of experimental trials was that the usual location of the keys was changed without the Giver being present. The Giver would then come in and behave as usual. The prediction was that if Dona was capable of understanding the Giver's knowledge concerning the whereabouts of the keys, in the experimental trials she should point not only to the food but also to the keys *before* the Giver tried to retrieve them from their usual location. The hiding places varied from trial to trial, so that they were rarely repeated. Control trials were carried out in which the Giver herself would change the location of the keys, so that, even if they were in a new location, the Giver knew about it and did not need any informative pointing. In all trials it was important to determine whether the animal pointed to the keys *before* there was any overt sign of the person trying to retrieve them from the wrong place. Otherwise, the animal could be responding to the behaviour, not to the knowledge of the person.

The results showed that in the normal trials (N=278), where Dona had no need to point to the keys, she pointed to the boxes in 85% occasions, and only 15% to the keys. In the experimental trials (N=21), however, she pointed to the keys in 64% occasions, whereas she pointed only to the boxes in 36%. In the control trials, where the Giver herself changed the location of the keys, the animal pointed to them in their new location only in 21% trials, whereas she pointed to the box in 79%.

Overall these results seem to show that the animal is capable of appreciating to some extent the covert mental state of a person, since she tends to provide this person with information about the location of the keys in those trials where the information is needed. A closer analysis shows this could be due to a process of adaptation to the ignorance situation. The first six experimental trials were failed by Dona, whereas from the seventh trial onward she was almost perfect. Since in the experimental trials the Giver tried to retrieve the keys from the usual place – the smaller box – if she was not instructed otherwise by Dona, the orang-utan had the opportunity to witness the consequences of the act of hiding the keys. In the first trial, she actually got no food, because she did not point to the new location of the keys after the Giver failed to find them in the usual place. In the next trials, however, she did point to the new location *after* the Giver tried to retrieve the keys from the wrong place, thereby eventually getting the food. This gave her an opportunity to learn the appropriate action when the keys were changed in location. Note, however, that even in the wrong trials she would eventually get the reward. If any learning was involved, it is more reminiscent of what is known as 'insight learning' than trial and error learning. Furthermore, it is noteworthy that Dona started being right when the key changes were made by a stranger. When the Stranger hid the keys, Dona was upset (she even spat at the Stranger in some of the trials!) and extremely attentive to his/her manipulations.

If we were to decide from her first responses whether or not Dona understood covert mental states, the conclusion should be a negative one. On the other hand, a relatively brief exposure to the consequences of false-belief situations seemed to lead to the development of some understanding. The coincidence of the first correct responses with the first trials where the change was made by a Stranger reinforces the hypothesis of some 'insightful' process, similar to those described by Köhler in object manipulation in response to specific 'aids' (e.g., the rebound effect in the roundabout-with-sticks problem; Köhler, 1927). Did Dona eventually understand the wrong representation of the other person and, therefore, did she have a theory of covert mental states? We cannot answer this question with the available evidence. However, even if Dona had clearly passed the test, what could we really conclude about her understanding of mind?

First, although this procedure was created with the aim of providing a non-verbal analogue of the false-belief task, it is not a real equivalent to it. To answer correctly the subject does not need to compute the false belief of the other person: it is enough for the subject to compute the *ignorance* of the Giver. In the false-belief task the subject has to point to the place where the target object *is not*. This is strong evidence of the ability to compute the false belief of the other person – to consider what is not the case. In our task, however, the subject has to point to the place where the target object *is* hidden. This may indeed be due to the subject's appreciation of the Giver's false belief. But it would be enough for the subject to compute the fact that the Giver *does not know* that the keys are in the new location, which need not include a false-belief computation. Thus, if anything, Dona would have an understanding of 'Knowing' versus 'Not Knowing'. What kind of understanding could this be? Again it is difficult to decide whether a procedure adapted to ignorance (like pointing to the keys when necessary) has to include a representation of 'Ignorance' or 'Not knowing' or whether this is merely implied by the contrast between 'Seeing X leads to Acting on X' versus 'Not seeing X leads to Not acting on X'. It is possible that the mind remains implicit in the very fact that such connections exist (Gómez, 1991), and that the task of a ToM mechanism is to draw the implications contained in the 'Seeing-Acting' procedures.

In summary, the experiment reported here, together with previous evidence from Premack and Premack (1983) and Povinelli *et al.* (1990), suggests that some understanding of covert mental states (at least ignorance and knowledge) may be within the reach of anthropoid apes. However, it is possible that this understanding is implicit in procedures connecting attentional states to actions.

6   Procedures and implicit representations

According to Karmiloff-Smith (1992), procedures involve sequences of actions which are successful in provoking certain results. Explicit knowledge is gained when these procedures are re-represented by the mind into different representational formats. We don't know whether the knowledge of anthropoid apes remains at the procedural level, as Karmiloff-Smith (1992) suggests. However, before this re-representation is carried out some interesting processes may operate at the level of procedures. For example, let's consider the case of non-verbal communicative procedures in which some representation of 'Seeing' or 'Attending' is included. There is a peculiarity of human one-year-olds that may be of interest in relation to the procedural embeddedness of 'seeing'. Besides 'proto-imperative' or request procedures, human infants also have 'proto-declarative' gestures (Bates *et al.,* 1975), i.e., procedures to show things to people for their own sake. In this they differ from apes, who apparently always use their procedures with the aim of making other people do things (Gómez *et al.,* 1993). Now, whereas a request should involve a representation with a final segment of the kind 'AGENT does X' (see above), a proto-declarative should be based upon representations whose final segments are of the kind 'AGENT sees X' or 'AGENT attends to X'. According to Karmiloff-Smith (1992), the end parts of procedures are the first to undergo re-representation in more explicit representational formats. Thus, proto-declarative procedures could represent a phylogenetic adaptation to facilitate the re-description of the representations of seeing and attending that remain implicit in the procedures involving attention manipulation.

    The problem of non-human ToMs has been frequently addressed with the assumption that the behaviours of apes that apparently require some mentalistic abilities will either turn out to be due to a real ToM, comparable to that of human children, or will turn out to be simple trial-and-error learnings devoid of any mentalistic understanding of others, much as the arithmetic feats of clever horses were shown to be mere trial-and-error tricks devoid of any genuine mathematical understanding at the beginning of this century (Boakes, 1984). However, between the learning of simple contingencies and theory-like cognition other sophisticated kinds of intelligent behaviour can be found. Wolfgang Köhler (1927) and

Jean Piaget (1936) suggested, long ago, that apes and human infants were capable of 'practical intelligence' in their dealings with the physical world. They spoke of 'naive physics', 'object concept', 'causality notions', etc., implying the existence of a systematic way to organise the subjects' intentional actions towards objects. They called this intelligence 'practical' to differentiate it from reflexive or conscious forms of understanding based upon explicit representations or concepts. In her re-formulation of the problem, Karmiloff-Smith (1992) speaks of the existence of a level of implicit representations or procedures that would correspond to practical intelligence. Knowledge is 'enveloped' in these procedures. An important part of cognitive development consists of 'unpacking' this knowledge, making it available to the cognitive system in the form of explicit representations.

The origins of ToM should lie in intelligent procedures adapted for dealing with the consequences of other people's minds. We have seen that anthropoid apes develop procedures that take into account the external signs of attention and inattention of other people. They also have procedures adapted to the practical consequences of having seen or not having seen something (amounting to a practical understanding of knowledge versus ignorance). These procedures are more complex than simple collections of trial-and-error habits, but, on the other hand, they need not involve a meta-representational theory of mind. However, these intelligent procedures may well constitute an implicit ToM, in the sense that they may *imply* ToM for an organism – or a system within the same organism – capable of developing these implications. 'Developing' here does not refer to an exercise in inference, but to a process of developmental change that may need an important biological anchorage, such as the presence of special procedures highlighting certain parts of the implicit representations for re-description. Cognitive primatology may give us cues as to the biological processes which build organisms with ToMs. The phylogeny of ToM could be understood partly as a process of making explicit what is implicit in behavioural procedures that emerged as adaptations to the mental properties of the social environment.

ACKNOWLEDGEMENTS

The research reported in this paper has been carried out under a DGICYT grant (PB92-0143-C02-02) from the Spanish Ministry of Education. I am grateful to S. Baron-Cohen for discussions bearing on the topics of the paper spanning a number of years. These discussions were facilitated by an Acciones Integradas grant from the British Council and The Spanish Ministry of Education. I am also grateful to E. Sarriá, M. Núñez, A. Rivière and the other members of the Theory of Mind research groups in Madrid for their stimulating and warm discussions.

NOTES

1 Furthermore, since the ape subjects in these experiments were exposed to gestures, expressions and behaviours produced by humans, they were being asked to apply their putative ToMs to human data. As pointed out by Carruthers (personal communication), even if a ToM similar to the human one had evolved in apes, the possibility exists that they are confused by the human ways of expression and behaviour.

2 Tomasello *et al.*'s (1993) 'enculturation' seems to refer mainly to the case of apes subject to formal training in artificial language or symbol use. However, they seem ready to include into this category apes who have been simply handreared. Probably different degrees or types of enculturation should be distinguished (Gómez, 1993).

3 There are reasons to argue that the representations supporting joint attention upon an object could involve a more complex structure than 'Self sees (Agent sees object)' (Gómez, 1994b). However, this point is not relevant for the present discussion.

20 Language and the evolution of mind-reading

Peter K. Smith

1 Introduction: a recent shift in views

Is 'theory of mind' unique to humans? Do great apes possess some form of mind-reading abilities? There has been a distinct shift in viewpoints on this recently. The evidence in favour of some mind-reading abilities at least in some great ape species had been accumulating through the 1980s. Thus, Premack (1988, p.179) argued that:

> We may need to distinguish three degrees of theory of mind: (a) species that make no attributions of any kind, presumably the case for the vast majority of species; (b) species whose attributions are unlimited in any respect except perhaps for number of embeddings . . . presumably the case for humans (by the time they are four years old); (c) species that make attributions but attributions that are limited in a number of respects, possibly the case for the chimpanzee.

Byrne and Whiten (1992, pp.624–5) went further, suggesting that:

> Great apes demonstrate an understanding of deception for which we have no good evidence in monkeys . . . our deception data are just part of a broad sweep of evidence that great apes have that ability, so central to human communication, to attribute certain intentional states – an ability also variously described as the ability to imagine other possible worlds, to empathize, to attribute mental states, to have a theory of mind, mind-reading, and second-order intentionality . . . *modern great apes may completely lack the formalizing systems of language, but they do not appear to lack understanding of what this kind of communication is about.* (my italics)

But the last few years have seen critiques of the interpretation of many studies, and a partial withdrawal of claims by some leading researchers. More sceptical views on the abilities of chimpanzees and other species are being voiced forcefully. Perhaps they are 'behaviourists' rather than 'mentalists'? Seyfarth and Cheney (1992, p. 84) suggest that 'Monkeys and perhaps even apes cannot communicate with the intent to modify the mental states of others because, apparently, they do not recognise that such mental states exist.'

And Povinelli and Eddy (in press b) argue that five to six-year-old chimpanzees apparently know very little about seeing as a mental event and that 'if, under the advancing scrutiny of improved experimental methods, the chimpanzee's theory of mind turns out to be a behavioral illusion . . . then we will be forced to conclude . . . that they simply do not share with us a suite of psychological dispositions that evolved exclusively in the human lineage.'

In this commentary on the papers in this section I shall argue that language – in the sense of an abstract, symbolic system of communication – has a crucial role to play in this debate, and that (*contra* the italicised quote from Byrne and Whiten, 1992 above) it is a precondition for explicit mind-reading skills to develop and evolve. Both Whiten (this volume) and Gómez (this volume) use the terms 'implicit' and 'explicit', with Gómez relating his use to that of Karmiloff-Smith (1992). Karmiloff-Smith, in her representational redescription (RR) model, posited representational levels I (implicit), E1 (explicit at level of cross-system availability of procedural components), and E2/3 (explicit at level of conscious access, E2, and verbal report, E3 – though these latter two levels are not clearly separated in Karmiloff-Smith's account). I shall argue that the kinds of mind-reading abilities in chimpanzees we can be sure of are those of 'very clever behaviourists', equivalent to implicit mind-reading (level I), though moving towards level E1 in enculturated chimpanzees. For fully explicit mind-reading in the sense of awareness of others' desires and beliefs, an individual would need language to convince us it had it, it would need language to develop it in ontogeny, and the species of which this individual is a part would need language, and explicit representations at level E2/3, for these mind-reading abilities to have evolved.

2 What kinds of mind-reading abilities can we be sure of in great apes?

I shall mainly focus here on evidence regarding chimpanzees, but the argument is a general one.

2.1 Anecdotal evidence

The most 'ecologically valid' evidence for mind-reading abilities in chimpanzees came from the 'anecdotal' or 'field' evidence collected outside experimental situations. These include the observations of high social intelligence in chimpanzees – forming alliances, 'chimpanzee politics' as it is termed by de Waal (1982); the deceitful behaviour shown by chimpanzees in Menzel's (1988) 'one-acre field' experiment; and Whiten and Byrne's (1988, Byrne and Whiten 1992) conclusion that high-level tactical deception occurs in great apes (but probably not in monkeys).

The behaviourist critique of these observations is that we do not know the prior reinforcement or learning history of the animals concerned; thus, any particular observation could be explained in terms of learning to respond to a behavioural situation in a way which has worked in the past. For example, 'Yeroen hobbles pitifully when in Nikkie's field of vision, but walks normally when out of sight' (as in de Waal, 1982), looks insightful given that Yeroen wants to avoid Nikkie's attacks, which are likely if Yeroen appears as a threat to Nikkie's dominance status. But this could be a learnt behaviour pattern arising from prior contingencies rather than a reading by Yeroen of Nikkie's state of mind or even of his perceptual knowledge. The rule in Yeroen's brain might simply be 'hobble pitifully while I can see Nikkie else he will attack me'.

The researchers concerned were not unaware of such objections. They described 'levels of deception'. For example Mitchell (1986) delineated four levels of deception: from an innate program (1) through stimulus-response (2) to learnt associations (3) to deliberate planning (4). Whiten and Byrne (1988) tried to demarcate higher levels by defining 'tactical deception' as 'acts from the normal repertoire of the agent, deployed such that another individual is likely to misinterpret what the acts signify, to the advantage of the agent' – that is, the acts are in the normal repertoire, but not used in the normal and expected way. Possibly Yeroen had hobbled before (he was an old chimpanzee!) but his hobbling only in front of Nikkie was tactical deception in this way.

As we can see from this example, even tactical deception need not necessarily imply explicit mind-reading in the sense of awareness of another's desires or beliefs (Whiten, this volume). In fact, Whiten and Byrne (1988) considered the above example as only 'level 1': *Creating an Image*. Level 1 also included *Concealment* (e.g. subordinate male inhibits normal copulatory call or female grooms another male out of sight of dominant male), *Distraction* (e.g. chased animal suddenly stops and stares into distance, as if at predator), and *Using Social Tool* (e.g. female baboon feeding, infant nearby screams, adult male chases off female, then infant feeds). All these can be rather readily explained by behavioural learning or what Whiten (this volume) calls implicit mentalism.

Whiten and Byrne (1988) tried to isolate higher levels of deception by looking for the animal having some understanding of the mechanism by which the deception worked. Perhaps how the world appears perceptually from another's viewpoint (level 1.5), or understanding the mechanism by which a tactic of deception worked, implying representation of mental state of other (level 2). The famous example of this is the counterdeception in which chimpanzee A avoided looking at a banana in a tree so that chimpanzee B, normally dominant, would not seize it. B went off, A finally took the banana, only to find B returning from hiding to take it.

However it is still possible to provide a behaviourist explanation of these anecdotes, including even those at level 2; in the banana example, B might have a learnt rule such as 'when A looks shifty, if I go away and come back I may get some food off him'. As Whiten and Byrne (1988) acknowledged, no particular episode provides watertight evidence in itself of being able to read another's mind. However they do suggest at the very least that *chimpanzees are very clever behaviourists*. They are aware of very subtle cues from conspecifics; and they appear to be able to learn a wide variety of ways of using these cues. For example the banana episode indicates B's sensitivity to behavioural cues which A may have been trying to conceal, plus a probably flexible way of utilising that information. The tactical deception anthology generally shows both of these – the variety of stimulus conditions acted upon, and the variety of response modes used (albeit usually by different individuals of the same species).

2.2   Experimental studies

A number of experimental studies have suggested that chimpanzees, and perhaps orang-utans and gorillas, do have some mind-reading qualities. These include the pioneering work of Premack and Woodruff (1978), of Gallup (1982) on mirror recognition, the subsequent studies by Premack (1988) on deception, Gómez (1991) on strategies of getting a human to open a door, and Povinelli *et al.* (1990, 1992) on informant/operator role-reversal in a pointing/food-getting task, and on an attribution of visual knowledge task (hider/leaver).

However, these studies have without exception been subject to critiques that there have either been procedural problems and/or alternative, 'behaviourist' explanations (see Heyes, 1993, 1994a). For example, the behaviour of the young gorilla studied by Gómez (1991) can be explained in terms of observables (Whiten, this volume). The informant/operator role-reversal experiment of Povinelli *et al.* (1992) can be explained in terms of learning outside the experimental situation (Heyes, 1993). The attribution of visual knowledge task (Povinelli, *et al.* 1990) can be explained in terms of learning of observable discriminating cues (Heyes, 1993).

These critiques have some force, and are acknowledged by Povinelli (this volume). So what can be learnt from the experimental studies? Again, some of them at least show that, even if we reject the mentalist interpretation, then chimpanzees must be very clever behaviourists. For example, consider the critique by Heyes (1993) of the Povinelli *et al.* (1990) hider/leaver study. In this, the chimpanzee has to choose between the pointing information of the hider (who has hidden the food) and the leaver (who left the room while the hiding took place). This was achieved, although only after several blocks of fifty trials. However, the best test of mind-reading, according to the authors, was when the leaver, instead of leaving, put a large paper bag over his head just before the food was hidden. This would test transfer to a new stimulus situation. Povinelli *et al.* (1990) reported success in this over thirty trials. Heyes (1993) pointed out that there might have been a decrement at the start of the thirty trials, followed by learning which could be explained behaviouristically. Indeed, Povinelli (1994a) confirmed that their performances were not above chance during the first few trials of the transfer test. Nevertheless, three of the four chimpanzees made only eight or nine errors out of thirty trials, so it does seem that the learning must have been quite rapid. In general, even the pessimistic picture from these experiments is that chimpanzees are at least very clever behaviourists, rapid learners of how to respond to new situations, if not actually explicit mind-readers.

2.3   Recent studies by Povinelli on a lack of understanding of visual knowledge in chimpanzees

A series of studies by Povinelli and Eddy (in press b; also Povinelli, this volume), by contrast, might seem to present chimpanzees as rather stupid. In these studies, young chimpanzees had to choose from one of two persons to beg for food from. One person could see them, the other person could not for a variety of reasons – facing away, bucket over head, blindfolded, hands over head, looking at ceiling. With the exception of the facing away person, the chimpanzees by and large failed to respond preferentially to the human who could see them. For example, they begged at someone with a bucket over his head as much as someone without. This suggests a lack of awareness of what others can see and therefore know, and actually appears rather stupid in the light of what chimpanzees can do in the wild (e.g. Whiten and Byrne's level 1: *Concealment* tactical deception, above). Indeed Povinelli and Eddy comment how the chimpanzees' poor performance surprised them, and how their trainers made excuses for the chimpanzees' poor performance in terms of an 'off day' or 'the weather'!

Povinelli notes possible reasons for their failure, including the young age of the chimpanzees concerned. I still find these results difficult to reconcile with the anecdotal evidence for tactical deception, or even with the rapid learning in the paper bag experiment referred to earlier. Developmental psychologists know well that it is easy to infer a lack of ability when in fact the experimental circumstances may hinder the participants – the Piagetian experiments are a classic example.

In the case of these recent studies on visual knowledge, I wonder if we are reading too much into the failure of the chimpanzees over a small number of trials; after all, they do succeed later on (Povinelli, this volume). Some persistency in begging from non-seeing humans may not be as stupid as it seems. In the wild, a begging response might be quite adaptive even if an animal is temporarily looking away – probably, it *will* look your way soon. Thus persistency in begging, despite the other animal initially ignoring you, might pay off after a while. Indeed, plate 3d in van Lawick-Goodall (1968) shows exactly such a situation – a chimpanzee with outstretched arm begging from above and behind another chimpanzee; the begging chimpanzee would see the top and back of the head of the other.

Another consideration in evaluating these 'begging' experiments is that we have privileged knowledge. *We* know that the experimental instructions were 'keep looking at the ceiling despite the begging gesture', or 'keep the bucket on your head for as long as it takes', but the chimpanzees were not to know this (at least in the early and unsuccessful trials; the chimpanzees did eventually learn not to beg from the person with the bucket – and the other non-seeing persons – it just took quite a number of trials to learn this). And outside these experimental situations, the chimpanzees might have experienced humans who did talk to them while not looking at them, who did turn round on hearing them. Indeed Gómez (this volume) found exactly this, that chimpanzees did try to attract the attention of humans who are turned away or have their eyes closed. One could ask, not entirely facetiously, who is being stupid, the chimpanzee begging from a human with a bucket over his head, or the human standing and keeping a bucket over his head despite the begging? Donaldson (1978) criticised some of Piaget's experiments for not making 'human sense'; do these experiments make 'chimpanzee sense'?

Against these justifications for the chimpanzees' 'failure', it might be argued that Povinelli and Eddy found that children aged just three years and up could do the tasks very quickly. However, children themselves have almost certainly had relevant prior training schedules. They will have played peek-a-boo games with parents, which would have been very good training for the hands-over-face or screen in front of face condition which they succeeded at better than the chimpanzees. The experiments showed that chimpanzees could learn these tasks with practice; maybe the children's practice had occurred earlier.

In summary, it appears that we cannot with certainty infer explicit mind-reading skills in chimpanzees (or other great apes) from the evidence to date. But we can infer that they are very clever behaviourists – apparently much cleverer than rhesus monkeys, for example, who routinely fail many of the tests we have considered.

3   Could we ever have a definitive experiment on mind-reading?

The experience of changing views on the evidence is salutary. Previously convincing evidence can be reinterpreted. Similarly, Gómez (this volume) describes the difficulties in interpretation of his giver/provider experiments with an orang-utan. In fact, I doubt that we can ever have a definitive study, or watertight experiment, that could convince us that chimpanzees or other great apes can or cannot explicitly mind-read – infer mental states in others and use them. I would argue that this is so, unless we could get them to communicate directly with us. In Povinelli and Eddy's (in press b) experiments, the reason the performance of the human children is convincing (for me) is not so much the rapid learning (since they have probably had relevant prior training) but the fact that they could verbalise their reasons ('your eyes aren't there', 'you can't see me'). By contrast, we are trying to infer from overt, non-verbal behaviour whether chimpanzees are using mental state information rather than overt non-verbal behaviour. A behaviourist will always come up with some reductionist explanation.

4   Is a 'very clever behaviourist' an implicit mentalist?

Both Heyes (1993) and Whiten (this volume) consider what kinds of evidence might be the most convincing for mind-reading in chimpanzees or other species. Heyes (1993) recommends what she calls *triangulation* – conditional discrimination learning followed by transfer tests. This in fact was the procedure in the Povinelli, Nelson, and Boysen (1990) hider/leaver studies – though as we saw (and Heyes points out), they failed to demonstrate the rapid transfer claimed to be needed to demonstrate mind-reading. On Heyes' argument, triangulation would give evidence of mental state attribution *if* the transfer was very rapid – effectively, without any decrement from before the transfer.

While *success* on such studies would certainly be more convincing than other evidence, it would probably not be conclusive. The informant/operator study of Povinelli, Nelson, and Boysen (1992) did attempt this paradigm with apparent success; but this was discounted by Heyes (1993) in terms of prior learning/training opportunities outside the experiment. It may well be possible for a sceptic to mount such a case, with varying degrees of plausability, for success in other studies of this kind. Equally, *failure* on a triangulation task could be ascribed to a temporary failure to realise the relevance of the new stimulus condition to the mental state being inferred. A chimpanzee might realise that it should point to the person who can see the food, but – for a few trials – not realise that a paper bag over the head prevents the person seeing (if it had not experienced the 'paper bag over the head situation' before, as would be intended to discount more simple learning explanations).

The idea of triangulation can be linked to Whiten's suggestion that mental states can be thought of as 'intervening variables' (this volume; figures 2 to 4). That is, if we can attribute a mental state of say, fear, to another animal, we can both infer this from a variety of stimulus inputs (e.g. facial expression, body posture, vocalisations) and predict a number of likely outcomes (no competition for food, failure to help). But how would we know that an animal is representing these intervening variables (IV's)? Triangulation as Heyes proposes could be a way of operationalising the idea. If you have an IV for 'the person does (not) know where the food is' then you should be able to transfer or switch rapidly between different stimulus predictors of this – e.g. his/her absence when the food was hidden, or presence while blindfolded.

5   Behaviourism, mentalism, and levels of representation

Any predictions of another's behaviour, at whatever level of representation or explicitness, must ultimately be based on behaviour observations (Whiten, this volume). Certainly for non-verbal species, any attributions we make about likely behaviour, or mental states, must be based on this – we think our cat is hungry when it vocalises or searches in a certain way. Ethologists have systematised just how motivational state, and future behaviour, can be inferred from particular behavioural displays. Animals generally respond in some way to such displays; and we can regard this as level I in Karmiloff-Smith's model ('procedures for analysing and responding to stimuli in the external environment', 1992, p. 20).

In intelligent species, considerable learning from observations may take place. Such learning could be associations between stimulus situations and desirable responses ('beg to someone whose face is visible'); and might go towards constructing IV's in Whiten's sense. Does having IV's constitute a level of explicit mind-reading? In Karmiloff-Smith's model, does it constitute level E1 ('representational redescription . . . for component parts [of a procedure] to become accessible to potential intra-domain links', 1992, p. 20)? There could be a case made that an animal which is a very clever behaviourist – which can build up complex links between stimulus situations which are similar, and can do reasonably well on transfer and triangulation tasks, is developing to an E1 level. Karmiloff-Smith herself believes that chimpanzees either do not go beyond the behavioural mastery of level I, or, 'the higher-level codes into which representations are translated during redescription are very impoverished' (1992, p. 192).

A lot of the evidence seems consistent with chimpanzees having some 'impoverished' or tentative E1 representations (generally, not just about mental states). Chimpanzees can achieve something like sensorimotor intelligence and deferred imitation, but do not naturally go beyond this to more advanced symbolic activity (Mignault, 1985). Nagell *et al.* (1993) found that chimpanzees could imitate the general functional relations of a demonstrated task, but not the actual component procedures (level I rather than level E1).

However there is stronger evidence for level E1 representations in enculturated chimpanzees (those reared by humans and with contact with a symbolic communication system). Tomasello *et al.* (1993) found that enculturated chimpanzees could show deferred imitation of means (component procedures) as well as ends.

It is also only in hand-reared chimpanzees that there is occasional evidence of pretend play – jabbing themselves in the arm following an inoculation at a doctors, hiding invisible 'objects' in piles of blankets, giving 'pretend' objects to others and watching, pretend eating, barking at 'pretend' animals. There is no reason to suppose this is fully metarepresentational pretend (level E2/3), any more than we need suppose this for the similar pretence of two-year-old children (Lillard, 1993; Jarrold, Carruthers, Smith, and Boucher, 1994). But it does suggest some shift from level I to level E1.

Similarly, chimpanzees have gaze-following and pointing abilities, and can show some shared attention (Gómez, this volume; Bard, 1994). These are not 'meta-representational' or E2/3 abilities, or true awareness of perception/knowledge relationship – such as Povinelli and Eddy found in three to four-year-old children who could talk about why they chose a seeing over a non-seeing person. But they are important staging posts; interestingly, Gómez (this volume) found some of these abilities also to be clearer in enculturated chimpanzees.

Any further mentalist capacities would require knowledge to be more explicit. A plausible way of achieving this would be if an animal could label its IVs. Some form of language or symbolic code would be necessary for this. Possession of such a symbolic code would obviously be necessary for E3 representations in Karmiloff-Smith's model, but I argue would also be necessary for the consolidation of E1 and development of E2 representations – necessary from both ontogenetical and phylogenetic arguments.

6   Does language have a crucial role in the ontogeny and phylogeny of mind-reading?

I have taken Whiten's (this volume) idea of IVs to correspond to Heyes (1993) views on triangulation and transfer abilities, and to indicate a level of very clever behaviourism; certainly level I and possibly 'impoverished' level E1. The best evidence for level E1 in chimpanzees comes from those exposed to a symbolic language code. I believe that this is not accidental, and is because some kind of language ability enables a chimpanzee to 'label' the IVs and thus to manipulate internally these IVs in its mind – including the IVs representing mental states.

If the labelling of IVs is a crucial step, this might suggest that the presence of words (or symbolic codes) for mental states, such as desires and beliefs, in the language of parents and caregivers, may be crucial. In fact, what I am arguing is that the *availability* of such codes is crucial for the developing individual to acquire mind-reading abilities (consolidated E1, and certainly E2/3). Various aspects of the care-giving environment will facilitate their use. I think that the *explicit use* of such codes by care-givers is likely to be important, but Harris (this volume) develops an alternative view about how conversation implies that people are recipients and providers of information.

Any argument for the importance of language in the ontogeny of mind-reading skills links to a corresponding argument for phylogeny. Whiten alludes to phylogeny, but considers that 'it is plausible that mental states must have been recognised in ancestral populations before words (names) came to be designated for them' (this volume). But we have seen how uncertain the evidence for this is in non-human species, beyond an implicit recognition; and how only enculturated chimpanzees give good evidence of E1 capacities.

There have been other candidates than language, for the crucial preconditions for mind-reading to develop. Gallup (1982) proposed that mirror self-recognition was the crucial indicator, implying an awareness of self which could lead via simulation to awareness of others. (The empirical evidence on this remains inconclusive; even if chimpanzees and orangutans do show enhanced self-directed behaviour in front of mirrors, this may simply show that the animal can use novel, displaced visual feedback about itself to guide behaviour; Menzel *et al.*, 1985; Heyes, 1994a). Harris (1989) earlier proposed that the preconditions for the ontogeny of mind-reading are self-awareness, the ability to pretend, and knowledge of the pretence-reality distinction.

I find these alternative proposals less convincing in considering the phylogeny of mind-reading. For this, some kind of bootstrappng exercise seems necessary. Young incipient mind-readers needed to be supported in their ontogenetic development of mind-reading skills. We need to consider as prerequisites *both* individuals who can develop mind-reading, *and* enculturation within a community which mind-reads. As the abilities of individuals evolved, so too the social support for mind-reading must have evolved.

Language seems the obvious candidate here. I have argued that it would help an individual ontogenetically by helping them label intervening variables/mental states of themselves and others; and it would help it phylogenetically, by the process of developing within a community of adults linguistically communicating about such states. It is not so clear that this phylogenetic scaffolding could be created by a community of creatures busy being self-aware or busy carrying out pretend simulations. Self-awareness and pretence of this kind are intrinsically solitary, whereas we need a social context for the evolution of mind-reading. Language seems to be the right candidate.

The likely importance of enculturation for mind-reading development in chimpanzees fits in well with the postulated role for language. Adult humans, and adult chimpanzees, behave very differently to young chimpanzees. In some ways the latter can benefit from human care-givers; they attend to and manipulate objects more (Bard and Vauclair, 1984), engage in longer bouts of mutual gaze (Bard, 1994), and show richer pretence and can be trained in simple forms of sign language. This demonstrates the powerful nature of the social environment in supporting the ontogeny of mind-reading skils. However they had to evolve too. Even chimpanzees with a lot of exposure to human care-givers (such as Sarah, who featured in the early Premack experiments) don't show unambiguous mind-reading skills. Enculturation in a ToM community is not sufficient for mind-reading. But it is very likely to be necessary; as Tomasello, Savage-Rumbaugh, and Kruger (1993) also suggest, if we could imagine a child being reared by chimpanzees, it might not develop an explicit theory of mind because of deficient enculturation.

In summary, only language seems likely to convince us – or sceptics among us – of mind-reading ability beyond the level of 'very clever behaviourist'; level I, with arguments about level E1, in Karmiloff-Smith's (1992) RR model. Only language would enable an individual to develop this through to explicit mind-reading; consolidating E1 and reaching E2/3. And only a linguistic community would have provided the phylogenetic scaffolding for this to happen. Only if chimpanzees could talk to each other about mental states would they have evolved mind-reading, and only if they could talk to us about mental states would we believe them.

ACKNOWLEDGEMENTS

I am grateful to Peter Carruthers for comments on an earlier version of this chapter.

References

American Psychiatric Association (1987). *Diagnostic and Statistical Manual of Mental Disorders* (3rd revised edition). Washington DC.

Amsterdam, B. (1972). Mirror self-image reactions before age two. *Developmental Psychobiology, 5*, 297–305.

Anselmi, D., Tomasello, M., and Acunzo, M. (1986). Young children's responses to neutral and specific contingent queries. *Journal of Child Language, 13*, 135–44.

Asendorpf, J. B., and Baudonniere, P. M. (1993). Self-awareness and other-awareness: mirror self-recognition and synchronic imitation among unfamiliar peers. *Developmental Psychology, 29*, 88–95.

Asperger, H. (1944). Die 'autistischen Psychopathen' im kindesalter. *Archiv fur Psychiatrie und Nervenkrankheiten, 117*, 76–136.

Astington, J. W. (1990). Narrative and the child's theory of mind. In B. Britton and A. Pellegrini (eds.), *Narrative Thought and Narrative Language*. Hillsdale, NJ: Erlbaum.

Astington, J. W., Harris, P. L., and Olson, D. R. (1988, eds.). *Developing Theories of Mind*. Cambridge, Cambridge University Press.

Astington, J. W., and Jenkins, J. M. (1995, March). Language and theory of mind: a theoretical review and a longitudinal study. Paper presented at the Biennial Meeting of the Society for Research in Child Development, Indianapolis, IN.

Avis, J., and Harris, P. L. (1991). Belief-desire reasoning among Baka children: evidence for a universal conception of mind. *Child Development, 62*, 460–7.

Baillargeon, R. (1987). Object permanence in 3.5 and 4.5 month old infants. *Developmental Psychology, 23*, 655–64.

Bakeman, R., and Adamson, L. (1984). Coordinating attention to people and objects in mother-infant and peer-infant interaction. *Child Development, 55*, 1278–89.

Baldwin, D.A. (1995). Understanding the link between joint attention and language aquisition. In C. Moore, and P. Dunham (eds.), *Joint Attention: Its Origins and Role in Development*. Hillsdale, NJ: Lawrence Erlbaum.

Baldwin, D. A., and Moses, L. J. (1994). Early understanding of referential intent and attentional focus: evidence from language and emotion. In C. Lewis and P. Mitchell (eds.), *Children's Early Understanding of Mind: Origins and Development*. pp 133–56. Hillsdale, NJ: Erlbaum.

Bard, K. A. (1994). Evolutionary roots of intuitive parenting: maternal competence in chmpanzees. *Early Development and Parenting, 3*, 19–28.

Bard, K. A., Platzman, Lester, B. M. and Suomi, S. J. (1992). Orientation to social and non-social stimuli in neonatal chimpanzees and humans. *Infant Behavior and Development*, *15*, 43–6.

Bard, K. A., and Vauclair, J. (1984). The communicative context of object manipulation in ape and human adult-infant pairs. *Journal of Human Evolution*, *13*, 181–90.

Barkow, J., Cosmides, L., and Tooby, J. (eds.), (1992). *The Adapted Mind: Evolutionary Psychology and the Generation of Culture*, Oxford: Oxford University Press.

Baron-Cohen, S. (1987). Autism and symbolic play. *British Journal of Developmental Psychology*, *5*, 139–48.

(1988). Social and pragmatic deficits in autism. Cognitive or affective? *Journal of Autism and Developmental Disorders*, *18*, 379–402.

(1989a). The autistic child's theory of mind: A case of specific developmental delay. *Journal of Child Psychology and Psychiatry*, *30*, 285–98.

(1989b). Perceptual role-taking and protodeclarative pointing in autism. *British Journal of Developmental Psychology*, *7*, 113–27.

(1989c). Are autistic children behaviourists? An examination of their mental-physical and appearance-reality distinctions. *Journal of Autism and Developmental Disorders*, *19*, 579–600.

(1990). Autism: A specific cognitive disorder of 'mind-blindness'. *International Review of Psychiatry*, *2*, 81–90.

(1991a). The development of a theory of mind in autism: Deviance and delay? *Psychiatric Clinics of North America*, *14*, 33–51.

(1991b). Do people with autism understand what causes emotion? *Child Development*, *62*, 385–95.

(1991c). Precursors to a theory of mind: Understanding attention in others. In A. Whiten (ed.), *Natural Theories of Mind: Evolution, Development and Simulation of Everyday Mindreading*, pp. 233–51. Oxford: Basil Blackwell.

(1992). Out of sight or out of mind: another look at deception in autism. *Journal of Child Psychology and Psychiatry*, *33*, 1141–55.

(1993). From attention-goal psychology to belief-desire psychology: the development of a theory of mind and its dysfunction. In S. Baron-Cohen, H. Tager-Flusberg, and D. J. Cohen (eds.), *Understanding Other Minds: Perspectives from Autism*. Oxford: Oxford University Press.

(1994). How to build a baby that can read minds: cognitive mechanisms in mind-reading. *Cahiers de Psychologie Cognitive/ Current Psychology of Cognition*, *13*, 513–52.

(1995a). *Mindblindness*. MIT Press/Bradford Books.

(1995b). The Eye-Direction Detector (EDD) and the Shared Attention Mechanism (SAM): two cases for evolutionary psychology. In C. Moore, and P. Dunham (eds.), *The Role of Joint Attention in Development*. Hillsdale, NJ: Erlbaum.

Baron-Cohen, S., Allen, J., and Gillberg, C. (1992). Can autism be detected at 18 months? The needle, the haystack, and the CHAT. *British Journal of Psychiatry*, *161*, 839–43.

Baron-Cohen, S., Campbell, R., Karmiloff-Smith, A., Grant, J., and Walker, J. (1995). Are children with autism blind to the mentalistic significance of the eyes? *British Journal of Developmental Psychology*. In press.

Baron-Cohen, S., Cox, A., Baird, G., Swettenham, J., Drew, A., and Charman, T. (1994). Psychological markers in the detection of autism in infancy, in a large population. Unpublished manuscript, University of Cambridge.

Baron-Cohen, S., and Cross, P. (1992). Reading the eyes: evidence for the role of perception in the development of a theory of mind. *Mind and Language*, *6*, 173-86.

Baron-Cohen, S., and Goodhart, F. (1994). The 'seeing leads to knowing' deficit in autism: the Pratt and Bryant probe. *British Journal of Developmental Psychology*, *12*, 397-402.

Baron-Cohen, S., Leslie, A., and Frith, U. (1985). Does the autistic child have a 'theory of mind'? *Cognition, 21*, 37-46.

(1986). Mechanical, behavioural and intentional understanding of picture stories in autistic children. *British Journal of Developmental Psychology*, *4*, 113-25.

Baron-Cohen, S., and Ring, H. (1994a). A model of the mindreading system: neuropsychological and neurobiological perspectives. In C. Lewis and P. Mitchell (eds.), *Children in Early Understanding of Mind: Origins and Development*. Hillsdale, NJ: Erlbaum.

(1994b). The relationship between EDD and ToMM: neuro-psychological and neurobiological perspectives. In C. Lewis, and P. Mitchell (eds.), *Children in Early Understanding of Mind: Origins and Development.* Hillsdale, NJ: Erlbaum.

Baron-Cohen, S., Tager-Flusberg, H., and Cohen, D. J. (eds.), (1993). *Understanding Other Minds. Perspectives from Autism*. Oxford: Oxford University Press.

Barresi, J., and Moore, C. (in press). Intentional relations and social understanding. *Behavioural and Brain Sciences*.

Bartsch, K., and Wellman, H. M. (1989). Young children's attribution of action to beliefs and desires. *Child Development, 60*, 946-64.

(1995). *Children Talk About the Mind*. New York: Oxford University Press.

Bates, E., Benigni, L., Bretherton, I., Camaioni, L., and Volterra, V. (1979). Cognition and communication from 9-13 months: correlational findings. In E. Bates (ed.), *The emergence of symbols: cognition and communication in infancy*. New York: Academic Press.

Bates, E., Camaioni, L., and Volterra, V. (1975). The acquisition of performatives prior to speech. *Merrill-Palmer Quarterly*, *21*, 205-26.

Baumrind, D. (1971). Current patterns of parental authority. *Developmental Psychology Monographs, 4* (1, Part 2).

Bennett, J. (1976). *Linguistic Behaviour*. Cambridge: Cambridge University Press.

(1978). Some remarks about concepts. *Behavioral and Brain Sciences, 1*, 557-60.

(1991). How to read minds in behaviour: a suggestion from a philosopher. In A. Whiten (ed.), *Natural Theories of Mind: Evolution, Development and Simulation of Everyday Mindreading*. Oxford: Basil Blackwell.

Bennett, K., and Harvey, P. (1985). Brain size, development and metabolism in birds and mammals. *Journal of Zoology, 207*, 491-509.

Bischof-Köhler, D (1988). Uber der Zusammenhang von Empathie und der Fahigkeit, sich im Spiegel zu erkennen [On the association between empathy and ability to recognize oneself in the mirror]. *Schhweizerische Zeitschrift für Psychologie, 47*, 147-59.

Bishop, D. (1989). Autism, Asperger's syndrome and senatic-pragmatic disorder:

where are the boundaries? *British Journal of Disorders of Communication, 24,* 107–21.

(1993). Autism, executive function and theory of mind. *Journal of Child Psychology and Psychiatry, 34,* 279–93.

Bishop, D., North, and Donlan, C. (in press). Genetic basis of specific language disorder: evidence from a twin study. *Developmental Medicine and Child Neurology.*

Bishop, D., and Rosenbloom, L. (1987). Classification of childhood language disorders. In W. Yule, and M. Rutter (eds.), *Language Development and Disorders. Clinics in Developmental Medicine.* London: Mac Keith Press.

Blackburn, S. (1992). Theory, observation and drama. *Mind and Language, 7,* 187–203.

Boakes, R. (1984). *From Darwin to Behaviourism: Psychology and the Minds of Animals.* Cambridge: Cambridge University Press.

Boden, M. (1990). *The Philosophy of Artificial Intelligence.* Oxford: Oxford University Press.

Bolton, P., and Rutter, M. (1990). Genetic influences in autism. *International Review of Psychiatry, 2,* 67–80.

Boucher, J. (1976). Is autism primarily a language disorder? *British Journal of Disorders of Communication, 11,* 135–43.

Bowler, D. M. (1992). 'Theory of mind' in Asperger's Syndrome. *Journal of Child Psychology and Psychiatry, 33,* 877–93.

Bowler, D. M., and Norris, M. (1993). Predictors of success on false belief tasks in pre-school children. Paper presented at the 6th European Conference on Developmental Psychology, Bonn.

Braverman, M. *et al.* (1989). Affect comprehension in children with pervasive developmental disorders. *Journal of Autism and Developmental Disorders, 19,* 301–16.

Brown, R. (1980). The maintenance of conversation. In D. R. Olson (ed.), *The Social Foundation of Thought and Language,* pp. 187–210. London: Norton.

Brown, J. R., and Dunn, J. (1991). 'You can cry, mum': The social and developmental implications of talk about internal states. *British Journal of Developmental Psychology, 9,* 237–56.

Brownell, C. A., and Carriger, M. S. (1990). Changes in cooperation and self-other distinction during the second year. *Child Development, 61,* 1164–74.

Bruner, J. (1983). *Child's talk: learning to use language.* Oxford: Oxford University Press.

(1990). *Acts of Meaning.* Cambridge, MA: Harvard University Press.

Bruner, J., and Feldman, C. (1993). Theories of mind and the problem of autism. In S. Baron-Cohen, H. Tager-Flusberg and D. Cohen (eds.), *Understanding Other Minds. Perspectives from Autism.* Oxford: Oxford University Press.

Burma, B. H. (1949). Reality, existence, and classification: A discussion of the species problem. *Madroño, 127,* 193–209.

Butterworth, G. (1991). The ontogeny and phylogeny of joint visual attention. In A. Whiten (ed.), *Natural Theories of Mind: Evolution, Development and Simulation of Everyday Mindreading.* Oxford: Basil Blackwell.

Butterworth, G., and Cochran, E. (1980). Towards a mechanism of joint visual attention in human infancy. *Int. J. Behav. Develop. 3.*

Butterworth, G. and Jarrett, N. (1991). What minds have in common is space: spatial mechanisms serving joint visual attention in infancy. *British Journal of Developmental Psychology.* 9.

Byrne, R. W., and Whiten, A. (eds.), (1988). *Machiavellian Intelligence: Social Expertise and the Evolution of Intellect in Monkeys, Apes, and Humans.* Oxford: Blackwell.

(1990). Tactical deception in primates: the 1990 database. *Primate Report, 27,* 1–101.

(1991). Computation and mindreading in primate tactical deception. In A. Whiten (ed.), *Natural Theories of Mind: Evolution, Development and Simulation of Everyday Mindreading.* Oxford: Basil Blackwell.

(1992). Cognitive evolution in primates: Evidence from tactical deception? *Man (N.S.), 27,* 609–27.

Carey, S. (1985). *Conceptual Change in Childhood.* Cambridge, MA: Bradford Books: MIT Press.

(1988). Conceptual differences between children and adults, *Mind and Language, 3(3),* 167–83.

Carruthers, P. (1992). *Human Knowledge and Human Nature.* Oxford: Oxford University Press.

(1996). *Language, Thought, and Consciousness: An Essay in Philosophical Psychology.* Cambridge: Cambridge University Press.

Case, R. (1985). *Intellectual Development.* Orlando, FL: Academic Press.

(1989, April). A neo-Piagetian analysis of the child's understanding of other people, and the internal conditions which motivate their behavior. Paper presented at the Biennial Meeting of the Society for Research in Child Development, Kansas City, MO.

Chance, M. R. A. (1967). Attention structure as the basis of primate rank orders. *Man, 2,* 503–18.

Chamberlin, T. C. (1897). The method of multiple working hypotheses. *Journal of Geology, 5,* 837–48.

Charman, T., and Baron-Cohen, S. (1992). Understanding drawings and beliefs: A further test of the metarepresentation theory of autism. *Journal of Child Psychology and Psychiatry, 33,* 1105–12.

Cheney, D. L., and Seyfarth, R. M. (1990a). Attending to behaviour versus attending to knowledge: Examining monkeys' attribution of mental states. *Animal Behaviour, 40,* 742–53.

(1990b). *How Monkeys See the World.* Chicago: University of Chicago Press.

(1991). Reading minds or reading behaviour? Tests for a theory of mind in monkeys. In A. Whiten (Ed.), *Natural Theories of Mind: Evolution, Development and Simulation of Everyday Mindreading,* pp. 175–94. Oxford: Basil Blackwell.

(1992). Characterizing the mind of another species. *Behavioral and Brain Sciences, 15,* 172-9.

Chevalier-Skolnikoff, S. (1983). Sensorimotor development in orang-utans and other primates. *Journal of Human Evolution, 12,* 545–61.

Chomsky, N. (1965). *Aspects of the theory of syntax.* Cambridge, MA: MIT Press.

(1980). *Rules and Representations.* New York: Columbia University Press.

(1986). *Knowledge of Language: Its Nature, Origin and Use.* New York: Preager.

Churchland, P. M. (1981). Eliminative materialism and the propositional attitudes. *Journal of Philosophy*, *78*, 67–90.

(1988). *Matter and Consciousness* (revised edition). Cambridge, MA.: MIT Press.

(1989). *A Neurocomputational Perspective*. Cambridge, MA: Bradford Books/MIT Press.

Clements, W. A., and Perner, J. (1994). Implicit understanding of belief. *Cognitive Development*, *9*, 377–95.

Cole, M., and Scribner, S. (1978). Introduction. In L. S. Vygotsky, *Mind in Society*. Cambridge, MA: Harvard University Press.

Collin, F. (1985). *Theory and Understanding*. Oxford: Basil Blackwell.

Collingwood, R. G. (1946). *The Idea of History*. Oxford: Oxford University Press.

Corkum, V., and Moore, C. (in press). In C. Moore and P. Dunham (eds.), *Joint Attention: Its Origin and Role in Development*, Hillsdale, NJ: Erlbaum.

Courschesne, E. (1992). A neurophysiological view of autism. In E. Schopler and G. Mesibov (eds.), *Neurobiological Issues in Autism*. New York: Plenum Press.

Cunningham, M. A. (1968). A comparison of the language of psychotic and non-psychotic children who are mentally retarded, *Journal of Child Psychology and Psychiatry*, *9*, 229–44.

Currie, G. (1990). *The Nature of Fiction*. New York: Cambridge University Press.

(1995). Imagination and simulation: Aesthetics meets cognitive science. In A. Stone and M. Davies (eds.), *Mental Simulation: Evaluations and applications*. Oxford: Basil Blackwell.

(forthcoming). Mental Imagery as the Simulation of Vision.

(In preparation). Mental Simulation: Theory and Evidence.

Davidson, D. (1980). Psychology as philosophy. In D. Davidson (ed.), *Essays on actions and events*. Oxford: Oxford University Press.

Davies, M. (1994). The mental simulation debate. *Proceedings of the British Academy*, *83*, 99–127.

Davies, M. and Stone, T. (eds.), (1995). *Folk Psychology and the Theory of Mind Debate: Core Readings*. Oxford: Basil Blackwell.

Dawson, G., and Lewy, A. (1989). Reciprocal subcortical influences in autism: the role of attentional mechanisms. In G. Dawson (ed.), *Autism: Nature, Diagnosis and Treatment*. New York: Guilford Press.

Dennett, D. C. (1978). Artificial intelligence as philosophy and psychology. In D. C. Dennett, *Brainstorms*. Cambridge, MA: Bradford Books/MIT Press.

(1981). Making sense of ourselves. *Philosophical Topics*, *12*, Number 1; reprinted as J.I. Biro and R.W. Shahan (eds.), *Mind, Brain, and Function: Essays in the Philosophy of Mind*, Brighton: Harvester Press, 1982, 63–81. Reprinted in *The Intentional Stance*. Cambridge, MA.: MIT Press, 83–101.

(1983). Intentional systems in cognitive ethology: The 'Panglossian paradigm' defended. *Behavioral and Brain Sciences*, *6*, 343–90.

(1987). *The Intentional Stance*. Cambridge, MA: MIT Press.

(1984). Cognitive wheels: the frame problem of AI. In C. Hookway (ed.), *Minds Machines and Evolution*. Cambridge: Cambridge University Press. Reprinted in Boden (1990).

(1988). The intentional stance in theory and practice. In R. W. Byrne, and A.

Whiten (eds.), *Machiavellian Intelligence: Social Expertise and the Evolution of Intellect*. Oxford: Oxford University Press.

De Villiers, J. G. (March, 1995). Steps in the mastery of sentence complements. Paper presented at the Biennial Meeting of the Society for Research in Child Development, Indianapolis, IN.

De Waal, F. B. M. (1982). *Chimpanzee Politics*. London: Jonathan Cape.

Doherty, M. (1994). Metalinguistic awareness and theory of mind: Two words for the same thing. Paper presented at the Hang Seng Theories of Theories of Mind Conference, Sheffield, 13–16th July, 1994.

Donaldson, M. (1978). *Children's Minds*. London: Fontana.

Doré, F., and Mercier, P. (1992). *Les Fondements de l'Apprentissage et de la Cognition*. Lille: Presses Universitaires de Lille.

Dreyfus, H. L., and Dreyfus, S. (1986). *Mind over Machine*. New York: Free Press, Macmillan.

Dunn, J. (1988). *The Beginnings of Social Understanding*. Cambridge, MA: Harvard University Press.

——— (1991). Understanding others: Evidence from naturalistic studies of children. In A. Whiten (ed.), *Naturalistic Theories of Mind: Evolution, Development and Simulation of Everyday Mindreading*, pp 233–51, Oxford: Basil Blackwell.

——— (1994). Changing minds and changing relationships. In C. Lewis and P. Mitchell (eds.), *Children's Early Understanding of Mind: Origins and Development*, pp. 297–310. Hove, U.K.: Erlbaum.

Dunn, J., Brown, J., and Beardsall, L. (1991). Family talk about feeling states and children's later understanding of others' emotions. *Developmental Psychology, 27*, 448–55.

Dunn, J., Brown, J., Slomkowski, C., Tesla, C., and Youngblade, L. (1991). Young children's understanding of other people's feelings and beliefs: individual differences and their antecedents. *Child Development, 62*, 1352–66.

Eddy, T. J., Gallup, G. G. Jr, and Povinelli, D. J. (1993). Attribution of cognitive states to animals: Anthropomorphism in comparative perspective. *Journal of Social Issues, 49*, 87–101.

Eisenmajer, R., and Prior, M. (1991). Cognitive linguistic correlates of 'theory of mind' ability in autistic children. *British Journal of Developmental Psychology, 9*, 351–64.

Eisenberg, N., and Strayer, J. (1987a). *Empathy and its Development*. New York: Cambridge University Press.

——— (1987b). Critical issues in the study of empathy. In Eisenberg and Strayer, *Empathy and its Development*. New York: Cambridge University Press.

Evans, G. (1982). *The Varieties of Reference*. Oxford: Oxford University Press.

Farah, M. (1984). The neurological basis of mental imagery: a componential analysis. *Cognition 18*, 245–72.

Fein, D., Pennington, B., Markowitz, P., Braverman, M., and Waterhouse, L. (1986). Toward a neuropsychological model of infantile autism: are the social deficits primary? *Journal of the American Academy of Child Psychiatry, 25*, 198–212.

Feldman, C. F. (1992). The new theory of theory of mind. *Human Development, 35*, 107–17.

Fivush, R., Gray, J. T., and Fromhoff, F. A. (1987). Two-year-olds talk about the past. *Cognitive Development, 2*, 393–409.

Flavell, J. H. (1988). From cognitive connections to mental representations. In J.W. Astington, P. L. Harris and D. R. Olson (eds.), *Developing Theories of Mind*, pp. 244–67. Cambridge, Cambridge University Press.

Flavell, J. H., Everett, B. A., Croft, K., and Flavell, E. R. (1981). Young children's knowledge about visual perception: further evidence for the level 1-level 2 distinction. *Developmental Psychology, 17*, 99–103.

Flavell, J. H., Flavell, E. R., and Green, F. L. (1987). Young children's knowledge about the apparent-real and pretend-real distinctions. *Developmental Psychology, 23*, 816–22.

Flavell, J. H., Flavell, E. R., Green, F. L., and Wilcox, S. A. (1980). Young children's knowledge about visual perception: effect of observer's distance from target on perceptual clarity of target. *Developmental Psychology, 16*, 10–12.

Fodor, J. (1968a). The appeal to tacit knowledge in psychological explanations, *Journal of Philosophy, 65*, 627–40.

(1968b). *Psychological Explanation*. New York: Random House.

(1975). *The Language of Thought*. New York: Thomas Y. Crowell.

(1983). *The Modularity of Mind: An Essay on Faculty Psychology*. Cambridge, MA: MIT Press.

(1987). *Psychosemantics: The Problem of Meaning in the Philosophy of Mind*. Cambridge, MA: MIT Press.

(1992). A theory of the child's theory of mind. *Cognition, 44*, 283–96.

Folstein, S., and Rutter, M. (1988). Autism: familial aggregation and genetic implications. *Journal of Autism and Developmental Disorders, 18*, 3–30.

Fox, M. W. (1982). Are most animals 'mindless automotons'? A reply to Gordon G. Gallup Jr. *American Journal of Primatology, 3*, 341–3.

Frankfurt, H. (1971). Freedom of the will and the concept of a person. *Philosophical Review, 68*, 5–20.

Frege, G. (1892). On sense and reference. *Zeitschrift fur Philosophie und philosophische Kritik, 100*, 25–50. Reprinted in P. Geach, and M. Black (eds., 1970). *Translations from the philosophical writings of Gottlob Frege*. Oxford: Basil Blackwell.

Frith, C. (1992). *The Cognitive Neuropsychology of Schizophrenia*. Hove, UK: Lawrence Erlbaum Associates.

Frith, U. (1989). *Autism: Explaining the Enigma*. Oxford: Basil Blackwell.

(Ed.), (1991). *Autism and Asperger's Syndrome*. Cambridge. Cambridge University Press.

Frith, U., and Happé, F. (1994). Autism: beyond 'theory of mind'. *Cognition, 50*, 115–32.

Frith, U., Happé, F., and Siddons, F. (1994). Autism and theory of mind in everyday life. *Social Development, 3*, 108–23.

Frith, U., and Hermelin, B. (1969). The role of visual and motor cues for normal, subnormal and autistic children. *Journal of Child Psychology and Psychiatry, 10*, 153–63.

Frith, U., Morton, J., and Leslie, A. M. (1991). The cognitive basis of a biological disorder: autism. *Trends in Neurosciences, 14*, 433–8.

Frye, D., Zelazo, P. D., and Palfai, T. (Unpublished manuscript). *The cognitive basis of theory of mind*. New York University.

Furrow, D., Moore, C., Davidge and Chiasson, L. (1992). Mental terms in mothers' and children's speech: similarities and relationships. *Journal of Child Language, 19,* 617–31.

Gallup, G. G., Jr (1970). Chimpanzees: self-recognition. *Science, 167,* 86–7.

(1982). Self-awareness and the emergence of mind in primates. *American Journal of Primatology,* 2, 237–48.

Gallup, G. G., Jr, Nash, R. F., and Ellison, A. L., Jr (1971). Tonic immobility as a reaction to predation: artificial eyes as a fear stimulus for chickens. *Psychonomic Science, 23,* 79–80.

Gallup, G. G., Jr, Povinelli, D. J., Suarez, S. D., Anderson, J. R., Lethmate, J., and Menzel, E. W. (in press). Further reflections on self-recognition in primates. *Animal Behaviour.*

Gallup, GG., Jr and Suarez, SD. (1986). Self-awareness and the emergence of mind in humans and other primates. In J. Suls and A.G. Greenwald (eds.). *Psychological Perspectives on the Self. Volume 3,* (pp 3–26). Hillsdale, NJ: Erlbaum.

Geertz, C. (1973). *The Interpretation of Cultures.* New York: Basic Books.

Ghiselin, M. T. (1975). A radical solution to the species problem. *Systematic Zoology, 23,* 536–44.

Gillberg, C. (1992). Autism and autistic-like conditions. Subclasses among disorders of empathy. *Journal of Child Psychology and Psychiatry, 33,* 813–42.

Goldman, A. (1989). Interpretation psychologized. *Mind and Language, 4,* 161–85.

(1992a). Empathy, mind, and morals. *Proceedings and Addresses of the American Philosophical Association, 66* (3).

(1992b). In defense of the simulation theory. *Mind and Language, 7,* 104–19.

(1993a). The psychology of folk psychology. *Behavioural and Brain Sciences, 16,* 15–28.

(1993b). *Philosophical Applications of Cognitive Science.* Boulder, CO: Westview Press.

Gómez, J. C. (1990). The emergence of intentional communication as a problem-solving strategy in the gorilla. In S. T. Parker and K. R. Gibson (eds.), *'Language' and Intelligence in Monkeys and Apes: Comparative Developmental Perspectives* (pp. 333–55). Cambridge, MA.: Cambridge University Press.

(1991). Visual behaviour as a window for reading the mind of others in primates. In A. Whiten (ed.), *Natural Theories of Mind: Evolution, Development and Simulation of Everyday Mindreading.* Oxford: Basil Blackwell.

(1992). *El desarrollo de la comunicación intencional en el gorila.* Ph.D. Dissertation, Universidad Autónoma de Madrid.

(1993). Intentions, agents and enculturated apes. Behavioural and Brain sciences, *16* (3), 520–1.

(1994). Shared attention in ontogeny and phylogeny: SAM, TOM, Grice, and the great apes. *Cahiers de Psychologie Cognitive/Current Psychology of Cognition, 13(5),* 590–8.

(in press). Ostensive behavior in the great apes: the role of eye contact. In A. Russon, S. Parker, and K. Bard (eds.), *Reaching into Thought,* Cambridge, MA.: Cambridge University Press.

Gómez, J. C., and Teixidor, P. (1992). Theory of mind in an orangutan: a nonverbal test of false-belief appreciation? Paper presented at the *XIV Congress of the International Primatological Society. Strasbourg, August.*

Gómez, J. C., Sarriá, E., and Tamarit, J. (1993). The comparative study of early communication and theories of mind: ontogeny, phylogeny and pathology. In S. Baron-Cohen, H. Tager-Flusberg, and D. Cohen (eds.), *Understanding Other Minds: Perspectives from Autism,* pp. 397–426. Oxford: Oxford University Press.

Goodman, N. (1947). The problem of counterfactual conditionals. *Journal of Philosophy 44,* 113–28.

Goodman, R. (1989). Infantile autism: A syndrome of multiple primary deficits? *Journal of Autism and Developmental Disorders, 19,* 409–24.

Gopnik, A. (1988). Conceptual and semantic development as theory change. *Mind and Language, 3(3),* 197–217.

(1990). Developing the idea of intentionality: Children's theories of mind. *Canadian Journal of Philosophy, 20,* 89–114.

(1993). How we know our minds: The illusion of first-person knowledge of intentionality. *Behavioral and Brain Sciences, 16,* 1–14.

Gopnik, A., and Astington, J. W. (1988). Children's understanding of representational change and its relation to the understanding of false belief and the appearance-reality distinction. *Child Development, 59,* 26–37.

Gopnik, A., and Graf, P. (1988). Knowing how you know: Young children's ability to identify and remember the sources of their beliefs. *Child Development, 59,* 1366–71.

Gopnik, A., and Melzoff, A. N. (1993). The role of imitation in understanding persons and in developing a theory of mind. In S. Baron-Cohen H. Tager-Flusberg and D. J Cohen (eds.), *Understanding Other Minds: Perspectives from Autism.* Oxford: Oxford University Press.

Gopnik, A., Melzoff, A. N., and Slaughter V. (1994) Changing your views: How understanding visual perception can lead to a new theory of mind. In C. Lewis and P. Mitchell (eds.), *Children's Early Undertaking of Mind,* Hilsdale, NJ: Erlbaum.

Gopnik, A., and Wellman, H. M. (1992). Why the child's theory of mind really *is* a theory. *Mind and Language, 7:*1–2, 145–71.

(1994). The 'theory theory'. In L. Hirshfield and S. Gelman, (eds.), *Domain-Specificity in Cultural Cognition.* New York: Cambridge University Press.

Gordon, R. M. (1986). Folk psychology as simulation. *Mind and Language, 1,* 158–71.

(1992a). The simulation theory: Objections and misconceptions. *Mind and Language, 7,* 11–34.

(1992b). Reply to Stich and Nichols. *Mind and Language, 7,* 85–97.

(1992c). Reply to Perner and Howes. *Mind and Language, 7,* 98–103.

(1995a). Simulation without introspection or inference from me to you. In T. Stone and M. Davies (eds.). *Mental simulation: Evaluations and Applications.* Oxford: Blackwell.

(1995b). Sympathy, simulation and the impartial spectator, *Ethics,* forthcoming. Reprinted in L. May, M. Friedman and A. Clark (eds.), *Mind and Morals,* Cambridge, Mass: MIT Press.

Gordon, R. M., and Barker, J. (1994). Autism and the theory of mind debate. In G. Graham and G. Stephens (eds.), *Philosophical Psychopathology.* Cambridge, MA: MIT Press.

Gould, S. J. (1977). *Ontogeny and Phylogeny*. Cambridge, MA: Harvard University Press.

Gould, S. J., and Vrba, E. (1982). Exaptation – a missing term in the science of form. *Paleobiology 8*, 4–15.

Greenfield, P. M., and Savage-Rumbaugh, S. (1990). Grammatical combination in *Pan paniscus*: processes of learning and invention in the evolution and development of language. In S. T. Parker and K. R. Gibson (eds.), *'Language' and Intelligence in Monkeys and Apes: Comparative Developmental Perspectives*, pp. 540–78. Cambridge: Cambridge University Press.

(1993). Comparing communicative competence in child and chimp: the pragmatics of repetition. *Journal of Child Language, 20*, 1–26.

Griffin, D. (1976). *The Question of Animal Awareness: Evolutionary Continuity and Mental Experience*. New York : Rockefeller University Press.

Hadwin, J., and Perner, J. (1991). Pleased and surprised: children's cognitive theory of emotion. *British Journal of Developmental Psychology, 9*, 215–34.

Hallock, M. B., Worobey, J. and Self, P. A (1989). Behavioural development in chimpanzees (*Pan troglodytes*) and human neonates across the first month of life. *International Journal of Behavioural Development, 12*, 527–40.

Halle, M., and Stevens, K. (1962). Speech recognition: a model and a program for research. In Fodor and Katz (eds.), *The Structure of Language: Readings in the Philosophy of Language*. Englewood Cliffs, NJ: Prentice-Hall.

Happé, F. G. E. (1993). Communicative competence and the theory of mind in autism. A test of relevance theory. *Cognition, 48*, 101–19.

(1994a). Current psychological theories of autism: the 'theory of mind' account and rival theories. *Journal of Child Psychology and Psychiatry. 35*, 215–30.

(1994b). Pretending and planning. In S. Baron-Cohen H. Tager-Flusberg and D. J Cohen (eds.), *Understanding Other Minds: Perspectives from Autism*. Oxford: Oxford University Press.

Harris, P. L. (1989). *Children and Emotion: The Development of Psychological Understanding*. Oxford: Basil Blackwell.

(1991). The work of the imagination. In A. Whiten (ed.), *Natural Theories of Mind: The Evolution, Development and Simulation of Everyday Mindreading*. Oxford: Basil Blackwell.

(1992). From simulation to folk psychology: The case for development. *Mind and Language, 7*, 120–44.

(1993). Pretending and planning. In S. Baron-Cohen H. Tager-Flusberg and D. J Cohen (eds.), *Understanding Other Minds: Perspectives from Autism*. Oxford: Oxford University Press.

Harris, P. L., Brown, E., Marriott, C., Whittall, S., and Harmer, S. (1991). Monsters, ghosts and witches: testing the limits of the fantasy-reality distinction in young children. *British Journal of Developmental Psychology, 9*, 105–23.

Harris, P. L., Johnson, C. N., Hutton, D., Andrews, G. and Cooke, T. (1989). Young children's theory of mind and emotion. *Cognition and Emotion, 3*, 379–400.

Harris, P. L., and Kavanaugh, R. D. (1993). Young children's understanding of pretence. *Society for Research in Child Development Monographs* (Serial No. 237).

Harris, P. L., Kavanaugh, R. D., and Meredith, M. (1994). Young children's comprehension of pretend episodes: the integration of successive actions. *Child Development, 65*, 16–30.

Haugeland, J. (1978). The nature and plausibility of cognitivism. *The Behavioral and Brain Sciences,* 1.

Heal, J. (1986). Replication and functionalism. In J. Butterfield (ed.), *Language, Mind, and Logic* (pp. 135–50). Cambridge, Cambridge University Press.

(1994). Simulation vs. theory-theory: what is at issue? *Proceedings of the British Academy, 83,* 129–44.

(1995). How to think about thinking. In T. Stone and M. Davies (eds.), *Mental Simulation: Evaluations and Applications.* Oxford: Basil Blackwell.

Heath, S.B. (1983). *Ways with Words.* Cambridge: Cambridge University Press.

Heelas, P., and Lock, A. (eds.), (1981). *Indigenous Psychologies.* London: Academic Press.

Heider, F. (1958). *The Psychology of Interpersonal Relations.* New York: Wiley.

Hermelin, B., and O'Connor, N.(1970). *Psychological Experiments with Autistic Children.* Oxford: Pergamon.

Hess, J., Novak, M. A., and Povinelli, D. J. (1993). 'Natural pointing' in a rhesus monkey, but no evidence of empathy. *Animal Behaviour, 46,* 1023–5.

Heyes, C. M. (1993). Anecdotes, training, trapping, and triangulating: do animals attribute mental states? *Animal Behaviour, 47,* 177–88.

(1994a). Reflections on self-recognition in primates. *Animal Behaviour, 47,* 909–19.

(1994b). Cues, convergence and a curmudgeon: a reply to Povinelli. *Animal Behaviour, 48,* 242–4.

Higginbotham, J. (1987). The autonomy of syntax and semantics. In J. Garfield (ed.), *Modularity in Knowledge Representation and Natural Language Understanding.* Cambridge MA: MIT Press.

Hobson, R. P. (1986). The autistic child's appraisal of expressions of emotion. A further study. *Journal of Child Psychology and Psychiatry, 27,* 671–80.

(1991). Against the theory of 'theory of mind'. *British Journal of Developmental Psychology, 9,* 33–51.

(1993a). *Autism and the Development of Mind.* Hove, UK: Erlbaum.

(1993b). Understanding persons: the role of affect. In S. Baron-Cohen, H. Tager-Flusberg and D. Cohen (eds.), *Understanding Other Minds: Perspectives from Autism.* Oxford University Press.

Hoffman, M. (1984). Interaction of affect and cognition in empathy. In C. Izard, J. Kagan, and R. Zajonc (eds.), *Emotions, Cognitions, and Behavior,* pp. 103–31. New York: Cambridge University Press.

(1987). The contribution of empathy to justice and moral judgement. In N. Eisenberg, and J. Strayer, (1987). *Empathy and its Development.* New York: Cambridge University Press.

Hoffman, W. L., and Prior, M. R. (1982). Neuropsychological dimensions of autism in children: a test of the hemispheric dysfunction hypothesis. *Journal of Clinical Neurology, 4,* 27–41.

Hogrefe, G., Wimmer, H., and Perner, J. (1986). Ignorance versus false belief: a developmental lag in attribution of epistemic states. *Child Development, 57,* 567–82.

Holland, D., and Quinn, N. (eds.), (1987). *Cultural Models in Language and Thought.* Cambridge: Cambridge University Press.

Holmes, H. A., Roldan, C., and Miller, S. A. (1994). *A cross-task comparison of false belief understanding in a Head Start population.* Unpublished manuscript, University of Florida.

Hood, L., and Bloom, L. (1979). What, when and how about why: a longitudinal study of early expressions of causality. *Monographs of the Society for Research in Child Development, 44*, Serial no 181.

Howes, C., and Matheson, C. C. (1992). Sequences in the development of competent play with peers. social and pretend play. *Developmental Psychology, 28*, 961–74.

Hresko, W. P., Reid, D. K., and Hammill, D. D. (1981). *The Test of Early Language Development (TELD)*. Austin, TX: Pro-Ed.

Hudson, J. A. (1990). The emergence of autobiographical memory in mother-child conversation. In R. Fivush and J. A. Hudson (eds.), *Knowing and Remembering in Young Children.* Cambridge: Cambridge University Press.

Hume, D. (1739/1978). *A Treatise of Human Nature*, 2nd edn., L.A. Selby-Bigge (ed.), with text rev. and variant readings by P. H. Nidditch, Oxford: Oxford University Press.

Hummer, P., Wimmer, H., and Antes, G. (1993). On the origins of denial negation. *Journal of Child Language, 20*, 607–18.

Hurlburt, R., Happé, F., and Frith, U. (1994). Sampling the form of inner experience of three adults with Asperger syndrome. *Psychological Medicine, 24*.

Jarrold, C., Boucher, J., and Smith, P. K. (in preparation). Generativity deficits in pretend play in autism.

(1994). Executive function deficits and the pretend play of children with autism. A research note, *Journal of Child Psychology and Psychiatry*, 1473–82.

Jarrold, C., Carruthers, P., Smith, P., and Boucher, J. (1994). Pretend play: is it metarepresentational? *Mind and Language, 9*, 445–68.

Jarrold, C., Smith, P. K., Boucher, J., and Harris, P. (1994). Children with autism's comprehension of pretence, *Journal of Autism and Developmental Disorders, 24*, No 4.

Jenkins, J. M., and Astington, J. W. (in press). Cognitive factors and family structure associated with theory of mind development in young children. *Development Psychology*.

Johnson, C. N. (1988). Theory of mind and the structure of conscious experience. In J. W. Astington, P. L. Harris, and D. R. Olson (eds.), *Developing Theories of Mind*. New York: Cambridge University Press.

(1991, April). From anticipation to reflection: biological, cognitive and social underpinnings of children's understanding of intentionality. Paper presented at the Biennial Meeting of the Society for Research in Child Development, Seattle, WA.

Johnson, D. B. (1982). Altruistic behavior and the development of the self in infants. *Merrill-Palmer Quarterly, 28*, 379–88.

Johnson, M. H., and Morton, J. (1991). *Biology and Cognitive Development: The Case of Face Recognition*. Cambridge, MA: Blackwell.

Johnson–Laird, P. (1983). *Mental Models: Towards a Cognitive Science of Language, Inference and Consciousness*. Cambridge, MA: Harvard University Press.

Kagan, J. (1981). *The Second Year: The Emergence of Self-Awareness*. Cambridge, MA: Harvard University Press.

Kahneman, D., and Tversky, A. (1982). The simulation heuristic. In D. Kahneman, P. Slovic, and A. Tversky (eds.), *Judgement Under Uncertainty*. Cambridge: Cambridge University Press.

Kanner, L. (1943). Autistic disturbances of affective contact. *Nervous Child, 2*, 217–50.

Karmiloff-Smith, A. (1988). The child is a theoretician, not an inductivist. *Mind and Language 3*, 183–95.

(1992). *Beyond Modularity*. Cambridge, MA: MIT Press.

Karmiloff-Smith, A., and Inhelder, B. (1974/5). If you want to get ahead, get a theory. *Cognition 3:3*, 195–212.

Keil, F. C. (1989). *Concepts, Kinds, and Cognitive Development*. Cambridge, MA Bradford Books: MIT Press.

Klin, A., and Volkmar, F. (1993). The development of individuals with autism: implications for the theory of mind hypothesis. In S. Baron-Cohen, H. Tager-Flusberg and D. Cohen (eds.), *Understanding Other Minds: Perspectives from Autism*. Oxford: Oxford University Press.

Köhler, W. (1927). *The mentality of apes*. N. York: Vintage. [Original: *Intelligenzprüfungen an Menschenaffen*. Berlin: Springer, 1921.]

Kosslyn, S. (1981). The medium and the message in mental imagery: A theory. *Psychological Review, 88*, 46–66.

(1983). *Ghosts in the Mind's Machine*. New York: Norton.

(1994). *Image and Brain*. Cambridge, MA: Bradford Books/MIT Press.

Krauss, R. M., and Glucksberg, S. (1969). The development of communication: competence as a function of age. *Child Development, 42*, 255–66.

Krebs, J. R., and Dawkins, R. (1984). Animal signals: mindreading and manipulation. In J. R. Krebs and N. B. Davies (eds.), *Behavioural Ecology: An Evolutionary Approach*. Oxford: Basil Blackwell.

La Fontaine, J. S. (1984). Person and individual: some anthropological reflections. In M. Carrithers, S. Collins, and S. Lukes (eds.), *The Category of the Person: Anthropology, Philosophy, History*, pp. 123–40, Cambridge: Cambridge University Press.

Lakatos, I. (1970). Falsification and the methodology of scientific research programmes. In I. Lakatos and A. Musgrave (eds.), *Criticism and the Growth of Knowledge*. Cambridge: Cambridge University Press.

(1978). *Philosophical Papers, volume 1. The Methodology of Scientific Research Programmes*. Edited by G. Currie and J. Worrall. Cambridge: Cambridge University Press.

Lamb, S. (1991). First moral sense: Aspects and contributors to a beginning morality in the second year of life. In W. Kurtines and J. Gewirtz (eds.), *Handbook of Moral Behavior and Development, 2: Research*. Hillsdale, NJ: Erlbaum.

Langer, E. (1975). The illusion of control. *Journal of Personality and Social Psychology 32*, 311–28.

Langer, S. K. (1942). *Philosophy in a New Key*. Cambridge, MA: Harvard University Press.

Leekam, S., Baron-Cohen, S., Brown, S., Perrett, D., and Milders, M., (1994). Eye-Direction Detection: a dissociation between geometric and joint-attention skills in autism. Unpublished ms, Institute of Social and Applied Psychology, University of Kent, Canterbury.

Lempers, J. D., Flavell, E. R., and Flavell, J. H. (1977). The development in very young children of tacit knowledge concerning visual perception. *Genetic Psychology Monographs*, *95*, 3–53.

Leslie, A. M. (1987). Pretence and representation: the origins of 'theory of mind'. *Psychological Review*, *94*, 412–26.

 (1988). Some implications of pretence for mechanisms underlying the child's theory of mind. In J. Astington, Harris, P. L., and Olsen, D. R. (eds.), *Developing Theories of Mind*. Cambridge: Cambridge University Press.

 (1991) The theory of mind impairment in autism: evidence for a modular mechanism of development? In Whiten, A (ed.), *Natural Theories of Mind: Evolution, Development and Simulation of Everyday Mindreading*. Oxford: Basil Blackwell.

 (1992). Autism and the 'theory of mind' module. *Current Directions in Psychological Science*, *1*, 18–21.

 (1994a). Pretending and believing: issues in the theory of ToMM. *Cognition*, *50*, 211–38.

 (1994b). ToMM, ToBy, and agency: core architecture and domain specificity. In L. Hirschfeld and S. Gelman (eds.), *Mapping the Mind: Domain Specificity in Cognition and Culture*, pp. 119–48. New York: Cambridge University Press.

Leslie, A. M., and Frith, U. (1988). Autistic children's understanding of seeing, knowing, and believing. *British Journal of Developmental Psychology*, *6*, 315–24.

 (1990). Prospects for a cognitive neuropsychology of autism. Hobson's choice, *Psychological Review*, *97*, 122–31.

Leslie, A. M., and German, T. P. (1995). Knowledge and ability in 'theory of mind': one-eyed overview of a debate. In T. Stone, and M. Davies (eds.), *Mental Simulation: Evaluations and applications*. Oxford: Blackwell.

Leslie, A. M., and Roth, D. (1993). What autism teaches us about metarepresentation. In S. Baron Cohen, H. Tager-Flusberg, and D. Cohen (eds.), *Understanding Other Minds: Perspectives from Autism*. Oxford: Oxford University Press.

Leslie, A., and Thaiss, L. (1992). Domain specificity in conceptual development. neuropsychological evidence from autism. *Cognition*, *43*, 225–51.

Lewis, D. (1966). An argument for the identity theory. *Journal of Philosophy*, *63*, 17–25.

 (1972). Psychophysical and theoretical identifications. *Australasian Journal of Philosophy*, *50*, 249–58. Reprinted in N. Block (ed.), *Readings in Philosophy of Psychology, Volume 1*. London: Methuen, 1980.

 (1973). *Counterfactuals*. Cambridge, MA: Harvard University Press.

Lewis, M. M. (1938). The beginning and early functions of questions in a child's speech. *British Journal of Educational Psychology, 8, 150–71*.

Lewis, M., and Brooks-Gunn, J. (1979). *Social Cognition and the Acquisition of the Self*. New York: Plenum Press.

Lewis, M., Sullivan, M. W., Stanger, C., and Weiss, M. (1989). Self-development and self-conscious emotions. *Child Development*, *60*, 146–56.

Lewis, V., and Boucher, J. (1988). Spontaneous, instructed, and elicited play in relatively able autistic children. *British Journal of Developmental Psychology*, *6*, 315–24.

Lillard, A. S. (1993). Pretend play skills and the child's theory of mind. *Child Development, 64,* 348–71.

Lin, A. C., Bard, K. A., and Anderson, J. R. (1992). Development of self-recognition in chimpanzees (*Pan troglodytes*). *Journal of Comparative Psychology, 106,* 120–7.

Lutz, C. (1985). Ethnopsychology compared to what? Explaining behavior and consciousness among the Ifaluk. In G. M. White and J. Kirkpatrick (eds.), *Person, Self, and Experience.* pp 35–59. Berkeley: University of California Press.

(1987). Goals, events, and understanding in Ifaluk emotion theory. In D. Holland and N. Quinn (eds.), *Cultural Models in Language and Thought.* Cambridge: Cambridge University Press.

Malcolm, N. (1958). Knowledge of other minds. *Journal of Philosophy,* 55.

Markman, K., Gavanski, I., Sherman, S., and McMullen, M. (1993). The mental simulation of better and worse possible worlds. *Journal of Experimental Social Psychology 29,* 87–109.

Marks, J. (1994). Blood will tell (won't it?): a century of molecular discourse on anthropological systematics. *American Journal of Physical Anthropology, 94:* 59–79.

Marr, D. C. (1977). Artificial Intelligence: A personal view. *Artificial Intelligence, 9,* 37–48. Reprinted in Boden (1990).

(1982). *Vision,* New York: W. H. Freeman.

Mathieu, M., and Bergeron, G. (1981). Piagetian assessment on cognitive development in chimpanzees (*Pan troglodytes*). In A. B. Chiarelli and R. S. Corruccini (eds.), *Primate Behavior and Sociobiology,* pp. 142–7. New York, Springer-Verlag.

Mauss, M. (1984). A category of the human mind: the notion of person; the notion of self. In M. Carrithers, S. Collins, and S. Lukes (eds.), *The Category of the Person: Anthropology, Philosophy, History.* pp 1–25. Cambridge, Cambridge University Press.

Mayr, E. (1957). Difficulties and importance of the biological species concept. In E. Mayr, (ed.), *The Species Problem,* pp 371–88. Washington DC: American Association for the Advancement of Science.

McCormick, P. (1994). Children's understanding of mind: a case for cultural diversity. Unpublished doctoral dissertation, University of Toronto (OISE), Toronto, Ont.

McDowell, J. (1985). Functionalism and anomalous monism. In E. LePore and B. P. McLaughlin (eds.), *Actions and Events: Perspectives on the Philosophy of Donald Davidson.* Oxford: Basil Blackwell, 387–98.

Meltzoff, A. (1993). Molyneux's babies: Cross–modal perception, imitation and the mind of the preverbal infant. In N. Eilan, R. McCarthy, and B. Brewer (eds.), *Spatial Representation.* Cambridge, MA: Blackwell.

Meltzoff, A., and Gopnik, A. (1993). The role of imitation in understanding persons and developing a theory of mind. In S. Baron-Cohen, H. Tager-Flusberg and D. J. Cohen (eds.), *Understanding Other Minds: Perspectives from Autism.* Oxford: Oxford University Press.

Meltzoff, A., and Moore, M. (1983). Newborn infants imitate adult facial gestures, *Child Development 54,* 702–9.

Menzel, E. W. (1988). A group of young chimpanzees in a one-acre field: leadership and communication. In R. W. Byrne and A. Whiten (eds.), *Machiavellian Intelligence: Social Expertise and the Evolution of Intellect*. pp. 155–9. Oxford: Clarendon Press.

Menzel, E. W., Jr and Johnson, M. K. (1976). Communication and cognitive organization in humans and other animals. *Annals New York Academy of Sciences, 280*, 131–46.

Menzel, E. W., Savage-Rumbaugh, E. S., and Lawson, J. (1985). Chimpanzee (*Pan troglodytes*) spatial problem solving with the use of mirrors and televised equivalents of mirrors. *Journal of Comparative Psychology, 99*, 211–17.

Mignault, C. (1985). Transition between sensorimotor and symbolic activities in nursery-reared chimpanzees (*Pan troglodytes*). *Journal of Human Evolution, 14*, 747–58.

Miller, N. E. (1959). Liberalization of basic S-R concepts. In S. Koch (ed.), *Psychology: A Study of a Science*. New York: McGraw Hill.

Miller, P. H. (1993). *Theories of Developmental Psychology* (3rd edition). New York: Freeman.

Millikan, R. G. (1993). The myth of the essential indexical. In her *White Queen Psychology and other Essays for Alice*. Cambridge, Mass.: MIT Press.

Minshew, N. (1992). Neurological localisation in autism. In E. Schopler and G. Mesibov (eds.), *High-Functioning Individuals with Autism*. New York: Plenum Press.

Mitchell, P., and Lacohée, H. (1991). Children's early understanding of false belief. *Cognition, 39*, 107–27.

Mitchell, R. W. (1986). A framework for discussing deception. In R. W. Mitchell and N. S. Thompson (eds.), *Deception: Perspectives on Human and Non-Human Deceit*. pp.3–40. Albany, N.Y.: SUNY Press.

(1993). Mental models of mirror-self-recognition: two theories. *New Ideas in Psychology, 11*, 295–325.

Mitchell, R. W., Parker, S. T., and Boccia, M. L. (1994). Mirror self-recognition and mental state attribution. *American Psychologist, 49*, 761–2.

Moore, C., Furrow, D., Chiasson, L., and Patriquin, M. (1994). Developmental relationships between production and comprehension of mental terms. *First Language, 14*, 1–17.

Moore, C., Pure, K., and Furrow, D. (1990). Children's understanding of the modal expressions of speaker certainty and uncertainty and its relation to the development of a representational theory of mind. *Child Development, 61*, 722–30.

Morton, A. (1991). The inevitability of folk psychology. In R. J. Bogdan (ed.), *Mind and Common Sense*. Cambridge: Cambridge University Press.

Morton, J. (1989). The origins of autism. *New Scientist, 1694*, 44–7.

Mundy, P., Sigman, M., Ungerer, J. A., and Sherman, T. (1986). Defining the social deficits in autism: the contribution of non-verbal communication measures. *Journal of Child Psychology and Psychiatry, 27*, 657–69.

Nagell, K., Olguin, R. S., and Tomasello, M. (1993). Processes of social learning in the tool use of chimpanzees (*Pan troglodytes*) and human children (*Homo sapiens*). *Journal of Comparative Psychology, 107*, 174–86.

Naito, M., Komatsu, S., and Fuke, T. (1995). Normal and autistic children's understanding of their own and others' false belief: a study from Japan. *British Journal of Developmental Psychology 13*.

Nisbett, R., and Ross, L. (1980). *Human Inference: Strategies and Shortcomings of Social Judgement.* Englewood Cliffs, NJ: Prentice-Hall.

O'Keefe, J., and Nadel, L. (1978). *The Hippocampus as a Cognitive Map.* Oxford: Clarendon Press.

O'Neill, D. K. (1993). *The ability of 2-year-olds to make informative requests.* Unpublished doctoral dissertation, Stanford University.

O'Neill, D. K., and Gopnik, A. (1991). Young children's ability to identify the sources of their beliefs. *Developmental Psychology, 27,* 390–7.

Olson, D. R. (1988). On the origins of belief and other internal states in children. In J. W. Astington, P. L. Harris and D. R. Olson (eds.), *Developing Theories of Mind,* pp. 414–26. New York: Cambridge.

(1993). The development of representations: The origins of mental life. *Canadian Psychology, 34,* 1–14.

(1994). *The World on Paper.* Cambridge: Cambridge University Press.

Ornitz, E. M., and Ritvo, E. R. (1968). Perceptual inconstancy in early infantile autism. *Archives of General Psychiatry, 18,* 76–98.

Oswald, D. P., and Ollendick, T. (1989). Role taking and social competence in autism and mental retardation. *Journal of Autism and Developmental Disorders, 19,* 119–28.

Ozonoff, S., Pennington, B., and Rogers, S. (1990). Are there specific emotion perception deficits in young autistic children? *Journal of Child Psychology and Psychiatry, 31,* 343–61.

(1991a). Executive function deficits in high-functioning autistic children. Relationship to theory of mind. *Journal of Child Psychology and Psychiatry, 32,* 1081–1106.

(1991b). Asperger's Syndrome. Evidence for an empirical distinction from high functioning autism. *Journal of Child Psychology and Psychiatry, 23,* 704–7.

Paley, V. G. (1984). *Boys and Girls: Superheroes in the Doll Corner.* Chicago, IL: Chicago University Press.

Parker, S. T., and Gibson, K. R. (1977). Object manipulation, tool use and sensorimotor intelligence as feeding adaptations in cebus monkeys and great apes. *Journal of Human Evolution, 6,* 623–41.

Parkin, L., and Perner, J. (1994). False directions in children's theory of mind: what it means to understand belief as representation. *Cognition, 46.*

Pea, R. (1982). Origins of verbal logic: spontaneous denials by two- and three-year-olds. *Journal of Child Language, 9,* 597–626.

Peacocke, C. (1983). *Sense and Content.* Oxford: Oxford University Press.

(1986). *Thoughts.* Oxford: Basil Blackwell.

(1991). *A Study of Concepts.* Cambridge, MA: MIT Press.

Peacocke, P. (1994). Introduction: The issues and their further development. In C. Peacocke (ed.), *Objectivity, Simulation and the Unity of Consciousness. Proceedings of the British Academy, 83,* xi–xxvi.

Perner, J. (1991a). *Understanding the representational mind.* Cambridge, MA: Bradford books: MIT Press.

(1991b). Letter of 24 September 1991 to Martin Davies with comments on papers by Goldman, Gordon, and Stich and Nichols for the Special Issue on Simulation in *Mind and Language.*

(1993). The theory of mind deficit in autism: rethinking the metarepresentation theory. In S. Baron-Cohen, H. Tager-Flusberg, and D. J. Cohen (eds.), *Understanding Other Minds: Perspectives from Autism*. Oxford: Oxford University Press.

(1994). The necessity and impossibility of simulation. *Proceedings of the British Academy, 83*, 129–44.

(submitted). The many faces of belief: reflections on Fodor's and the child's theory of mind. *Cognition*.

Perner, J., Baker, S., and Hutton, D. (1994). Prelief: the conceptual origins of belief and pretence. In C. Lewis and P. Mitchell (eds.), *Children's Early Understanding of Mind: Origins and Development*. Hove, UK. Erlbaum.

Perner, J., Frith, U., Leslie, A. M., and Leekam, S. R. (1989). Exploration of the autistic child's theory of mind: knowledge, belief and communication. *Child Development, 60*, 689–700.

Perner, J., and Howes, D. (1992). 'He thinks he knows'; and more developmental evidence against the simulation (role-taking) theory. *Mind and Language, 7*, 72–86.

Perner, J., Leekam, S. R., and Wimmer, H. (1987). Three-year olds' difficulty with false belief: The case for a conceptual deficit. *British Journal of Developmental Psychology, 5*, 125–37.

Perner, J., Ruffman, T., and Leekam, S. R. (1994). Theory of mind is contagious: you catch it from your sibs. *Child Development, 65*, 1228–38.

Peskin, J. (1993). *Pretence and deception: preschoolers' predictions of counterfactual actions*. Unpublished manuscript, University of Toronto.

Peterson, C. (1990). The who, when and where of early narratives. *Journal of Child Language, 17*, 433–55.

Pettit, P. (1986). Broad-minded explanation and psychology. In P. Pettit and J. McDowell (eds.), *Subject, Thought, and Context*. Oxford: Oxford University Press, 17–58.

Phillips, W. (1993). *Understanding intention and desire by children with autism*. Unpublished PhD thesis, Institute of Psychiatry, University of London.

Phillips, W., Baron-Cohen, S., and Rutter, M. (1994). To what extent can children with autism understand desire? Paper submitted for publication.

Piaget, J. (1936). *La Naissance de l'Intelligence Chez l'Enfant*. Neuchatel: Delachaux et Niestlé.

(1937). *La Construction du Réel Chez l'Enfant*. Neuchâtel: Delachaux et Niestlé.

Pillow, B. H. (1989). Early understanding of perception as a source of knowledge. *Journal of Experimental Child Psychology, 47*, 116–29.

Pinder, S. (1984). *Language Learnability and Language Development*, Cambridge, MA: Harvard University Press.

Pinker, S. (1994). *The Language Instinct*. Harmondsworth: Penguin.

Poti, P., and Spinozzi, G. (1994). Early sensorimotor development in chimpanzees (*Pan troglodytes*). *Journal of Comparative Psychology, 108*, 93–103.

Povinelli, D. J. (1991). *Social intelligence in monkeys and apes*. Doctoral dissertation, Yale University, New Haven, Connecticut.

(1993). Reconstructing the evolution of mind. *American Psychologist, 48*, 493–509.

(1994a). Comparative studies of animal mental state attribution: a reply to Heyes. *Animal Behaviour, 48*, 239–41.

(1994b). How to create self-recognizing gorillas (but don't try it on macaques). In S. Parker, R. Mitchell, and M. Boccia (eds.), *Self-Awareness in Animals and Humans*, pp 291–4. Cambridge: Cambridge University Press.

Povinelli, D.J., and deBlois, S. (1992a). Young children's (*Homo sapiens*) understanding of knowledge formation in themselves and others. *Journal of Comparative Psychology*, *106*, 228–38.

(1992b). On (not) attributing mental states to monkeys: first, know thyself. *Behavioral and Brain Sciences*, *15*, 164–6.

Povinelli, D. J., and Eddy, T. J. (1994). The eyes as a window: what young chimpanzees see on the other side. *Cahiers de Psychologie Cognitive/Current Psychology of Cognition*, *13*, 695–705.

(In press a). Chimpanzees: Joint visual attention. *Psychological Science*.

(In press b). What young chimpanzees know about seeing. *Monographs of the Society for Research in Child Development*.

Povinelli, D. J., and Godfrey, L. R. (1993). The chimpanzee's mind: How noble in reason? How absent of ethics? In M. Nitecki and D. Nitecki (eds.), *Evolutionary Ethics*. pp 277–324. Albany, SUNY Press.

Povinelli, D. J., Nelson, K. E., and Boysen, S. T. (1990). Inferences about guessing and knowing by chimpanzees (Pan troglodytes). *Journal of Comparative Psychology*, *104*, 203–10.

(1992). Comprehension of role reversal in chimpanzees: evidence of empathy? *Animal Behaviour*, *43*, 633–40.

Povinelli, D. J., Parks, K. A., and Novak, M. A. (1991). Do rhesus monkeys (Macaca mulatta) attribute knowledge and ignorance to others? *Journal of Comparative Psychology*, *105*, 318–25.

(1992). Role reversal by rhesus monkeys, but no evidence of empathy. *Animal Behaviour*, *43*, 269–81.

Povinelli, D. J., Rulf, A. B., and Bierschwale, D. T. (1994). Absence of knowledge attribution and self-recognition in young chimpanzees (Pan troglodytes). *Journal of Comparative Psychology*, *108*, 74–80.

Povinelli, D. J., Rulf, A. R., Landau, K. R., and Bierschwale, D. T. (1993). Self-recognition in chimpanzees (*Pan troglodytes*): distribution, ontogeny, and patterns of emergence. *Journal of Comparative Psychology*, *107*, 347–72.

Pratt, C., and Bryant, P. E. (1990). Young children understand that looking leads to knowing (so long as they are looking into a single barrel). *Child Development*, *61*, 973–82.

Premack, D. (1984). Pedagogy and aesthetics as sources of culture. In M. S. Gazzaniga (ed.), *Handbook of Cognitive Neuroscience*. pp.15–35. New York, Plenum Press.

(1988). 'Does the chimpanzee have a theory of mind?' revisited. In R.W. Byrne and A. Whiten (eds.), *Machiavellian Intelligence: Social Expertise and the Evolution of Intellect*, pp.160–79. Oxford: Oxford University Press.

Premack, D., and Dasser, V. (1991). Perceptual origins and conceptual evidence for theory of mind in apes and children. In A. Whiten (ed.), *Natural Theories of Mind: Evolution, Development and Simulation of Everyday Mindreading*, pp. 253–66. Oxford: Basil Blackwell.

Premack, D., and Premack, A. J. (1983). *The Mind of an Ape*. N. York: Norton.

Premack, D., and Woodruff, G. (1978). Does the chimpanzee have a theory of mind? *The Behavioral and Brain Sciences*, *1*, 515–26.

Preston, B. (1993). Behaviorism and mentalism: is there a third alternative? *Synthese, 79.*

Prior, M. R., Dahlstrom, B., and Squires, T. (1990). Autistic children's knowledge of thinking and feeling states in other people. *Journal of Child Psychology and Psychiatry, 31,* 587–601.

Przetacznik-Gierowska, M., and Likeza, M. (1990). Cognitive and interpersonal functions of children's questions. In G. Conti-Ramsden and C. E. Snow (eds.), *Children's Language, vol 7*, pp. 69–101. Hillsdale, N.J.: Erlbaum.

Pylyshyn, Z. (1973). What the mind's eye tells the mind's brain: a critique of mental imagery. *Psychological Bulletin, 80,* 1–24.

—— (1978). When is attribution of beliefs justified? *Behavioural and Brain Sciences, 1,* 592–3.

—— (1980). Computation and cognition: issues in the foundations of cognitive science. *Behavioral and Brain Sciences 3,* 111–32.

—— (1981). The imagery debate: Analog media versus tacit knowledge. In N. Block (ed.), *Imagery*. Cambridge, MA: MIT Press.

Raver, C. C., and Leadbeater, B. J. (1993). The problem of the other in research on theory of mind and social development. *Human Development, 36,* 350–62.

Reddy, V. (1991). Playing with others' expectations: teasing and mucking about in the first year. In Whiten, A. (ed.), *Natural Theories of Mind: Evolution, Development and Simulation of Everyday Mindreading.* Oxford: Basil Blackwell.

Reed, T., and Peterson, C. (1990). A comparative study of autistic subjects' performance at two levels of visual and cognitive perspective taking. *Journal of Autism and Developmental Disorders, 20,* 555–68.

Ricks, D., and Wing, L. (1976). Language, communication and the use of symbols. In L.Wing (ed.), *Early Childhood Autism: Clinical, Educational and Social Aspects* (2nd edn). New York: Pergamon Press.

Rimland, B. (1971). The differentiation of childhood psychosis. *Journal of Autism and Childhood Schizophrenia, 1,* 161–74.

Robinson, W. P. (1986). Children's understanding of the distinction between messages and meanings: Emergence and implications. In M. Richards and P. Light (eds.), *Children of Social Worlds*. Cambridge, England: Polity Press.

Roese, N., and Olson, J. (1993). The structure of counterfactual thought, *Personality and Social Psychology Bulletin, 19,* 312–19.

Rogers, S. J., and Pennington, B. F. (1991). A theoretical approach to the deficits in infantile autism. *Development and Psychopathology, 3,* 137–62.

Rogoff, B., Chavajay, P., and Matusov, E. (1993). Questioning assumptions about culture and individuals. *Behavioral and Brain Sciences, 16,* 533–4.

Rollin, B. E. (1989). *The Unheeded Cry: Animal Consciousness, Animal Pain and Science.* Oxford: Oxford University Press.

Roth, D., and Leslie, A. M. (1991). The recognition of attitude conveyed by utterance: a study of preschool and autistic children. *British Journal of Developmental Psychology, 9,* 315–30.

Ruffman, T. K. (1994). Do children understand the mind by means of simulation or a theory?: Evidence from their understanding of inference. Unpublished manuscript, Laboratory of Experimental Psychology, University of Sussex.

Ruffman, T. K., and Olson, D. R. (1989). Children's ascriptions of knowledge to others. *Developmental Psychology, 25,* 601–6.

Rumsey, J. M. (1985). Conceptual problem solving in highly verbal, nonretarded men. *Journal of Autism and Developmental Disorders, 15*, 23–6.

Rumsey, J. M., and Hamburger, S. D. (1988). Neurological findings in high-functioning men with infantile autism, residual state. *Journal of Clinical and Experimental Neuropsychology, 10*, 201–21.

Russell, J., Mauthner, N., Sharpe S., and Tidswell, T. (1991). The 'Windows Task' as a measure of strategic deception in preschoolers and autistic subjects. *British Journal of Developmental Psychology, 9*, 331–50.

Rutter, M. (1968). Concepts of autism: a review of research. *Journal of Child Psychology and Psychiatry , 9*, 1–25.

(1978). Diagnosis and definition. In M. Rutter and E. Schopler (eds.), *Autism: a Reappraisal of Concepts and Treatment*. New York: Plenum Press.

Samet, J. (1993). Autism and theory of mind: Some philosophical perspectives. In S. Baron-Cohen, H. Tager-Flusberg, and D. Cohen (eds.), *Understanding Other Minds: Perspectives from Autism*. Oxford: Oxford University Press.

Savage-Rumbaugh, E. S. (1986). *Ape Language: From Conditioned Response to Symbol*. New York: Columbia University Press.

Savage-Rumbaugh, E. S., Murphy, J., Sevcik, R. A., Brakke, K., Williams, S. L., and Rumbaugh, D. M. (1993). Language comprehension in ape and child. *Monographs of the Society for Research in Child Development, 58*, Serial No. 233.

Savic, S. (1975). Aspects of adult-child communication: the problem of question acquisition. *Journal of Child Language, 2*, 25–260.

Scaife, M., and Bruner, J. (1975). The capacity for joint visual attention in the infant. *Nature, 253*, 265–6.

Schaffer, R. H. (1984). *The Child's Entry into a Social World* (Trad. cast.: *Interacción y Socialización*. Madrid: Visor, 1989, Trans.). London: Academic Press.

Scheiffelin, B. B., and Ochs, E. (1986). *Language Socialization Across Cultures*. Cambridge: Cambridge University Press.

Schiffer, S. (1981). Truth and the theory of content. In H. Parret and J. Bouverese (eds.), *Meaning and Understanding*. Berlin: Walter de Gruyter.

Scott, F., Baron-Cohen, S., and Leslie, A. M. (1994). Can pigs fly? A study of counterfactual reasoning in normal, autistic and Down's syndrome children. Manuscript.

Seyfarth, R. M., and Cheney, D. (1992). Meaning and mind in monkeys. *Scientific American, 267* (Dec), 78–84.

Shah, A. (1988). Visuo–spatial islets of abilities and intellectual functioning in autism. Ph.D. Dissertation, University of London.

Shatz, M., and O'Reilly, A. W. (1990). Conversational or communicative skill? A reassessment of two-year-olds' behaviour in miscommunication episodes. *Journal of Child Language, 17*, 131–46.

Shatz, M., Wellman, H. M., and Silber, S. (1983). The acquisition of mental terms: A systematic investigation of the first reference to mental state. *Cognition, 14*, 301–21.

Sigman, M., Ungerer, J. M., Mundy, P., and Sherman, T. (1986). Social interactions of autistic, mentally retarded, and normal children and their caregivers. *Journal of Child Psychology and Psychiatry, 27*, 647–56.

(1987). Cognition in autistic children. In D. Cohen, A. Donnellan, and R. Paul (eds.), *Handbook of Autism and Atypical Developmental Disorders*. Silver Springs, MD: V.H. Winston.

Silverman, P. S. (1986). Can a pigtail macaque learn to manipulate a thief? In R. W. Mitchell and N. S. Thompson (eds.), *Deception: Perspectives on Human and Nonhuman Deceit*. pp.151–67. Cambridge: Cambridge University Press.

Simner, M. (1971). Newborn's response to the cry of another infant, *Developmental Psychology 5*, 136–50.

Slaughter V. (1994). Conceptual coherence in the child's theory of mind, University of California at Berkeley doctoral dissertation.

Smith, P. K. (1982). Does play matter? Functional and evolutionary aspects of animal and human play. *Behavioural and Brain Sciences*, 5, 139–84.

Sodian, B., and Wimmer, H. (1987). Children's understanding of inference as a source of knowledge. *Child Development, 58*, 424–33.

Sodian, B., and Frith, U. (1992). Deception and sabotage in autistic, retarded and normal children. *Journal of Child Psychology and Pychiatry*, *33*, 591–605.

Spelke, E., Breinlinger K., Macomber J., and Jacobson, K. (1992). Origins of knowledge, *Psychological Review*, 4.

Spinozzi, G. (1993). Development of spontaneous classificatory behavior in chimpanzees (*Pan troglodytes*). *Journal of Comparative Psychology*, *107*, 193–200.

Spitz, R. A. (1965). *The First Year of Life*. New York, International Universities Press.

Spitz, R. A., and Wolf, K. M. (1946). The smiling response: a contribution to the ongenesis of social relationships. *Genetic Psychology Monographs*, *34*, 57–125.

Stalnaker, R. (1968). A theory of conditionals. In N. Rescher, *Studies of Logical Theory*. Oxford: Blackwell.

Steel, J. G., Gorman, R., and Flexman, J. E. (1984). Neuropsychiatric testing in an autistic idiot-savant. Evidence for nonverbal abstract capacity. *Journal of the American Academy of Child Psychiatry*, *23*, 704–7.

Stich, S. P. (1978). Beliefs and subdoxastic states. *Philosophy of Science, 45*, 499–518.

(1981). Dennett on intentional systems. *Philosophical Topics*, *12*, Number 1; reprinted as J. I. Biro and R. W. Shahan (eds.), *Mind, Brain, and Function: Essays in the Philosophy of Mind*, Brighton: Harvester Press, 1982, 39–62.

(1983). *From Folk-Psychology to Cognitive Science*. Cambridge, MA: MIT Press.

Stich, S. P., and Nichols, S. (1992). Folk psychology: simulation or tacit theory? *Mind and Language*, *7*, 35–71.

(1995). Second thoughts on simulation. In T. Stone and M. Davies, (eds.), *Mental Simulation: Evaluations and applications*. Oxford: Basil Blackwell.

Stone, T., and Davies, M. (eds.), (1995). *Mental Simulation: Evaluations and Applications*. Oxford: Basil Blackwell.

Stotland, E. (1969). Exploratory investigations of empathy. In L. Berkowitz (ed.), *Advances in Experimental Social Psychology, 4*. New York: Academic Press.

Sullivan, K., and Winner, E. (1993). Three-year-olds' understanding of mental states: The influence of trickery. *Journal of Experimental Child Psychology, 56*, 135–48.

Swartz, K. B., and Evans, S. (1991). Not all chimpanzees show self-recognition. *Primates, 32*, 483–96.

Tager-Flusberg, H. (1992). Autistic children's talk about psychological states:

deficits in the early acquisition of a theory of mind. *Child Development, 63,* 161–72.

(1993). What language reveals about the understanding of minds in children with autism. In Baron-Cohen S., Tager-Flusberg H., and Cohen D. J. (eds.), *Understanding Other Minds: Perspectives from Autism.* Oxford: Oxford University Press.

(1995, March), Language and the acquisition of a theory of mind: evidence from autism and Williams syndrome. Paper presented at the Biennial Meeting of the Society for Research in Child Development, Indianapolis, IN.

(1994). Social-cognitive abilities in Williams syndrome. Paper presented at the Conference of the Williams Syndrome Association, San Diego, CA, 27 July.

Tan, J., and Harris, P. L. (1991). Autistic children understand seeing and wanting. *Development and Psychopathology, 3,* 163–74.

Thompson, R. (1987). Empathy and emotional understanding: the early development of empathy. In N. Eisenberg and J. Strayer (eds.), *Empathy and its Development.* New York: Cambridge University Press.

Tomasello, M. (1988). The role of joint attentional processes in early language development. *Language Sciences, 10,* 69–88.

(In press). The power of culture: evidence from apes. *Human Development.*

Tomasello, M., and Call, J. (1994). Social cognition of monkeys and apes. *Yearbook of Physical Anthropology, 37,* in press.

Tomasello, M., Savage-Rumbaugh, S., and Kruger, A. C. (1993). Imitative learning of actions on objects by children, chimpanzees, and enculturated chimpanzees. *Child Development, 64,* 1688–705.

Tomasello, M., Kruger, A., and Ratner, H. H. (1993). Cultural learning. *Behavioral and Brain Sciences, 16,* 495–552.

Trevarthen, C. B. (1977). Descriptive analyses of infant communicative behaviour. In H. R. Schaffer (ed.), *Studies in Mother-Infant Interaction.* London: Academic Press.

(1993). Predispositions on cultural learning in young infants. *Behavioral and Brain Sciences, 16,* 534.

Tyack, D., and Ingram, D. (1977). Children's production and comprehension of questions. *Journal of Child Language, 4,* 211–24.

Vaidyanathan, R. (1991). Development of forms and functions of negation in the early stages of language acquisition: a study in Tamil. *Journal of Child Language, 18,* 51–66.

van Lawick-Goodall, J. (1968). The behaviour of free-living chimpanzees in the Gombe Stream reserve. *Animal Behaviour Monographs, 1,* 161–311.

Vauclair, J., and Bard, K. A. (1983). Development of manipulations with objects in ape and human infants. *Journal of Human Evolution, 12,* 631–45.

Vrba, E. (1989). Levels of selection and sorting with special reference to the species level. In R. Dawkins and M. Ridley (eds.), *Oxford Surveys in Evolutionary Biology.* New York: Oxford University Press.

Vygotsky, L. S. (1962). *Thought and Language.* Cambridge, MA: MIT Press.

(1967). Play and its role in the mental development of the child. *Soviet Psychology, 5,* 6–18. Reprinted in J. K. Gardner (ed.), *Readings in Developmental Psychology.* Boston, MA: Little, Brown, 1978.

(1978). *Mind in Society.* Cambridge, MA: Harvard University Press.

(1981). The genesis of higher mental functions. In J. V. Wertsch (ed.), *The Concept of Activity in Soviet Psychology,* pp.144–88. Armonk, NY: Sharpe.

Wellman, H. M. (1990) *The Child's Theory of Mind.* Cambridge MA: MIT Press.

(1991). From desires to beliefs: acquisition of a theory of mind. In A. Whiten. (ed.), *Natural Theories of Mind: Evolution, Development and Simulation of Everyday Mindreading.* Oxford: Basil Blackwell.

Wellman, H. M., and Estes, D, (1986). Early understanding of mental entities: a reexamination of childhood realism. *Child Development, 57,* 910–23.

Wertsch, J. V. (1985). *Vygotsky and the Social Formation of Mind.* Cambridge, MA: Harvard University Press.

Wertsch, J. V., and Tulviste, P. (1992). L. S. Vygotsky and contemporary developmental psychology. *Developmental Psychology, 28,* 548–57.

Whiten, A. (1993). Evolving theories of mind: the nature of non-verbal mentalism in other primates. In S. Baron-Cohen, H. Tager-Flusberg, and D. Cohen (eds.), *Understanding Other Minds: Perspectives from Austism,* pp.367–96. Oxford: Oxford University Press.

(1994). Grades of mindreading. In C. Lewis and P. Mitchell (eds.), *Children's Early Understanding of Mind: Origins and Development.* Hove UK: Erlbaum.

(in press). The evolution and development of emotional states, emotional expressions and emotion-reading in human and non-human primates. In B. Shore and C. Worthman (eds.), *Emotions: a Bio-Cultural Perspective.* Cambridge: Cambridge University Press.

(1991: ed.) *Natural Theories of Mind: Evolution, Development and Simulation of Everyday Mindreading.* Oxford: Basil Blackwell.

Whiten, A., and Byrne, R. W. (1988). Tactical deception in primates. *Behavioral and Brain Sciences, 11,* 233–44.

(1991). The emergence of metarepresentation in human ontogeny and primate phylogeny. In A. Whiten (ed.), *Natural Theories of Mind: Evolution, Development and Simulation of Everyday Mindreading,* pp. 267–81. Oxford: Blackwell.

Widman, L., and Loparo, K. (1989). Artificial intelligence, simulation, and modeling: a critical survey. In L. Widman, K. Loparo, and N. Nielsen (eds.), *Artificial Intelligences, Simulation, and Modeling.* New York: John Wiley.

Wimmer, H., Hogrefe, G.-J., and Perner, J. (1988). Children's understanding of informational access as source of knowledge. *Child Development, 59,* 386–96.

Wimmer, H., Hogrefe, G.-J., and Sodian, B. (1988). A second stage in children's conception of mental life: understanding sources of information. In J. W. Astington, P. L. Harris, and D. R. Olson (eds.), *Developing Theories of Mind,* 173–92. New York: Cambridge University Press.

Wimmer, H. and Perner, J. (1983). Beliefs about beliefs: representation and constraining function of wrong beliefs in young children's understanding of deception. *Cognition, 13,* 103–28.

Wimmer, H., and Weichbold, V. (1994). Children's theory of mind: Fodor's heuristics examined. *Cognition, 53,* 45–57.

Wing, L. (1981). Asperger Syndrome: a clinical account. *Journal of Psychological Medicine, 11,* 115–29.

(1988). The continuum of autistic characteristics. In E. Schopler and G. Mesibov (eds.), *Diagnosis and Assessment in Autism.* New York: Plenum Press.

Wing, L., and Gould, J. (1979). Severe impairments of social interaction and associated abnormalities in children: epidemiology and classification. *Journal of Autism and Developmental Disorders, 9,* 11–29.

Wittgenstein, L. (1953). *Philosophical Investigations.* Oxford: Basil Blackwell.

Wolpert, L. (1992). *The Unnatural Nature of Science.* London: Faber.

Wood, D. J., Bruner, J. S., and Ross, G. (1976). The role of tutoring in problem solving. *Journal of Child Psychology and Psychiatry, 17,* 89–100.

Woodfield, A. (1994, July). Which concepts of mind do pre-school children use? Paper presented at the conference on Theories of Theories of Mind, Sheffield University, England.

Woodruff, G., and Premack, D. (1979). Intentional communication in the chimpanzee: the development of deception. *Cognition, 7:* 333–62.

World Health Organisation (1987). *International Classification of Diseases* (9th edition). Geneva.14

Yirmiya, N., Sigman, M., Kasari, C., and Mundy, P. (1992). Empathy and cognition in high-functioning children with autism. *Child Development, 63,* 150–60.

Zahn-Waxler, C., and Radke-Yarrow, M. (1982). The development of altruism: alternative research strategies. In N. Eisenberg (ed.), *The Development of Prosocial Behavior.* New York: Academic Press.

Zaitchik, D. (1990). When representations conflict with reality: The preschooler's problem with false beliefs and 'false' photographs. *Cognition, 35,* 41–68.

Author index

Subject index